# perspectives

## Child Development

# perspectives

## Child Development

Academic Editors

**Pamela Ludemann**

**T. Bridgett Perry**

*Framingham State College*

coursewise
publishing
inc.

St. Paul • Bellevue • Boulder • Dubuque • Madison

Our mission at **coursewise** is to help students make connections—linking theory to practice and the classroom to the outside world. Learners are motivated to synthesize ideas when course materials are placed in a context they recognize. By providing gateways to contemporary and enduring issues, **coursewise** publications will expand students' awareness of and context for the course subject.

For more information on **coursewise,** visit us at our web site: http://www.coursewise.com

To order an examination copy:
Houghton Mifflin Sixth Floor Media  800-565-6247 (voice) / 800-565-6236 (fax)

## coursewise publishing editorial staff

Thomas Doran, ceo/publisher: Journalism/Marketing/Speech
Edgar Laube, publisher: Political Science/Psychology/Sociology
Linda Meehan Avenarius, publisher: **courselinks**™
Sue Pulvermacher-Alt, publisher: Education/Health/Gender Studies
Victoria Putman, publisher: Anthropology/Geography/Environmental Science
Tom Romaniak, publisher: Business/Criminal Justice/Economics
Kathleen Schmitt, publishing assistant

## coursewise publishing production staff

Lori A. Blosch, permissions coordinator
Mary Monner, production coordinator
Victoria Putman, production manager

**Note:** Readings in this book appear exactly as they were published.
Thus, inconsistencies in style and usage among the different readings are likely.

Cover photo: Copyright © 1997 T. Teshigawara/Panoramic Images, Chicago, IL. All Rights Reserved.

Interior design and cover design by Jeff Storm

Printed in the United States of America by **coursewise publishing,** Inc.
1559 Randolph Avenue, St. Paul, MN 55105

10 9 8 7 6 5 4 3 2 1

# from the
# Publisher

## Edgar Laube

*coursewise publishing*

As the father of three young children, I am continually amazed by their ability to absorb elements from their environment. For years I had occasionally heard new parents talk about their babies being "sponges" and such, and some parenting books dwell on this topic. It's need-to-know stuff for a parent. But it wasn't until my oldest daughter adopted the habit of uttering a certain profanity every time she got frustrated, which was often, that I began to pay close attention. She was 18 months old at the time and had no clue about the meaning of her words.

The message is that even very young children are functioning human beings. Maybe they can't walk or talk or read or play the clarinet, but they process an enormous amount of information between their ears. Recognizing this reality is critically important not only for parents, but for all sorts of people whose professional lives touch children—teachers, nurses, social workers, police, even psychologists. Our children live in environments we construct for them, whether it's the womb, the classroom, or the video arcade. They watch us and mimic us and are a reflection of us. That's why the study of child development is so important. Understanding the way children develop and the challenges they face is a critical perspective for anyone who hopes that tomorrow will be better than today.

The Academic Editors of this volume are committed teachers who are devoted to the study of children's development. Pam Ludemann is an associate professor of psychology at Framingham State College, Framingham, Massachusetts. She has a doctorate in developmental psychology from Purdue and spent several years as a post-doctoral fellow at the National Institutes of Health—National Institute of Child Health and Human Development. Pam is a firm believer in challenging students (that's you) to do more than you think you can do. She's the founder and editor of a departmental journal of student research. Her goal in editing this reader was to provide an up-to-date and digestible addition to more formal modes of presentation.

T. Bridgett Perry is the chair of the psychology department at Framingham State College. She has a doctorate in experimental psychology from Oklahoma University. It was during some years spent as a staff psychologist at a children's hospital that Bridgett developed her long-term interest in understanding the forces that shape children and how children cope. Her research in peer relations and self-concept development has extended to the areas of school, family, and the larger culture.

I am delighted with the work of these two dedicated professionals. Their efficiency and can-do attitude certainly made life a bit simpler for me. More important, however, their judgment about issues and readings to include always seemed apt, and the interests of students were usually uppermost in their minds. My thanks to both Pam and Bridgett.

Onward! Students, I hope you enjoy this reader and, in the process, develop a sense of how important and lasting are the decisions we make and the behaviors we adopt toward our most impressionistic citizens. Don't forget about the **courselinks**™ site, which provides many more resources than can be contained in this reader. And for gosh sakes, let me know what you think. You can reach me at www.coursewise.com.

*Pamela Ludemann*

*T. Bridgett Perry*

# from the
# Academic Editors

## Pamela Ludemann
## T. Bridgett Perry
*Framingham State College*

Children are an integral part of our everyday lives, regardless of our age, marital status, race, or gender. Most of you have had or currently have younger siblings with whom you are forever trying to get along and understand. In addition, many of you will enter professions such as teaching, coaching, counseling, and nursing that involve daily work with children. Some of you may already be facing the challenges of parenthood, and many more of you will face those challenges in the future. In addition, many of you would benefit from understanding some of the issues you faced in your own childhood years. A well-structured course in child development should provide you with some of the information you need to meet these challenges.

As advocates for understanding children and promoting children's rights, we feel that a child development course prepares you for one of the most important tasks of your lives—that of understanding and promoting healthy child development in the communities within which you live and work. One way to effect positive change in the lives of children is to understand their development—both typical and atypical—by becoming educated consumers of the vast research literature in the field. The mass media are a second source of information. Sometimes, the media provide information based on empirical research, but more often, they offer a layperson's perspective on current issues facing the world's children. We believe that *Perspectives: Child Development* links popular sources of child development information with the typical research-based texts students read in most classrooms.

We hope that this reader will be an informative and stimulating resource to supplement lectures and promote discussion. We have gathered a series of readings from some of the most widely read magazines and journals. These readings reflect what we feel are some of the most controversial issues in child development, as well as some of the long-standing theories on these issues. In addition, the readings celebrate the competencies and resiliency of children, while also highlighting the distressing circumstances that some children face. The web site activities we have provided will help you to further integrate into classroom discussion the everyday issues of growing up and will encourage you to think critically about the many issues surrounding the study and rearing of children.

# Editorial Board

We wish to thank the following instructors for their assistance. Their many suggestions not only contributed to the construction of this volume, but also to the ongoing development of our Child Development web site.

# WiseGuide Introduction

## Critical Thinking and Bumper Stickers

The bumper sticker said: Question Authority. This is a simple directive that goes straight to the heart of critical thinking. The issue is not whether the authority is right or wrong; it's the questioning process that's important. Questioning helps you develop awareness and a clearer sense of what you think. That's critical thinking.

Critical thinking is a new label for an old approach to learning—that of challenging all ideas, hypotheses, and assumptions. In the physical and life sciences, systematic questioning and testing methods (known as the scientific method) help verify information, and objectivity is the benchmark on which all knowledge is pursued. In the social sciences, however, where the goal is to study people and their behavior, things get fuzzy. It's one thing for the chemistry experiment to work out as predicted, or for the petri dish to yield a certain result. It's quite another matter, however, in the social sciences, where the subject is ourselves. Objectivity is harder to achieve.

Although you'll hear critical thinking defined in many different ways, it really boils down to analyzing the ideas and messages that you receive. What are you being asked to think or believe? Does it make sense, objectively? Using the same facts and considerations, could you reasonably come up with a different conclusion? And, why does this matter in the first place? As the bumper sticker urged, question authority. Authority can be a textbook, a politician, a boss, a big sister, or an ad on television. Whatever the message, learning to question it appropriately is a habit that will serve you well for a lifetime. And in the meantime, thinking critically will certainly help you be course wise.

Question Authority

## Getting Connected

This reader is a tool for connected learning. This means that the readings and other learning aids explained here will help you to link classroom theory to real-world issues. They will help you to think critically and to make long-lasting learning connections. Feedback from both instructors and students has helped us to develop some suggestions on how you can wisely use this connected learning tool.

## WiseGuide Pedagogy

A wise reader is better able to be a critical reader. Therefore, we want to help you get wise about the articles in this reader. Each section of *Perspectives* has three tools to help you: the WiseGuide Intro, the WiseGuide Wrap-Up, and the Putting It in *Perspectives* review form.

## WiseGuide Intro

In the WiseGuide Intro, the Academic Editor introduces the section, gives you an overview of the topics covered, and explains why particular articles were selected and what's important about them.

Also in the WiseGuide Intro, you'll find several key points or learning objectives that highlight the most important things to remember from this section. These will help you to focus your study of section topics.

WiseGuide Intro

At the end of the WiseGuide Intro, you'll find questions designed to stimulate critical thinking. Wise students will keep these questions in mind as they read an article (we repeat the questions at the start of the articles as a reminder). When you finish each article, check your understanding. Can you answer the questions? If not, go back and reread the article. The Academic Editor has written sample responses for many of the questions, and you'll find these online at the **courselinks**™ site for this course. More about **courselinks** in a minute. . . .

## WiseGuide Wrap-Up

Be course wise and develop a thorough understanding of the topics covered in this course. The WiseGuide Wrap-Up at the end of each section will help you do just that with concluding comments or summary points that repeat what's most important to understand from the section you just read.

In addition, we try to get you wired up by providing a list of select Internet resources—what we call R.E.A.L. web sites because they're **R**elevant, **E**xciting, **A**pproved, and **L**inked. The information at these web sites will enhance your understanding of a topic. (Remember to use your Passport and start at http://www.courselinks.com so that if any of these sites have changed, you'll have the latest link.)

## Putting It in *Perspectives* Review Form

At the end of the book is the Putting It in *Perspectives* review form. Your instructor may ask you to complete this form as an assignment or for extra credit. If nothing else, consider doing it on your own to help you critically think about the reading.

Prompts at the end of each article encourage you to complete this review form. Feel free to copy the form and use it as needed.

## The courselinks™ Site

The **courselinks**™ Passport is your ticket to a wonderful world of integrated web resources designed to help you with your course work. These resources are found at the **courselinks** site for your course area. This is where the readings in this book and the key topics of your course are linked to an exciting array of online learning tools. Here you will find carefully selected readings, web links, quizzes, worksheets, and more, tailored to your course and approved as connected learning tools. The ever-changing, always interesting **courselinks** site features a number of carefully integrated resources designed to help you be course wise. These include:

- **R.E.A.L. Sites** At the core of a **courselinks** site is the list of R.E.A.L. sites. This is a select group of web sites for studying, not surfing. Like the readings in this book, these sites have been selected, reviewed, and approved by the Academic Editor and the Editorial Board. The R.E.A.L. sites are arranged by topic and are annotated with short descriptions and key words to make them easier for you to use for reference or research. With R.E.A.L. sites, you're studying approved resources within seconds—and not wasting precious time surfing unproven sites.

- **Editor's Choice** Here you'll find updates on news related to your course, with links to the actual online sources. This is also where we'll tell you about changes to the site and about online events.

- **Course Overview** This is a general description of the typical course in this area of study. While your instructor will provide specific course objectives, this overview helps you place the course in a generic context and offers you an additional reference point.

- **www.orksheet** Focus your trip to a R.E.A.L. site with the www.orksheet. Each of the 10 to 15 questions will prompt you to take in the best that site has to offer. Use this tool for self-study, or if required, email it to your instructor.

- **Course Quiz** The questions on this self-scoring quiz are related to articles in the reader, information at R.E.A.L. sites, and other course topics, and will help you pinpoint areas you need to study. Only you will know your score—it's an easy, risk-free way to keep pace!

- **Topic Key** The Topic Key is a listing of the main topics in your course, and it correlates with the Topic Key that appears in this reader. This handy reference tool also links directly to those R.E.A.L. sites that are especially appropriate to each topic, bringing you integrated online resources within seconds!

- **Web Savvy Student Site** If you're new to the Internet or want to brush up, stop by the Web Savvy Student site. This unique supplement is a complete **courselinks** site unto itself. Here, you'll find basic information on using the Internet, creating a web page, communicating on the web, and more. Quizzes and Web Savvy Worksheets test your web knowledge, and the R.E.A.L. sites listed here will further enhance your understanding of the web.

- **Student Lounge** Drop by the Student Lounge to chat with other students taking the same course or to learn more about careers in your major. You'll find links to resources for scholarships, financial aid, internships, professional associations, and jobs. Take a look around the Student Lounge and give us your feedback. We're open to remodeling the Lounge per your suggestions.

## Building Better Perspectives!

Please tell us what you think of this *Perspectives* volume so we can improve the next one. Here's how you can help:

1. Visit our **coursewise** site at: http://www.coursewise.com

2. Click on *Perspectives*. Then select the Building Better *Perspectives* Form for your book.

3. Forms and instructions for submission are available online.

Tell us what you think—did the readings and online materials help you make some learning connections? Were some materials more helpful than others? Thanks in advance for helping us build better *Perspectives*.

## Student Internships

If you enjoy evaluating these articles or would like to help us evaluate the **courselinks** site for this course, check out the **coursewise** Student Internship Program. For more information, visit:

http://www.coursewise.com/intern.html

# Brief Contents

**section 1**   Prenatal Development and Birth   1

**section 2**   The Newborn and Infant   16

**section 3**   Early Social-Emotional Development   37

**section 4**   Cognitive Development   53

**section 5**   Problems in Learning   74

**section 6**   Language Development   90

**section 7**   Socialization   105

**section 8**   Family Issues   131

**section 9** **Family Stressors** 152

**section 10** **Children's Health** 185

**section 11** **Issues in Identity** 198

# Contents

## section 1

## Prenatal Development and Birth

**WiseGuide Intro**    1

1   **Your Baby Has a Problem,** Robina Riccitiello and Jerry Adler. *Newsweek,* Spring/Summer 1997.
Three out of every one hundred newborns suffer birth defects that seriously affect their health and quality of life. Medical advances and preventative practices have reduced the occurrence or severity of some malformations, though not all.    **3**

2   **Building a Better Baby?** Mark Cohen. *Parenting,* November/December 1997.
Estimates indicate that each person carries a small number of potentially harmful genes. Though healthy themselves, individuals may pass these "bad" genes on to offspring. Genetic engineering may soon enable the "fixing" of genetic defects in the embryo or in the father's sperm. This potential for treating certain hereditary illnesses is not without concerns. Questions arise regarding how far some people will take this new technology as they compete for "better babies," the technology's effects on the human gene pool, and possible health insurance mandates.    **6**

3   **When I'm Sixty-Four,** Katha Pollitt. *The Nation,* May 26, 1997.
In 1997, modern medical science enabled a 63-year-old woman to give birth. As the nation focuses on this case, many important issues go undiscussed. These issues include our sexist attitudes that applaud advanced-age fathers but not the "Miracle Mom," our for-profit health care system that will put resources into creating babies but not into providing prenatal care to the one in six women who cannot afford it, and the many children who live in poverty, foster care, and abusive homes.    **9**

4   **When Does Life Begin? The Supreme Court Ponders the Rights of a Fetus,** D'arcy Jenish. *MacLean's,* July 1, 1997.
Questions concerning whether or not a pregnant woman can abuse her unborn child and the behaviors labeled as potentially abusive are controversial. Some argue that allowing the legal system to control the actions of expectant women is a serious infringement on the rights of women. Others contend that the fetus is entitled to be born in as healthy a state as possible.    **11**

5   **Labor Day: A Complete Guide to Your Hospital Birth,** Candy Schulman. *Parents,* October 1995.
Every birth is a unique experience, but knowing the basics of what to expect during labor is valuable. This reading provides a step-by-step account of hospital routines and common labor and postpartum events. Topics include when to arrive at the hospital, labor medications and monitoring, giving birth, and recovery.    **13**

**WiseGuide Wrap-Up**    **15**

**WiseGuide Intro      16**

**6    Fertile Minds,** J. Madeleine Nash. *Time,* February 3, 1997.
The rapid development of the fetal brain is explained and linked to the dramatic changes
that occur after birth. The interaction of genes and environment is demonstrated by the
contrasting effects of deprived versus enriched environments on brain development. The
malleability of the human brain during the first 10 years of life stresses the importance of
appropriate infant stimulation, child care, and education, as well as the potentially harmful
effects of childhood neglect and abuse and maternal depression.      **18**

**7    A Baby's First 48 Hours,** Laura Flynn McCarthy. *Parenting,* November 1997.
Just what happens immediately after a baby is born? This reading provides a look at the
hour-to-hour experiences, tests, and examinations an infant goes through before discharge
from the hospital. The value of these tests in promoting optimal health during the
newborn period and throughout life is discussed.      **25**

**8    Baby's-Eye View,** Paula Spencer. *Parenting,* March 1997.
What does the world really look like to a newborn? The author reviews what researchers
have discovered about infants' needs and their abilities to sense, remember, and show
preferences. Having such knowledge may allow new parents to better appreciate their
babies' perspectives and to respond more sensitively and competently to their early
behaviors.      **29**

**9    The Nursery's Littlest Victims,** Sharon Begley with Anne Underwood
and John F. Lauerman. *Newsweek,* September 22, 1997.
The question of whether instances of multiple-child deaths in families are cases of Sudden
Death Infant Syndrome (SIDS) or infanticide has arisen. A 1972 paper indicating that SIDS
runs in families put blinders on the medical community until recently. It is now believed
that 5 to 10 percent of the three thousand diagnosed SIDS deaths each year may, in fact,
be infanticides: cases of Münchhausen by proxy.      **32**

**10   Fragile: Handle with Care,** Dr. Alvin F. Poussaint and Susan Linn. *Newsweek,*
Spring/Summer 1997.
Each year, thousands of young children suffer brain injury or die from being violently
shaken. Shaken baby syndrome (SBS) is often caused by individuals overwhelmed by the
demands of child care and who are not chronic abusers. Tragically, ignorance as to
appropriate caregiving methods lies at the heart of the problem.      **34**

**WiseGuide Wrap-Up      36**


**WiseGuide Intro      37**

**11   Encouraging Positive Social Development in Young Children,**
Donna Sasse Wittmer and Alice Sterling Honig. *Young Children,* July 1994.
When care providers implement curricula that promote interpersonal consideration and
cooperation, children begin to display more of these behaviors in their play. Through adult
modeling, labeling, and praising, children internalize the value of prosocial behaviors. This
reading offers specific advice on how to respond to children's feelings, how to encourage
perspective taking and problem solving, and how to use positive discipline in the
classroom.      **39**

**12   Shyness, Sadness, Curiosity, Joy. Is It Nature or Nurture?**
Marc Peyser and Anne Underwood. *Newsweek,* Spring/Summer 1997.
Scientists are beginning to discover that genetics and environment work together to
determine personality. Although genes may control predispositions to respond in
particular ways, experiences may alter the final outcomes. Studies of twins and shy
offspring highlight the power of experience.      **47**

# section
# 2

## The Newborn
## and Infant

# section
# 3

## Early Social-
## Emotional
## Development

13 **Peppermint Prozac,** Arianna Huffington. *U.S. News & World Report,*
August 18/August 24, 1997.
Thousands of children are now being prescribed antidepressants without the requirement
of psychiatric evaluations. Though some children truly benefit from antidepressants, there is
concern that such medications may be prescribed as false cures for normal aspects of
childhood and adolescence. The "quick fix" of drugs may also interfere with children
learning to cope effectively with life experiences.   **50**

**WiseGuide Wrap-Up   52**

**WiseGuide Intro   53**

14 **How Smart Is Your Baby?** Susan Ochshorn. *Parenting,* February 1995.
Research indicates that infants arrive with inborn abilities to make sense of information
and with thinking processes already underway. Fetal sensory systems are functional during
the last months of pregnancy and ready the newborn to respond to stimulation. Early
reflexes, a preference for novelty, and the ability to detect differences and similarities are at
the center of infant thinking and problem solving. From these primitive starts, the toddler
gains a sense of self and begins to speak and to understand how the world works.   **55**

15 **Teaching *All* Children: Four Developmentally Appropriate Curricular and
Instructional Strategies in Primary-Grade Classrooms,** David W. Burchfield.
*Young Children,* November 1996.
Educators are actively searching for ways to meet the varied educational needs of all
children. Moving away from grade-level thinking toward more child-sensitive approaches to
school achievement has become a focus in many primary schools. This reading examines
four curricular and instructional strategies that hold promise, including Gardner's multiple
intelligences, the project approach, a writer's workshop, and a cuing system for promoting
literacy.   **60**

16 **Why Children Talk to Themselves,** Laura E. Berk. *Scientific American,*
November 1994.
When children talk aloud, it is not meaningless babble. Self-talk, or private speech,
according to Vygotsky, mimics the kinds of instructions parents provide as they help their
children solve problems and maintain focus. Gradually, private speech is internalized and
becomes the inner voice we all use to guide our actions. Studies examining self-guiding
private speech and parenting style, math achievement, sustained task attention, and
children with learning disabilities are discussed.   **67**

**WiseGuide Wrap-Up   73**

**WiseGuide Intro   74**

17 **Computers Should Be Made Available to Children of Low-Income Families,**
Robert J. Walker. *USA Today,* September 1997.
In the area of technology, U.S. families fit into two groups, one in which young children
have access to computers and another in which they do not. Most families with yearly
incomes under $20,000 do not have computers, placing their children at a technological
disadvantage in school and future job markets. The value of computer literacy and
programs to promote computer use in low-income homes is discussed.   **76**

18 **Hope for 'Snow Babies,'** Sharon Begley. *Newsweek,* September 29, 1997.
Babies born to cocaine-addicted mothers face an assortment of early life risks and
potential school-age attention and behavior problems. However, careful analysis indicates
that child outcomes are influenced more by these children's home environments than by
how much or when their mothers used the drug. Given these children's altered brains,
which make them overly sensitive to distractions, it is important to consider environmental
factors that might hinder their development.   **80**

# section
# 4

## Cognitive
## Development

# section
# 5

## Problems in Learning

**19 Children Who Burn Too Brightly,** David J. Welsh. *Early Childhood News,*
November/December 1997.
Estimates indicate that over 2 million school-aged children are diagnosed with attention
deficit hyperactivity disorder (ADHD), many of whom are prescribed medications to
control an underlying disorder. Unfortunately, diagnosis often hinges on adults' perceptions
of what constitutes excessive or inappropriate behaviors. This reading expresses concern
over the desire to promote uniformity in classrooms and to extinguish behaviors that fall
outside narrowly defined boundaries. **82**

**20 Dyslexia,** Sally E. Shaywitz. *Scientific American,* November 1996.
New research indicates that dyslexia is a language-processing problem and not a defect in
the visual system. Specifically, dyslexics show deficits in the ability to process linguistic units,
or phonemes, the individual sounds that make up all spoken and written words. Using a
case example and research, this reading explains how language is processed and where it
breaks down for dyslexics when reading and retrieving information from memory. **84**

**WiseGuide Wrap-Up    89**


**WiseGuide Intro    90**

**21 New Insights into How Babies Learn Language,** Marcia Barinaga.
*Science,* August 1, 1997.
The sound exaggerations of parentese may enable infants to learn the key features of
speech sounds and, ultimately, language. At each stage of language learning, the infant's
brain appears to become more efficient at making rules for what to notice and what to
ignore. Cross-cultural comparisons of mother-infant vocal interactions and developmental
changes in children's responses to sounds are described. **92**

**22 Why Is This Baby Crying?** Eugenie Allen. *Parenting,* October 1996.
Infants and young children cry for many reasons, and there are wide variations in how
much individual children cry. Research indicates that what matter most are the consistent
efforts caregivers make to console the crying child. Such efforts communicate to children
that someone is there for them. Normative changes in crying behaviors, colic, and
methods of comforting are discussed. **94**

**23 The Language Explosion,** Geoffrey Cowley. *Newsweek,* Spring/Summer 1997.
This reading provides an overview of language development, from the prenatal period
through the preschool years. Language begins with infants' early abilities to distinguish
language sounds and babble syllables. In a short time, words are linked to meaning, and
vocabulary blossoms. Ultimately, children decipher the rules for stringing words together
meaningfully. Specific processes underlying each stage of language acquisition are
described. **98**

**24 Starting Point,** George Butterworth. *Natural History,* May 1997.
Pointing with the index finger is an early developing gesture used to communicate. Simply
by extending a finger, a child is able to make a point, ask a question, or share an
experience. Recent evidence suggests that the onset of pointing may be related to a child's
rate of language acquisition. **102**

**WiseGuide Wrap-Up    104**

# section

# 6

# Language
# Development

# section 7

# Socialization

**WiseGuide Intro    105**

25  **Vygotsky's Theory: The Importance of Make-Believe Play,** Laura E. Berk.
*Young Children,* November 1994.
Vygotsky forged a sociocultural theory that bridges the gap between cognition and social development. He viewed representational play as a means by which children grapple with unrealizable desires and learn to follow social rules for behavior. Thus, play contributes to the development of a diverse array of capabilities, including separation of thought from actions, impulse control, memorization, language, and imagination. In fact, Vygotsky suggested that play is the preeminent educational activity of childhood and that adult scaffolding promotes play complexity by supporting children's zone of proximal development.    **107**

26  **Why Cool Rules,** David Laskin. *Parents,* June 1997.
While fads change every year, the need to be accepted is timeless. Being cool serves as the first step in separating from family and forming an individual identity. Cool involves conveying a certain style, attitude, wit, social adeptness, or appearance. Between the ages of 7 and 10 years, fitting in is more important than being original. Tips for helping children fit in while maintaining family values are offered.    **116**

27  **Friendship and Friends' Influence in Adolescence,** Thomas J. Berndt.
*Current Directions in Psychological Science,* October 1992.
The influence of friends on children and adolescents is best represented by both the psychological and social benefits of close relationships and the negative repercussions of peer conflicts and pressure. Recent findings suggest that a more integrative approach to studying friendships should include the investigation of friendship features, developmental changes, and the mutual influences of friends, positive and negative.    **119**

28  **The Age of Cliques,** Karen Levine. *Parents,* December 1995.
The middle-school years mark a child's transition out of an insulated world of family life and into the world of peers. The peak of conformity comes around age 13. Membership in a clique may help a child feel safe and protected, while exclusion can be painful and cruel. Suggestions for parents on discussing peer group membership with their children are discussed.    **124**

29  **Lonely Children,** Janis R. Bullock. *Young Children,* September 1993.
Children who are lonely due to poor peer relations are at risk for social maladjustment. Concepts of loneliness that children report are similar to those that adults report and can be reliably assessed. Loneliness in childhood may be the result of losing someone or something of importance, a problem at home, or a continual sense of being an outsider. Socially rejected and socially isolated children are at greater risk for loneliness than children accepted by their peers.    **126**

**WiseGuide Wrap-Up    130**

# section 8

# Family Issues

**WiseGuide Intro    131**

30  **Make Room for Daddy,** David Ruben. *Parenting,* June/July 1996.
A father's active involvement in childrearing tasks results in positive outcomes for the entire family. While traditional father roles are changing, mothers still spend more time with their children than fathers. Moreover, fathers have no single childrearing task for which they bear primary responsibility. Statistics suggest that moms still perform two-thirds of all parenting tasks. However, research suggests that, the more involved a dad becomes, the more competent their children become socially, intellectually, and emotionally.    **133**

31  **Discipline: The New Rules,** Mary Conners. *Parents,* February 1998.
The new rules of discipline may be making parents more confused and conflicted than ever, but their effectiveness is on the rise. Parents understand that different children and different circumstances call for different techniques. Today, time-out procedures have replaced spanking. Two major issues discussed are the importance of consistency in discipline and the control of parental anger while disciplining.    **138**

**32  The Secret World of Siblings,** Erica Goode. *U.S. News & World Report,* January 1994.
Surveys suggest that 80 percent of all Americans have at least one sibling. Sibling
relationships outlast marriages, survive deaths of parents, and resurface after quarrels that
would sink any friendship. However, research on the effects of sibling interactions is limited.
It is known that parenting style, age, birth order, number of siblings, and cultural and ethnic
expectations affect the quality of sibling relationships. Changes in sibling relationships over
the lifespan are discussed.   **142**

**33  The National Television Violence Study: Key Findings and
Recommendations.** *Young Children,* March 1996.
Televised violence does not have a uniform effect on viewers. The outcome of media
violence depends on the nature of the depictions and the sociological and psychological
makeup of the audience. This reading addresses risks, the percentage of violent content on
different channels, and the positive and negative effects of viewing violence. In addition,
recommendations are made for the television community, policy and public interest
leaders, and parents.   **148**

**WiseGuide Wrap-Up    151**

# section
# 9

## Family Stressors

**WiseGuide Intro    152**

**34  American Child Care Today,** Sandra Scarr. *American Psychologist,* February 1998.
Child care has two purposes: mother's employment and children's development.
Affordable child care fosters maternal employment and gender equality. However, the
questions of quality daycare, affordable daycare, and how much is too much daycare
remain issues for debate. Beneficial effects of daycare may be greatest for disadvantaged
children, whose homes put them at developmental risk. Issues in quality care and
government policies are examined.   **154**

**35  Corporate-Sponsored Child Care: Benefits for Children, Families, and
Employers,** Rebecca Oekerman. *Early Childhood Education Journal,* February 1997.
By the year 2000, 81 percent of all mothers with preschool- and school-aged children are
expected to be working outside the home. The demand for corporate-sponsored child
care is on the rise, and some corporations have responded to the need. Benefits for
employers include less on-the-job employee stress, less employee absenteeism, and
improved morale and work performance. Parents and children benefit from the
maintenance of close contact and immediate accessibility. Children may also benefit from
receiving quality, monitored child care.   **170**

**36  Parenting Q&A: Divorce.** *The Boston Parent's Paper,* November 1997.
Children's reactions to divorce are likely to vary in accordance with their age, sex,
temperament, and level of development. Young children are unlikely to understand issues
surrounding parental divorce. However, they are likely to show how they are feeling by
acting out or by engaging in developmentally immature behaviors. Older children are likely
to ask questions and want honest answers. Suggestions for how to help children adjust to
parental separation and divorce are offered.   **174**

**37  Kids with Gay Parents,** Joseph P. Shapiro with Stephen Gregory. *U.S. News & World
Report,* September 16, 1996.
As lawmakers battle over the legalization of gay marriages, much of the debate centers on
the issue of raising children in gay family environments. Information on the effects of being
raised in gay households is limited, and long-term effects have not been thoroughly
researched. Anecdotal evidence suggests that numerous factors affect the developmental
outcome of children raised by gay parents.   **176**

**38  Homeless Children in the United States: Mark of a Nation at Risk,**
Ann S. Masten. *American Psychological Society,* April 1992.
One of the biggest social issues to affect our nation's children is homelessness. In 1988, the
National Institute of Medicine estimated that more than 100,000 children were homeless
on any given night. Stressors, health issues, educational risks, developmental problems, and
mental health concerns are considered.   **179**

**WiseGuide Wrap-Up    184**

# section 10

## Children's Health

# section 11

## Issues in Identity

**WiseGuide Intro    185**

39  **You've Come a Long Way, Baby,** Russell Watson and Brad Stone. *Newsweek,*
Spring/Summer 1997.
The top ten health worries of parents include the common cold, wheezing, ear infection,
fevers, vomiting, dehydration, diarrhea, rash, skin infection, falls, and growth rates. These
worries are identified, with tips for parents. In addition, information on the chicken pox
vaccination debate and crib death is presented.    **187**

40  **The Case Against Baby Fat,** Laura Nathanson. *Parents,* September 1996.
Childhood is the only time when weight gain can be slowed, allowing a child to "grow"
into a healthy weight for his or her height. Strategies for slowing down weight gain during
toddlerhood and young adulthood in a fun, healthy manner are presented.    **190**

41  **Malnutrition, Poverty, and Intellectual Development,** J. Larry Brown
and Ernesto Pollitt. *Scientific American,* February 1996.
The impact of malnutrition on the healthy development of children is discussed.
Malnutrition has always been thought to hinder mental development in general by
producing permanent structural damage to the brain. However, new evidence suggests
that malnutrition may impact intellectual development in multiple ways. Results from
cross-cultural studies and the long-term effects of hunger on development are
discussed.    **193**

**WiseGuide Wrap-Up    197**


**WiseGuide Intro    198**

42  **Raising Sons, Raising Daughters,** Leslie Bennetts. *Ladies' Home Journal,* June 1997.
Most experts agree that the key to an individual's development, especially in the area of
gender identity, lies in the interaction of nature and nurture. However, there are distinct
sex-based physical and cognitive differences in the brains of boys and girls. Our society is
attempting to equalize the playing fields for the sexes through more egalitarian parenting
and socialization strategies. Suggestions are made for "emboldening our daughters and
taming our sons."    **200**

43  **Becoming Sexual: Differences between Child and Adult Sexuality,**
Fred Rothbaum, Avery Grauer, and David J. Rubin. *Young Children,* September 1997.
Most concerns regarding children's sexuality and its normality stem from
misunderstandings of how it is different from that of adults. Children's sexual behavior can
be distinguished from adults' in three areas: curiosity and play versus knowing and
consequential behavior; spontaneity and openness versus self-consciousness and privacy;
and sensuality and excitement versus passion and eroticism. Ideas for talking to children
about sexual matters are offered.    **204**

44  **Gay Students in Middle School,** Norma J. Bailey and Tracy Phariss. *Education Digest,*
October 1996.
Educators have become acutely aware of the need to provide a safe and sensitive
environment for youths of every sexual orientation. Barriers that still hinder the creation
of this type of environment include lack of information about the needs of young gays, lack
of courage on the part of adults and youth, and the failure of school systems to confront
controversial issues, especially in the areas of youth sexuality. Steps to create a safer
environment are outlined.    **210**

45  **Will These Kids Ever Be Wanted? The New Adoption Crisis,** Amy Engeler.
*Redbook,* July 1997.
The issues that arise when adoption involves children other than infants are discussed.
There are an estimated 100,000 older children living in foster homes across the country
who are hoping to be adopted. Strategies such as "adoption parties" for placing older
children are presented and highlight frustrations. In addition, reasons for the system's
failures and possible remedies are described.    **213**

**WiseGuide Wrap-Up    220**


**Index    221**

# Topic Key

This Topic Key is an important tool for learning. It will help you integrate this reader into your course studies. Listed below, in alphabetical order, are important topics covered in this volume. Below each topic, you'll find the reading numbers and titles, and R.E.A.L. web site addresses, relating to that topic. Note that the Topic Key might not include every topic your instructor chooses to emphasize. If you don't find the topic you're looking for in the Topic Key, check the index or the online topic key at the **courselinks**™ site.

## Adolescence
6 Fertile Minds
27 Friendship and Friends' Influence in Adolescence
28 The Age of Cliques
30 Make Room for Daddy
36 Parenting Q&A: Divorce

Youth Studies in Australia
http://www.acys.utas.edu.au/ncys/ysa

## Adoption and Foster Care
45 Will These Kids Ever Be Wanted? The New Adoption Crisis

## Attachment and Separation
8 Baby's-Eye View
32 The Secret World of Siblings
35 Corporate-Sponsored Child Care: Benefits for Children, Families, and Employers

## Birth Defects
1 Your Baby Has a Problem
2 Building a Better Baby?
4 When Does Life Begin?
6 Fertile Minds
10 Fragile: Handle with Care
18 Hope for 'Snow Babies'

Down Syndrome
http://www.nas.com/downsyn/index.html

## Brain Development
6 Fertile Minds
8 Baby's-Eye View
12 Shyness, Sadness, Curiosity, Joy. Is It Nature or Nurture?
14 How Smart Is Your Baby?
18 Hope for 'Snow Babies'
20 Dyslexia
23 The Language Explosion
24 Starting Point
41 Malnutrition, Poverty, and Intellectual Development

## Child Care
6 Fertile Minds
30 Make Room for Daddy
34 American Child Care Today
35 Corporate-Sponsored Child Care: Benefits for Children, Families, and Employers

Disney Resources
http://family.disney.com

Child Development Policy Advisory Committee of California
http://www.cdpac.ca.gov/

## Cognitive Development
14 How Smart Is Your Baby?
15 Teaching All Children: Four Developmentally Appropriate Curricular and Instructional Strategies in Primary-Grade Classrooms
16 Why Children Talk to Themselves
17 Computers Should Be Made Available to Children of Low-Income Families
18 Hope for 'Snow Babies'
24 Starting Point
25 Vygotsky's Theory: The Importance of Make-Believe Play
30 Make Room for Daddy
34 American Child Care Today
40 The Case Against Baby Fat

APA Monitor
http://www.apa.org/monitor/mar97/crit.htm

Rising Scores on Intelligence Tests
http://www.97articles/neisser.html

Piaget
http://www.uniqe.ch/piaget/presentg.html#

Down Syndrome
http://www.nas.com/downsyn/index.html

## Divorce
29 Lonely Children
36 Parenting Q&A: Divorce

Divorce
http://www.divorceinfo.com

Stepfamilies
http://www.studyweb.com/family/famstp.htm

Divorce
http://www.studyweb.com/family/famdiv.htm

## Education Issues
6 Fertile Minds
11 Encouraging Positive Social Development in Young Children
15 Teaching All Children: Four Developmentally Appropriate Curricular and Instructional Strategies in Primary-Grade Classrooms
17 Computers Should Be Made Available to Children of Low-Income Families
18 Hope for 'Snow Babies'
19 Children Who Burn Too Brightly
25 Vygotsky's Theory: The Importance of Make-Believe Play
27 Friendship and Friends' Influence in Adolescence
38 Homeless Children in the United States: Mark of a Nation at Risk
41 Malnutrition, Poverty, and Intellectual Development
44 Gay Students in Middle School

APA Monitor
http://www.apa.org/monitor/mar97/crit.htm

America's Homeless Children: Will Their Future Be Different?
http://nch.ari.net/edsurvey97/

## Environmental Influences
6 Fertile Minds
12 Shyness, Sadness, Curiosity, Joy. Is It Nature or Nurture?
14 How Smart Is Your Baby?
18 Hope for 'Snow Babies'
19 Children Who Burn Too Brightly
23 The Language Explosion
25 Vygotsky's Theory: The Importance of Make-Believe Play

## Fathers

5   Labor Day: A Complete Guide to Your Hospital Birth
30  Make Room for Daddy

Single Fathers
http://www.singlefathers.com/header.html

## Fetal Development/Newborns

4   When Does Life Begin?
6   Fertile Minds
7   A Baby's First 48 Hours
8   Baby's-Eye View
14  How Smart Is Your Baby?
23  The Language Explosion

Kidsource-Newborns
http://www.kidsource.com/kidsource/pages/newborns.web.html

## Gender Issues

3   When I'm Sixty-Four
4   When Does Life Begin?
27  Friendship and Friends' Influence in Adolescence
30  Make Room for Daddy
32  The Secret World of Siblings
36  Parenting Q&A: Divorce
42  Raising Sons, Raising Daughters

Girls and the Media
http://www.girlsinc.org/programs/recast.html

## Genetics

1   Your Baby Has a Problem
2   Building a Better Baby?
3   When I'm Sixty-Four
40  The Case Against Baby Fat

## Health

9   The Nursery's Littlest Victims
22  Why Is This Baby Crying?
37  Kids with Gay Parents
38  Homeless Children in the United States: Mark of a Nation at Risk
39  You've Come a Long Way, Baby
40  The Case Against Baby Fat
41  Malnutrition, Poverty, and Intellectual Development
44  Gay Students in Middle School

Bandaids and Blackboards
http://funrsc.fairfield.edu

## Infant-Toddler Development

8   Baby's-Eye View
14  How Smart Is Your Baby?

22  Why Is This Baby Crying?
24  Starting Point

Child Behavior Problems
http://www.studyweb.com/mental/menchild.htm

## Language, Communication, and Literacy

8   Baby's-Eye View
14  How Smart Is Your Baby?
15  Teaching All Children: Four Developmentally Appropriate Curricular and Instructional Strategies in Primary-Grade Classrooms
16  Why Children Talk to Themselves
20  Dyslexia
21  New Insights into How Babies Learn Language
22  Why Is This Baby Crying?
23  The Language Explosion
24  Starting Point
25  Vygotsky's Theory: The Importance of Make-Believe Play

Kidshealth
http://kidshealth.org/index2.html

Fostering Speech and Language Skills
http://family.disney.com/Features/family_1998_05/char/char58speech/char58speech.html

America's Homeless Children: Will Their Future Be Different?
http://nch.ari.net/edsurvey97/

## Learning Problems

16  Why Children Talk to Themselves
18  Hope for 'Snow Babies'
19  Children Who Burn Too Brightly
20  Dyslexia
38  Homeless Children in the United States: Mark of a Nation at Risk
41  Malnutrition, Poverty, and Intellectual Development

Disabilities: Attention Deficit Disorder (ADD)
http://www.kidsource.com/kidsource/pages/dis.add.html

## Media

17  Computers Should Be Made Available to Children of Low-Income Families
32  The Secret World of Siblings

Girls and Media
http://www.girlsinc.org/programs/recast.html

Disney Resources
http://family.disney.com

## Nature-Nurture Issue

6   Fertile Minds
12  Shyness, Sadness, Curiosity, Joy. Is It Nature or Nurture?
21  New Insights Into How Babies Learn Language
32  The Secret World of Siblings
40  The Case Against Baby Fat
42  Raising Sons, Raising Daughters

Nature, Nurture and Nature via Nurture
http://www.crispian.demon.co.uk/05.htm

## Parenting and Family Issues

3   When I'm Sixty-Four
12  Shyness, Sadness, Curiosity, Joy. Is It Nature or Nurture?
15  Teaching All Children: Four Developmentally Appropriate Curricular and Instructional Strategies in Primary-Grade Classrooms
21  New Insights into How Babies Learn Language
22  Why Is This Baby Crying?
23  The Language Explosion
24  Starting Point
25  Vygotsky's Theory: The Importance of Make-Believe Play
26  Why Cool Rules
28  The Age of Cliques
30  Make Room for Daddy
31  Discipline: The New Rules
33  The National Television Violence Study: Key Findings and Recommendations
36  Parenting Q&A: Divorce
37  Kids with Gay Parents
40  The Case Against Baby Fat
41  Malnutrition, Poverty, and Intellectual Development
42  Raising Sons, Raising Daughters
43  Becoming Sexual: Differences between Children and Adult Sexuality
45  Will These Kids Ever Be Wanted?

Goodkids
http://www.flash.net/~goodkids/

Child Development Policy Advisory Committee of California
http://www.cdpac.ca.gov/

Grandparents
http://seniors-site.com/grandpar/

Single Fathers
http://www.singlefathers.com/header.html

## Play, Peers and Friends

25 Vygotsky's Theory: The Importance of Make-Believe Play
26 Why Cool Rules
27 Friendship and Friends' Influence in Adolescence
28 The Age of Cliques
29 Lonely Children
36 Parenting Q&A: Divorce
43 Becoming Sexual: Differences Between Child and Adult Sexuality

Abused Children Have More Conflicts with Friends
http://www.apa.org/monitor/jun97/friends.html

Beating Peer Pressure
http://family.disney.com/Features?family_1997_05/hudv/hudv57peer/hudv57peer.html

## Prenatal Care/Pregnancy

3 When I'm Sixty-Four
4 When Does Life Begin?
5 Labor Day: A Complete Guide to Your Hospital Birth

Age of Fertility
http://www.fertilitext.org/age_fert.htm

## Problems and Disorders

4 When Does Life Begin?
6 Fertile Minds
9 The Nursery's Littlest Victims
10 Fragile: Handle with Care
13 Peppermint Prozac
18 Hope for 'Snow Babies'
22 Why Is This Baby Crying?

39 You've Come a Long Way, Baby
45 Will These Kids Ever Be Wanted?

Bandaids and Blackboards
http://funrsc.fairfield.edu

Kidshealth
http://kidshealth.org/index2.html

Anxiety Disorders in Children and Adolescents
http://www.adaa.org

Something Fishy—Eating Disorders
http://www.somthing_fishy.com/ed.htm

Child Behavior Problems
http://www.studyweb.com/mental/menchild.htm

National Information, Support and Referral Service on Shaken Baby Syndrome
http://www.capcenter.org/service.htm

## Punishment and Discipline

10 Fragile: Handle with Care
11 Encouraging Positive Social Development in Young Children
31 Discipline: The New Rules

## Self and Self-Esteem

14 How Smart Is Your Baby?
29 Lonely Children
36 Parenting Q&A: Divorce
40 The Case Against Baby Fat

Disney Resources
http://family.Disney.com

Socioemotional Development
http://www.valdosta.peachnet.edu/~whuitt/psy702/affsys/erikson.html

## Social Class

17 Computers Should Be Made Available to Children of Low-Income Families
34 American Child Care Today
38 Homeless Children in the United States: Mark of a Nation at Risk
41 Malnutrition, Poverty, and Intellectual Development
45 Will These Kids Ever Be Wanted?

## Temperament and Personality

11 Encouraging Positive Social Development in Young Children
12 Shyness, Sadness, Curiosity, Joy. Is It Nature or Nurture?
22 Why Is This Baby Crying?
29 Lonely Children
32 The Secret World of Siblings

Shyness
http://www.shyness.com

Temperament
http://www.temperament.com/bdi.com.html

## Violence and Conflict

9 The Nursery's Littlest Victims
10 Fragile: Handle with Care
11 Encouraging Positive Social Development in Young Children
27 Friendship and Friends' Influence in Adolescence
29 Lonely Children
32 The Secret World of Siblings
33 The National Television Violence Study: Key Findings and Recommendations

Children and Television Violence
http://helping.apa.org/kidtvviol.html

# section

1

## Learning Objectives

- Present some of the benefits and risks posed by advances in medical technologies.

- Review information on a few common birth disorders.

- Provide information that will enable readers to become informed consumers of birth-related services.

- Discuss ethical and legal issues surrounding the rights of women and, specifically, of mothers.

- Stress the importance of considering all sides of an issue, even if some are distasteful.

# Prenatal Development and Birth

**WiseGuide Intro**

The prenatal period involves approximately 40 weeks of rapid development. Early in this period, the precursors of all bodily systems form. These early systems elaborate and grow, enabling the fetus to react to stimuli, move, and even learn. The prenatal period ends at the point at which enough refinement has occurred that a viable life apart from the mother is possible. Through an as yet unknown interaction of fetal size and activity, maternal hormones, and placental aging, the processes of labor and, ultimately, birth begin.

Today, many alternative forms of delivery are available. Each has its proponents and is associated with benefits and limitations. Being an educated consumer is, thus, a new facet of parenthood. With an understanding of childbirth procedures and alternatives, parents to–be are able to ask pertinent questions and make satisfying choices. The "one-size-fits-all" birth experience is clearly a notion of the past.

Advances in modern medicine are also providing new hope for the 11% to 25% of couples coping with infertility problems. Even postmenopausal women are discovering that giving birth late in life is possible. Needless to say, many of these procedures are still experimental and costly and carry certain risks. There are also no guarantees of success. Controversies and ethical questions surround such medical interventions and bring to mind the constant balancing of benefits and costs.

Though the majority of pregnancies are uncomplicated and produce healthy newborns, problems do arise. Whether the result of heredity, accident, or unknown factors, 3 out of 100 newborns suffer birth defects. Awareness of potential risk factors and therapies may assist individuals contemplating parenthood or facing a pending birth as they make a multitude of decisions. Are there medications, food, and activities a pregnant woman should avoid? Is genetic counseling and testing warranted? If there is a family history of illness, should biological parenthood even be considered? If prenatal test results indicate the existence of a problem, is abortion a better alternative to carrying a pregnancy to term? What fetal and early life birth defects can medical science correct? These are among the many questions that flood the minds of prospective parents. There are no certain answers to many, but awareness of the facts and issues surrounding each can alleviate some of the anxiety about the final choices made.

Finally, our new knowledge about how many teratogens reach the developing fetus and cause sometimes preventable harm adds a new element, concern about fetal rights. We have long asked the question of when life begins. New is the question of when maternal responsibility and liability for the life within her womb begin.

## Questions

**Reading 1.** What can a pregnant woman do to increase the likelihood that her baby will be born healthy?

What options currently exist for families whose baby is born with a birth defect?

Pick a disorder and describe the interventions available.

**Reading 2.** Explain two benefits and two risks associated with future advances in gene therapy.

Why are the ethics of technologies that may someday be used to treat hereditary illnesses in question?

**Reading 3.** What are the three "good" reasons given for enabling older women to have babies?

What are the three "bad" reasons given for enabling older women to have babies?

**Reading 4.** What is the pro-choice position on fetal rights?

What is the pro-life position on fetal rights?

**Reading 5.** Describe the typical sequence of hospital-based labor and delivery events of a noncomplicated pregnancy.

Describe the newborn's first experiences within minutes after birth.

## Thinking Beyond the Facts

As you read through the articles of this section on prenatal development and birth, consider the issues presented. A wealth of information is available for today's parents-to-be, from prenatal care and labor options to the potential hazards of a variety of substances and activities. Prenatal testing, for instance, has dramatically improved in recent years. These tests allow parents to make some important life decisions before the birth of their child. On the one hand, early warning of a birth defect allows parents to seek-out information and support groups. Advanced knowledge may also enable medical personnel to anticipate the special needs of the newborn. On the other hand, studies have shown that the majority of people who discover that their fetus has an uncorrectable disorder terminate the pregnancy. Some are concerned that selective termination of pregnancies may, in time, have negative consequences for the human gene pool. Relatedly, prenatal tests are not 100% accurate or without risks. Healthy babies may be lost to misdiagnoses and permissible statistical error. Given the multitude of concerns, should the option to "know" be available? As technology improves, how far should parents' right to know go? Is selection of fetuses for sex, intelligence, personality, and other traits desirable? Should selection be limited only to traits that permit normal quality of life? Who is to define the limits of what is normal? It is not unthinkable that arguments favoring alternation of *any* trait that might improve a child's quality of life would be voiced.

Along with parental rights, the question of fetal rights has come to the forefront. More is known about the importance of quality prenatal care in assuring a healthy start. The fetus is no longer thought of as safely tucked away in the mother's womb. It is now known that many substances that the mother takes can directly reach the developing baby. A portion of these cause mild to profound birth defects. Does our level of understanding about teratogens create new forms of child abuse and neglect? If the answer is yes, to what extent is this to be carried? Is the taking of an occasional aspirin comparable to heroin addiction? Is a missed prenatal care visit neglect? Is the decision to abort infanticide by the mother and murder by the physician? Are they conspiring to commit this crime by scheduling the procedure? Consider the many other circumstances in which a woman may not be doing everything to serve as the ideal incubator to her developing child. Visit web sites related to fetal alcohol syndrome, teenage pregnancy, advanced-age motherhood, and work-related stress.

What can a pregnant woman do to increase the likelihood that her baby will be born healthy? What options currently exist for families whose baby is born with a birth defect? Pick a disorder and describe the interventions available.

# Your Baby Has a Problem

**Robina Riccitiello and Jerry Adler**

"There is a problem", the doctors say. But even before the words are out you've seen it in their eyes, sensed in the way they peered at the baby as it struggled into life, bearing the mark of a moment when, in the twining dance of chromosomes that we call conception, something microscopic stuck or came undone. A problem. Two soft folds of tissue, groping toward one another in the darkness of the womb, failed to meet, somewhere in the three-dimensional complexities of the embryonic heart. Or the skein of nerves, spreading intricately from the bulb of the brain, left an unaccountable gap where no sensations flow, no muscles feel the impulse to move. And of all the things you might have wished for your child—wisdom or beauty or simple happiness—you are left forever after with one simple desire, a word that now embodies all your hope and longing: normal.

But these problems are a part of the human condition, exactly as prevalent now as they were when the United States began keeping detailed statistics in the 1960s, or for that matter in studies that go back to the 1890s: out of 100 babies, on average three are born with anomalies that will seriously affect their health. In one sense, this should be reassuring for expectant mothers who get nervous driving under electrical-power lines: while there is no doubt that drugs, radiation or industrial chemicals are capable of causing birth defects, these events are so rare as to be statistically negligible. (To the degree that birth defects are caused by environmental toxins, says Dr. Godfrey Oakley, head of the division of birth defects and developmental disabilities at the federal Centers for Disease Control, danger is more likely to be found in molds, vegetables or something else that has been with humanity for much longer than Alar or saccharin.) On the other hand, the great advances of the last 25 years in genetic science and embryology haven't done much to bring the rate of birth defects down, either. Surprisingly little research has been done on birth defects specifically, as distinct from human genetics; it was just last year that the CDC committed a modest $3 million to set up five centers to study the estimated 75 percent of birth defects whose causes remain a mystery.

Some problems are very well understood and can be prevented, although the prevention in some cases takes the form of an abortion. Abolishing fetal alcohol syndrome, which afflicts one baby in 1,000 with developmental problems, is as easy, and as difficult, as getting pregnant women to control their drinking. Four hundred micrograms daily of folic acid, taken before and during pregnancy, cuts by two thirds the risk of have a baby with neural-tube defects such as spina bifida, a crippling failure of the spinal cord to close. Yet "the best evidence we have is that only one out of four women is actually following that advice," Oakley says. One problem: the vitamin must be taken in the very first weeks after conception; starting only after a pregnancy is confirmed may be too late. In the last four years, Oakley adds, there were more preventable birth defects resulting from folic-acid deficiency in the United States than in the infamous epidemic of thalidomide poisoning in Europe 40 years ago,

## When Things Go Wrong: Birth Defects

Birth defects can arise from inherited genetic abnormalities as is the case with sickle cell anemia, from viruses such as those responsible for rubella, from poor prenatal care—or from reasons so mysterious they can only be labeled fate:

| Most Common Birth Defects* | Occurrence | Other Birth Defects | Occurrence |
|---|---|---|---|
| Congenital heart defects | 1/110 | Spina bifida | 1/2,000 |
| Narrow stomach/intestine junction | 1/250 | Cystic fibrosis | 1/2,000** |
| Congenital hip dislocation | 1/400 | Fragile X syndrome | 1/2,000++ |
| Sickle cell anemia | 1/400+ | Congenital HIV infection | 1/2,400 |
| Cerebral palsy | 1/500 | Missing/underdeveloped limbs | 1/2,500 |
| Cleft lip/cleft palate | 1/730 | Duchenne muscular dystrophy | 1/3,500*** |
| Clubfoot | 1/735 | Anencephaly | 1/8,000+++ |
| Down syndrome | 1/900 | Congenital rubella syndrome | 1/100,000 |
| Fetal alcohol syndrome | 1/1,000 | | |
| Hearing impairment | 1/1,000 | | |

*Live births in the U.S.
+Black babies
**White babies
++Mostly boys
***Boys
+++Occurs in 12,000 total pregnancies, but babies are often stillborn or aborted.

Sources: The March of Dimes, Centers for Disease Control

when a drug prescribed to ease morning sickness turned out to cause babies to be born with flippers for arms and legs.

A more complicated case is that of cerebral palsy, a nerve disorder that can effect voluntary movements including walking, writing and speech. Many cases result from maternal infections during pregnancy, and when doctors began controlling these a generation ago they expected cerebral palsy to eventually disappear. Instead, the rate has increased by 20 percent in 20 years, to approximately two in 1,000 births. This is because doctors are now keeping alive many more very premature and low-weight babies, who are prone to brain damage from lack of oxygen at birth. Yet a recent study showed a virtual elimination of cerebral palsy in at-risk babies whose mothers received the drug magnesium sulfate, which

appears to protect the brain against the toxic effects of oxygen deprivation. Thus the partial conquest of this crippling condition may yet be at hand, allowing for the fact that it can also be caused by lead poisoning, head injuries, encephalitis and probably several other things that we don't even know about yet.

But cerebral palsy is far from the worst problem a baby can be born with. The very worst things that can go wrong with an embryo are never encountered, because they are lethal long before birth, in some cases before the woman even knows she has conceived. By definition, a fetus born alive is a survivor, although sometimes the parents have no choice but to start mourning there and then. Babies born without brains (anencephaly) or with extra copies of chromosomes (trisomy) rarely live for more than a few days or

weeks, except in some special cases, of which the best known is Down syndrome.

These conditions are rare, however. The most common lethal defects, although still accounting for only a fraction of 1 percent of all births, are malformations of the heart. Fortunately, these are problems that surgeons have learned to treat (chart). Few conditions are more devastating than hypoplastic left-heart syndrome, in which the main pumping chamber fails to develop, and as recently as 15 years ago it was invariably fatal. But a three-stage operation developed by Dr. William I. Norwood, in which the right ventricle is made to do the job of its undeveloped partner, now keeps some of these children alive, at least until they can receive a transplant. Transposition of the aorta and pulmonary artery, which results in the heart's recirculating unoxgenated blood out to the body, used to be fatal about 90 percent of the time, but now has a 90 percent survival rate after surgery. Advances such as these, plus better neonatal intensive care generally have contributed to what Dr. Richard B. Johnston, medical director of the March of Dimes, says is a 50 percent drop in deaths from birth defects since the 1960s.

Down syndrome in theory is completely preventable, in the sense that there is a reliable test for the extra chromosome known to be its cause, after which the pregnancy can be terminated. Of course, that's not a solution to everyone's taste, and around 10 percent of women who know their babies will be born with Down syndrome go on to have them anyway, says Dr. Barbara K. Burton, director of the genetics center at Columbia Michael Reese Hospital in Chicago. But even though the other 90 percent do have abortions, the number of Down syndrome babies born each year is not declining, because more women are becoming pregnant later in life, when the chance of having a Down syndrome child rises dramatically. Burton estimates that only 6 to 8 percent of pregnant mothers get the tests — amniocentesis or chorionic villus sampling — that can detect the extra chromosome. Some of them may be put off by the slight risk of miscarriage, but a new test that may be available as early as next year promises to end that danger, according to Dr. Allen Horwitz of the University of Illinois College of Medicine. The procedure involves locating the infinitesimal quantity of fetal cells that cross the placenta into the mother's bloodstream, so only a sample of her blood would be required. "It's a way of finding samples of genes or chromosomes of the fetus without invading the uterus," says Horwitz.

And what of the mothers who have their babies anyway? A generation ago they would have been told that their child might never learn to speak, was certainly ineducable and probably should be sent to an institution — where, says David Patterson, president of the Eleanor Roosevelt Institute (which promotes genetic research), life expectancy was around 9 years. Unnumbered thousands of children perished in neglect that way, before an astounding paradigm shift that began in the 1970s, with parents who insisted on taking their Down syndrome babies home with them. With adequate care, it turned out, Down syndrome children didn't have to die before the age of 10; life expectancy now is 58 and rising, according to Patterson. With someone willing to teach them, most could learn to read, and some, says Lori Atkins of the National Down Syndrome Society, even have driver's licenses. It is possible, in short, for a Down syndrome child to hold a job and live at least a version of the sort of life that every parent dreams of from the moment he or she hears the fateful news that a child has "a problem."

A normal life.

 **Article Review Form at end of book.**

Explain two benefits and two risks associated with future advances in gene therapy. Why are the ethics of technologies that may someday be used to treat hereditary illnesses in question?

# Building a Better Baby?

**Mark Cohen**

They don't seem like the sort of parents who'd bet a child's health on a biological experiment. From all appearances, Ron Scanlon,* a naval technician, and his wife, Karen,* a preschool teacher, seem to be living an unremarkable suburban life in Virginia Beach, Virginia—except that their two dauthters, ages 4 and 1, have cystic fibrosis (CF), a hereditary lung disease whose victims seldom live past the age of 30.

Though healthy themselves, both Ron and Karen carry the gene for CF. And that means their next child—and they do want another—runs a one in four chance of inheriting the disease. It's a chance neither parent is willing take.

"Both of my children are wonderful, and it would break my heart if either one wasn't here," says Karen. "But if there was something we could do to make sure our next child wouldn't have CF, I'd be comfortable with that."

Unfortunately, the Scanlons don't feel they have a lot of options. They're not interested in adopting. And using prenatal testing to determine their unborn child's health and then possibly aborting the fetus is out of the question: both Ron and Karen consider this wrong. They've also ruled out an elaborate technique called preimplantation diagnosis, in which doctors fertilize several eggs, check the embryos for genetic abnormalities, and then implant a healthy embryo in the uterus, disposing of the flawed embryos.

What's left? An even more radical technique: *fixing* a genetic defect in the embryo or in the father's sperm before an egg is fertilized. The technology to achieve this may be available within the next couple of decades, and the Scanlons, now in their twenties, are thinking of waiting for it.

In other words, Ron and Karen Scanlon's next baby could be the product of human genetic engineering.

## Knowing Where to Stop

Genetic technology is a little like nuclear energy—the potential for both good and evil is enormous.

On the good side is the awesome power to cure that could come from addressing genetic defects at the earliest possible stage of human development. Even now, some researchers are inserting healthy genes in sick children and adults in an effort to treat a handful of potentially fatal illnesses, including cancer. But this "gene therapy" is limited in the kinds of problems it can fix.

Genetic engineering, also called "germ-line therapy," goes way beyond gene therapy in that it may be able to fix a problem almost before it exists. How? By allowing scientists to replace a single faulty gene with a normal one in a handful of sperm or fertilized eggs in a petri dish. As a result, genetic engineering has the potential to eliminate Fragile X syndrome (a leading genetic cause of mental retardation) by getting at the root of the problem before an embryo's brain has fully developed; it might someday provide a way to treat schizophrenia without drugs or to cure colon cancer without surgery or radiation. And because eggs and sperm are unique in their ability to pass on DNA, or genetic material, to later generations, genetic engineering could also make changes that, literally, would last forever. Parents

*These names have been changed.

might never have to worry about such devastating killers as CF, Tay-Sachs, or hereditary breast cancer again.

The terrifying part comes from the fear that people won't know where to stop. With the list of identified human genes growing almost by the week, the menu of diseases and traits that might someday be controlled by genetic engineering runs into the thousands. Permitting parents to eliminate their families' CF gene may seem like an easy call. But what about eliminating the gene for obesity? Or endowing an unborn child with the genes for blond hair and taller stature? Will the government need to step in and impose limits? And if so, how?

## From Animals to Humans

Germ-line genetic engineering requires making changes in the cells that ultimately give rise to every other cell in the body, so even the slightest mistake could lead to such disasters as arms growing where legs should be. A decade ago, a technique was developed that has proved to be pretty accurate—it can deliver a gene to an exact spot in a cell. But certain ethical complications seemed to preclude it from being applied to humans: Among other things, it requires mixing cells from two embryos to create one being.

University of Pennsylvania biologist Ralph Brinster may have found a way around this problem. He focuses on genetically altering the sperm rather than the embryo. Brinster's experiments on mice show that he can use sperm "stem" cells (the cells that create sperm) from one mouse to refill the sterile testicles of another and

produce healthy babies. His next step will be to see if he can grow enough sperm stem cells in a petri dish to replace faulty genes with healthy ones before injecting the sperm back into a mouse's testicles (see "Fixing Genes *Before* Conception").* At that point, he's likely to help other scientists apply his technique to lab animals and farm livestock.

And then? "I would bet some human reproductive specialists already are thinking about how they can use the technique," says Art Caplan, a bioethicist at the University of Pennsylvania. "From their perspective, there's almost no reason not to plunge ahead. No one has any compunction about experimenting on sperm."

Nor is Brinster's the only avenue that has been opened. Neal First, a reproductive physiologist at the University of Wisconsin, is working on another approach involving the fusing of a single cell from a genetically altered cow embryo into an unfertilized egg. Since it appears that the DNA of the embryo cell almost totally dominates that of the egg, First's technique—now being tested on livestock—addresses defects passed down from the mother's side.

## Beyond Genetic Roulette

How will society handle the ethical issues raised by all this research? In Europe, the leading scientific body has issued a policy that discourages its members from working on human germ-line therapy. In this country, the debate is still low key. Nevertheless, no research is currently being done on human genetic engineering that affects the gene pool, nor

*Does not appear in this publication.

will the federal government fund such trials.

It's easy to see why. Heaven forbid that another dictator like Hitler ever get his hands on the secrets to building "perfect" humans. And even in a free society, the technology could sorely test the social order. "This is bound to be an expensive technology," says LeRoy Walters, director of the Kennedy Institute of Ethics at Georgetown University. "We know what people will do to give their kids an advantage in life, like setting up trust funds or getting them into the best schools. I'd hate for these parents to compete to see who can provide the best head start for their children through genetic intervention." Since it's unlikely that health insurers would pay for cosmetic applications of genetic engineering—such as ensuring good looks or taller stature—the result could destabilize society, says Walters.

John Fletcher, a bioethicist at the University of Virginia, foresees another troubling marriage of genetic engineering and health insurance. "I can imagine a time when some HMOs will require their members to go through genetic testing and genetic therapy for certain costly genetic illnesses," he says. "If you weren't willing to go through such testing, they might not cover you."

And there are more concerns. James Neel, a professor emeritus of human genetics at the University of Michigan, is worried that there may be hidden dangers in deleting certain genes from the population. "Some of these harmful genes may have other functions that are good and right for us but that we just don't yet understand," he says. There is some evidence, for example, that the same genes that cause sickle cell disease and thalassemia help guard against malaria; and that the cystic fibrosis gene may help healthy carriers who later contract cholera from becoming dehydrated. "The fact is," Neel says, "we're just starting to gain the most feeble insights into what's really an extremely complicated machine—the human body."

Still, as much as he shared Neel's concern about the need for caution, Walters would hate to see the power of genetic engineering halted. "I think it's a risk worth taking," he says. "The goal should be to give everyone a chance to lead a full life, safeguarded against cancer or heart disease."

Caplan agrees. "I don't see any compelling ethical argument why the technology should not be used to treat certain tragic hereditary illnesses," he says. As experts and ordinary people alike begin wrestling with where to draw the line between, for instance, altering genes for depression and height, Tay-Sachs and baldness, "the question they have to keep asking themselves," says Caplan, "is, 'What kind of world do we want to create?'"

For the Scanlons, the issue of genetic engineering is no abstraction. "I don't agree with changing the genes for things like IQ or eye color," says Karen. "I'm not comfortable tampering with whatever natural traits a child is supposed to have."

Ron Scanlon is a little less confident of his convictions—but only a little. He admits he might feel a pang of keeping-up-with-the-Joneses if all of his friends and relatives were genetically altering their offspring to be smarter, faster, better looking. But he says he'd stop at altering anything that didn't seriously threaten his child's health.

"I think one of the most important ways we grow is by overcoming adversity," he says. "If you take away nature's ability to give us obstacles to conquer, then you're taking away someone's chance of being everything he's intended to be."

 **Article Review Form at end of book.**

What are the three "good" reasons given for enabling older women to have babies? What are the three "bad" reasons given for enabling older women to have babies?

# When I'm Sixty-Four

## Katha Pollitt

For the past two weeks everyone in America has been completely occupied in writing letters to the editor explaining why the 63-year-old woman who recently had a baby thanks to the wonders of modern science is to be commended or scourged. Try it yourself: Sixty-three-year-old women having babies is GOOD, because it (a) maximizes human choices, (b) makes women more equal to men, who have been fathering kids as geezers with younger women since time immemorial to approving smirks, (c) reminds us that postmenopausal women are still sexual beings. Or: Sixty-three-old-old women having babies is BAD, because it (a) violates the limits of nature and life cycle, (b) further defines women as having only reproductive value, (c) reminds us that postmenopausal women are still sexual beings.

By now we can all recite the arguments on any side at an instant's notice. Is Miracle Mom selfish? Ahem. For the affirmative: When Miracle Baby is a surly Miracle Teen, Mom will be practically 80, with Dad only slightly younger. How will she be able to stand the horrible music that will surely be all the rage among the gilded youth of 2015? What if she's sick, senile, dead? Blah, blah, blah. For the negative: She's got great genes. Plenty of younger parents can't keep up with their kids; tragedy can strike at any age. And what about all those start-over dads? They'll be keeling over by the dozens by the time their kids are out of diapers. Yak, yak, yak.

Let's just cut to the finish line. Of course it's sexist to criticize Miracle Mom while congratulating 77-year-old Tony Randall or 70-year-old George Plimpton (whose young brides, interestingly, never seem to make it into the family photo shoot—their role in the media debate is to be on standby for the post-keel-over moment). It's even an illusion to see start-over dads as more natural than postmenopausal moms: Without modern medicine (not to mention Nautilus machines, plastic surgery, money and celebrity) most septuagenarians would be in no condition to attract younger women, much less impregnate them. On the other hand, it's reasonable to wonder if geriatric parenting on the part of either sex is such a great idea for children, although in an era that features as parents anyone from 12-year-old rape victims to vials of posthumously preserved sperm, why fuss about a few wrinkles?

But the real point is, Who cares? Why are we even talking about this? Post-retirement babies are not going to be a popular option for either sex, any time soon. Most people in their 60s with the necessary cash, leisure and vigor have other plans—playing the slots, driving around the country in R.V.s, writing angry letters to their representatives about attempts to recalculate the consumer price index. If every now and then a woman feels driven to put herself through gynecological hell (according to the *National Enquirer*, Miracle Mom had five in vitros, at a total cost of $32,000), why can't we just add it to the very long list of oddball things people do and leave the whole Miracle Family alone?

The amazing thing about the story is that for all the endless stream of verbiage about it, the important issues it raises still go undiscussed. Just think, for example, about the society that has

Reprinted with permission from the 1997 issue of *The Nation* magazine.

produced a health care system with the resources to create this baby but that "cannot afford" prenatal care for one in six women, and that is now congratulating itself over proposals to provide medical insurance for half the 10 million children who lack it—never mind the other half, or the rest of the family, either. I'm not attacking Miracle Mom—as long as we have for-profit medicine, why shouldn't she be able to buy a childbirth? But her story certainly illustrates the weird distortions the profit motive has introduced into health care. How come medical ethicists, ever ready with a pious sound-bite, don't talk about that?

The truth is, medical ethics, like the media, and like medicine itself, treats individual cases as if they were about personal choices when they really represent masked social decisions. Behind Miracle Mom is a huge medical machinery that we have chosen to render invisible, just as behind the start-over dads is a huge so-cial machinery (not just the young wives but nannies, house-keepers, private schools, wealth) that is similarly unacknowledged and that permits them to limit their fatherhood to its ceremonial aspects.

The Miracle Mom brouhaha obscures another reality too. Like the ongoing sensation of the JonBenet Ramsey murder case, it allows an outlet for self-congratulatory outrage on behalf of children while having almost nothing to do with the conditions in which children actually live. It feels good to fire off a letter about how foolish a late-middle-aged woman is to imagine she can keep up with an active toddler, and how sad it will be for her child to spend her youth caring for aged parents or mourning their deaths. And yet we live placidly in a nation in which thousands upon thousands of poor children are being raised by their grandmothers, under truly grim conditions, and in which, indeed, those grandmothers may be all that stands between those children and the new for-profit foster care businesses permitted under welfare reform. (According to Nina Bernstein's spectacular exposé in *The New York Times,* it was a Democrat, Senator John Breaux of Louisiana, who engineered this coup.) In the same way, the tabloid spotlight focused on the awful life and death of JonBenet serves as a substitute for the spotlight that should be focused on all abused children, and the circumstances that permit abuse to flourish.

In the time the nation's spent obsessing over Miracle Mom, how many babies have been born to girls in foster care? To women living in homeless shelters? On the streets? These questions, unlike those of Miracle Mom's longevity and Miracle Teen's happiness, have answers. Maybe that's why we prefer not to ask them.

 **Article Review Form at end of book.**

What is the pro-choice position on fetal rights? What is the pro-life position on fetal rights?

# When Does Life Begin?

## The Supreme Court ponders the rights of a fetus

### D'arcy Jenish

William G, as he is known, is a six-month-old Winnipeg boy who survived a perilous journey into this world. His mother, a 23-year-old reformed glue and solvent sniffer identified only as Ms. G, had previously given birth to three other children—two suffering mental damage as a result of her addiction. William, who is living with his parents, is said to be healthy and developing normally. Nevertheless, he remains at the centre of a stormy legal battle that has the potential both to limit the rights of pregnant women and, for the first time, bestow legal rights on fetuses.

The issue arose last summer when a Winnipeg social agency obtained a court order forcing Ms. G—then five months pregnant and still sniffing solvents—to seek medical treatment for her addiction. An appeal court later overturned the order. But last week, the case moved to the Supreme Court of Canada, which heard arguments on several hotly controversial issues, including the rights of fetuses and mandatory medical treatment for pregnant women. "The case could lead to a huge change in the law," says Winnipeg lawyer David Phillips, who represents Ms. G. "Potentially, everything a pregnant woman does could be subject to court scrutiny."

With so much at stake, 13 organizations and government agencies presented their arguments before the Supreme Court. Women's groups, pro-choice organizations and the Canadian Civil Liberties Association argued that allowing the state to control the actions of an expectant mother was a serious infringement on the rights of women. Such a power, they said, could potentially be used to curtail access to abortion. Child welfare agencies, pro-life groups and such religious organizations as the Evangelical Fellowship of Canada argued in favor of recognizing the fetus as a person entitled to the full protection of the law—something the Supreme Court has avoided doing in several decisions over the past decade. "If a woman decides to carry a child to term, that child is entitled to be born in as healthy a state as possible," maintains David Brown, a Toronto lawyer representing the Evangelical Fellowship. "You simply can't ignore the child."

The nine-member court is not likely to deliver a decision for several months. But officials with Winnipeg Child and Family Services, the agency that obtained the initial court order, and lawyers for the Manitoba government reject the notion that it could have broad implications for women. Donna Miller, director of the constitutional law branch with the provincial department of justice, says the government simply wants the authority to order women into treatment in the rare cases in which their conduct threatens the health or survival of the fetus. "We're talking about an exceptional remedy," says Miller. "We're not talking about any interference in the decision a woman makes about carrying the child to term."

But other lawyers say that a decision siding with the Winnipeg agency and the Manitoba government would fundamentally change the law by recognizing the unborn child as a person, independent of its mother. As such, says Phillips, the fetus would automatically acquire legal rights that could be exercised against others, including the mother. Child welfare workers could, for example, seek court protection for the fetus in cases where the mother smokes during pregnancy, he suggests.

According to some women's groups, recognition of fetal rights would in turn renew the battle over access to abortion. "You have five or six pro-life groups intervening in this case," says Carissima Mathen, a staff lawyer with the Toronto-based Women's Legal Education and Action Fund. "There's definitely a link between this case and the bigger question of whether a woman can decide to continue a pregnancy or not." Jo Dufay, executive director of the Toronto-based Canadian Abortion Rights Action League, adds that conferring legal rights on fetuses would inevitably lead to a battle to define and expand those rights. "It could lead to a situation where a man intervenes because he doesn't think it is right for a woman to have an abortion," she says.

But apart from those concerns, many women's groups staunchly oppose the notion of court-ordered medical treatment for pregnant women—even when the objective is to protect the fetus. Governments should instead put the resources into addiction treatment and counselling, says Mathen. And, cautions Dufay, pregnant women with addictions could avoid doctors and social agencies if they face the prospect of obligatory treatment.

"You can't lock a woman up because she's pregnant and you don't like the way she's behaving," says Dufay.

In Ms. G's case, she decided to stay in the Winnipeg treatment centre even after the Appeal Court ruled she could not be held against her will. She has been free of her addiction for about nine months, says her lawyer, and receives regular visits from child welfare officials. Now, church and pro-life groups say it is time for the Supreme Court to define a balance between a pregnant woman's rights and her responsibilities to the fetus. "You can't find another human relationship where you have such a closeness between two people," said Brown. "That closeness gives rise to a duty of care." It has also given rise to a complex case that will undoubtedly tax the collective wisdom of the highest court in the land.

 **Article Review Form at end of book.**

Describe the typical sequence of hospital-based labor and delivery events of a noncomplicated pregnancy. Describe the newborn's first experiences within minutes after a birth.

# Labor Day

## A complete guide to your hospital birth

**Candy Schulman**

As your pregnant belly grows, you're bound to hear an endless array of labor stories—ranging from "My baby came out so fast, my doctor didn't have time to put on her gown!" to "Forty-six hours of labor—never again!" Every birth experience is different and unpredictable, just the way every newborn is one-of-a-kind. However, it you're prepared for what to expect at the hospital—and if you feel free to ask any questions you have once you get there—you'll be more relaxed throughout labor and delivery.

### You'll Be Examined When You Arrive at the Hospital

Your doctor will probably suggest that you go to the hospital when contractions are five minutes apart. Usually in a separate exam room on the labor floor, a doctor, resident (staff doctor), or nurse will perform a vaginal exam to determine how dilated your cervix is, and if you're ready to be admitted. Even if you've filled out pre-admission forms, your part-ner must leave you to go to the admissions office.

You won't be alone, though. You'll most likely be with your labor nurse, who will be a great source of support, information, and advice during labor and de-livery. You'll see and count on her more than your obstetrician—pos-sibly even more than your hus-band, who may feel helpless when he sees you in pain.

Although your doctor won't be very far away, your nurse is al-ways close by. In between visits when he announces, "You're five centimeters dilated now," your doctor may be seeing patients in his office, napping nearby (if it's nighttime) or delivering another baby.

"Your physician monitors all medical care; your nurse executes the care and communicates essen-tial information to your doctor," says Betty Tannin Dicker, M.S.N., senior nurse clinician and child-birth educator at Tisch Hospital/New York University Medical Center. Nursing care also includes checking vital signs, such as pulse and blood pressure, and overseeing fetal monitors and IVs. In a teaching hospital, your labor may also be monitored by a resi-dent, but most medical decisions are still made in consultation with your doctor.

### Most of Your Time Will Be Spent in the Labor Room

Many hospitals now have birthing rooms, often with cozy decor, which are combination labor/de-livery rooms. When you're about ready to give birth, the lower half of the birthing bed breaks away so your doctor can move in close to you. Birthing rooms may be re-served for low-risk pregnancies and given out on a first-come, first-served basis.

If you're in a traditional labor room, you'll stay there until right before delivery. Most hospitals no longer require shaving of the vagi-nal area or routine enemas, but you may be hooked up to an IV to give you extra fluids and nutri-ents. In order to make sure your baby is tolerating labor well, you'll probably be attached to an elec-tronic fetal monitor for about 20 minutes (and possibly again later on). Two belts are placed around your abdomen; one records your contractions, and the other uses ultrasound to measure how the baby's heart rate changes in re-sponse to the contractions. Unless your doctor says you need to stay on a monitor (if fetal distress is suspected, for example), you'll be able to get up and move around, even with an IV. Gravity helps speed labor along.

The most popular pain-relief option is an epidural, a nerve block that causes numbness from the waist down. While you're sitting up and bending forward or lying on your side, the anesthesiologist numbs the area on your back before inserting a needle into the space between the spinal cord and its outer membrane. A small tube is threaded through the needle, which is removed, leaving the tube in place. That way, you can be given low doses of the drug continuously, although the medication will be stopped in time for you to regain sensation for pushing. Once you've had an epidural, you can no longer stand up, and you'll need to have fetal monitoring, frequent blood-pressure checks, and possibly a urinary catheter.

When you're finally ten centimeters dilated, you should feel the urge to start pushing. The most common pushing position is semi-upright, knees bent, feet resting on the nurse and doctor's shoulders. However, a semi-sitting or semi-squatting position, which works along with gravity, may be the most efficient for pushing.

## Just Before the Birth, You'll Move to the Delivery Room

Soon after the baby's head has crowned, you may be wheeled into a larger delivery room, which resembles an operating room. If an episiotomy is necessary, a local anesthetic may be injected into the perineum before the incision is made; most women find this painless.

With one or two more pushes, your baby arrives! You may be able to hold your baby before the umbilical cord is cut; when hospitals don't allow this, the doctor will cut the cord first and suction the baby's nose and mouth to eliminate any mucus. Your doctor will then ask you to push again in order to expel the placenta before he stitches up the episiotomy site.

A nurse or doctor will give your newborn an initial exam, including using the Apgar scale to evaluate his condition (heart rate, breathing, color, muscle tone, reflex), weighing, measuring, taking footprints, giving eyedrops to prevent infection, cleaning, and fastening matching ID bracelets onto your and the baby's wrists.

If your doctor recommends a cesarean section, most hospitals will allow your spouse to attend the birth—except in emergencies when general anesthesia is used. Usually, you'll be awake and given regional anesthesia (epidural or spinal). Your partner will sit by your head, and his view of the surgery is shielded by a screen. Although it takes about 10 to 15 minutes until your baby is delivered, the entire procedure lasts more than an hour.

## You Can Relax for a While in the Recovery Room

The next hour or two is usually spent in the recovery room, although, depending on the hospital, you may go directly to your room on the maternity floor. Your vital signs, such as blood pressure, will be monitored, and you'll be given pain-relief medication if necessary. If you've had an epidural, you must stay in the recovery room until the anesthesia wears off and you can feel your legs completely. Meanwhile, you

can hold and nurse your baby, take photographs, and muse over whose nose she has.

## Maternity Ward Nurses Care for You and Your Baby

Since most insurance companies allow hospitalization for only 24 to 48 hours after a vaginal delivery and four days after a cesarean, try to blend recuperation with education. Don't be afraid to admit that you know little about caring for a newborn; the nurses will be happy to help you with breast-feeding or demonstrate basics like diapering, bathing and umbilical-stump care.

Be prepared for the discharge of blood (lochia) after delivery, which may be heavier than a menstrual period for three days and pinker by the week's end. Sanitary pads, not tampons, should be used; you may prefer to bring your own. You'll experience uterine cramps (as the uterus returns to its normal size), and possibly have difficulty with urination and bowel movements for a few days, and soreness around the episiotomy site. Nurses will give you a squirt bottle to cleanse the perineal area with warm water after urination to prevent infection. Sitz baths can soothe episiotomies and hemorrhoids. Pain medication ranges from acetaminophen to IV Demerol; if you're nursing, check with your doctor to make sure that any drug is compatible with breast-feeding.

Rest is absolutely essential. It's often difficult, though, because visitors and flowers arrive . . . and you can't stop adoring, stroking, and snuggling your baby. The end of labor is a remarkable new beginning.

 **Article Review Form at end of book.**

# WiseGuide Wrap-Up

- Out of 100 babies, 3 are likely to be born with birth defects. The underlying causes are many and often unknown.

- New advancements in gene therapy are making real the possibility of someday repairing birth defects in the womb or of preventing their occurrence at all. Of concern is how far the technology should be taken. Though few would argue against the use of technology to treat tragic hereditary illnesses, how is the line to be drawn when considering other traits, such as intelligence and personality?

- Since a 63-year-old woman gave birth with the help of fertility experts, many have debated the ethics of modern science. Some view this advancement as furthering equality of the sexes and maximizing choice. Others see such interventions as unnatural, as burdening young offspring with the care of elderly parents and as the product of our *for-profit* healthcare system.

- As we have learned more about the vulnerability of the fetus, attention has turned to situations in which pregnant women knowingly act in ways that are potentially harmful to their unborn babies. The courts are now testing whether the rights of pregnant women may be restricted for the sake of the fetus.

- Though every labor is unique, there are some very probable experiences. Availability of birthing rooms, labor coaches, and fetal monitoring is now common place. Many women will also make the decision to use some form of labor medication and to breastfeed.

## R.E.A.L. Sites

This list provides a print preview of typical **coursewise** R.E.A.L. sites. There are over 100 such sites at the **courselinks**™ site. The danger in printing URLs is that web sites can change overnight. As we went to press, these sites were functional using the URLs provided. If you come across one that isn't, please let us know via email to: webmaster@coursewise.com. Use your Passport to access the most current list of R.E.A.L. sites at the **courselinks**™ site.

**Site name:** Down Syndrome
**URL:** http://www.nas.com/downsyn/index.html
**Why is it R.E.A.L.?** A major concern of new parents is whether or not their fetus is healthy. The most common birth defect for mothers over 40 is Down syndrome. This web site is designed to provide the best information available on the World Wide Web regarding Down syndrome. Healthcare guidelines for people with Down syndrome, medical essays and issues common to children with Down syndrome, and an extensive listing of other Down syndrome web sites are included. Visit this web site to discover the issues facing parents of children with Down syndrome in the United States and other countries. Are children with Down syndrome treated differently in other countries? Identify any issues that might be the result of cultural differences.

**Site name:** Age of Fertility
**URL:** http://www.fertilitext.org/age_fert.htm
**Why is it R.E.A.L.?** The most recent controversy included in this section of readings is the one regarding age of motherhood. How old is too old to experience biological motherhood? Visit this site and read the most recent research regarding factors influencing the outcome of pregnancies of older women. Before you visit the site, make a list of the issues you think are most critical. For example, you might question the viability of eggs that have been in the womb for over 40 years. What does the research say about this and other questions you develop? Are there "real" major concerns for the birth of children to older mothers, or is it merely a question of societal prejudices against older mothers?

# section

## 2

### Learning Objectives

- Provide a simplified explanation of brain development.

- Present information on how to provide optimal early environments for children.

- Explain common hospital-based events during and following a birth.

- Provide information on the amazing abilities of infants and young children.

- Discuss child abuse issues.

# The Newborn and Infant

**WiseGuide Intro**

A baby is born and there's a flurry of activity, anticipation, uncertainty, and joy! We no longer conceive of the newborn as a "blank slate", ready to be molded by the whims of caregivers, nor do we believe that infants are confronted with a whirling blur of disorganized stimulation or that the secret to a child's final outcome is written in the genes. Today, we know that nature and nurture work together to influence development. Biological events occurring during the gestational period prepare the infant to learn from stimulation present in the world outside the womb. The provision of developmentally appropriate experiences for infants and young children can profoundly affect brain development. Rich experiences really do produce rich brains. The dramatic changes that occur in the brain during the first years of life have profound implications for parents and policymakers. Questions concerning the impact of poor prenatal care, impoverished and understimulating home environments, child abuse and neglect, and the high turnover rates and substandard training of child care providers on children's long-term development abound.

How can new parents be confident that they are providing their newborn with the best start at life? Knowledge of what is normal may be one answer, and that begins with familiarity with hospital routines. Various procedures are more or less standard in American hospitals following a birth. In the first moments and hours of life, tests are run and observations are made. Any signs of abnormality are double-checked by hospital personnel. Along with initial assessments of the newborn's health status, newborn reflexes, sleep patterns, and feeding responses are noted. Blood screenings for serious illnesses are completed and the first immunizations are given. The medical community should remain an important part of the child's life even after discharge at 2–5 days of age.

Once home, it is helpful to know about the newborn's capabilities. Such knowledge may help new parents provide the stimulation needed to boost development. Infants' sensory systems, though immature, are functioning well and collecting information. Babies see, hear, smell, and taste. They also feel pain, are uncomfortable if too hot or cold, and respond positively to consistent, loving care. Babies also remember and begin to form expectations based on their experiences within the first months of life.

Unfortunately, not all caregivers are able to respond appropriately to the early signals of the children in their charge. Though most child deaths are due to illness and accident, some infants and toddlers die or are seriously impaired at the hands of their care providers. In recent years, cases of infanticide as a result of child abuse, parental mental illness, and inappropriate methods of handling have been highlighted in the media. Many questions surround how cases of infanticide are distinguished from natural or accidental deaths.

## ? Questions ?

**Reading 6.** What major changes does the brain undergo in the first years of life?

Describe at least two types of home experiences found to negatively affect the development of a child's brain.

**Reading 7.** Upon birth, what positive signs of newborn health is the doctor looking for?

Why is it important that mothers and their newborns remain in the hospital for a minimum of 48 hours?

**Reading 8.** Some responses of newborns suggest that learning is occurring in the womb. Give an example and the bodily system involved.

How do babies come to love their parents?

Describe the infant and parent behaviors involved in the process of attachment.

**Reading 9.** Why are cases of Sudden Infant Death Syndrome being reexamined?

What does the American Academy of Pediatrics currently recommend for helping infants to sleep?

**Reading 10.** What caregiver circumstances are most associated with instances of Shaken Baby Syndrome?

Who is at greatest risk for being a victim of Shaken Baby Syndrome?

## Thinking Beyond the Facts

Consider the issues presented in this section on the newborn and infant. The rapid development of the brain during infancy and early childhood suggests that as a society we are failing to provide for a large number of our young citizens. Many American children live in poverty, with parents who struggle to provide the basics in terms of food, shelter, and medical care. Often these parents lack the means or knowledge necessary to provide developmentally appropriate stimulation. Unfortunately, these children are also likely to live in unhealthy or dangerous environments, to be enrolled in poor-quality child care programs, and later to attend inadequately funded schools. With welfare reforms in progress, there is much uncertainty. Breaking the cycle of dependence, hopefully, will not result in further cognitive losses for these children. What are your views about welfare supports and Aid to Dependent Families? Do you think welfare reform will help or hurt children in the short and long run? What are your state's current welfare requirements for families with children?

Though it may be comforting to believe that children at risk belong only to the poorest of inner-city parents, the truth is that risk factors exist at all income levels and in all regions of the country. Teenage pregnancy, out-of-wedlock births, substance abuse, and low level of education are among the factors strongly associated with early childhood risks. However, affluence is not a guarantee of knowing how to care for a child. Under the right circumstances, anyone might abuse a child or even commit infanticide. Recent cases of Shaken Baby Syndrome highlight the news and make clear the difficulty of determining intent to cause harm. Cases of SIDS are being reexamined, as psychological disorders of parents are linked to infant deaths. As it has been said, people must obtain licenses to own a dog and drive a car, but anyone can become a parent. Should new parents be monitored for stress-related factors that might lead to child abuse or neglect? Should high school curricula require parenting and child care classes? What other widely available means to educate future parents might be considered? Perhaps punishment is the answer. Would imprisonment of those caught or suspected of actions against children stop future offenses and offenders? Visit web sites on child abuse, SIDS, child care options, and new baby care for more information on these early life topics.

What major changes does the brain undergo in the first years of life? Describe at least two types of home experiences found to negatively affect the development of a child's brain.

# Fertile Minds

## J. Madeleine Nash

Rat-a-tat-tat. Rat-a-tat-tat. Rat-a-tat-tat. If scientists could eavesdrop on the brain of a human embryo 10, maybe 12 weeks after conception, they would hear an astonishing racket. Inside the womb, long before light first strikes the retina of the eye or the earliest dreamy images flicker through the cortex, nerve cells in the developing brain crackle with purposeful activity. Like teenagers with telephones, cells in one neighborhood of the brain are calling friends in another, and these cells are calling their friends, and they keep calling one another over and over again, "almost," says neurobiologist Carla Shatz of the University of California, Berkeley, "as if they were autodialing."

But these neurons—as the long, wiry cells that carry electrical messages through the nervous system and the brain are called—are not transmitting signals in scattershot fashion. That would produce a featureless static, the sort of noise picked up by a radio tuned between stations. On the contrary, evidence is growing that the stac-cato bursts of electricity that form those distinctive rat-a-tat-tats arise from coordinated waves of neural activity, and that those pulsing waves, like currents shifting sand on the ocean floor, actually change the shape of the brain, carving mental circuits into patterns that over time will enable the newborn infant to perceive a father's voice, a mother's touch, a shiny mobile twirling over the crib.

Of all the discoveries that have poured out of neuroscience labs in recent years, the finding that the electrical activity of brain cells changes the physical structure of the brain is perhaps the most breathtaking. For the rhythmic firing of neurons is no longer assumed to be a by-product of building the brain but essential to the process, and it begins, scientists have established, well before birth. A brain is not a computer. Nature does not cobble it together, then turn it on. No, the brain begins working long before it is finished. And the same processes that wire the brain before birth, neuroscientists are finding, also drive the explosion of learning that occurs immediately afterward.

At birth a baby's brain contains 100 billion neurons, roughly as many nerve cells as there are stars in the Milky Way. Also in place are a trillion glial cells, named after the Greek word for glue, which form a kind of honeycomb that protects and nourishes the neurons. But while the brain contains virtually all the nerve cells it will ever have, the pattern of wiring between them has yet to stabilize. Up to this point, says Shatz, "what the brain has done is lay out circuits that are its best guess about what's required for vision, for language, for whatever." And now it is up to neural activity—no longer spontaneous, but driven by a flood of sensory experiences—to take this rough blueprint and progressively refine it.

During the first years of life, the brain undergoes a series of extraordinary changes. Starting shortly after birth, a baby's brain, in a display of biological exuberance, produces trillions more connections between neurons than it can possibly use. Then, through a process that resembles Darwinian competition, the brain eliminates connections, or synapses, that are seldom or never used. The excess synapses in a child's brain undergo a draconian pruning, starting around the age of 10 or earlier, leaving behind a mind whose patterns of emotion and thought are, for better or worse, unique.

Deprived of a stimulating environment, a child's brain suffers. Researchers at Baylor College of Medicine, for example, have found that children who don't play much or are rarely touched develop brains 20% to 30% smaller than normal for their age. Laboratory animals provide another provocative parallel. Not only do young rats reared in toy-strewn cages exhibit more complex behavior than rats confined to sterile, uninteresting boxes, researchers at the University of Illinois at Urbana-Champaign have found, but the brains of these rats contain as many as 25% more synapses per neuron. Rich experiences, in other words, really do produce rich brains.

The new insights into brain development are more than just interesting science. They have profound implications for parents and policymakers. In an age when mothers and fathers are increasingly pressed for time—and may already be feeling guilty about how many hours they spend away from their children—the results coming out of the labs are likely to increase concerns about leaving very young children in the care of others. For the data underscore the importance of hands-on parenting, of finding the time to cuddle a baby, talk with a toddler and provide infants with stimulating experiences.

The new insights have begun to infuse new passion into the political debate over early education and day care. There is an urgent need, say child-development experts, for preschool programs designed to boost the brain power of youngsters born into impoverished rural and inner-city households. Without such programs,

they warn, the current drive to curtail welfare costs by pushing mothers with infants and toddlers into the work force may well backfire. "There is a time scale to brain development, and the most important year is the first," notes Frank Newman, president of the Education Commission of the States. By the age of three, a child who is neglected or abused bears marks that, if not indelible, are exceedingly difficult to erase.

But the new research offers hope as well. Scientists have found that the brain during the first years of life is so malleable that very young children who suffer strokes or injuries that wipe out an entire hemisphere can still mature into highly functional adults. Moreover, it is becoming increasingly clear that well-designed preschool programs can help many children overcome glaring deficits in their home environment. With appropriate therapy, say researchers, even serious disorders like dyslexia may be treatable. While inherited problems may place certain children at greater risk than others, says Dr. Harry Chugani, a pediatric neurologist at Wayne State University in Detroit, that is no excuse for ignoring the environment's power to remodel the brain. "We may not do much to change what happens before birth, but we can change what happens after a baby is born," he observes.

Strong evidence that activity changes the brain began accumulating in the 1970s. But only recently have researchers had tools powerful enough to reveal the precise mechanisms by which those changes are brought about. Neural activity triggers a biochemical cascade that reaches all the way to the nucleus of cells and the coils of DNA that encode specific genes. In fact, two of the

genes affected by neural activity in embryonic fruit flies, neurobiologist Corey Goodman and his colleagues at Berkeley reported late last year, are identical to those that other studies have linked to learning and memory. How thrilling, exclaims Goodman, how intellectually satisfying that the snippets of DNA that embryos use to build their brains are the very same ones that will later allow adult organisms to process and store new information.

As researchers explore the once hidden links between brain activity and brain structure, they are beginning to construct a sturdy bridge over the chasm that previously separated genes from the environment. Experts now agree that a baby does not come into the world as a genetically preprogrammed automaton or a blank slate at the mercy of the environment, but arrives as something much more interesting. For this reason the debate that engaged countless generations of philosophers—whether nature or nurture calls the shots—no longer interests most scientists. They are much too busy chronicling the myriad ways in which genes and the environment interact. "It's not a competition," says Dr. Stanley Greenspan, a psychiatrist at George Washington University. "It's a dance."

## The Importance of Genes

That dance begins at around the third week of gestation, when a thin layer of cells in the developing embryo performs an origami-like trick, folding inward to give rise to a fluid-filled cylinder known as the neural tube. As cells in the neural tube proliferate at the astonishing rate of 250,000 a minute, the brain and spinal cord

The Newborn and Infant   **19**

assemble themselves in a series of tightly choreographed steps. Nature is the dominant partner during this phase of development, but nurture plays a vital supportive role. Changes in the environment of the womb—whether caused by maternal malnutrition, drug abuse or a viral infection—can wreck the clockwork precision of the neural assembly line. Some forms of epilepsy, mental retardation, autism and schizophrenia appear to be the results of developmental processes gone awry.

But what awes scientists who study the brain, what still stuns them, is not that things occasionally go wrong in the developing brain but that so much of the time they go right. This is all the more remarkable, says Berkeley's Shatz, as the central nervous system of an embryo is not a miniature of the adult system but more like a tadpole that gives rise to a frog. Among other things, the cells produced in the neural tube must migrate to distant locations and accurately lay down the connections that link one part of the brain to another. In addition, the embryonic brain must construct a variety of temporary structures, including the neural tube, that will, like a tadpole's tail, eventually disappear.

What biochemical magic underlies this incredible metamorphosis? The instructions programmed into the genes, of course. Scientists have recently discovered, for instance, that a gene nicknamed "sonic hedgehog" (after the popular video game Sonic the Hedgehog) determines the fate of neurons in the spinal cord and the brain. Like a strong scent carried by the wind, the protein encoded by the hedgehog gene (so called because in its absence, fruit-fly embryos sprout a coat of prickles)

diffuses outward from the cells that produce it, becoming fainter and fainter. Columbia University neurobiologist Thomas Jessell has found that it takes middling concentrations of this potent morphing factor to produce a motor neuron and lower concentrations to make an interneuron (a cell that relays signals to other neurons, instead of to muscle fibers, as motor neurons do).

Scientists are also beginning to identify some of the genes that guide neurons in their long migrations. Consider the problem faced by neurons destined to become part of the cerebral cortex. Because they arise relatively late in the development of the mammalian brain, billions of these cells must push and shove their way through dense colonies established by earlier migrants. "It's as if the entire population of the East Coast decided to move en masse to the West Coast," marvels Yale University neuroscientist Dr. Pasko Rakic, and marched through Cleveland, Chicago and Denver to get there.

But of all the problems the growing nervous system must solve, the most daunting is posed by the wiring itself. After birth, when the number of connections explodes, each of the brain's billions of neurons will forge links to thousands of others. First they must spin out a web of wirelike fibers known as axons (which transmit signals) and dendrites (which receive them). The objective is to form a synapse, the gaplike structure over which the axon of one neuron beams a signal to the dendrites of another. Before this can happen, axons and dendrites must almost touch. And while the short, bushy dendrites don't have to travel very far, axons—the heavy-duty cables of the nervous system—must traverse distances that are the microscopic equivalent of miles.

What guides an axon on its incredible voyage is a "growth cone," a creepy, crawly sprout that looks something like an amoeba. Scientists have known about growth cones since the turn of the century. What they didn't know until recently was that growth cones come equipped with the molecular equivalent of sonar and radar. Just as instruments in a submarine or airplane scan the environment for signals, so molecules arrayed on the surface of growth cones search their surroundings for the presence of certain proteins. Some of these proteins, it turns out, are attractants that pull the growth cones toward them, while others are repellents that push them away.

## The First Stirrings

Up to this point, genes have controlled the unfolding of the brain. As soon as axons make their first connections, however, the nerves begin to fire, and what they do starts to matter more and more. In essence, say scientists, the developing nervous system has strung the equivalent of telephone trunk lines between the right neighborhoods in the right cities. Now it has to sort out which wires belong to which house, a problem that cannot be solved by genes alone for reasons that boil down to simple arithmetic. Eventually, Berkeley's Goodman estimates, a human brain must forge quadrillions of connections. But there are only 100,000 genes in human DNA. Even though half these genes—some 50,000—appear to be dedicated to constructing and maintaining the nervous system, he observes, that's not enough to specify more than a tiny fraction of the connections required by a fully functioning brain.

In adult mammals, for example, the axons that connect the brain's visual system arrange themselves in striking layers and columns that reflect the division between the left eye and the right. But these axons start out as scrambled as a bowl of spaghetti, according to Michael Stryker, chairman of the physiology department at the University of California at San Francisco. What sorts out the mess, scientists have established, is neural activity. In a series of experiments viewed as classics by scientists in the field, Berkeley's Shatz chemically blocked neural activity in embryonic cats. The result? The axons that connect neurons in the retina of the eye to the brain never formed the left eye-right eye geometry needed to support vision.

But no recent finding has intrigued researchers more than the results reported in October by Corey Goodman and his Berkeley colleagues. In studying a deceptively simple problem—how axons from motor neurons in the fly's central nerve cord establish connections with muscle cells in its limbs—the Berkeley researchers made an unexpected discovery. They knew there was a gene that keeps bundles of axons together as they race toward their muscle-cell targets. What they discovered was that the electrical activity produced by neurons inhibited this gene, dramatically increasing the number of connections the axons made. Even more intriguing, the signals amplified the activity of a second gene—a gene called CREB.

The discovery of the CREB amplifier, more than any other, links the developmental processes that occur before birth to those that continue long after. For the twin processes of memory and learning in adult animals,

Columbia University neurophysiologist Eric Kandel has shown, rely on the CREB molecule. When Kandel blocked the activity of CREB in giant snails, their brains changed in ways that suggested that they could still learn but could remember what they learned for only a short period of time. Without CREB, it seems, snails—and by extension, more developed animals like humans—can form no long-term memories. And without long-term memories, it is hard to imagine that infant brains could ever master more than rudimentary skills. "Nurture is important," says Kandel. "But nurture works through nature."

## Experience Kicks In

When a baby is born, it can see and hear and smell and respond to touch, but only dimly. The brain stem, a primitive region that controls vital functions like heartbeat and breathing, has completed its wiring. Elsewhere the connections between neurons are wispy and weak. But over the first few months of life, the brain's higher centers explode with new synapses. And as dendrites and axons swell with buds and branches like trees in spring, metabolism soars. By the age of two, a child's brain contains twice as many synapses and consumes twice as much energy as the brain of a normal adult.

University of Chicago pediatric neurologist Dr. Peter Huttenlocher has chronicled this extraordinary epoch in brain development by autopsying the brains of infants and young children who have died unexpectedly. The number of synapses in one layer of the visual cortex, Huttenlocher reports, rises from around 2,500 per neuron at birth

to as many as 18,000 about six months later. Other regions of the cortex score similarly spectacular increases but on slightly different schedules. And while these microscopic connections between nerve fibers continue to form throughout life, they reach their highest average densities (15,000 synapses per neuron) at around the age of two and remain at that level until the age of 10 or 11.

This profusion of connections lends the growing brain exceptional flexibility and resilience. Consider the case of 13-year-old Brandi Binder, who developed such severe epilepsy that surgeons at UCLA had to remove the entire right side of her cortex when she was six. Binder lost virtually all the control she had established over muscles on the left side of her body, the side controlled by the right side of the brain. Yet today, after years of therapy ranging from leg lifts to math and music drills, Binder is an A student at the Holmes Middle School in Colorado Springs, Colorado. She loves music, math and art—skills usually associated with the right half of the brain. And while Binder's recuperation is not 100%—for example, she has never regained the use of her left arm—it comes close. Says UCLA pediatric neurologist Dr. Donald Shields: "If there's a way to compensate, the developing brain will find it."

What wires a child's brain, say neuroscientists—or rewires it after physical trauma—is repeated experience. Each time a baby tries to touch a tantalizing object or gazes intently at a face or listens to a lullaby, tiny bursts of electricity shoot through the brain, knitting neurons into circuits as well defined as those etched onto silicon chips. The results are those behavioral mileposts that never cease to delight and awe parents. Around the age of two months, for example, the motor-control centers of the brain develop to the point that infants can suddenly reach out and grab a nearby object. Around the age of four months, the cortex begins to refine the connections needed for depth perception and binocular vision. And around the age of 12 months, the speech centers of the brain are poised to produce what is perhaps the most magical moment of childhood: the first word that marks the flowering of language.

When the brain does not receive the right information—or shuts it out—the result can be devastating. Some children who display early signs of autism, for example, retreat from the world because they are hypersensitive to sensory stimulation, others because their senses are underactive and provide them with too little information. To be effective, then, says George Washington University's Greenspan, treatment must target the underlying condition, protecting some children from disorienting noises and lights, providing others with attention-grabbing stimulation. But when parents and therapists collaborate in an intensive effort to reach these abnormal brains, writes Greenspan in a new book, *The Growth of the Mind* (Addison-Wesley, 1997), three-year-olds who begin the descent into the autistic's limited universe can sometimes be snatched back.

Indeed, parents are the brain's first and most important teachers. Among other things, they appear to help babies learn by adopting the rhythmic, high-pitched speaking style known as Parentese. When speaking to babies, Stanford University psychologist Anne Fernald has found, mothers and fathers from many cultures change their speech patterns in the same peculiar ways. "They put their faces very close to the child," she reports. "They use shorter utterances, and they speak in an unusually melodious fashion." The heart rate of infants increases while listening to Parentese, even Parentese delivered in a foreign language. Moreover, Fernald says, Parentese appears to hasten the process of connecting words to the objects they denote. Twelve-month-olds, directed to "look at the ball" in Parentese, direct their eyes to the correct picture more frequently than when the instruction is delivered in normal English.

In some ways the exaggerated, vowel-rich sounds of Parentese appear to resemble the choice morsels fed to hatchlings by adult birds. The University of Washington's Patricia Kuhl and her colleagues have conditioned dozens of newborns to turn their heads when they detect the *ee* sound emitted by American parents, vs. the *eu* favored by doting Swedes. Very young babies, says Kuhl, invariably perceive slight variations in pronunciation as totally different sounds. But by the age of six months, American babies no longer react when they hear variants of *ee*, and Swedish babies have become impervious to differences in *eu*. "It's as though their brains have formed little magnets," says Kuhl, "and all the sounds in the vicinity are swept in."

## Tuned to Danger

Even more fundamental, says Dr. Bruce Perry of Baylor College of Medicine in Houston, is the role parents play in setting up the neural circuitry that helps children regulate their responses to stress. Children who are physically abused early in life, he observes, develop brains that are exquisitely tuned to danger. At the slightest threat, their hearts race, their stress hormones surge and their brains anxiously track the nonverbal cues that might signal the next attack. Because the brain develops in sequence, with more primitive structures stabilizing their connections first, early abuse is particularly damaging. Says Perry: "Experience is the chief architect of the brain." And because these early experiences of stress form a kind of template around which later brain development is organized, the changes they create are all the more pervasive.

Emotional deprivation early in life has a similar effect. For six years University of Washington psychologist Geraldine Dawson and her colleagues have monitored the brain-wave patterns of children born to mothers who were diagnosed as suffering from depression. As infants, these children showed markedly reduced activity in the left frontal lobe, an area of the brain that serves as a center for joy and other light-hearted emotions. Even more telling, the patterns of brain activity displayed by these children closely tracked the ups and downs of their mother's depression. At the age of three, children whose mothers were more severely depressed or whose depression lasted longer continued to show abnormally low readings.

Strikingly, not all the children born to depressed mothers develop these aberrant brain-wave patterns, Dawson has found. What accounts for the difference appears to be the emotional tone of the exchanges between mother and child. By scrutinizing hours of videotape that show depressed mothers interacting with their babies, Dawson has attempted to identify the links between maternal behavior and children's brains. She found that mothers who were disengaged, irritable or impatient had babies with sad brains. But depressed mothers who managed to rise above their melancholy, lavishing their babies with attention and indulging in playful games, had children with brain activity of a considerably more cheerful cast.

When is it too late to repair the damage wrought by physical and emotional abuse or neglect? For a time, at least, a child's brain is extremely forgiving. If a mother snaps out of her depression before her child is a year old, Dawson has found, brain activity in the left frontal lobe quickly picks up. However, the ability to rebound declines markedly as a child grows older. Many scientists believe that in the first few years of childhood there are a number of critical or sensitive periods, or "windows," when the brain demands certain types of input in order to create or stabilize certain long-lasting structures.

For example, children who are born with a cataract will become permanently blind in that eye if the clouded lens is not promptly removed. Why? The brain's visual centers require sensory stimulus—in this case the stimulus provided by light hitting the retina of the eye—to maintain their still tentative connections. More controversially, many linguists believe that language skills unfold according to a strict, biologically defined timetable.

Children, in their view, resemble certain species of birds that cannot master their song unless they hear it sung at an early age. In zebra finches the window for acquiring the appropriate song opens 25 to 30 days after hatching and shuts some 50 days later.

## Windows of Opportunity

With a few exceptions, the windows of opportunity in the human brain do not close quite so abruptly. There appears to be a series of windows for developing language. The window for acquiring syntax may close as early as five or six years of age, while the window for adding new words may never close. The ability to learn a second language is highest between birth and the age of six, then undergoes a steady and inexorable decline. Many adults still manage to learn new languages, but usually only after great struggle.

The brain's greatest growth spurt, neuroscientists have now confirmed, draws to a close around the age of 10, when the balance between synapse creation and atrophy abruptly shifts. Over the next several years, the brain will ruthlessly destroy its weakest synapses, preserving only those that have been magically transformed by experience. This magic, once again, seems to be encoded in the genes. The ephemeral bursts of electricity that travel through the brain, creating everything from visual images and pleasurable sensations to dark dreams and wild thoughts, ensure the survival of synapses by stimulating genes that promote the release of powerful growth factors and suppressing genes that encode for synapse-destroying enzymes.

By the end of adolescence, around the age of 18, the brain has declined in plasticity but increased in power. Talents and latent tendencies that have been nurtured are ready to blossom. The experiences that drive neural activity, says Yale's Rakic, are like a sculptor's chisel or a dressmaker's shears, conjuring up form from a lump of stone or a length of cloth. The presence of extra material expands the range of possibilities, but cutting away the extraneous is what makes art. "It is the overproduction of synaptic connections followed by their loss that leads to patterns in the brain," says neuroscientist William Greenough of the University of Illinois at Urbana-Champaign. Potential for greatness may be encoded in the genes, but whether that potential is realized as a gift for mathematics, say, or a brilliant criminal mind depends on patterns etched by experience in those critical early years.

Psychiatrists and educators have long recognized the value of early experience. But their observations have until now been largely anecdotal. What's so exciting, says Matthew Melmed, executive director of Zero to Three, a nonprofit organization devoted to highlighting the importance of the first three years of life, is that modern neuroscience is providing the hard, quantifiable evidence that was missing earlier. "Because you can see the results under a microscope or in a PET scan," he observes, "it's become that much more convincing."

What lessons can be drawn from the new findings? Among other things, it is clear that foreign languages should be taught in elementary school, if not before. That remedial education may be more effective at the age of three or four than at nine or 10.

That good, affordable day care is not a luxury or a fringe benefit for welfare mothers and working parents but essential brain food for the next generation. For while new synapses continue to form throughout life, and even adults continually refurbish their minds through reading and learning, never again will the brain be able to master new skills so readily or rebound from setbacks so easily.

Rat-a-tat-tat. Rat-a-tat-tat. Rat-a-tat-tat. Just last week, in the U.S. alone, some 77,000 newborns began the miraculous process of wiring their brains for a lifetime of learning. If parents and policy-makers don't pay attention to the conditions under which this delicate process takes place, we will all suffer the consequences—starting around the year 2010.

 **Article Review Form at end of book.**

Upon birth, what positive signs of newborn health is the doctor looking for? Why is it important that mothers and their newborns remain in the hospital for a minimum of 48 hours?

# A Baby's First 48 Hours

**Laura Flynn McCarthy**

It's that crucial moment in delivery—your baby's head is crowning. You give one last push and out he slides, looking like he's just been through a battle, which, in a sense, he has.

Suddenly, nurses and doctors initiate a whirlwind of procedures designed to ensure that your newborn is healthy and normal. Knowing ahead of time what generally will happen over the next two days may help explain why everyone seems to want to get their hands—and stethoscopes—on your precious bundle.

## First Breath

As soon as the baby's head emerges from the birth canal, the obstetrician will suction amniotic fluid out of his nose and mouth with a small rubber bulb to help him begin to breathe. Some newborns cry upon entering the world; others are born coughing, whimpering, or quietly breathing. The practice of slapping the rump has been outmoded for years, but doctors may rub an infant's back or hand if he doesn't begin breathing right away.

Along with amniotic fluid and possibly some of your blood, most healthy newborns are partially covered with a sticky white protective coating—called the vernix caseosa—which is produced in utero by oil glands in the fetus's skin. The face may appear wrinkled and disgruntled-looking from the wetness and pressure of birth.

The umbilical cord is clamped and cut, causing no pain to you or the baby since it lacks nerve endings. At this point, the baby stops receiving oxygen from your blood. Shortly thereafter, you'll deliver the placenta. The portion of the umbilical cord still attached to the infant continues to pulsate for several minutes and then stops beating.

## 5 Minutes

Because the first few minutes of life are critical to the baby's overall health, doctors perform a series of routine checks, called the Apgar newborn scoring system (see "Newborn Tests," page 27).

Your pediatrician or obstetrician will probably also conduct a quick physical, looking for obvious congenital abnormalities—a cleft palate, Down syndrome, ab-

normal genitalia (a misplaced urethra or undescended testicles, for example). The doctor also checks for signs of maturity such as well-developed breast tissue, fully formed ears with strong cartilage, well-creased soles, and skin that's not too thin and translucent (a sign of prematurity) or excessively wrinkled and peeling (which signals postmaturity). Following this brief exam, a nurse usually weighs the newborn, measures his length and head circumference, takes his temperature, and washes him with mild soap and water. She'll then dry, diaper, and swaddle him, topping him off with a cap.

Most babies receive eyedrops containing 1 percent silver nitrate or a less irritating antibiotic eye ointment to prevent infections caused by possible exposure to gonorrhea or chlamydia during birth. (A mother may unknowingly carry these sexually transmitted diseases.) A newborn also receives his first shot—an injection of vitamin K—which helps establish normal blood clotting. Doctors may conduct these procedures before giving the mother her baby, but some hospitals will delay them to give parents time to cuddle with their newborn.

## 60 Minutes

"Healthy newborns are surprisingly alert in the first hour of life," says Rita Harper, M.D., professor of pediatrics at New York University Medical School. "They move their arms and legs readily and look around the room. They may even make eye contact with Mom and Dad for the first time."

Although a mother's milk won't flow for a few days, those who choose to breast-feed may be given the option to nurse during this alert stage. Early feeding encourages the baby's sucking reflex and presents an opportunity to bond, and colostrum, a thin yellow fluid that precedes breast milk, is rich in proteins and protective antibodies. If the baby was delivered by emergency C-section and the mother received general anesthesia, the doctor may recommend waiting until the drug wears off and the mother feels strong enough to nurse.

## 1 to 6 Hours

Usually, if there are no medical problems, you can request to see your baby whenever you wish. If your newborn is healthy, he may remain in your room or stay in the nursery for the first few hours, visiting you for feeding (typically every three to four hours).

Exhausted from the delivery, most babies enter a deep sleep within a couple of hours after birth and are difficult to awaken. "This transition marks the beginning of a new period of close observation by the hospital staff," says Richard Molteni, M.D., chairman of pediatrics at Geisinger Medical Center, in Danville, PA. "Every half hour or so, nurses will check the infant's temperature, respiration, heart and circulation, muscle tone, and activity and con-

## Extra Care for Preemies

Most babies who are born premature receive the same tests as a full-term newborn, plus additional monitoring of vital signs. A doctor may order extra blood tests to check for infections picked up during delivery, such as staphylococcus and streptococcus (both treated with antibiotics), as well as blood levels of sodium and other electrolytes. She may also order tests for blood levels of oxygen and carbon dioxide (supplementary oxygen may be necessary and levels of bilirubin, an orange or yellowish pigment responsible for jaundice (particularly common in preemies). Preemies may also receive help with:

### Regulating Body Temperature

Babies born preterm have greater difficulty staying warm at normal room temperatures, so they're often placed in a temperature-controlled enclosed bed (Isolette).

### Breathing

Those born a month or more early are at a particularly high risk for respiratory distress syndrome, in which the small air sacs in the lungs collapse. When doctors suspect an early delivery, they may give the mother injections of a corticosteroid that helps the fetus produce surfactant, which encourages lung development. Preterm babies may also need oxygen or additional respiratory support.

### Feeding

Very premature babies can't coordinate their sucking and swallowing reflexes, and consequently have trouble feeding; they may need to receive nutrients intravenously. Doctors recommend that breast-feeding mothers express their milk for future use and to maintain the supply.

sciousness level. They'll also look at skin color—in babies with white or olive skin, the color goes from beet red to pale; in black infants, the color shift is more subtle." These checks continue until the baby's condition is stable, then become less frequent.

## Rounding Out Day 1

When the newborn awakens from the restorative sleep, he may fuss and need to be fed and changed. He may also fixate on your face for several minutes.

Generally, a pattern evolves: The baby sleeps for two to three hours, wakes and cries to be fed, wets his diaper, wants affection, and then falls back to sleep. Those who don't develop this pattern are often reevaluated for possible problems—congenital abnormalities (like a heart defect) or the presence of an infection.

Within 24 hours after birth, most babies pass urine for the first

time and have their initial bowel movement, called meconium, which has a tar-like consistency. If your infant is staying in your room and you notice abnormal secretions or no urination or bowel movement, tell the nurse or doctor. Within the first 12 to 18 hours, a pediatrician will thoroughly examine your baby and recheck vital signs.

## The Second Day

Sometime during the first two days your newborn will undergo a series of tests, including standard blood tests, which screen for rare but serious illnesses. When treated early, the consequences of these diseases can be minimized or completely avoided. Doctors will place about six drops of the baby's blood (obtained by pricking the bottom of his foot) on a piece of filter paper, which is then sent to a lab. The tests vary, depending on your state's laws and your family's history of certain diseases (see "Newborn Tests"). Some hospitals have also started checking a newborn's hearing by placing a pair of headphones over his ears and observing neurological responses to soft sounds. A doctor will probably conduct at least one more physical before you leave the hospital.

During the hospital stay, many parents choose to have their baby receive the first of three hepatitis B vaccinations and, if the baby is a boy, decide whether or not to have him circumcised (in which the foreskin around his penis is surgically removed). Circumcisions are usually performed by an obstetrician or pediatrician during the baby's first two days. In Jewish families, it's often performed on the eighth day in a bris ceremony by an experienced practitioner called a mohel. Many doctors once believed that circumcision was an absolute necessity, but today pediatricians disagree about whether the procedure offers definite preventive health benefits. If you choose to circumcise, ask your doctor to use a topical analgesic cream, which may reduce the baby's pain.

# Heading Home

Most doctors recommend that mothers and newborns remain in the hospital for a minimum of 48 hours after a normal vaginal delivery and three to four days following a cesarean. This allows time for doctors and nurses to notice problems that aren't immediately apparent. In fact, a recent study from the University of Washington in Seattle found that among healthy newborns, at least 8 percent of rehospitalizations within the first week of life could be attributed to early discharge. Thirty-two states currently have

## Newborn Tests

Within the first two days, most infants undergo some of the following tests.

### Apgar Newborn Scoring System

A doctor or nurse measures five components of a newborn's health at one minute and again at five minutes after birth, including color, (more pink than blue), heart rate (should be over 100 beats per minute), breathing (good strong cry), muscle tone (active flexing of arms and legs), and reflex response (grimace, cough, or sneeze when a catheter or bulb syringe is put in the nose).

The score derived from the five vital signs ranges from 0 (an unresponsive baby) to 10 (a baby that requires no special attention). Two scores of 7 or above indicate good health and usually no further testing is necessary. For newborns with one-minute scores under 7, the doctor will attempt to improve whatever needs attention. He may help the baby with his breathing by suctioning his airways and placing an oxygen mask on or near his face. Low heart rate, poor reflexes, and weak muscle tone may be stimulated by rubbing the infant gently. If the five-minute score remains low, the doctor will continue to try to improve the baby's state, testing him again at 10 minutes, and if necessary at 15 minutes.

### Blood Test for Enzyme Deficiencies

Tests for diseases such as galactosemia, phenylketonuria (PKU), and maple syrup urine disease (MSUD), which result from low-levels or improperly functioning enzymes—substances that regulate chemical reactions in the body. Untreated, these diseases can cause retardation or eye or liver problems. Once diagnosed, babies are put on a special formula.

### Blood Test for Hypothyroidism

Screens for an absent or poorly functioning thyroid gland. Undiagnosed, the condition can lead to stunted growth and mental retardation. If caught early,

children can be treated with thyroid hormones.

### Blood Glucose Test

Checks for hypoglycemia (abnormally low blood sugar). Recommended for small babies or those born of diabetic mothers. Babies may be given glucose intravenously or sugar water orally.

### Tests for Blood Incompatibility

If your blood is Rh-negative, the doctor may give your infant an Rh-incompatibility test. If your blood is type O, he'll recommend the ABO (Coombs') test. Both look for a reaction between your blood and your baby's blood that could cause the newborn to develop a type of anemia often accompanied by jaundice (which causes the skin to turn yellow). An Rh-negative mother may be given an injection to protect future babies. In severe cases the baby may need a transfusion; the jaundice usually clears up after a couple days' treatment with fluorescent lights.

### Blood Tests for Sickle-Cell Anemia

Found chiefly among blacks, this blood disease becomes a problem later in life, causing anemia, infections, jaundice, and leg and joint pain. It's usually treated symptomatically.

### Blood Test for Human Immunodeficiency Virus (HIV)

Currently required only in New York state, this is a test for the virus that causes AIDS. Early drug intervention may slow or even prevent the development of AIDS in babies.

### Blood Count (Hematocrit)

Measures the volume of red blood cells in the baby's blood. The test is generally reserved for babies at high risk for anemia (low red blood cell count) or polycythemia (abnormally high red blood cell count). In rare cases, babies may require a transfusion.

laws to protect mothers from early dismissal. Starting in 1998, a federal law will require insurance companies to cover at least two

days of hospitalization for the mother and child after a normal vaginal delivery and four days after a C-section. This time also enables parents to get acquainted with their baby in the presence of experts, who can offer advice on new skills, like breast-feeding.

"In terms of one's health, it's been said that the most critical times in a person's life are the last few years and the first two days," says Dr. Molteni. "Those first forty-eight hours are an important time, in which doctors can assess and care for the newborn in ways that could affect his health and development—not only through- out childhood but for the rest of his life.

 **Article Review Form at end of book.**

Some responses of newborns suggest that learning is occurring in the womb. Give an example and the bodily system involved. How do babies come to love their parents? Describe the infant and parent behaviors involved in the process of attachment.

# Baby's-Eye View

## Paula Spencer

Propped against my knees in the delivery room, my son, minutes old, peered at me with wide, unblinking eyes. He looked so intent. So serious. So thoughtful.

What could earth's freshest arrival possibly be thinking about? Maybe he was wondering who all the giants looming over him might be, especially the pair with the goofy grins who kept counting his fingers and toes over and over. Maybe his head still ached from the incredibly narrow trip out of my womb. Maybe he was asking himself, "Hey, who turned on the lights?"

It's hard to know how the world appears to a new baby. But in recent years, researchers have deduced plenty about what infants sense, remember, prefer, and need. And such knowledge is more than academic for new parents. "The essence of good parenting is the ability to see things from a baby's-eye view and to respond to the baby from that point of view," says Martha Cox, a developmental psychologist at the University of North Carolina.

In other words, by putting yourself in your baby's booties, you can better understand his behaviors and needs in those often mystifying first months. Thanks to a wealth of new research, it's now possible to answer many of the most common, vexing questions about the first months of life.

## Does He Remember Anything from the Past Nine Months in My Womb?

A fetus can hear, taste, smell, and even sense light while in utero. By the seventh month of pregnancy, for example, an unborn baby can hear. Dr. Marshall Klaus, author of *The Amazing Newborn* and an adjunct professor of pediatrics at the University of California, San Francisco, tells of a pianist who practiced a difficult concerto solo over and over while pregnant. Once her baby was born, that particular piece of music calmed his crying. What's more, babies clearly prefer high-pitched voices. Some researchers theorize that this is because they have spent nine months listening to the distinct pitch of a female voice (male voices are too low and distant to be heard over the noisy sounds inside the womb). Other experts believe that a preference for the female voice may be inborn, a kind of survival mechanism.

A newborn can also distinguish the scent of his own mother from that of other women, possibly because of associations made in the womb, says Klaus. In a famous British study, when six-day-old infants were placed between two breast pads, one worn by their mother and the other worn by another mother, the babies consistently turned toward the pad their mother wore. When their mother's breast milk was placed on an unworn pad, the infants showed no preference, indicating that it was the scent of their mother's body rather than that of her breast milk that they recognized.

A baby's associations with smells may start even before birth. If you ate a lot of garlic or other strongly scented foods while pregnant, Klaus says, your baby may like such odors. Generally, though, babies are born with a natural preference for sweets and show disdain for bitter flavors.

Reprinted with the permission of the author, Paula Spencer, Contributing Editor of PARENTING MAGAZINE, where this article first appeared.

There's another reason a baby's primitive senses develop in the womb: Sight, smell, hearing, taste, and touch are his primary means of collecting information about his world after birth. In fact, using sensory perception to relate to the world and situate himself within it is the first big milestone in a child's emotional development, according to Dr. Stanley Greenspan, a child psychiatrist and the author of *First Feelings*.

## Am I Special to My Baby Yet?

Given a newborn's preference for mother's voice and smell, you'd think your baby would adore you from day one. But mutual love is a gradual process. "It's not that newborns have a fondness and attachment for the mother, it's more that they like what's familiar," says Karen Barrett, a professor of human development at Colorado State University.

Babies don't have the sense of self-awareness that adults do. Their perceptions are immediate and physical: *When I feel hunger, there's a breast in my mouth*, or *When I'm cold, I get covered up*. "In infancy a child begins to develop a sense of predictability and consistency as well as a reliance on the caregiver's responsiveness to his needs," says Jay Belsky, a professor of human development and family studies at Pennsylvania State University. "The child is learning whether he can—or can't—count on this specific individual." These are the roots of attachment and love.

By three or four months, a baby knows whether or not the person holding him is familiar, Belsky says. But he doesn't have much of a grasp of people as individuals yet. That will come later,

at around six to eight months. A recent major daycare study by the National Institute of Child Health and Human Development found that being cared for consistently by familiar people reinforces a child's sense of security, Belsky adds.

What about those "social smiles" that first flash at you around four to six weeks? Alas, not even those heart-warming grins are evidence that your baby is singling you out. "Babies have a sort of prewired response to eyes," says Barrett. "It's a stimulus response that nature built in so that they tune in to their parent's face." By four to six months, though, a baby's smile becomes selective—reserved only for special people.

## What Can My Baby See?

At birth, babies are very nearsighted; the world is a blur beyond 7 to 12 inches (which is, not coincidentally, the distance to a mother's face when she holds her baby). They can see color but prefer the sharp contrast of black and white. They also respond more to curved shapes than to straight-edged ones and are attracted to faces (especially eyes), brightly lit objects, and things that move.

Zoologist Desmond Morris, author of *Babywatching*, calls this selective eyesight "the height of efficiency." Since an infant is so helpless, Morris says, there's no advantage in his knowing what dangers lurk beyond the comfort of the parental face.

Gradually, binocular eyesight (the ability to focus on objects that are both near and far away) improves. At first the baby takes a greater interest in his immediate surroundings—say, a pattern on his bumper pad or his mobile. By the end of the first

year, a baby's vision nearly matches that of an adult's.

## Why Does My Baby Cry So Much?

Most babies aren't always miserable. But a huge number of things can set them off compared with their minimal means of communicating distress. In the first six months, an infant has a very limited ability to regulate things like hunger, temperature, or feelings. "He can't go to the fridge or fetch a blanket; he can't even soothe himself when he's upset," says psychologist Cox. "Crying is how a baby lets his parents know something isn't right."

Hunger, fatigue, cold, and dirty diapers aren't the only things to cry about: Loud noises, bright lights, or too much intense play may overstimulate a baby, provoking tears.

Follow your instinct to attend to cries swiftly, Cox recommends. You'll be teaching your infant that she can count on you for a quick, helpful response, which builds confidence. And numerous studies have shown that when parents respond quickly to crying, the baby cries less over time—a reflection of her growing trust in you.

## Does She Think about Me When I'm Not There with Her?

Early on, you'll miss your baby more than she misses you. That's because an infant hasn't yet developed a sense of you as a separate person, someone who continues to exist after you walk out the door.

"A two- or three-month-old may recognize that someone new is holding her, but she won't pine for you," says Carol Harding, director of the Center for Children, Families, and Community at Loyola University Chicago. In fact, she'll probably be quite content, provided her immediate needs for food and comfort are being met.

As early as four to six months, a baby begins to demonstrate a preference for her mother, whose scent, looks, and feel are now both very familiar and comforting. But it's not until around eight to ten months (sometimes earlier) that babies tend to cry and appear visibly distressed by separations.

Although the mother-baby bond is indelible, similarly close attachments develop with the father, siblings, caregiver, and other special people whom the baby sees regularly. Consistency and warmth are important in helping a baby feel secure, Harding says. She cites as an example babies reared in orphanages in the 1950s who had their basic needs met but lacked predictable emotional support, and consequently grew up insecure. That's why, if you work outside the home, you should encourage a baby's closeness to his sitter rather than worry that he'll

like the sitter more than you, says Belsky. "The baby is better off with lots of secure attachments."

## How Much Does My Baby Remember?

Young babies don't have a reflective memory that lets them think back on events and imbue them with meaning. And without words, they lack the ability to record their impressions (which is believed to be in large part why we forget so much of our own infancy). Still, babies remember more than you might expect, because they are able to take note of things around them.

"Even newborns have demonstrated the ability to recall a particular face," says Klaus. A mother who wore glasses during delivery and the first days of her baby's life, for example, may see a puzzled expression flicker across his face if she suddenly switches to contacts.

By as early as two or three months, babies begin forming assumptions based on their experience. Instead of waiting for the bottle to be inserted into their lips, they reach out toward it or get excited at the mere sight of it.

According to psychologist Marshall Haith of the University of Denver, babies don't just respond when things happen, they form expectations. In Haith's experiments, he presents babies with a series of pictures in predictable patterns (such as a face appearing first on the left side of a screen, then on the right, then on the left again) while monitoring their eye movements. Even two-month-olds have shown they can anticipate what will happen next in a given sequence by moving their eyes to the location where they expect the image to appear. In everyday terms, you can see this in the way a baby plays peekaboo, learning from experience to anticipate your reappearing face.

A baby's memory, like his attachment to you, builds gradually, nurtured by predictability and consistency. "Relationships develop over the whole first year and thereafter," Belsky says. "If the baby's needs are met, it's like a ball rolling down a hill. Things just start to move along."

 **Article Review Form at end of book.**

Why are cases of Sudden Infant Death Syndrome being reexamined?
What does the American Academy of Pediatrics currently
recommend for helping infants to sleep?

# The Nursery's Littlest Victims

Hundreds of cases of 'crib death,' or SIDS, may in fact be infanticide.

## Sharon Begley

*With Anne Underwood in New York and
John F. Lauerman in Boston*

There was talk, of course—how could there not be when all five children in one family died as babies? But doctors, police and neighbors accepted Waneta Hoyt's explanation: her little Eric and James and Julie and Molly and Noah, she said, were all victim of crib death, or sudden infant death syndrome (SIDS). Even after Hoyt was convicted of five counts of murder, in 1995, it seemed like an isolated instance of a disturbed woman almost getting away with murder.

But the Hoyt case may have been even deadlier than anyone thought, claiming—indirectly—many more than five young lives. According to a new book, "The Death of Innocents" (*632 pages. Bantam. $24.95*), by reporters Richard Firstman and Jamie Talan, the deaths of the last two Hoyt babies became the basis for a SIDS paper so influential that it put blinders on pediatricians and researchers for 25 years, preventing most of them from considering homicide when babies died

for no apparent reason. In that paper, published in the journal Pediatrics in 1972, Dr. Alfred Steinschneider, who had cared for Molly and Noah Hoyt, argued that SIDS runs in families and is caused by prolonged sleep apnea (a cessation of breathing for 15 seconds or more). The paper became an instant classic. It gave birth to a multimillion-dollar apnea-monitor industry. But it also provided cover for families where more than one child died of SIDS. A quarter-century later, Dr. Jerold Lucey, editor of Pediatrics then and now, writes in the October issue, "We should never have published this article . . . [S]ome physicians still believe SIDS runs in families. It doesn't—murder does."

Every year in the United States more than 3,000 infant deaths are listed as SIDS, while 300 or so are identified as infanticides. Now two scientific papers suggest that some in the first category belong in the second:

- In a study scheduled for publication in *Pediatrics* in November, Dr. David Southall of City General Hospital in Stoke-on-Trent, England,

describes how he set up video cameras in the hospital rooms of children brought in after parents reported that they had stopped breathing and nearly died. The cameras captured 39 instances of mothers trying to smother their babies. Fully one third of these "near-miss SIDS" cases, Southall estimates, are actually cases of Münchhausen by proxy, in which a parent injuries a child in a bid for attention and sympathy. Overall, Southall concludes, 5 to 10 percent of SIDS deaths are in fact infanticides.

- In an unpublished study, Dr. Thomas Truman concludes that as many as one third of repeated near-SIDS cases at what may be the most prestigious SIDS center in the United States may be cases of Münchhausen by proxy. While serving a fellowship at Massachusetts General Hospital from 1993 to 1996, Truman told Firstman and Talan, he analyzed the medical records of 155 children treated in MGH's apnea program. In 56 of these cases, says Truman, the child's chart contained circumstantial evidence of possible abuse. One baby suffered repeated breathing crises at home, turning blue and limp—but only when the mother, and no one else, was present. Another had no breathing problems during the six months he spent in a local hospital; the day he went home, alone with his mother, he had a life-threatening breathing emergency. When Truman alerted New York authorities to the possibility of abuse in the case of "Emily," 1, his superior dismissed it. Emily died one year after being sent home from MGH.

None of these cases prompted formal investigations. As a result, it is impossible to determine what really happened to the children. Last week MGH declined to respond to the allegations beyond issuing a statement that SIDS is "constantly debated within our department." The doctors who run the apnea program refused to be interviewed.

Whatever the individual pathology of mothers who kill their children, there is a larger pathology at work here: the medical community's. Perhaps the most important pages in "Death of Innocents" explore how "misguided science . . . arguably shielded countless other infanticides" besides Waneta Hoyt's. In a chilling demonstration of the power of a scientific paradigm to blind researchers to reality, the medical establishment embraced the apnea-runs-in-families hypothesis uncritically. As a result, few doctors entertained the possibility that their SIDS and near-

SIDS cases were murder or Münchhausen. Yet as early as 1982 Southall presented data that should have sunk the apnea idea. He had monitored, for 24 hours, the breathing of 9,251 babies; 27 later died of SIDS. Not a single little victim had had prolonged apnea. But the idea that apnea causes SIDS was so powerful, says Dr. Marie Valdes-Dapena, a pediatric pathologist, that she and the rest of the scientific community "bought it hook, line and sinker."

With the claims that SIDS runs in families and is caused by apnea now in tatters, the hope that it can be prevented with a monitor is also on the ropes. Since the 1970s worried parents have been relying on these electronic devices to signal when a sleeping baby stops breathing. In one ongoing study, Dr. John Keens of the University of Southern California School of Medicine has found that some babies indeed stopped breathing while they slept and died. Monitors sounded, but the children could not be revived. That suggests that death (perhaps from heart defects) caused their apnea, rather than apnea causing death. No studies have found monitors to save lives of normal babies (they do protect preemies). "Huge amounts of time and money have been wasted over the last 25 years in a useless attempt to 'do something' for SIDS victims by monitoring", editorializes Lucey in the upcoming *Pediatrics*. Neither Steinschneider nor Healthdyne, the leading monitor

manufacturer, responded to *Newsweek's* requests for comment.

Although apnea monitors are saving few babies, SIDS cases fell 30 percent, from 4,891 to 3,279, between 1992 and 1995. In 1992, the American Academy of Pediatrics recommended that babies sleep on their backs or sides rather than their stomachs. Yet even today Steinschneider's organization, the American SIDS Institute, does not include that advice in its brochure on preventing SIDS.

No one denies that thousands of babies do die in their sleep of natural, if mysterious, causes. Some may have cardiac defects; others may have rebreathed oxygen-poor air formed by pockets in their cribbing. SIDS support groups worry that grieving families who have already suffered the tragedy of a baby's dying will now be subjected to suspicions that the death was actually murder. "The kinds of cases they're sensationalizing are few and far between," says Phipps Cohe of the SIDS Alliance. How few? Last week Massachusetts authorities said they would study Truman's allegations before deciding whether to reopen any cases of infant deaths. And, thankfully, videotaping is becoming standard practice at hospitals' apnea clinics. But no one, of course, is watching what goes on at home.

 **Article Review Form at end of book.**

What caregiver circumstances are most associated with instances of Shaken Baby Syndrome? Who is at greatest risk for being a victim of Shaken Baby Syndrome?

# Fragile
## Handle with care

**Dr. Alvin F. Poussaint
and Susan Linn**

Each year, thousands of young children suffer brain injury or die from being violently shaken. Children as old as 5 are vulnerable to shaken-baby syndrome (SBS), but infants between 2 and 4 months are especially at risk. Although inflicting SBS is a crime punishable by imprisonment, rates continue to rise. Since 1980 annual reported incidents of child abuse and neglect have risen threefold, to more than 3 million. Children under 1 account for one third of reported physical-abuse cases, with head trauma the most frequent cause of disability or death. Clearly, the threat of criminal prosecution is not enough: any plan to prevent this kind of abuse must include public-education and intervention programs.

SBS, first described as a syndrome in 1974, can be lethal: approximately one shaken baby in four dies from the injuries. Those who survive may suffer blindness caused by bleeding around the brain and eyes, or disabling brain damage, including mental retardation, paralysis, seizure disor-

ders, and speech and learning disabilities. SBS is especially tragic because it often stems from ignorance. According to a nationwide study by Dr. Jacy Showers of the SBS Prevention Plus Program, 37 percent of parents and other caregivers are unaware that shaking babies is dangerous. Many people who injure babies in this fashion are not chronic abusers but adults overwhelmed by the demands of child care.

It is no easy task to care for an infant. Newborns cry an average of one to four hours a day. Not surprisingly, the vast majority of SBS incidents occur when an infant is crying: people who violently shake babies cannot tolerate their inability to control the infant's cries, and may even believe that the baby is purposely crying to be annoying or to get attention. Others interpret sustained crying as a sign that the baby is "spoiled," and think that he needs to be physically disciplined. A vicious cycle begins when a caregiver becomes ever more exasperated and angry and shakes the baby in a misguided effort to stop the crying. Anyone can experience transient anger toward a crying baby. But if the impulse to shake or hit is strong and

recurrent, call an agency such as CHILDHELP (800-4-ACHILD) or the National Child Abuse Hotline (800-422-4453).

Helping parents and caregivers better understand infant behavior and manage their frustrations could significantly reduce the occurrence of SBS and other abuse. Since a major precursor to SBS is loss of control, caregivers who believe they are "losing it" should avoid touching the child. Instead, after making sure the baby is safe, step back or leave the room briefly to cool down. Consider possible causes for the crying. Is she ill, hungry, soiled, teething, injured or frightened? Try proven soothing techniques, such as patting, holding, talking or singing. Parents who know which calming techniques work for their baby should share the information with others caring for the infant. When a baby's crying sounds unusual or seems excessive, contact the pediatrician.

Of those charged with shaken-baby abuse, 60 percent are either the baby's father or the mother's boyfriend and are mostly young, in their 20s. Clearly, prevention efforts must reach out to men—through prenatal classes, clinics and schools and with information provided in workplace and recreational sites. Home visiting programs by social agencies show an impressive success rate for families at risk for child abuse and neglect. Hawaii's Healthy Start program has reduced abuse to 1 percent in high risk families, compared with 20 percent in such families nationwide. Shaken Baby Syndrome Prevention Plus (800-858-5222) can provide information about starting local prevention programs. The small start-up cost pales beside the cost of a single case of SBS: up to $1 million in medical care, special-education programs and other public services over the first few years of a child's life. Protecting our most helpless children is the least we can do for them.

 **Article Review Form at end of book.**

# WiseGuide Wrap-Up

- Nature and nurture work together to mold each child's brain during the prenatal period and in the first years after birth.

- Varied and developmentally appropriate stimulation promotes optimal brain development during early childhood. Children's brains may suffer, in contrast, when their environments are impoverished due to poverty or exposure to stressors, such as abuse, neglect, and maternal depression.

- Hospital-based births include a number of routine procedures designed to assure the optimal health of newborns. APGAR tests, health and appearance checks, alertness and sleep observations, as well as first immunizations, are among the common experiences of babies discharged from most U.S. hospitals.

- Newborns can demonstrate a range of skills. All sensory systems, though immature, are functioning. Babies remember, communicate with cries and quieting, and have preferences.

- New questions are arising about the realities of Sudden Infant Death Syndrome (SIDS). New research suggests that 5 to 10% of cases initially though to be SIDS-related are, in fact, infanticides.

- Shaken Baby Syndrome is now a well-recognized form of abuse, most often occurring when caregivers are overwhelmed by the demands of infants in their care.

## R.E.A.L. Sites

This list provides a print preview of typical **coursewise** R.E.A.L. sites. There are over 100 such sites at the **courselinks**™ site. The danger in printing URLs is that web sites can change overnight. As we went to press, these sites were functional using the URLs provided. If you come across one that isn't, please let us know via email to: webmaster@coursewise.com. Use your Passport to access the most current list of R.E.A.L. sites at the **courselinks**™ site.

**Site name:** Kidsource—Newborns: Websites

**URL:** http://www.kidsource.com/kidsource/pages/newborns.web.html

**Why is it R.E.A.L.?** This web site provides a list of summaries of articles and links to other web sites with information on newborns. Visit this site and compare the issues facing parents of premature infants with those of full-term infants. Continue to explore this site and visit the *American Academy of Pediatric Dentistry* site to explore the concerns of thumb, finger, and pacifier habits. Did you or your siblings use one of these techniques to calm yourself as an infant? Discover what advice professional are giving parents today on this topic.

**Site name:** National Information, Support and Referral Service on Shaken Baby Syndrome

**URL:** http://www.capcenter.org/service.htm

**Why is it R.E.A.L.?** One of the most controversial issues of our time is whether or not Shaken Baby Syndrome is really a syndrome at all. This web site provides the most current information to parents and professionals on this mysterious cause of death. The newsletter that this organization publishes provides articles on a variety of aspects of this syndrome. Visit this site and link to numerous sites that provide medical, legal, and social perspectives on this cause of infant and toddler death.

# section

# 3

- Present information on the normal stresses and strains of parenthood.

- Discuss stranger and separation anxieties and factors affecting their occurrences.

- Provide an overview of the nature and nurture of children's behaviors.

- Review suggested methods for promoting the emotional well-being of children.

- Provide information on childhood depression and controversies surrounding treatment.

# Early Social-Emotional Development

 **WiseGuide Intro**

Young children crying and clinging to their parents is a common sight to most caregivers. The early emergence of such reactions is called stranger anxiety. Stranger anxiety and, later, separation anxiety, are normal signs of children's growing cognitive abilities and healthy attachments to their parents. Children vary widely in the onset, intensity, and persistence of such reactions. The child's temperament, experiences with strangers and outings, and birth order seem to influence separation anxiety reactions. Also important are parental reactions to children's distress.

Many other aspects of children's social development are also influenced by the opportunities that caregivers make available and by caregivers' reactions to children's behaviors. Of particular importance to many parents and teachers is that children get along well with one another. New curricula emphasize prosocial behavior—encouraging perspective taking, kindness, sharing, and cooperation. Lessons in prosocial behaviors come more naturally when there are clear expectations for positive interactions, adult modeling, and the labeling and reinforcing of desirable encounters.

Though scientists have demonstrated that some aspects of personality and behavior may be genetically programmed, even the most passive or aggressive child is not immune to environmental influences. Shy children have been shown to outgrow this predisposition with sensitive parenting. Similarly, not all aggressive children reach adulthood as criminals. But sometimes parents cannot solve the emotional difficulties children experience. Improved methods of diagnosing and treating emotional disorders are now available. For instance, once unrecognized, childhood depression is now routinely noted as a mental health problem of the young. Questions arise, however, as to whether adult-based treatments are appropriate for children. Also of concern is whether emphasis on quick-fix, drug-based remedies for a variety of ailments is not limiting our ability to see and seek alternative interventions. Are we running the risk of overmedicating our children and preventing them from experiencing some of the normal turmoil inherent in growing up?

## Thinking Beyond the Facts

In this section on early social-emotional development, questions concerning what's normal come to mind. Though it may be unpleasant to hear and see the distress of children separated from their parents, such reactions are normal and do not do "irrevocable harm." In fact, the cries may be harder on the parents than on the children. Fear of the dark, of bugs, of strangers, or of nearly anything are also common. Similarly, sharing a family bed regularly or sporadically, cuddling security objects,

**Reading 11.** Define, with examples, the difference between social behaviors in general and prosocial behaviors specifically.

Chris has just pushed Jamie to the floor in order to be first in line for a snack. Describe how one would respond to this event in a victim-centered manner.

What do these words and actions teach?

**Reading 12.** Give an example of what a parent of an aggressive child might do to counter the child's genetic tendencies.

Give an example of how parents sometimes promote personality traits in their children that they feel are not desirable.

**Reading 13.** Why are people concerned that providing children with antidepressants when they are feeling bad may ultimately have more negative than positive effects?

Why do some people view the quick fix of drugs to relieve the stresses of childhood a potential new form of child abuse?

having temper tantrums and using "bad words," sucking the thumb, and talking to imaginary friends are among the many (often unspoken) occurrences within normal families.

Normal parenting can also vary from child to child, based on personality, age, or other circumstances. Shy children may need unusually tender guidance. Outgoing children may need to learn restraint. Older children need freedoms and responsibilities that would be inappropriate at earlier ages. Discuss your family rituals, good and bad. How did your parents handle your personality type? If you have brothers or sisters, were any treated differently because of special traits or talents? Are there any specific events that helped you learn about the importance of being cooperative, giving, or sharing? Are there any experiences that you think may have influenced you to behave negatively? As a parent, will (or did) you do things differently? Also consider whether medication to "take the edge off" development transition (e.g., the terrible-twos or the turmoil of puberty) should be widely available. What potential outcomes, good and bad, might a "cure" for some of the stressors of childhood and family life pose? To learn more about the normal trials and tribulations of parenting, visit websites presenting information on dealing with bedtime problems, "lovies," shyness, aggression, tantrums, and imaginary play.

Define, with examples, the difference between social behaviors in general and prosocial behaviors specifically. Chris has just pushed Jamie to the floor in order to be first in line for a snack. Describe how one would respond to this event in a victim-centered manner. What do these words and actions teach?

# Encouraging Positive Social Development in Young Children

## Donna Sasse Wittmer and Alice Sterling Honig

*A toddler, reaching for a toy, got his finger pinched in the hinge on the door of a toy shelf in his child care classroom. He cried loudly; his pacifier fell from his mouth. Another toddler, obviously distressed by the sounds of pain coming from his playmate, picked up the pacifier and held it in the crying toddler's mouth in an apparent attempt to help and comfort the injured toddler.*

This example, shared by a child care provider, is one of many exciting prosocial events that have been observed in young toddlers, preschoolers, and primary-age children as they interact together in group settings. Caregivers of young children notice events such as the one above as they live and work with very young children. If adults implement curriculum that promotes interpersonal consideration and cooperation in children, we see even more of these behaviors.

Social development was seen as the core of the curriculum in nursery schools and kindergartens until a cognitive emphasis was brought into the field in the late 1960s; social development, has recently been getting renewed attention by early childhood education leaders. Skilled teachers of young children implement prosocial goals for young children as they attempt to facilitate children's positive social interactions. Prosocial goals that teachers emphasize include

- showing sympathy and kindness,
- helping,
- giving,
- accepting food or toys,
- sharing,
- showing positive verbal and physical contact,
- comforting another person in distress,
- donating to others who are less fortunate,
- showing concern,
- responding to bereaved peers,
- taking the perspective of another person,
- showing affection, and
- cooperating with others in play or to complete a task.

The adults in children's lives play an important role in helping children develop these prosocial attitudes and behaviors.

Not surprisingly, if caregivers and teachers take time to encourage, facilitate, and teach prosocial behaviors, children's prosocial interactions increase and aggression decreases (Honig 1982). In an interesting study, children who attended, from 3 months to kindergarten, an experimental child care program that focused on intellectual growth were rated by their kindergarten teachers as more aggressive than a control group of children who attended community child care programs during their preschool years for less amount of time (Haskins 1985). But when a prosocial curriculum entitled "My

Friends and Me" was implemented, the next groups of child care graduates did not differ in aggression rates from control-group children. Emphasizing and encouraging prosocial behaviors made a difference in how children learned to interact and play with each other. A number of other intriguing research studies concerning teacher educators and curriculum intended to enhance positive social development in young children are described in our book *Prosocial Development in Children: Caring, Sharing, & Cooperating*.

## Focus on Prosocial Behaviors: Value, Model, and Acknowledge

Need it be said? What the adults who are important in children's lives value, model, and encourage in children influences them. What values do we value and encourage?

## Value and Emphasize Consideration for Others' Needs

Children become aware at an early age of what aspects of life their special adults admire and value. Research on toddlers (Yarrow & Waxler 1976) and boys with learning disabilities (Elardo & Freund 1981) shows that when parents encourage their children to have concern for others, the children behave more prosocially.

As every experienced teacher knows, emphasizing the importance of children helping others whenever possible results in children undertaking more helping activities (Grusec, Saas-Kortsaak, & Simultis 1978). Children whose parents esteem altruism highly are more frequently considered by peers as highly prosocial (Rutherford & Mussen 1968).

## Model Prosocial Behaviors

"Practice what you preach," "Do as I say, not as I do," and "Monkey see, monkey do" are tried-and-true sayings that remind us that children model many behaviors that we do—and do not!—want them to imitate. Adults who model prosocial behaviors influence children's willingness to behave prosocially (Bandura 1986). A teacher who patiently tied his toddlers' shoelaces day after day observed that toddlers who saw a peer tripping over laces would bend down and try to twist their friend's sneaker laces in an attempt to help. Bryan (1977) stresses that children imitate helping activities whether the models are living people or fictional characters. Over the years, modeling has proven more powerful than preaching. Traditionally we have called it *setting a good example*. How caregivers and parents act—kind, considerate, and compassionate, or cruel, thoughtless, and uncaring—influences young children to imitate them.

Children who frequently observe and are influenced by family members and teachers who behave prosocially will imitate those special adults. "Mama," observed 3-year-old Dana, "that was a very good job you did buckling my seat belt." How often Mama had used just such encouraging words with her preschooler!

## Label and Identify Prosocial and Antisocial Behaviors

We all love it when our positive deeds are acknowledged. Notice the positive interactions, however small, that occur between children and encourage them through your comments. When adults label behaviors, such as "considerate toward peers" and "cooperative with classmates," children's dialogues and role-taking abilities increase (Vorrath 1985). Rather than just saying "That's good" or "That's nice" to a child, be specific in identifying prosocial behaviors and actions for children. Saying "You are being helpful" or "You gave him a tissue, he really needed it to wipe his nose" will be most helpful to children.

## Attribute Positive Social Behaviors to Each Child

Attributing positive intentions, such as "You shared because you like to help others" or "You're the kind of person who likes to help others whenever you can," results in children donating more generously to people in need (Grusec, Kuczynski, Rushton, & Simultis 1978; Grusec & Redler 1980).

After 8-year-olds had shared their winnings from a game with "poor" children, the children who were given positive attributions (e.g., "You're the kind of person who likes to help others whenever you can"), as opposed to social reinforcers (just being told that it was good to share with others), were more likely to share at a later time (Grusec & Redler 1980).

Skilled teachers personalize attributions so that each child feels special. Say such things as "You are a very helpful person," "You are the kind of person who likes to stick up for a child who is being bothered," and "You really try to be a buddy to a new child in our class who is shy at first in finding a friend."

Children from punitive homes may need help understanding how to make attributions that are true rather than assuming that others have evil intentions. For example, you might ask, "Did your classmate step on your homework paper in the schoolyard to be mean or to keep it from blowing away?" Focus children's thinking on attributes and intentions of others' actions as a way to prevent children from unthinkingly lashing out at others in angry response.

## Notice and Positively Encourage Prosocial Behaviors, but Do Not Overuse External Rewards

In research by Rushton and Teachman (1978), social reinforcement for sharing increased sharing among young children even when the experimenter was no longer present. Goffin (1987) recommends that teachers notice when children share mutual goals, ideas, and materials, as well as when they negotiate and bargain in decision making and accomplishing goals. When caregivers and parents use external reinforcement too much, however, children's prosocial behaviors may decrease. Fabes, Fultz, Eisenberg, May-Plumlee, and Christopher (1989) reported that mothers who like using rewards may undermine their children's internalized *desire* to behave prosocially by increasing the salience of external rather than internal rewards.

Teachers have reported that offering stickers for prosocial behaviors to one child in a classroom often backfires when other children become upset that they didn't also get stickers. A kindergarten child went home from school one day and told his grandmother, "I've got it figured out now. First you have to be bad,

and then good, and then you get a sticker." Commenting on positive behaviors and attributing positive characteristics to children rather than using external rewards help young children internalize prosocial responses.

---

# Encourage Understanding of Children's Own and Others' Feelings and Perspectives

Skilled teachers understand how to do these things:

## Acknowledge and Encourage Understanding and Expression of Children's Feelings

The ability to empathize with a peer who is experiencing sadness, anger, or distress may depend on a child having had a prior similar experience with those feelings (Barnett 1984). Children from ages 3 to 8 are becoming aware of *happy feelings* (3 1/2 years), *fear* (3 1/2 to 4 years), and *anger and sadness* (3 to 8 years) (Borke 1971).

Caregivers need to help children put feelings into words and to understand their feelings. Teachers can acknowledge and reflect children's feelings by making comments such as "It seems as if you are feeling so sad" or "You look like you are feeling angry. You want my attention *now*. As soon as I change Luanne's diaper, I can read to you." This calm observation by a child care provider wiped the thunder off a toddler's face. He looked amazed that his teacher had understood his feelings. He relaxed when she reassured him with a promise to come back in a few minutes and read with him.

## Facilitate Perspective- and Role-Taking Skills and Understanding Others' Feelings

Helping young children notice and respond to the feelings of others can be quite effective in teaching them to be considerate of others. A preschool teacher kneeled to be at eye level with a child who had just socked another child during a struggle for a bike. The teacher pointed out the feelings of the other child: "He's very sad and hurt. What can you do to make him feel better?" The aggressor paused, observed the other child's face, and offered the bike to the crying child.

A child's ability to identify accurately the emotional state of another, as well as the empathic ability to experience the feelings of another, contribute to prosocial behavior. Children who are altruistic and more willing to help others display more empathy and perspective-taking skills (a cognitive measure) (Chalmers & Townsend 1990).

Feshbach (1975) reported that two training techniques that promoted understanding in children of other children's feelings were *role playing* and *maximizing the perceived similarity* between the observer and the stimulus person. The latter is what antibias education is about.

Encourage children to act out stories dramatically. Children who act out different stories become aware of how the characters feel. Switching roles gives children a different perspective on the feelings and motives of each character. Acting out roles, as in "The Three Billy Goats Gruff" or "Goldilocks and the Three Bears" gives children a chance to understand each story character's point of view (Krogh & Lamme 1983). A first- or second-grade class may want to write a letter of apology from Goldilocks to the Bear family!

Trovato (1987) created the puppets "Hattie Helper," "Carl Defender," "Robert Rescuer," "Debra Defender," "Kevin Comforter," and "Sharon Sharer" for adults to use to help young children learn prosocial behaviors with other children. Crary (1984) also promotes the use of puppets for teachers and children to use in role playing different social situations that may arise in the classroom.

Perspective taking is not enough to ensure children's development of prosocial behaviors. Children who are low in empathy but high in perspective taking may demonstrate Machiavellianism (a tendency to take advantage in a negative way of knowledge concerning another person's feelings and thoughts) (Barnett & Thompson 1985). Although Howes and Farber's (1987) research with toddlers ages 16 to 33 months of in child care showed that 93% of toddlers responded prosocially to peers who showed distress, George and Main (1979) reported that abused toddlers looked on impassively or reacted with anger when a playmate was hurt or distressed. Vulnerable children urgently need help understanding and acknowledging their range of often very strong feelings and empathizing with other people's feelings.

## Use Victim-Centered Discipline and Reparation: Emphasize Consequences

Other-oriented techniques focus a child on the effects of hurtful and antisocial behaviors, such as hit-ting or pinching. Results of a study of how children learned altruism at home revealed that parents of the most prosocial toddlers had emphasized the negative consequences of their toddlers' aggressive acts on other children (Pines 1979). Point out the consequences of the child's behavior. Emphasize to the aggressor the results of hurtful actions upon another person. Choose statements such as "Look—that hurt him!" "He is crying" and "I cannot let you hurt another child, and I do not want anyone to make you hurt; we need to help each other feel happy and safe in this class."

## Help Children Become Assertive Concerning Prosocial Matters

If a child has high-perspective-taking skills and is assertive, then the child is likely to be prosocial. In contrast, if a child has high-perspective-taking skills and is timid, then the child is less likely to be prosocial (Barrett & Yarrow 1977). In the book *Listen to the Children* (Zavitkovsky, Baker, Berlfein, & Almy 1986, 42), the authors shared a true story about two young girls, Dolores and Monica, who were washing their hands before lunch. Eric was waiting for his turn to wash his hands. Out of the blue, he shouted crossly into Monica's face, "You're not pretty." The author and observer reported that out of the stillness came Dolores's firm voice, "Yes, she is. She looks just right for her." Dolores was demonstrating both perspective-taking skills—knowing that Monica's feelings were hurt—and prosocial defending skills. As teachers notice and acknowledge prosocial behaviors, children's self-confidence concerning prosocial interactions will increase.

## Encourage Problem Solving and Planfulness for Prosocial Behaviors

You have heard this before, but it takes time, effort, and planfulness to *do* it.

## Encourage Means-Ends and Alternative-Solution Thinking in Conflict Situations

Help children think through, step-by-step, their reasoning about how to respond when they are having a social problem with a peer. What are the steps by which they figure out how to get from the conflict situation they are in to peaceful, friendly cooperation or a courteous live-and-let-live situation?

Shure (1992) provides daily lessons for teachers to help children discover when their feelings and wishes are the *same* or *different* from other children's, or whether *some* or *all* of the children want to play the game that *one* prefers. Teachers who use these daily lesson plans with emphasis on encouraging children to think of alternative solutions to their social conflicts and to imagine the consequences of each behavior or strategy they think of can help aggressive and shy children become more positively social within three months. Increased positive social functioning is associated with children's ability to think of more strategies rather than with the quality of the social solutions they devise (Shure & Spivak 1978).

## Use Socratic Questions to Elicit Prosocial Planfulness and Recognition of Responsibility

When a child is misbehaving in such a way as to disturb his own or class progress, quietly ask, "How does that help you?" This technique, recommended by Fugitt (1983), can be expanded to encourage group awareness by asking the child, "How is that helping the group?" or "How is that helping your neighbor?" This strategy is designed to help children recognize and take responsibility for their own behaviors.

## Show Pictured Scenes of Altruism, and Ask Children to Create Verbal Scenarios

Show children pictured scenes of children being helpful, cooperative, generous, charitable, patient, courteous, sharing, and kind. Working with a small group of children, call on each child to make up a scenario or story about the child or children in the picture. Ask, "What do you think is happening here?" Be sure to help children become aware of how the child being helped feels and how the child who has been helpful or generous will feel about herself or himself.

## Provide Specific Behavioral Training in Social Skills

Cartledge and Milburn (1980) recommend defining skills to be taught in behavioral terms assessing children's level of competence. Then teach the skills that are lacking, evaluate the results of teaching, and provide opportunities for children to practice and generalize the transfer of

these new social skills to other situations.

McGinnis and Goldstein use structured "skillstreaming" strategies to teach prosocial skills to preschool (1990) and elementary school (1984) children. Skills such as listening, using nice talk, using brave talk, saying thank you, asking for help, greeting others, reading others, waiting one's turn, sharing, offering help, asking someone to play, and playing a game are a few of the "beginning social skills" and "friendship making skills." Other skills help children deal with feelings and provide them with alternatives to aggression. Preschool children who received training and were encouraged to (1) use politeness words, (2) listen to who is talking, (3) participate with a peer in an activity, (4) share, (5) take turns, and (6) help another person have fun were more sociable in the training classroom and at follow-up (Factor & Schilmoeller 1983).

Teaching concern for others is a familiar idea to teachers of children from infancy through 8 years!

---

# Use Positive Discipline for Promoting Prosocial Behaviors and Less Aggression

We have to educate children about socially desirable behaviors, as about many other things.

## Use Positive Discipline Strategies, Such as Induction and Authoritative Methods

When teachers use positive discipline techniques—such as reasoning, use of positive reinforcement, and empathic listening—and *au-*

*thoritative* strategies (Baumrind 1977)—loving, positive commitment to the child plus use of firm, clear rules and explanations—children are more likely to behave prosocially. The more nonauthoritarian and nonpunitive the parent, the higher the child's level of reasoning (Eisenberg, Lennon, & Roth 1983). Discipline that is *emotionally intense but nonpunitive* is effective with toddlers (Yarrow & Waxler 1976).

## Positive Discipline: A Protection against Media Violence

As one might guess, a relationship has been found between parent's positive discipline techniques and the effects of prosocial and antisocial television programs on children. Using Hoffman's terms to describe parenting styles, Abelman (1986) reported that parents who are most *inductive* (who use reasoning) and who rarely use love withdrawal or power assertion have children who are *most* affected by prosocial and *least* affected by antisocial television. The reverse is also true. Positive discipline, then, is a powerful buffer against the negative effects of antisocial media materials.

## Respond to and Provide Alternatives to Aggressive Behaviors

This has been a basic principle of nursery and kindergarten education since their beginning. Writing much more recently, Caldwell (1977) advises caregivers not to ignore aggression or permit aggression to be expressed and assume that this venting will "discharge the tension." For example, bullying that is ignored does not disappear. Caldwell writes, "In order to control aggression, we must strengthen altruism" (1977, 9). Teach children what they can do to help others feel good.

*Redirect* antisocial actions to more acceptable actions. A child who is throwing a ball at someone may be redirected to throw a beanbag back and forth with another child.

Teach angry, acting-out children to *use words* to express feelings. When children are feeling aggrieved, tell them, "Use your words" instead of hurtful actions. Help children learn "I" statements to express their feelings or wishes and to express how they perceive a situation of distress or conflict (Gordon 1970). Give children words and phrases to use, such as "I feel upset when our game is interrupted," "I cannot finish my building if you take away these blocks," or "I was using that Magic Marker first. I still need it to finish my picture."

Ask children to restate classroom rules about not hitting or hurting others (Honig 1985). Preschool children, however, may interpret the rules from an egocentric viewpoint and not always understand the reasons for rules. Deanna, a preschooler, went home from school and told her mother, "Matthew pinched me." After talking about the classroom rule, "Don't pinch or hit back," Deanna's mother tried to get Deanna to problem-solve other solutions to the problem, such as telling Matthew that it hurt when he pinched. The next day, when her mom picked her up from school, Deanna reported angrily, "Matthew pinched me back." When asked why she pinched him, Deanna restated the classroom rule, "That doesn't matter; he's not supposed to pinch me back."

## Offer Children Choices

This is another "basic" of professional work with young children. Toddlers and preschoolers struggling to assert newly emergent autonomy cooperate more easily with caregiver requests if they feel empowered to make choices. Adults can decide on the choices to be offered. For the toddler having trouble settling at naptime, the offer "Would you like to sleep with your head at this end of your cot or the other end?" may empower him enough to decide cheerfully just how he wants to lie down for naptime. Gilligan observed that "The essence of the moral decision is the exercise of choice and the willingness to accept responsibility for that choice" (1982, 58). Often adults forget that if they carefully craft choices, children may more readily cooperate in the home and in the classroom. During snacktime adults can offer a choice of "darker or lighter toast," "apple or orange juice" to the finicky eater who generally resists food simply set down without her being allowed some choice. When children want to practice throwing a small basketball into a preschooler-size net, discuss the need for a turn-taking rule and offer a choice: "Do you want to take two or three throws for your turn?" Later, comment on how the children followed the rule. Ask them how they think the rule helped their game go more peaceably.

## Provide Opportunities for Social Interactions Through Play— Pair "Social Isolates" with Sociable Children

Place a child who is experiencing social problems with a friendly socially skilled playmate, preferably a younger one, to increase the social isolate's positive peer interactions (Furman, Rahe, & Hartup 1978). Pair an assertive, gregarious, but gentle child (who is the recipient of many prosocial overtures and is likely to offer help and friendliness) with a very shy child.

## Create Good Adult-Child Relationships

Children learn to enjoy being with other people when they experience adults who are positive, caring, loving, and responsive. When adults respond to a child in affectionate, kind, empathetic ways, the child learns how to be a communicative partner who knows how to take turns, listen, negotiate, and help others; common sense tells us that this is logical. Park and Waters (1989) found that two children who had experienced affirmative first relationships with their mothers engaged in more harmonious, less controlling, more responsive, and happier play together than did children who had not experienced positive first relationships.

## Provide Body Relaxation Activities

Create a relaxed classroom climate to further harmonious interactions. Relaxation exercises can restore harmony when children are fussy or tense. Back rubs help. Sand play and water play promote relaxation in some children who have a difficult time acting peaceably.

Children may lie down on mats and wiggle each limb separately, in turn, to relax and ease body tension. Many classical music pieces, such as the Brahms *Lullaby* or Debussy's *Reverie*, can be useful in helping children imagine peaceful scenes. Focused imagery activities can reduce tensions. Have children close their eyes and imagine being in a quiet forest glade, listening to a stream flow nearby and feeling the warm sunshine on their faces.

Group movement to music adds another dimension of relaxation. Dancing partners need to tune in to each other's motions and rhythmic swaying as they hold hands or take turns imitating each other's gestures.

## Use Technology to Promote Prosocial Behaviors

Unlike most of the familiar principles for promoting social development reviewed in this article, *this* idea will be new to many teachers. Videotape children who are behaving prosocially to facilitate sharing. A video camera in the classroom can help promote altruism. Third-grade children viewed videotapes of themselves and models in situations involving sharing. This technique was effective in increasing sharing immediately following training and one week later (Devoe & Sherman 1978). Maybe some teachers who like trying new things will try this idea with *younger* children.

## Conclusion

As teachers focus on and facilitate prosocial behaviors, the whole ambience of a classroom may change. As teachers model kindness and respect, express appreciation for prosocial actions, promote cooperation, teach children how their behaviors affect others, point out each child's prosocial behaviors with admiration to the other children, and en-

courage children to help each other, prosocial deeds and attitudes will increase. Adults' interactions with young children make a powerful difference in the atmosphere and climate of the classroom.

## References

Abelman, R. 1986. Children's awareness of television's prosocial fare: Parental discipline as an antecedent. *Journal of Family Issues* 7:51–66.

Bandura, A. 1986. *The social foundation of thought and action: A social cognitive theory.* Englewood Cliffs, NJ: Prentice-Hall.

Barnett, M. 1984. Similarity of experience and empathy in preschoolers. *The Journal of Genetic Psychology* 145: 241–50.

Barnett, M., & S. Thompson. 1985. The role of perspective-taking and empathy in children's Machiavellianism, prosocial behavior, and motive for helping. *The Journal of Genetic Psychology* 146: 295–305.

Barrett, D.E., & M.R. Yarrow. 1977. Prosocial behavior, social inferential ability, and assertiveness in young children. *Child Development* 48: 475–81.

Baumrind, D. 1977. Some thoughts about childrearing. In S. Cohen & T. J. Comiskey (Eds.), *Child development: Contemporary perspectives.* Itasca, IL: F. E. Peacock.

Borke, H. 1971. Interpersonal perception of young children: Egocentrism or empathy? *Developmental Psychology* 5: 263–9.

Bryan, J. H. 1977. Prosocial behavior. In H. L. Hom, Jr., & P. A. Robinson, eds. *Psychological processes in early education.* New York: Academic.

Caldwell, B. 1977. Aggression and hostility in young children. *Young Children* 32(2): 4–14.

Cartledge, G., & J. F. Milburn, eds. 1980. *Teaching social skills to children.* New York: Pergamon.

Chalmers, J., & M. Townsend. 1990. The effects of training in social perspective taking on socially maladjusted girls. *Child Development* 61: 178–90.

Crary, E. 1984. *Kids can cooperate: A practical guide to teaching problem solving.* Seattle, WA: Parenting Press.

Devoe, M., & T. Sherman. 1978. A microtechnology for teaching prosocial behavior to children. *Child Study Journal* 8(2): 83–92.

Eisenberg, N., R. Lennon, & K. Roth. 1983. Prosocial development: A longitudinal study. *Developmental Psychology* 19: 846–55.

Elardo, R., & J. J. Freund. 1981. Maternal childrearing styles and the social skills of learning disabled boys: A preliminary investigation. *Contemporary Educational Psychology* 6: 86–94.

Fabes, R. A., J. Fultz, N. Eisenberg, T. May-Plumlee, & F.S. Christopher. 1989. Effect of rewards on children's prosocial motivation: A socialization study. *Developmental Psychology* 25: 509–15.

Factor, D., & G. L. Schilmoeller. 1983. Social skill training of preschool children. *Child Study Journal* 13(1): 41–56.

Feshbach, N. 1975. Empathy in children: Some theoretical and empirical considerations. *The Counseling Psychologist* 5: 25–30.

Fugitt, E. 1983. *"He hit me back first!" Creative visualization activities for parenting and teaching.* Rolling Hills Estates, CA: Jalmar.

Furman, W., D. F. Rahe, & W. W. Hartup. 1978. Rehabilitation of low-interactive preschool children through mixed-age and same-age socialization. In H. McGurk, ed., *Issues in childhood social development.* Cambridge: Methuen.

George, C., & M. Main. 1979. Social interactions of young abused children: Approach, avoidance, and aggression. *Child Development* 50: 306–18.

Gilligan, C. 1982. *In a different voice.* Cambridge, MA: Harvard University Press.

Goffin, S. G. 1987. Cooperative behaviors: They need our support. *Young Children* 42(2): 75–81.

Gordon, T. 1970. *Parent effectiveness training.* New York: Wyden.

Grusec, J. E., & E. Redler. 1980. Attribution, reinforcement, and altruism. *Developmental Psychology* 16: 525–34.

Grusec, J., P. Saas-Kortsaak, & Z. Simultis. 1978. The role of example and moral exhortation in the training of altruism. *Child Development* 49: 920–3.

Grusec, J., J. Kuczynski, P. Ruston, & Z. Simultis. 1978. Modeling, direct instruction, and attributions: Effects on altruism. *Developmental Psychology* 14: 51–7.

Haskins, R. 1985. Public school aggression among children with varying day care experience. *Child Development* 56: 689–703.

Honig, A. S. 1982. Research in review. Prosocial development in children. *Young Children* 37(5): 51–62.

Honig, A. S. 1985. Research in review. Compliance, control, and discipline. Part 1. *Young Children* 40(2): 50–8.

Honig, A. S., & D. S. Wittmer. 1992. *Prosocial development in children: Caring, sharing, & cooperating: A bibliographic resource guide.* New York: Garland.

Howes, C., & J. Farber. 1987. Toddlers' responses to the distress of their peers. *Journal of Applied Developmental Psychology* 8: 441–52.

Krogh, S., & L. Lamme. 1983 (January-February). Learning to share: How literature can help. *Childhood Education* 59(3): 188–92.

McGinnis, E., & A. Goldstein. 1984. *Skillstreaming the elementary school child: A guide to prosocial skills.* Champaign, IL: Research Press.

McGinnis, E., & A. Goldstein. 1990. *Skillstreaming in early childhood. Teaching prosocial skills to the preschool and kindergarten child.* Champaign, IL: Research Press.

Park, K., & E. Waters. 1989. Security of attachment and preschool friendships. *Child Development* 60: 1076–81.

Pines, M. 1979. Good Samaritans at age two? *Psychology Today* 13: 66–77.

Rushton, J. P., & G. Teachman. 1978. The effects of positive reinforcement, attributions, and punishment on model induced altruism in children. *Personality and Social Psychology Bulletin* 4: 322–5.

Rutherford, E., & P. Mussen. 1968. Generosity in nursery school boys. *Child Development* 39: 755–65.

Shure, M. B. 1992. *I can problem solve: An interpersonal cognitive problem-solving program.* Champaign, IL: Research Press.

Shure, M., & G. Spivack. 1978. *Problem-solving techniques in childrearing.* San Francisco: Jossey-Bass.

Trovato, C. 1987. Teaching today's kids to get along. *Early Childhood Teacher* 34: 43.

Vorrath, H. 1985. *Positive peer culture.* New York: Aldine.

Yarrow, M. R., & C. Z. Waxler. 1976. Dimensions and correlates of prosocial behavior in young children. *Child Development* 47: 118–25.

Zavitkovsky, D., K. R. Baker, J. R. Berlfein, & M. Almy. 1986. *Listen to the children.* Washington, DC: NAEYC.

**Article Review Form at end of book.**

Give an example of what a parent of an aggressive child might do to counter the child's genetic tendencies. Give an example of how parents sometimes promote personality traits in their children that they feel are not desirable.

# Shyness, Sadness, Curiosity, Joy

## Is it nature or nurture?

**Marc Peyser
and Anne Underwood**

If any child seemed destined to grow up afraid of her shadow and just about anything else that moved, it was 2-year-old Marjorie. She was so painfully shy that she wouldn't talk to or look at a stranger. She was even afraid of friendly cats and dogs. When Jerome Kagan, a Harvard professor who discovered that shyness has a strong genetic component, sent a clown to play with Marjorie, she ran to her mother. "It was as if a cobra entered that room," Kagan says. His diagnosis: Marjorie showed every sign of inherited shyness, a condition in which the brain somehow sends out messages to avoid new experiences. But as Kagan continued to examine her over the years, Marjorie's temperament changed. When she started school, she gained confidence from ballet classes and her good grades, and she began to make friends. Her parents even coaxed her into taking horseback-riding lessons. Marjorie may have

been born shy, but she has grown into a bubbly second grader.

For Marjorie, then, biology—more specifically, her genetic inheritance—was not her destiny. And therein lies our tale. In the last few years scientists have identified genes that appear to predict all sorts of emotional behavior, from happiness to aggressiveness to risk-taking. The age-old question of whether nature or nurture determines temperament seems finally to have been decided in favor of Mother Nature and her ever-deepening gene pool. But the answer may not be so simple after all. Scientists are beginning to discover that genetics and environment work together to determine personality as intricately as Astaire and Rogers danced. "If either Fred or Ginger moves too fast, they both stumble," says Stanley Greenspan, a pediatric psychiatrist at George Washington University and the author of "The Growth of the Mind." "Nature affects nurture affects nature and back and forth. Each step influences the next." Many scientists now believe that some experiences can actually alter the structure of the brain. An ag-

gressive toddler, under the right circumstances, can essentially be rewired to channel his energy more constructively. Marjorie can overcome her shyness—forever. No child need be held captive to her genetic blueprint. The implications for child rearing—and social policy—are profound.

While Gregor Mendel's pea plants did wonders to explain how humans inherit blue eyes or a bald spot, they turn out to be an inferior model for analyzing something as complex as the brain. The human body contains about 100,000 genes, of which 50,000 to 70,000 are involved in brain function. Genes control the brain's neurotransmitters and receptors, which deliver and accept mental messages like so many cars headed for their assigned parking spaces. But there are billions of roads to each parking lot, and those paths are highly susceptible to environmental factors. In his book, "The New View of Self," Dr. Larry Siever, a psychiatry professor at Mount Sinai Medical Center, writes about how the trauma of the Holocaust caused such intense genetic scrambling in some survivors that their children inherited the same stress-related abnormalities. "Perhaps the sense of danger and uncertainty associated with living through such a time is passed on in the family milieu and primes the biological systems of the children as well," says Siever. He adds that that might explain why pianist David Helfgott, the subject of the movie "Shine," had his mental breakdown.

A gene is only a probability for a given trait, not a guarantee. For that trait to be expressed, a gene often must be "turned on" by an outside force before it does its job. High levels of stress apparently activate a variety of genes, including those suspected of being involved in fear, shyness and some mental illnesses. Children conceived during a three-month famine in the Netherlands during a Nazi blockade in 1945 were later found to have twice the rate of schizophrenia as did Dutch children born to parents who were spared the trauma of famine. "Twenty years ago, you couldn't get your research funded if you were looking for a genetic basis for schizophrenia, because everyone knew it was what your mother did to you in the first few years of life, as Freud said," says Robert Plomin, a geneticist at London's Institute of Psychiatry. "Now you can't get funded *unless* you're looking for a genetic basis. Neither extreme is right, and the data show why. There's only a 50 percent concordance between genetics and the development of schizophrenia."

Scientists have been devoting enormous energy to determining what part of a given character trait is "heritable" and what part is the result of socialization. Frank Sulloway's book, "Born to Rebel," which analyzes the influence of birth order on personality, opened a huge window on a universal—and largely overlooked—environmental factor. But that's broad brushstroke. Most studies focus on remarkably precise slivers of human emotions. One study at Allegheny University in Pennsylvania found that the tendency for a person to throw dishes or slam doors when he's angry is 40 percent heritable, while the likelihood a person will yell in anger is only 28 percent heritable. The most common method for determining these statistics is studying twins. If identical twins are more alike in some way than are fraternal twins, that trait is believed to have a higher likelihood of being inherited. But the nature-nurture knot is far from being untied.

The trick, then, is to isolate a given gene and study the different ways environment interacts with it. For instance, scientists believe that people with the longer variety of a dopamine-4 receptor gene are biologically predisposed to be thrill seekers. Because the gene appears to make them less sensitive to pain and physical sensation, the children are more likely to, say, crash their tricycles into a wall, just to see what it feels like. "These are the daredevils," says Greenspan. But they need not be. Given strict boundaries, Greenspan says, thrill-seeking kids can be taught to modulate and channel their overactive curiosity. A risk-taking child who likes to pound his fist into hard objects can be taught games that involve hitting softly as well. "If you give them constructive ways to meet their needs," says Greenspan, "they can become charismatic, action-oriented leaders."

Shyness has been studied perhaps more than any other personality trait. Kagan, who has monitored 500 children for more than 17 years at Harvard, can detect telltale signs of shyness in babies even before they're born. He's found that the hearts of shy children in the womb consistently beat faster than 140 times a minute, which is much faster than the heartbeats of other babies. The shy fetus is already highly reactive, wired to overmonitor his environment. But he can also outgrow this predisposition if his parents gently but firmly desensitize him to the situations that cause anxiety, such as encouraging him to play with other children or, as in Marjorie's fear of animals, taking her to the stables and teaching her to ride a horse. Kagan has found that by the age of 4, no more than 20 percent of the previously shy children remain that way.

Will the reprogramming last into adulthood? Because evidence of the role of genes has been discovered only recently, it's still too early to tell. But studies of animals give some indication. Stephen Suomi at the National Institute of Child Health and Human Development works with rhesus monkeys that possess the same genetic predisposition to shyness that affects humans. He's shown that by giving a shy monkey to a foster mother who is an expert caregiver, the baby will outgrow the shyness. Even more surprising, the once shy monkey will become a leader among her peers and an unusually competent parent, just like the foster mom. Though she will likely pass along her shyness genes to her own child, she will teach it how to overcome her predisposition, just as she was taught. And the cycle continues—generations of genetically shy monkeys become not just normal, but superior, adults and parents. The lesson, says Suomi: "You can't prejudge anyone at birth. No matter what your genetic background, a negative characteristic you're born with may even turn out to be an advantage."

But parents aren't scientists, and it's not always easy to see how experiences can influence a child's character. A baby who smiles a lot and makes eye contact is, in part, determining her own environment, which in turn affects her temperament. As her parents coo and smile and wrinkle their noses in delighted response, they are reinforcing their baby's sunny disposition. But what about children who are born with low muscle tone, who at 4 months can barely hold up their own heads, let alone smile? Greenspan has discovered that mothers of these kids smile at the baby for a while, but when the affection isn't returned, they give up. And so does the baby, who over time fails to develop the ability to socialize normally. "If you move in the wrong patterns, the problem is exacerbated," Greenspan says. He has found that if parents respond to nonsmiling babies by being superanimated—like Bob Barker hosting a game show—they can engage their child's interest in the world.

The ramifications of these findings clearly have the potential to revolutionize child-rearing theory and practice. But to an uncertain end. "Our society has a strong belief that what happens in childhood determines your fate. If you have a happy childhood, everything will be all right. That's silly," says Michael Lewis, director of the Institute for the Study of Child Development in New Jersey and the author of "Altering Fate." Lewis estimates that experience ultimately rewrites 90 percent of a child's personality traits, leaving an adult with only one tenth of his inborn temperament. "The idea that early childhood is such a powerful moment to see individual differences in biology or environment is not valid," he says. "We are too open to and modifiable by experience." Some scientists warn that attempting to reprogram even a narrow sliver of childhood emotions can prove to be a daunting task, despite research's fascinating new insights. "Children are not a 24-hour controlled experiment," says C. Robert Cloninger, a professor of psychiatry and genetics at the Washington University School of Medicine in St. Louis. "If you put a child in a Skinner box, *then* maybe you could have substantial influence." So, mindful of the blinding insights of geneticists and grateful for the lingering influences of environment, parents must get on with the business of raising their child, an inexact science if ever there was one.

 **Article Review Form at end of book.**

Why are people concerned that providing children with antidepressants when they are feeling bad may ultimately have more negative than positive effects? Why do some people view the quick fix of drugs to relieve the stresses of childhood a potential new form of child abuse?

# Peppermint Prozac

### Arianna Huffington

Is your daughter depressed about acne? Soon, you may be able to take her to a dermatologist for peppermint-flavored Prozac. Is your son blue over an ingrown toenail? Take him to a podiatrist for some antidepressants. Is he angry about having to wear braces? His orthodontist may soon be handing out pills along with a dinosaur toothbrush.

Already, at least 580,000 children are being prescribed antidepressants—and those numbers are likely to increase dramatically. For now, doctors can prescribe Prozac to kids but Eli Lilly, which manufactures the drug, can't market it as a children's remedy. According to the *Medical Sciences Bulletin*, however, "the FDA is currently evaluating Prozac for use as an antidepressant in children." If the FDA gives its blessing, Eli Lilly will be free to peddle "children's" Prozac—especially now that the FDA is about to clear the way for TV advertising of prescription drugs. The company already has on the market a peppermint-flavored version of Prozac. And where Prozac leads, other antide-pressants, such as Zoloft and Paxil, are sure to follow.

Doctors may prescribe antidepressants to children without any psychiatric evaluation. Yet the symptoms used to identify depression in a recent Prozac ad range from feeling "unusually sad or irritable" to finding it "hard to concentrate." I have two healthy little girls, ages 6 and 8, both of whom have experienced these symptoms. Indeed, I don't know any normal children who haven't.

No doubt there are children and teenagers who could genuinely benefit from antidepressants. But it's easy to see how millions might wind up taking antidepressants as a false cure for childhood and adolescence. One father in Southern California wrote to me recently to say that one of his son's friends is on antidepressants "because her parents are 'too strict' and she is depressed at not being able to do what other kids do."

## A Passing Cloud

Signs of depression may be nothing more than a passing cloud—or an indication of unresolved grief and loss. A doctor spending a few minutes with a child cannot possibly know the difference. "It's part of the human condition to feel crummy if something bad is happening in one's life," says Harold Koplewicz, vice chairman of psychiatry at the New York University Medical Center. "But that is very different from having a clinical disorder."

Indeed, substituting the quick fix of a drug for the often frustrating reality of parenting can be a subtle form of child abuse. It is our job as parents to help our kids navigate life's emotional roller coaster. Their mental health depends not only on their life experiences—good and bad—but on how they learn to cope with them.

Children behave notoriously in line with the expectations of the adults around them. If we think they can't cope without a pill, they will grow up believing that. If we teach our children that pills will make them feel better, how can we then tell them not to try a joint or a few drinks to lift their spirits?

It may not be long before stressed parents and teachers, bombarded with ads promising immediate relief for their kids—and themselves—will turn to

Prozac with alarming frequency. Forty percent of American children live without a father in the house. How tempting antidepressants will seem to those overwhelmed mothers.

One psychologist, Barbara Ingersoll, recently proclaimed that before long "mood disorders will be treated not as exotic, uncommon conditions in children but more like [cavities] or poor vision . . . There won't be a stigma for kids on Prozac—the stigma will be on not taking Prozac." In the past, the upper classes typically dealt with the stresses of childhood by sending their kids to boarding school.

Now, instead of being sent to Hotchkiss, children can be transported to Camp Prozac.

There are so many forces pushing us to accelerate the use of antidepressants for children. But we need to slow down. "Children are so vulnerable," says Michael Faenza, president and CEO of the National Mental Health Association. "We don't have a good body of research yet about how antidepressants will affect them long term." Even in Aldous Huxley's *Brave New World*, Soma—the drug that kept everyone manageably numb—wasn't put in the kids' bottles.

Here is a modest solution. Until much more is known about the effects of antidepressants on children's brains, why can't doctors simply refuse to prescribe the drugs without a full psychiatric evaluation? Since Eli Lilly claims to be concerned primarily with the mental health of its customers—as opposed to opening an enormous new market for Prozac—company executives would no doubt agree to such a restriction. And if they find that pill too hard to swallow, maybe the FDA could give it to them in a nice peppermint-flavored version.

 **Article Review Form at end of book.**

# WiseGuide Wrap-Up

- Between ages 7 to 12 months and through age 3 years, children typically experience separation anxiety, demonstrated by the crying, clinging, and reduced play behaviors of children when their caregivers depart.

- Prosocial classroom goals involve the facilitation of children's positive social interactions, including helping, sharing, cooperating and perspective taking. Within normal classroom routines, teachers can model, reinforce, and label prosocial behaviors for children. When dealing with conflicts, victim-centered discipline and assisted problem solving help promote cooperative interactions and reduce aggression.

- Children are born with differing temperaments, from shy to aggressive. However, genetic predispositions are not set in stone.

Gentle but firm interventions can desensitize the shy child and appropriately channel the behaviors of an aggressive child.

- Childhood depression is now well recognized and is being treated with antidepressants. There is some concern that we too willingly offer medications rather than encouraging children to cope with normal highs and lows.

## R.E.A.L. Sites

This list provides a print preview of typical **coursewise** R.E.A.L. sites. There are over 100 such sites at the **courselinks**™ site. The danger in printing URLs is that web sites can change overnight. As we went to press, these sites were functional using the URLs provided. If you come across one that isn't, please let us know via email to: webmaster@coursewise.com. Use your Passport to access the most current list of R.E.A.L. sites at the **courselinks**™ site.

**Site name:** Shyness
**URL:** http://www.shyness.com

**Why is it R.E.A.L.?** This web site is the home page sponsored by the Shyness Institute. This site provides links to resources on shyness, organizations, and services offering information on shyness. Shyness is a serious problem for a number of children and adults in our culture. A reading list of self-help and research materials is available. Select one or more articles to read and then try one of the online quizzes to examine your own level of shyness.

**Site name:** Things to do @ b-di.com & temperament.com
**URL:** http://www.temperament.com/b-di.com.html

**Why is it R.E.A.L.?** This web site is a clearinghouse for research and practical information on temperamental characteristics to be used by parents, students, and professionals who have an interest in temperament. Review sample items used on questionnaires to measure temperament. Can you identify any of these traits in your own personality? Ask your parents about your temperament in infancy and early childhood. What traits remain with you today? Why?

# section

# 4

## Learning Objectives

- Introduce readers to the biological basis of intelligent behaviors.

- Provide information on the early cognitive abilities of children.

- Review current views on how to stimulate and facilitate cognitive development in young children.

- Provide an overview of sample programs thought to promote optimal learning for all children.

- Discuss the origins and cognitive benefits of self-directed speech.

# Cognitive Development

**WiseGuide Intro**

Well before children begin to recite the ABCs, calculate 2 + 2, or call out the colors of the rainbow, they are problem solving and learning. The intelligence of a young child is different from that tapped by IQ and achievement tests. The fetus and newborn experience the world through their senses. The older infant touches, vocalizes, socializes, and moves. Through the combined influences of biological maturation and environmental stimulation, intelligent behavior evolves. Among the earliest signs of intelligence is the infant's ability to distinguish familiar and unfamiliar events, objects, and people. Weeks later, infants demonstrate great pleasure upon discovering that their actions make interesting events happen. Laughter at games such as peek-a-boo and persistent searches for lost toys indicate that object permanence and goal-oriented planning have emerged. By the start of the second year, language and independent walking emerge. With the former, the child enters the world of concepts, begins to pretend, and develops a sense of self. From the latter, the areas and perspectives to explore expand and further influence what is learned.

Parents' and teachers' roles in the emergence of intelligence behavior are clear. Adults provide children with opportunities to discover. They also nurture children's strengths and build on their weaknesses. Studies have shown that the types of interactions children have with their parents early in life influence later IQ scores. Talking to children about their interests, responding to their questions, and providing guidance are as important parenting tasks as are discipline and safety matters. The instructional styles parents use as they demonstrate and explain are also mimicked in children's self-instructions. Referred to as "private speech" by Vygotsky, how children come to internalize language and use it for self-regulation has gained much attention. Similarly, educators are taking Gardner's and others' theories stressing diversity of learning style seriously. Particularly among those concerned with children from low-income families or experiencing academic difficulties, the broadening of our definition of normal intelligence provides hope. It also open doors to and legitimizes alternative instructional methods.

## Thinking Beyond the Facts

Wondering if your child will "measure up" in the world of academics is a common preoccupation of American parents. Intelligence testing has flourished in our determination to separate the "haves" and "have nots." As this section on cognitive development suggests, developmental experts are now explaining how babies and children learn best, pointing to family factors that seem to promote cognitive growth, and encouraging schools to develop curriculum variety to foster the optimal development of all styles of learners. Even when children's learning is within norms, parents now seek-out tutorial services with the hopes of providing the greatest possible advantages for their offspring.

# Questions

**Reading 14.** What form of intelligence does the fetus show? Give some examples.

By the end of the second year of life, what kinds of intellectual abilities can the toddler demonstrate?

**Reading 15.** Describe the seven intelligences that Gardner proposed and explain why it is important to recognize this diversity of abilities.

What basic elements do the project approach and writer's workshop have in common?

**Reading 16.** How do Piaget and Vygotsky differ in their views of the function and value of private speech?

How might encouragement of the use of private speech benefit children with learning problems?

How important is being the smartest? Think about your family. Did your parents enroll you in any programs designed to spur your development? Did they have a favorite reference book or magazine for advice on parenting? Was your development compared with that of your siblings, your cousins, or neighborhood children? From your school experiences, did the brightest children have advantages beyond good report cards? Were they the happiest and most well adjusted in the classrooms? Did less bright students suffer and, if so, how? Were children grouped as college-prep, honors, or problem learner? How might such groupings affect children's academic confidence and motivation, as well as self-esteem? To learn more, visit web sites on child cognitive development, self-esteem, intelligence testing, tutorial services, and educational after-school and summertime programs for children.

Beyond your personal experiences, consider efforts today to promote bilingual education, classroom inclusion of children with a range of learning problems, school choice, and individualized education programs. Schools are also taking an active role in the teaching of values and the provision of substance abuse and sex education. How are more open attitudes toward individuality and individual needs of benefit to children? Are schools able to meet the needs of everyone and still enable the majority to gain the skills needed to succeed in college and in the workforce? Why are our children academically falling behind the children of other nations on standardized test scores? Finally, where should the lines be drawn between family and school responsibilities when it comes to nonacademic topics? Check websites on alternative schooling programs, bilingual education, and sex and drug education for more specific information and examples of model programs.

What form of intelligence does the fetus show? Give some examples. By the end of the second year of life, what kinds of intellectual abilities can the toddler demonstrate?

# How Smart Is Your Baby?

**Susan Ochshorn**

Blank slates, lumps of clay, empty vessels. These descriptions of newborn babies have prevailed through the centuries. Even so, the internal workings of the child—what is really going on in the minds of the junior members of our species—have always been a matter of fascination and speculation for both researchers and proud new parents.

Over the past several decades, professionals in the field of child development, led by advances in neuroscience, have ventured deep into the virtually uncharted territory of how a child's brain development affects thinking. The latest studies show that babies do indeed arrive with inborn, or preprogrammed, abilities. They come into the world with their senses primed to take in information, and with the thinking process already well under way.

## In the Beginning

The first glimmers of cognitive skills, those abilities associated with learning and thinking, appear in the womb. Between con-ception and delivery, billions of brain cells form, including those that will become the cerebral cortex, the part of the brain that contains specialized areas for analyzing time, space, and language (as well as for controlling sensory and motor functions). The fetus' responses are primitive, but they are the first step in cognitive development. "A fetus will kick in response to a loud sound, and then, as the sound is repeated, will stop kicking," says Daphne Maurer, a professor of psychology at McMaster University in Ontario and coauthor of *The World of the Newborn*. This action represents learning in its most rudimentary form.

## A Stimulating Environment

The womb—long believed to be quiet and stable—is thought of as the home no one wants to leave. But this cozy notion of the womb isn't correct, says Maurer. Actually, life in the uterus is noisy, unsettling, and foul-tasting. Researchers who have plumbed its depths with microphones confirm noises that reach as high as 95 decibels, equivalent to standing next to a lawn mower. Mom's voice resonates deep within, her heart chugs like a heavy-duty pump, her stomach churns and gurgles like a waterfall. "The womb is not the peaceful, insulated place that people envision. There's a lot going on, and a fetus' senses are constantly working," says Anthony DeCasper, a professor of psychology at the University of North Carolina at Greensboro.

In fact, fetal intelligence is purely sensory. The fetus experiences his world through taste, touch, vision, and hearing. With all the activity going on inside the womb, he is remarkably adapted and primed to respond to stimulation of all kinds. And many parents happily (often unknowingly) provide it. Pregnant women touch and stroke their bellies repeatedly and commune with the developing fetus. "The first one we kind of doted on in utero," says Sarah Kahn, a mother of four in New Canaan, Connecticut. "We talked to him in there and called him 'the Cheeseburger.' " Some people go even further—reading stories, speaking in foreign languages, playing complex segments of postmodern music. Is there any value to all of this? Probably not, says DeCasper. "In the normal course of development, the fetus gets plenty of stimulation," he says. "There's no need to expose it to more than it ordinarily gets."

## Wired for Sound

By the seventh month, the fetus begins responding to sound. In a classic Japanese study, researchers generated tones directly against expectant mothers' bellies and found that during the third trimester the fetal pulse rate quickened—evidence of the ability to hear.

Other experiments have suggested that the fetus can actually remember what he's heard in utero. DeCasper asked a group of pregnant women to read a portion of a book (for example, Dr. Seuss' *The Cat in the Hat*) twice daily to their babies in utero over the last six weeks of pregnancy. Less than three days after birth, the babies listened to the same passage that had been read to them, plus a passage that had not been read to them. The majority of the newborns indicated—by sucking more vigorously on a pacifier—a preference for the tale they had heard while they were in the womb. Like Maurer and others who study fetal behavior, DeCasper is convinced that learning does occur during the prenatal period. "It's perceptual learning, or learning through the senses," he says.

## The First Year

Once out of the womb, the newborn's challenges increase dramatically. The first year brings a series of rapid-fire changes—all fueled by a baby's myriad new experiences. Jerome Kagan, a professor of developmental psychology at Harvard University, likens the process of cognitive development to the production of flowers: "A baby needs a variety of stimuli and the opportunity to use her growing competencies. Just as a

seed needs water and sunshine to become a flower, a young infant needs to crawl, play, vocalize, smile, and interact with others for her abilities to fully develop."

For much of early childhood, babies' intellectual exploration continues to be very much rooted in the senses and motor skills. A new toy immediately goes into the mouth. A furry blanket gets the fingers moving and stroking. Objects and movements attract her attention, and she looks at things that interest her.

## Early Learning

Grasping, rooting, sucking, and stepping, the infant is born with a bundle of reflexes that provide her first responses to external stimuli. For example, rooting—the way a baby turns her head when touched on the cheek—stimulates the infant to nurse. And grasping, involuntary in the newborn, becomes intentional as the baby develops. Carolyn Krall, a mother of three in Minneapolis, was struck immediately by the power of her youngest daughter's grasp. "If Simone grabbed hold of something," Krall recalls, "she'd hang on so tightly that it was hard to get her to let go."

Babies seem almost comical in the first days after birth, their movements awkward and undirected. Within weeks, however, they've learned to take more control of their limb movement. In a study by Carolyn Rovee-Collier, a professor of psychology at Rutgers University in New Brunswick, New Jersey, and the editor of *Infant Behavior and Development*, researchers attached a ribbon from a baby's foot to the mobile above her crib. "These babies soon learned to kick their foot in order to make the mobile move," Rovee-Collier says.

At what experts call the "two-and-a-half-month shift," the brain undergoes major physiological changes that affect babies' behavior. Infants begin spending more of their time awake, their awareness of outside stimuli increases, and they begin to react in slightly less random ways. The infant starts to remember objects she encountered just a second or two before. Her vision, which was extremely limited at birth, improves to the point that she can now focus on a face and maintain eye contact. "Once Simone was two and a half months, she could definitely recognize me," says Krall. "When I first get up in the morning, I don't wear my glasses, and although Simone would eat and go through her whole nursing routine, she didn't smile. Because I wasn't wearing my glasses, she would look at me as if she wasn't quite sure who I was."

One of a baby's earliest challenges is detecting the similarities and differences among objects and actions in her environment. The image of Mom's face quickly becomes familiar to the newborn, while a change in the mother's appearance can be temporarily distressing. The infant needs to integrate the difference into her original image of Mom. The process of habituation—by which a baby grows accustomed to a particular object, sensation, or event—is a primitive form of learning, one skill in her limited but significant repertoire.

Another major development at this stage, says Dr. Robert Emde, a professor of psychiatry at the University of Colorado Health Sciences Center in Denver, is the emergence of the social smile. "An infant is now apt to greet people with a warm smile and may even coo in their presence. It's an awakening of the child's sociability, the beginning of rewarding social interaction. At this point, a baby becomes more of a person in her parents' eyes."

As babies continue to take in sights and experiences—faces, voices, movements, patterns, tastes—they make them their own, forming what are called "mental schemas," or ways of remembering past events and using them to solve problems. "My daughter has a toy trumpet," says Suzanne deYoung, a Manhattan mother of a ten-month-old. "When I blow into it, the air comes out and hits her face—she loves it. Today when I picked up the trumpet, she winced and smiled, as if she knew the air was about to come out."

But it's the novel or unusual events that stretch the brain and transform the familiar schemas. The child who looks at the same old mobile, with the same objects, day after day, will soon become bored. Change the objects that hang from it, though, and she'll stay interested. "With each day, an infant acquires more knowledge of her world, becoming sensitive to deviations from what she knows," says Kagan. "If you show a baby a picture of a familiar face, she might be interested, but present her with a picture of an upside-down face and she'll be very attentive."

What's needed for intellectual growth, then, is a balance between familiarity and novelty. In order to understand the stimuli around her, a young baby has to do things over and over again. "We need some repetition to learn," says Maurer. "The nervous system doesn't usually change from doing something once. There's often rhythm in a baby's actions—that's true of sucking, kicking, or grasping a toy." Such repetitive actions help organize the brain and set the stage for more complex thinking. DeYoung learned this when her daughter was about two months old. "She discovered the toy bar on her bouncy chair when she accidentally bumped it," she says. "After that she would intentionally knock it and grin from ear to ear."

## Mobility and Memory

With a baby's increased mobility and control of her body come greater interaction with the world as well as an improved understanding of the nature of how things work and how she can affect events. Jean Piaget—the Swiss psychologist who conducted landmark studies in cognitive development from the 1920s through the 1970s—labeled the period from birth to two years the sensorimotor period, the first of four periods in the development of intelligence. His observations of his own three children—which he recorded in rich detail—convinced him of the inextricable link between activity and cognitive skills.

In the second half of the first year, infants make great strides. The brain continues to mature, which allows for enhanced learning ability. Six-month-olds now comprehend, with great pleasure, that their actions can affect their environment. Still, the ability to intentionally produce a desired effect is not firmly established. It is not until about eight months that the infant will consciously decide to kick the bars and make the bells ring. "Sophie knew that crying or rattling her crib would get Mom or Dad to pick her up," says New York City father Sean O'Connor. "She'd also initiate a game of peekaboo by putting a sheet over her head, knowing we'd come to take it off."

At about the same time, babies begin to solidify, a sense of object permanence, or the knowledge that something exists even when it is out of sight. As early as four months, an infant realizes that her beloved koala bear hasn't vanished when it falls behind the crib, even though she is unable to act on her understanding and reach under the crib to get it. As a result, she quickly forgets about it. However, the nine-month-old, more accomplished at reaching, is not distracted by the fact that the bear is out of sight for the moment. She can remember the location of her furry companion.

That's what Lucy Barnard observed her daughter, Paris, accomplish at nine months. "She had a hand-shaped toy that she liked to chew on," says the Houston mother of three. "One day she left it on the floor, and the next morning, after I got her dressed, she crawled right to the toy and started to chew on it." Paris had acquired what experts label "recall memory." "When babies use recall memory, they're calling up something that isn't present," says Jane Healy, author of *Your Child's Growing Mind: A Practical Guide to Brain Development and Learning From Birth to Adolescence*. "That could be a visualization of an object or a past event, or a nonvisual memory of a piece of information, such as a word."

## First Words

Once a child can form mental pictures of her world, she is on her way to a higher level of thinking. She will soon be able to recognize common characteristics among objects—the beginning of categorization, a critical skill for language and math. And, perhaps most important, she will begin to play symbolically, another critical building block in the development of language.

Most children utter their first words by the time they are one year old—but they are already skilled conversationalists. Through cooing and babbling, in wordless dialogues with Mom, Dad, and others, the baby has learned the art of communication. "One of the things we do as people is converse with each other," says Naomi S. Baron, a professor of linguistics at American University in Washington, D.C., and the author of *Growing Up With Language*. "The baby learns, 'Aha, when you're with people, you talk,' " says Baron. The infant has adopted the "conversational imperative" and is now ready to take on the infinitely rich world of words.

## The Second Year

Although the achievements of the second year—toddlerhood—are striking, their evolution tends to be slower than those of the newborn's first few months. The work during this period is more complex, and the time it takes for children to reach each level varies enormously. Some toddlers walk early and talk late; others are verbally precocious but happily creep and crawl until the middle of the second year. Whatever the timetable, the mind and body are flowering, and learning is nonstop.

The 13- to 15-month-old is an entirely different creature than he was as a newborn. His brain is now better organized, and the different cognitive systems within it, which have been maturing at different rates, are reaching a kind of equilibrium. But the defining physical feature of a toddler is his ever-increasing mobility.

"The most exciting part of the transition from the first into the second year is the mastery of walking," says Daniel Stern, a professor of psychology at the University of Geneva in Switzerland and the author of *Diary of a Baby*. "Learning to explore opens up the world for children. They can now look at things from different perspectives and start to understand that the same thing can be experienced in different ways." An upright and mobile toddler has a much different view of the world of objects, people, and events. He is more of a participant with far more control over his environment. "When they can finally walk, they're so thrilled," says Carolyn Krall. "They stand up and realize 'OK, I can make things happen on my own!' "

## Love of Language

With greater physical and mental control comes a whole new set of intellectual skills as well as the refinement of already-developing abilities. Most experts agree that the strides made in language are one of the major achievements of the second year. Says Stern, "Language structures experience. If you can't put an experience into words, it can never be examined fully."

The early schemas, or mental models, that infants construct are useful for learning many things, but they are limited in ways that language is not. "Language is the unique tool that makes humans go forward cognitively," says Stern. Quincy Cotton, a New York City mother of two, remembers how at age two her son, Luke, could speak in complete sentences and begin to express his emotions. "When I would drop him off, he would say things like, 'I don't want you to go.' "

According to Baron, children take one of two approaches to language. Some begin with a single word and go on to sentences; others begin with sentences and then attribute meaning to the words. "In this culture, children tend to start with one word. A lot of people around them are saying, 'Can you say *ball*?' " explains Baron. "But in cultures where parents are less concerned about whether their children are going to speak at a certain time," she adds, children are more likely to start with "sentences," sometimes unintelligible, that have the structure of speech. Some of those children don't say individual words until they've spoken sentences.

However children approach language, conscientious parents are often distressed by what they perceive to be delays in speech. But, says Baron, "the most critical thing to remember is that there is an incredible amount of variation." The two older children of Rachel Warner were extremely late talkers. "Both of them spoke only two- to three-word sentences until they were three," says the mother of three in Arlington, Virginia. "Then their speech took flight."

In the twilight of what Piaget called the sensorimotor period, from about 18 to 24 months, the toddler's mental actions increase and get stronger. He no longer depends on his senses alone to understand what is happening around him; he can represent the world inside his mind. And he has words to express his thoughts. "At the end of the second year, children start to grasp general concepts and understand the way things work in the world," says Stern. "For the first time, they can understand abstract ideas: not only that *this* tree is green, for instance, but that *all* trees are green."

## Categorically Speaking

While the nine-month-old recognizes similarities and differences among objects, a child twice his age can actually create his own distinct categories. Researchers have discovered that this intellectual ability evolves slowly, over the second and into the third year. In a study by Susan Sugarman, a professor of psychology at Princeton University, children ranging in age from one to three years were given a group of objects—four boats and four dolls, for example. When asked to rearrange them, some of the one-year-olds would randomly pick up a boat, look it over, and touch it to the other boats, one at a time. The 18-month-olds would handle two or three objects of the same kind in sequence. The two-year-olds, however, divided the objects into two separate categories.

"Categorization is basic to the way we operate—we think by comparing and contrasting," says Sugarman. Being able to put things in categories might make it easier for a child to share. For example, a toddler can give a cookie to a playmate if he understands that there are *other* cookies where that one came from. It might also help him understand a sibling—that's *another* child in the family."

Toddlers can not only organize objects, they are also discovering that some things (like hats and balls) have different purposes and that others (like cups and saucers or spoons and forks) are related. In pretend play, toddlers invent their own versions of objects and events in their world. "In this type of play, which typically appears during the last half of the second year, a child discovers how to take all those things that are going on in his life and cut them down to size. He's creating a small-scale reality," says Jerome Singer, a professor of psychology at Yale University and coauthor of *The House of Make-Believe: Children's Play and the Developing Imagination.*

At first, the creations are quite simple: An 18-month-old child might pretend to drink water from an empty cup or use a real fork to pretend to eat a piece of invisible cake. By the end of the second year, however, a child is capable of substituting one object for another. He might use a stuffed dinosaur to represent another child, or a wooden block for a table. As the child plays in this way, his imagination soars—and when he speaks aloud, he reveals glimpses of what he's thinking.

In order to pretend to be something he is not, a child has to know who he is. Along with a cache of new intellectual skills, the toddler is developing a sense of self. By a year and a half, he recognizes himself in the mirror. At 20 months, he can describe his own behavior. "Mike did it," he'll say, or "Finished." "At this age, children also start to use pronouns like *me, mine,* and *I,*" says Stern. "That indicates the formation of a self that can be referred to, called the 'self-reflective self.'" And by the end of the second year, he has become sensitized to adult standards, the way adults think things should be done.

In studies with kids of this age group, Kagan asked adults to demonstrate various activities that they wanted the children to imitate. He found real distress, starting at 18 months, among those toddlers who could not do what the adults had done. The child now knows that there is an expected way to do things, and he is determined to get it right. Whether building a tower or putting in the final piece of a puzzle, he is goal-driven. When he accomplishes it, his delight is reflected in what Kagan calls the "smile of mastery."

To parents, the changes of the first two years are nothing short of miraculous: A toddler's incredible curiosity—and formidable new learning skills—will lay the foundation for a lifetime of exploration. Yet the pace of a child's progress can also be a source of anxiety for mothers and fathers. Most professionals simply advise parents not to worry and to let their baby develop according to his own timetable. "Although milestones can be important markers of intellectual growth or flagging development, they have little meaning by themselves," says Virginia Casper, a developmental psychologist at the Bank Street College of Education in New York City. "Every child goes about learning in his own way. What really matters is knowing your child and how he learns—and then using that information to help him along."

 **Article Review Form at end of book.**

Describe the seven intelligences that Gardner proposed and explain why it is important to recognize this diversity of abilities. What basic elements do the project approach and writer's workshop have in common.

# Teaching *All* Children

## Four developmentally appropriate curricular and instructional strategies in primary-grade classrooms

**David W. Burchfield**

The classrooms of our nation's public schools are becoming increasingly diverse places. Old models and traditional structures for teaching and learning are not working well for all children entering our school doors, nor are these approaches challenging children to reach their full potential so that they may succeed in school, the workplace, and in life.

Teachers and support staff in schools and school systems, major professional organizations, and many parents attest to this claim (NASBE 1988; Bredekamp & Rosegrant 1992; Davis 1992; NCREL 1992). Educators and communities are actively searching for ways to meet the varied

educational needs of their children. The future of public education and of our society rests in part on the ability of educators and concerned community members to develop and implement ways to support and teach *all* children well.

As even our graded classrooms begin demographically to take on the characteristics of one-room schoolhouses, practioners must continue sharing with each other *what is working* in the context of teaching and learning that encourages children to learn and reach their potential. Educators of primary-school children are embracing more and more the idea of moving away from grade-leveled thinking toward more *child-focused* (Burchfield 1994) or *child-sensitive* (Katz 1992) attitudes and approaches.

Teachers must be given opportunities to develop, implement, and evaluate developmentally appropriate curricular and instructional strategies that go beyond the traditional "high-middle-low group" way of looking at, organizing, and teaching the children in their classroom communities (Burchfield & Burchfield 1992).

Whether we work with and advocate for children in communities that are exploring new models, such as nongraded and multi-age structures (Goodlad & Anderson 1987; Katz, Evangelou, & Hartman 1990) or are involved in conversations in graded-school communities that acknowledge the challenge of heterogeneity, we must continually examine our philosophies and belief systems about children and teaching and learning to ensure that they are

Reprinted with permission from the National Association for the Education of Young Children.

developmentally appropriate and child focused. It will be a consequence that we develop new models of curriculum and innovative instructional strategies for the sake of our children and their learning.

For the past decade I have been fortunate in having opportunities (as a preschool and primary-grade teacher, early childhood grant administrator, consultant, and now a principal) to learn about and implement strategies that have worked with children, from whom I have learned so much. What I learned and now practice is the consequence of my own interaction with and observation of children; many professional development opportunities; much reading, research, and reflection; and a result of collaboration with other educators and members of school communities.

For much of this century, leading early childhood educators have been advocating that we view children in more diverse ways than those represented by narrow and traditional IQ measures, that we engage primary-school children in authentic project work, that we involve children in meaningful writing for a variety of reasons, and that we challenge young readers to develop a repertoire of decoding strategies while learning to read. The theorists and researchers cited in *this* article, however, represent current best practice in the field and have particularly served as useful to this author.

The four curricular and instructional strategies outlined and described below have improved my understanding of children and increased the quality of my teaching and their learning so that all have had the opportunity to succeed in the primary years and beyond.

## 1. Multiple Intelligences and Different Ways of Knowing

A number of years ago, in my graduate studies, I became familiar with Howard Gardner's theory concerning multiple intelligences (Gardner 1983) and what is now often referred to as "different ways of knowing."

Gardner's theory holds that children and all people are much more complex than once viewed by traditional theories of intelligence, learning, and development. The premise of Gardner is that people naturally have specific areas of both strength and weakness and that ability and intelligence exist in not only the traditional curricular focus areas of language and numero-mathematics (which are also the aim of most instruction, assessment, and reporting), but also in five other areas of development or ways of knowing: bodily-kinesthetic, spatial, musical, interpersonal, and intrapersonal.

Gardner's theory is related to the seemingly all-too-simple and yet quite profound premise that *children are different* and they are much more capable than previously was conceptualized. A theory of difference asserts that people learn on a continuum from novice to expert in any given domain of learning and development (Hatano & Inagaki 1983; Walsh 1991).

If we truly adopt the belief that children are different and unique; if we expand our view to include a broader concept of intelligence and then accept the idea that there may be as many as seven "ways of knowing" and understanding what we learn, dramatic implications consequently result for the whole scope of teaching and learning.

No longer can we conduct themes or units of study with our students by simply sequencing for a period of a week or two teacher-directed activities that seem to go in no specific direction. Nor can we narrowly focus our unit study solely on reading, writing, and math or demand that most or all children do the same thing at the same time. When we gather together young people (who vary on a continuum from novice to expert) to be involved in and to think about a topic, question, or skill for an extended period of time, we must build in a progression for learning, such as the one advocated by DeVries and Kohlberg (1987), which outlines four major steps in the learning cycle: awareness, exploration, inquiry, and utilization.

Children first are made aware of the idea and can discover what they already know and have experienced about the topic. Students will ask lots of questions, design ways of figuring out some answers, and become involved in making decisions about the ways they inquire and share what they learn and understand.

A unit of study designed by practitioners who hold Gardner's theory to be true would allow children to experience a concept or skill in a variety of ways and demonstrate their learning and understandings by using their strong suits *and* by being challenged to develop their ability in areas identified (by parents, teachers, and even the children) for more emphasis and improvement.

During a unit of study about parks, for example, children could demonstrate their understandings in the following ways:

- sing a song or compose an original piece of music about their study,

- build a model of their park,

- share a drawing or a piece of writing about a field trip to their park,

- listen to read-alouds of picture books about animals that live in their park,

- represent in dramatic play the way a worm moves through earth,

- interview a groundskeeper about her responsibilities and report the findings,

- share their feelings about the homeless people who live in the park, or

- estimate the number of trees in the whole park based upon study of a small area.

The possibilities are endless.

Gardner's theory is being considered and put into practice in many schools across the country. Gardner and organizations such as the Galef Institute (1994) have created comprehensive ways of organizing curriculum, instruction, and assessment and reporting of children's progress based on the seven ways of knowing. Gardner's theory, along with an acceptance of the belief that children are different, has far-reaching implications for teaching and learning in classrooms and schools where difference is not only valued but viewed as an asset for the community of learners.

## 2. The Project Approach

The most mature, balanced, and practical model that complements Gardner's theory is the Project Approach proposed by Katz and Chard (1989), which builds on a long history of process-oriented project work and a focus on integrated teaching and learning in early childhood education.

The Project Approach encourages *meaningful* and relevant engagement in units of study chosen cooperatively by teachers and children, depending upon the needs of the school and school system. The units of study can be extensively interdisciplinary in nature or be adapted to explore one angle of the curriculum if the local school district demands a separate focus on other skills and domains of learning (such as math and language arts—reading, writing, and spelling/word study).

The greatest strength of the Project Approach, perhaps, is this: It is a flexible and adaptable model and process that can fit with local curricular demands. Katz and Chard (1989) acknowledge that it may not be possible or even desirable to integrate all skills and areas of learning into every unit of study in which we become engaged. The Project Approach is a real-world, user-friendly guide to organizing purposeful, social, active, and engaging units of study that allow children to be involved in making decisions about the direction, implementation, and evaluation of their learning.

Once I had read the Project Approach, my own classroom practice began a transformation. I finally had a process and a scaffolding for unit studies substantial enough to hold onto, a model that gave me an actual process to work through with children (and for a teacher who desperately wanted to move beyond the superficial).

Similar to the learning cycle outlined by DeVries and Kohlberg (1987) and to the Transformational Curriculum advocated by Rosegrant and Bredekamp (1992), Katz and Chard's approach encourages teachers and children, in

the context of the classroom community, to be involved as scientists in significant studies.

Initial awareness of an idea or skill is built through active discussion, brainstorming, webbing, and shared experience. Children and teachers then wonder and ask questions that form the basis for further investigation.

Something sets the Project Approach apart from other related approaches and processes: Children are encouraged to be involved in the discussion and planning of ways to inquire about the chosen topic and in devising methods to investigate the questions generated or those that arise. "Projects" for individuals, small groups, or the whole class are designed and negotiated that allow children to inquire and then demonstrate and utilize their learning and understandings.

There may be some non-negotiable activities, experiences, and, projects that are built in by the teacher over the course of the unit of study. The powerful motivators for the children, however, are that they are involved in decisions about the course of the study, the topic at hand is relevant, and the children are actively and socially involved in making sense out of the concepts and skills.

## 3. The Writer's Workshop

Although the use of the "writing process" and children writing for authentic reasons have been advocated for decades, a way of thinking about the teaching of writing, using the "writer's workshop," (Calkins 1983; Graves 1983) has spread like wildfire and now affects thousands of classrooms and millions of children.

Teachers have been trained in "writing projects" at universities and colleges and have read influential authors who have thoroughly researched the movement and been involved in teacher-training themselves (Newkirk & Atwell 1988; Short, Harste & Burke 1988; Calkins 1991, 1994; Graves 1991; Routman 1991; Harwayne 1992).

What began as a fledgling movement to encourage authorship in children by allowing them to use the writing process has now developed in many locations into classrooms and schools deeply involved in authentic and meaning-based writer's (and reader's) workshops. The writer's workshop is often the favorite, cherished time of the day by both children and teachers who regularly practice the model in classroom communities.

Carved out of an often-dissected day, the workshop is a place dedicated to the individual making sense out of significant moments and ideas, using the written word. In my own classroom the writer's workshop was so revered and powerful that, if a field trip or assembly displaced its position in the day, the children would often demand to miss recess in favor of making up the workshop and having the opportunity for written expression.

Topics and reasons for writing emerge from many sources along a continuum from child to teacher. With young children in the primary grades, the most motivating sources come from their own experiences and ideas. Topical or thematic units of study, author studies, and even genre studies of tales, picture books, songs, rhymes, and poems (and many others) also provide the impetus for inspiration.

Ironically, perhaps the least-effective way to encourage meaningful, relevant, and child-sensitive writing is the typical "story starter" on the blackboard (which many of us experienced in school ourselves during an occasional creative writing lesson). Such a teacher-driven written command narrows both the choice of topic and the reason to write at all and often leads to a boring product accomplished only to "get your seat work done," to please the teacher, or to receive external rewards, such as stickers, smiley faces, or grades.

It is difficult to develop new knowledge and skills in an area of teaching (such as writing) with which we ourselves most likely had little significant experience or success as students in our early years of schooling. Yet Lucy Calkins (1994) challenges us to allow writing not to be desk work, but "lifework," to create an intimate atmosphere in our workshops where "significance is grown" and we as teachers and children hold onto a time, place, and process to "make sense of our lives."

The workshop can vary in length from 45 minutes to two hours, depending upon the age of the children, the time of the year, and other demands on the classroom schedule. The time often begins with a brief (five to eight minutes) minilesson (or group time) in which the class may focus on examples of children's work or ideas, revisit and reflect upon a quality piece of children's literature, or focus upon a skill that will lead the class forward in their technical ability in writing.

During the heart of the workshop is a lengthy time for writing, reading, and conferring. Children draw and write about topics mostly of their own choice and yet may draw on classroom-based or teacher-guided ideas and suggestions. The teacher confers with children during this time about the content, process, design, or evaluation of their writing. The greatest challenge while conferring with a child is to truly listen first and then to respond in a child-focused way that challenges the child, if necessary, to explore a new idea, book, or skill that might assist with the development of their idea or piece of writing.

The workshop concludes with an "author's chair" or "author's circle," as children talk about their drawings and ideas. Young authors also share pieces of writing that are in process or may be nearing completion and possible publication.

The writer's workshop taps a powerful desire on the part of the child to express relevant and significant ideas. In fact, it is my experience that children, when allowed to write from their earliest years in school, choose to write more than read, quite possibly as a result of the basic human need for expression and the yearning we have in this life to truly be heard. The writer's workshop is an age-appropriate place for the individual to flourish while both learning to write by writing and making sense of significant ideas.

## 4. Develop a Balance of Reading Strategies/ Cueing Systems

Teachers nationwide are being asked to make reading instruction more whole and relevant, whether the source of text is the traditional basal textbook, emergent literacy reading material, or trade books. Staff development in this process is often aimed at learning how to assess a student's instructional level in reading ability, then matching child and text so that the reader is operating on the margin of development. Focus is placed on what children read and how to determine a reader's instructional ability level, and often not as much on how the child attacks new words in the text.

In my own development as a teacher of young readers, I became aware of the work of Marie Clay, a New Zealander and creator of the Reading Recovery Program (Clay 1979), which advocates that teachers build on what children can do and know in their learning to read.

Clay's idea is that although children typically develop two major cueing systems or decoding strategies (semantic and graphophonemic), at least two more approaches (syntax and visual clues) exist. She encourages teachers of young readers to develop all of these strategies with children, which will encourage readers to be increasingly independent in comprehending and decoding text of a given instructional level.

In addition to Clay, Strickland (1994) and Goodman (1993) also advocate a balanced approach to helping children develop strategies for unlocking new words while reading.

As a teacher it became clear to me that the question is not: Is it phonics *or* meaning *or* whole word? Rather we must ask, "How can I understand what my students already know and can do, and then help them develop a repertoire of strategies upon which to draw to maximize their reading development and ability?"

As a consequence of this new understanding I developed a schema (based on Clay's model)

for organizing my thinking and for my children's reference as we were involved in reading. I challenged myself and the children to draw upon these strategies while unlocking new words. The strategies (Figure 1) are listed in order of priority and in the language we used in the classroom.

In the context of reading instruction, these strategies (posted on charts) became reference points for children's learning. Eventually and with much practice, the strategies become more habitual and automatic with young readers.

The first strategy, "What makes sense," draws upon meaning and context clues. Children are encouraged to figure out unknown words by looking at the pictures or by going back to the beginning of the sentence and rereading the text and coming up to the unknown word with increased fluency, expression, and understanding.

The second strategy, "What the letters tell us," primarily asks very young readers to "get your mouth ready to say the word." Instead of isolating a sound and beginning to break the word apart by sounding it out at the beginning of the word, which often does not really represent the sound the letter makes as a part of the whole word, the reader is asked to learn how to form the mouth properly to begin to pronounce the word.

For example, the word *monkey* can be started by putting the lips together, but without making an *m* sound. The child learns to form the mouth to get ready to say letters and blends. Young readers in the classroom, for some reason, learned the *th* formation particularly quickly. I told them that the only time they were allowed to stick their tongue out at the teacher

## Figure 1 — Strategies to Unlock New Words

1. **What makes sense** (context, meaning, semantics)
   - using pictures to make sense of our new words
   - reread: go back to the beginning of the sentence and start again

2. **What the letters tell us** (graphophonemics)
   - beginning letters: "get your mouth ready to say the word"
   - vowel patterns

3. **Words we use often** (see Figure 2)
   - high-frequency sight words
   - 36 words make up 50% of all the words we read

4. **How words are built** (structure)
   - length of the word
   - compound words (block out one part of the word)
   - prefixes and suffixes

5. **How our language works**
   - repeat the sentence back to the child as it is read
   - can we say it that way?

was when they were beginning a word that began with *th*!

In the debate between advocates of phonics and advocates of meaning, another important strategy, widely used for 40 years or more, had been lost: high-frequency sight words or, as we referred to them, "words we use often." Practitioner colleagues and I recognized that it was these short, rather meaningless words that often gave children the most trouble, even while engaged in reading meaningful text (including words such as *it, was, saw, but, of, who,* etc.).

As we decided to focus more on these words, the idea of creating "Club 22" and "Club 60" was born. These clubs, membership in which depends upon the child calling these high-frequency

## Figure 2   Words We Use Often

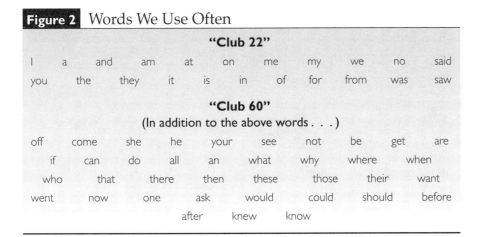

**"Club 22"**

| I | a | and | am | at | on | me | my | we | no | said |
|---|---|-----|-----|-----|----|-----|-----|-----|-----|------|
| you | the | they | it | is | in | of | for | from | was | saw |

**"Club 60"**
(In addition to the above words . . . )

| off | come | she | he | your | see | not | be | get | are |
|-----|------|-----|-----|------|-----|-----|-----|-----|-----|
| if | can | do | all | an | what | why | where | when | |
| who | that | there | then | these | those | their | want | | |
| went | now | one | ask | would | could | should | before | | |
| | | after | knew | know | | | | | |

words in isolation from word cards and listing on a chart in the classroom (see Figure 2), were motivators for children to learn these basic sight words. Children were not highlighted as "in" or "out" of the club, although it was celebrated when every child reached a new plateau (even intermittent) in word knowledge.

As the young readers in the classroom community developed from emergent to beginning-reading levels, children began to work on the other two strategies: "How words are built," which emphasizes such ideas as compound words and knowledge of prefixes and suffixes, and "How our language works," which asks children to listen to how they read a sentence and to reflect as to whether or not it sounded right (grammar and usage rules).

The result of shifting from believing that only one or two ways exist to teach young readers (and that these ways are necessarily antithetical) to understanding that children bring different strengths and weaknesses to the act of reading was powerful in practice. This understanding was more consistent with my emerging knowledge base and beliefs about children, teaching, and learning and with my goal of

helping each child reach his or her potential as an individual.

## Summary

As practitioners search for ways to challenge individual children to learn and reach their potential in meaningful and age-appropriate ways, we must share with each other what is working in order to promote best practice.

The existing challenges of diversity and heterogeneity are most likely here to stay. As grade-leveled thinking is broken down, we must develop, implement, and evaluate more child-focused and child-sensitive curricular and instructional methods and strategies that encourage teachers and children to achieve their best for the sake of learning.

Howard Gardner offers a useful and real-world way to look at children, their intelligence and ability and consequently a framework in which to organize curriculum. The Project Approach complements well this view of children and offers the teacher a user-friendly way to engage children in relevant and meaningful units of study.

By implementing the writer's workshop and offering young readers a repertoire of strategies in the primary years, we can better

respond to the individual learners who inhabit our communities and create more literate classrooms and children as well.

As educators, we must rise to the challenge of the diversity and the heterogeneity in our schools and classrooms. Inherent in the philosophy of developmental appropriateness is the ultimate and most important call: *To maintain our focus on children.* Then practices, like those above, that encourage success for *all* will follow.

## References

Bredekamp, S., & T. Rosegrant. eds. 1992, *Reaching potentials: Appropriate curriculum and assessment for young children, volume 1.* Washington, DC: NAEYC.

Burchfield, D.W. 1994. What's working now?/Challenges we face. Speech presented at the Elementary Principals' Institute, April. Jefferson County, Kentucky.

Burchfield, D.W., & B.C. Burchfield. 1992. Two primary teachers learn and discover through a process of change. In *Reaching potentials: Appropriate curriculum and assessment for young children, volume 1,* eds, S. Bredekamp, & T. Rosegrant, 150–58. Washington, DC: NAEYC.

Calkins, L.M. 1983. *Lessons from a child.* Portsmouth, NH: Heinemann.

Calkins. L.M. 1991. *Living between the lines.* Portsmouth, NH: Heinemann.

Calkins, L.M. 1994. *The art of teaching writing.* New ed. Portsmouth, NH: Heinemann.

Clay, M. 1979. *The early detection of reading difficulties.* Portsmouth, NH: Heinemann.

Davis, R. 1992. *The nongraded primary: Making schools fit children.* Arlington, VA: American Association of School Administrators.

DeVries, R., & L. Kohlberg. 1987. *Constructivist early education: Overview and comparison with other programs.* Washington, DC: NAEYC.

Galef Institute. 1994. *Different ways of knowing.* (Brochure describing the Galef Institute and the Kentucky Collaborative for Elementary Learning's professional development program). Louisville, KY: Author.

Gardner, H. 1983. *Frames of mind: The theory of multiple intelligences.* New York: Basic.

Goodlad, J.I., & R.H. Anderson. 1987. *The non-graded elementary school.* 2d ed. New York: Teachers College Press.

Goodman, K. 1993. *Phonics phacts.* Portsmouth, NH: Heinemann.

Graves, D.H. 1983. *Writing: Teachers and children at work.* Portsmouth, NH: Heinemann.

Graves, D.H. 1991. *Build a literate classroom.* Portsmouth, NH: Heinemann.

Harwayne, S. 1992. *Lasting impressions: Weaving literature into the writing workshop.* Portsmouth, NH: Heinemann.

Hatano, G., & K Inagaki. 1983. Two courses of expertise. *Annual Report of the Research and Clinical Center for Child Development.* Sapporo, Japan: Hokkaido University.

Katz, L. 1992. Future visions for early childhood education. Speech presented at the NAEYC Leadership Conference, April 10–12, Washington, D.C.

Katz, L., & S. Chard. 1989. *Engaging children's minds: The project approach.* Norwood, NJ: Ablex.

Katz, L., D. Evangelou, & J.A. Hartman. 1990. *The case for mixed-age grouping in early education.* Washington, DC: NAEYC.

National Association of State Boards of Education (NASBE). 1988. *Right from the start: The report of the NASBE Task Force on Early Childhood Education.* Alexandria, VA: Author.

North Central Research Educational Laboratory (NCREL) & the PBS Elementary/Secondary Service. 1992. *Schools that work: The research advantage—Meeting children's needs.* (5th of an 8-part video conference series; guidebook available). Oakbrook, IL: NCREL.

Newkirk, T., & N. Atwell. eds. 1988. *Understanding writing: Ways of observing, learning, and teaching.* 2d ed. Portsmouth, NH: Heinemann.

Rosegrant, T., & S. Bredekamp. 1992. Reaching individual potentials through transformational curriculum. In *Reaching potentials: Appropriate curriculum and assessment for young children, volume 1.* eds. S. Bredekamp & T. Rosegrant, 66–73. Washington, DC: NAEYC.

Routman, R. 1991. *Invitations: Changing as teachers and learners K–12.* Portsmouth, NH: Heinemann.

Short, K.G., J.C. Harste, & C. Burke. 1988. *Creating classrooms for authors: The reading-writing connection.* Portsmouth, NH: Heinemann.

Strickland, D.S. 1994. Reinventing our literacy programs: Books, basics, balance. *The Reading Teacher* 48 (4): 294–302.

Walsh, D. 1991. How children learn. *Virginia Journal of Education* 84: 7–11.

 **Article Review Form at end of book.**

How do Piaget and Vygotsky differ in their views of the function and value of private speech? How might encouragement of the use of private speech benefit children with learning problems?

# Why Children Talk to Themselves

## Laura E. Berk

As any parent, teacher, sitter or casual observer will notice, young children talk to themselves—sometimes as much or even more than they talk to other people. Depending on the situation, this private speech (as modern psychologists call the behavior) can account for 20 to 60 percent of the remarks a child younger than 10 years makes. Many parents and educators misinterpret this chatter as a sign of disobedience, inattentiveness or even mental instability. In fact, private speech is an essential part of cognitive development for all children. Recognition of this fact should strongly influence how both normal children and children who have trouble learning are taught.

Although private speech has presumably been around as long as language itself, the political climate in Russia in the 1930s, and the authority of a great Western cognitive theorist, prevented psychologists and educators from understanding its significance until only very recently. In Russia more than six decades ago, Lev S. Vygotsky, a prominent psycholo-

gist, first documented the importance of private speech. But at that time, the Stalinist regime systematically persecuted many intellectuals, and purges at universities and research institutes were common.

In fear, Soviet psychologists turned on one another. Some declared Vygotsky a renegade, and several of his colleagues and students split from his circle. According to the recollections of one of Vygotsky's students, the Communist party scheduled a critical "discussion" in which Vygotsky's ideas would be the major target. But in 1934, before Vygotsky could replicate and extend his preliminary studies or defend his position to the party, he died of tuberculosis. Two years later the Communist party banned his published work.

In addition to not knowing about Vygotsky, Western psychologists and educators were convinced by the eminent Swiss theorist Jean Piaget that private speech plays no positive role in normal cognitive development. In the 1920s, even before Vygotsky began his inquiries, Piaget had completed a series of seminal studies in which he carefully recorded the verbalizations of

three- to seven-year-olds at the J. J. Rousseau Institute of the University of Geneva. Besides social remarks, Piaget identified three additional types of utterances that were not easily understood or clearly addressed to a listener: the children repeated syllables and sounds playfully, gave soliloquies and delivered what Piaget called collective monologues.

Piaget labeled these three types of speech egocentric, expressing his view that they sprang only from immature minds. Young children, he reasoned, engage in egocentric speech because they have difficulty imagining another's perspective. Much of their talk then is talk for themselves and serves little communicative function. Instead it merely accompanies, supplements or reinforces motor activity or takes the form of non sequiturs: one child's verbalization stimulates speech in another, but the partner is expected neither to listen nor understand. Piaget believed private speech gradually disappears as children become capable of real social interaction.

Although several preschool teachers and administrators

openly questioned Piaget's ideas, he had the last word until Vygotsky's work reached the West in the 1960s. Three years after Joseph Stalin's death in 1953, Nikita S. Khrushchev criticized Stalin's "rule by terror" and announced in its place a policy that encouraged greater intellectual freedom. The 20-year ban on Vygotsky's writings came to an end. In 1962 an English translation of Vygotsky's collection of essays, *Thought and Language*, appeared in the U.S. Within less than a decade, a team led by Lawrence Kohlberg of Harvard University had compiled provocative evidence in support of Vygotsky's ideas.

In the late 1970s some American psychologists were becoming disenchanted with Piaget's theory, and at the same time, a broader range of Vygotsky's writings appeared in English. These conditions, coupled with Kohlberg's results, inspired a flurry of new investigations. Indeed, since the mid-1980s the number of studies done on private speech in the West has increased threefold. Most of these studies, including my own, corroborate Vygotsky's views.

In his papers Vygotsky' described a strong link between social experience, speech and learning. According to the Russian, the aspects of reality a child is ready to master lie within what he called the zone of proximal (or potential) development. It refers to a range of tasks that the child cannot yet accomplish without guidance from an adult or more skilled peer. When a child discusses a challenging task with a mentor, that individual offers spoken directions and strategies. The child incorporates the language of those dialogues into his or her private speech and then uses it to guide independent efforts.

"The most significant moment in the course of intellectual development," Vygotsky wrote, ". . . occurs when speech and practical activity, two previously completely independent lines of development, converge." The direction of development, he argued, is not one in which social communication eventually replaces egocentric utterances, as Piaget had claimed. Instead Vygotsky proposed that early social communication precipitates private speech. He maintained that social communication gives rise to all uniquely human, higher cognitive processes. By communicating with mature members of society, children learn to master activities and think in ways that have meaning in their culture.

As the child gains mastery over his or her behavior, private speech need not occur in a fully expanded form; the self, after all, is an extremely understanding listener. Consequently, children omit words and phrases that refer to things they already know about a given situation. They state only those aspects that still seem puzzling. Once their cognitive operations become well practiced, children start to "think words" rather than saying them. Gradually, private speech becomes internalized as silent, inner speech—those conscious dialogues we hold with ourselves while thinking and acting. Nevertheless, the need to engage in private speech never disappears. Whenever we encounter unfamiliar or demanding activities in our lives, private speech resurfaces. It is a tool that helps us overcome obstacles and acquire new skills.

Currently two American research programs, my own and that of Rafael M. Diaz at Stanford University, have sought to confirm and build on Vygotsky's findings. Our respective efforts began with similar questions: Do all children use private speech? Does it help them guide their actions? And does it originate in social communication? To find out, I chose to observe children in natural settings at school; Diaz selected the laboratory.

Ruth A. Garvin, one of my graduate students, and I followed 36 low-income Appalachian five- to 10-year-olds, who attended a mission school in the mountains of eastern Kentucky. We recorded speech in the classroom, on the playground, in the halls and in the lunchroom throughout the day—paying special attention to those remarks not specifically addressed to a listener.

Our findings revealed that egocentric speech, Piaget's focus, seldom occurred. Most of the comments we heard either described or served to direct a child's actions, consistent with the assumption that self-guidance is the central function of private speech. Moreover, the children talked to themselves more often when working alone on challenging tasks and also when their teachers were not immediately available to help them. In either case, the children needed to take charge of their own behavior.

Furthermore, we found evidence suggesting that private speech develops similarly in all children and that it arises in social experience. The private speech of the Appalachian students changed as they grew older in ways that were much like those patterns Kohlberg reported a decade and a half earlier.

Middle-class children, such as those Kohlberg observed, speak out loud to themselves with

## Varieties of Private Speech

| Category | Description |
|---|---|
| Egocentric communication | Remarks directed to another that make no sense from the listener's perspective. |
| Fantasy play | A child role-plays and talks to objects or creates sound effects for them. |
| Emotional release | Comments not directed to a listener that express feelings, or those that seem to be attempts to review feelings about past events or thoughts. |
| Self-direction | A child describes the task at hand and gives himself or herself directions out loud. |
| Reading aloud | A child reads written material aloud or sounds out words. |
| Inaudible muttering | Utterances so quiet that an observer cannot understand them. |

increasing frequency between four and six years of age. Then, during elementary school, their private speech takes the form of inaudible muttering. The Appalachian children moved through this same sequence but did so more slowly. At age 10, more than 40 percent of their private speech remained highly audible, whereas Kohlberg's 10-year-olds spoke out loud to themselves less than 7 percent of the time.

To explain the difference, we studied Appalachian culture and made a striking discovery. Whereas middle-class parents frequently converse with their children, Appalachian parents do so much less often. Moreover, they usually rely more on gestures than on words. If Vygotsky's theory is correct, that private speech stems from social communication, then this taciturn home environment might explain the slow development of private speech in Appalachian children.

While our Appalachian study was under way, Diaz and one of his graduate students, Marnie H. Frauenglass, videotaped 32 three- to six-year-olds in the laboratory as the youngsters matched pictures and solved puzzles. Frauenglass and Diaz also found that private speech becomes less audible with age. Yet their results, along with those of other researchers, posed serious challenges to Vygotsky's theory. First, many children emitted only a few utterances, and some none at all—seeming proof that private speech is not universal.

Another difficulty arose. If private speech facilitates self-regulation, as Vygotsky believed, then it should relate to how a child behaves while working and how well the child performs. Yet in Frauenglass and Diaz's study, children who used more private speech did worse on the tasks set before them! Other researchers had reported weak and sometimes negative associations between private speech and performance as well.

Diaz crafted some insightful explanations for these outcomes. After a close look at Vygotsky's definition of the zone of proximal development, Diaz concluded that perhaps the tasks typically given in the laboratory were not suitable for evoking private speech in all children. Some children may have been so familiar with solving puzzles and matching pictures that the cognitive operations they needed to succeed were already automatic. Other children may have found these tasks so difficult that they could not master them without help. In either case, self-guiding private speech would not be expected. Furthermore, Diaz reasoned that since private speech increases when children encounter difficulties, it would often coincide with task failure. He suggested that the beneficial impact of private speech might be delayed.

Returning to the classroom—this time, to the laboratory school at Illinois State University—I embarked on a series of studies to test these intriguing possibilities. My team of observers carefully recorded the private speech and task-related actions of 75 first to third graders as they worked alone at their desks on math problems. Their teachers considered this work to be appropriately challenging for each child. Graduate student Jennifer A. Bivens and I then followed the first graders and monitored their behavior as second and third graders.

Every child we observed talked to himself or herself—on average 60 percent of the time. Also, as in previous studies, many children whose remarks described or otherwise commented on their activity received lower scores on homework and achievement tests taken that same year. Yet private speech that was typical for a particular age predicted gains in math achievement over time. Specifically, first graders who made many self-guiding comments out loud or quietly did better at second grade math. Likewise, second graders who often muttered to themselves grasped third-grade math more easily the following year.

Also, the relationship we noted between a child's use of private speech and his or her task-related behavior bolstered Vygotsky's hypothesis that self-guiding comments help children direct their actions. Children whose speech included a great deal of task-irrelevant wordplay or emotional expression often squirmed in their seats or chewed on or tapped their pencils against their desks.

In contrast, children who frequently made audible comments about their work used more nonverbal techniques to help them overcome difficulties, such as counting on fingers or tracking a line of text using a pencil. Finally, children who most often used quiet private speech rarely fidgeted and were highly attentive. Overall, children who progressed most rapidly from audible remarks to inner speech were more advanced in their ability to control motor activity and focus attention. The development of private speech and task-related behavior thus went hand in hand.

In a later investigation, Sarah T. Spuhl, another of my graduate students, and I attempted to witness in the laboratory the dynamic relationship Vygotsky highlighted between private speech and learning—namely, private speech diminishes as performance improves. We added a new dimension to our research as well: an exploration of how the interaction between a child and an adult can foster self-regulation through private speech.

We asked 30 four- and five-year-olds to assemble Lego pieces into a reproduction of a model. Each subject attempted the exercise in three 15-minute sessions, scheduled no more than two to four days apart. This timing permitted us to track their increasing

competence. We pretested each child to ensure that the Lego tasks would be sufficiently challenging something, that had not been done before. Only novice Lego builders participated. Two weeks before the sessions began, we videotaped each mother helping her child with activities that required skills similar to those involved in Lego building, such as fitting blocks together and matching their colors and shapes.

Next we evaluated the communication between the mothers and their children as they solved problems together. According to previous research, parenting that is warm and responsive but exerts sufficient control to guide and encourage children to acquire new skills promotes competence. (Psychologists term such parenting authoritative.) In contrast, both authoritarian parenting (little warmth and high control) and permissive parenting (high warmth and little control) predict learning and adjustment problems. Based on this evidence, we thought that the authoritative style might best capture those features of adult teaching we wished to identify.

Our results revealed that children who have authoritative mothers more often used self-guiding private speech. Among the four-year-olds, those experiencing authoritative teaching showed greater improvement in skill over the course of the three Lego-building sessions. Furthermore, we did a special statistical analysis, the outcome of which suggested that private speech mediates the relationship between authoritative parenting and success—a finding consistent with Vygotsky's assumptions.

Unlike previous laboratory research, every child in our sample used private speech. As expected, the children's comments became more internalized over the course of the three sessions as their skill with the Lego blocks increased. And once again, private speech predicted future gains better than it did concurrent task success. In particular, children who used private speech that was appropriate for their age—audible, self-guiding utterances at age four and inaudible muttering at age five—achieved the greatest gains.

Next I turned my attention to children having serious learning and behavior problems. Many psychologists had concluded that elementary school pupils who were inattentive, impulsive or had learning disabilities suffered from deficits in using private speech. To treat these children, researchers had designed and widely implemented training programs aimed at inducing children to talk to themselves. In a typical program, children are asked to mimic a therapist acting out self-guiding private speech while performing a task. Next the therapist demonstrates lip movements only and finally asks the children to verbalize covertly.

Despite the intuitive appeal of this training, the approach most often failed. I suspected that the design of these treatments might have been premature. The procedures were not grounded in systematic research on how children having learning and behavior problems use private speech. The spontaneous self-regulatory utterances of such children remained largely uninvestigated.

To fill this gap in our knowledge, my graduate student Michael K. Potts and I studied 19 six- to 12-year-old boys who had been clinically diagnosed with attention-deficit hyperactivity disorder (ADHD), a condition characterized by severe inattentiveness, impulsivity and overactivity. Once again, we observed private speech as the subjects worked on mathematics problems at their desks. We compared these observations to the private speech of 19 normal boys matched in age and verbal ability.

Contrary to the assumptions underlying self-instructional training, ADHD boys did not use less private speech. Instead they made substantially more audible, self-guiding remarks than did normal boys. Furthermore, we examined age-related trends and found that the only difference between the two groups was that ADHD boys made the transition from audible speech to more internalized forms at a later age.

We uncovered a possible explanation for this developmental lag. Our results implied that ADHD children's severe attention deficit prevented their private speech from gaining efficient control over their behavior. First, only in the least distractible ADHD boys did audible self-guiding speech correlate with improved attention to math assignments. Second, we tracked a subsample of ADHD subjects while they were both taking and not taking stimulant drug medication, the most widely used treatment for the disorder. (Although stimulants do not cure ADHD, a large body of evidence indicates that they boost attention and academic performance in most children who take them.) We found that this medication sharply increased the maturity of private speech in ADHD boys. And only when these children were medicated did the most mature form of private speech, inaudible muttering, relate to improved self-control.

The promising nature of these findings encouraged me to include children having learning disabilities in the research. My colleague Steven Landau joined me in observing 112 third to sixth graders working on math and English exercises at their desks. Half of the children met the Illinois state guidelines for being classified as learning disabled: their academic achievement fell substantially below what would be expected based on their intelligence. The other half served as controls. As in the ADHD study, we found that the children who had learning disabilities used more audible, self-guiding utterances and internalized their private speech at a later age than did children who did not have a disability. When we looked at a subgroup of learning disabled children who also displayed symptoms of ADHD, this trend became even more pronounced.

Research on children suffering from persistent learning difficulties vigorously supports Vygotsky's view of private speech. These children follow the same course of development as do their unaffected age mates, but impairments in their cognitive processing and ability to pay attention make academic tasks more difficult for them. This difficulty in turn complicates verbal self-regulation. Our findings suggest that training children who have teaming and behavior problems to talk to themselves while performing cognitive tasks amounts to no more than invoking a skill they already possess. Furthermore, interventions that push children to move quickly toward silent self-communication may be counterproductive. While concentrating, ADHD and learning-disabled pupils show heightened dependence on audible private speech in an effort to compensate for their cognitive impairments.

How can our current knowledge of private speech guide us in teaching children who learn normally and those who have learning and behavior problems? The evidence as a whole indicates that private speech is a problem-solving tool universally available to children who grow up in rich, socially interactive environments. Several interdependent factors—the demands of a task, its social context and individual characteristics of a child—govern the extent and ease with which any one child uses self-directed speech to guide behavior. The most profitable intervention lies not in viewing private speech as a skill to be trained but rather in creating conditions that help children use private speech effectively.

When a child tries new tasks, he or she needs communicative support from an adult who is patient and encouraging and who offers the correct amount of assistance given the child's current skills. For example, when a child does not understand what an activity entails, an adult might first give the child explicit directions. Once the child realizes how these actions relate to the task's goal, the adult might offer strategies instead. Gradually, adults can withdraw this support as children begin to guide their own initiatives.

Too often inattentive and impulsive children are denied this scaffold for learning. Because of the stressful behaviors they bring to the adult-child relationship, they are frequently targets of commands, reprimands and criticism, all of which keep them from learning how to control their own actions.

Finally, parents and teachers need to be aware of the functional value of private speech. We now know that private speech is healthy, adaptive and essential behavior and that some children need to use it more often and for a longer period than others. Still, many adults continue to regard private speech as meaningless, socially unacceptable conduct—even as a sign of mental illness. As a result, they often discourage children from talking to themselves. At home, parents can listen to their child's private speech and thus gain insight into his or her plans, goals and difficulties. Likewise, teachers can be mindful of the fact that when pupils use more private speech than is typical for their age, they may need extra support and guidance. Certainly, we have much more to discover about how children solve problems using spontaneous private speech. Nevertheless, Vygotsky's theory has greatly deepened our understanding of this phenomenon. Today it is helping us design more effective teaching methods for all children and treatments for children suffering from learning and behavior problems. One can only regret that earlier generations of psychologists and educators—and those they might have helped—did not have the advantage of Vygotsky's insights.

 **Article Review Form at end of book.**

# WiseGuide Wrap-Up

- Today, there is growing emphasis on developing school programs that motivate and facilitate learning for all children. Several approaches are being explored, including Gardner's multiple intelligences, project-based assignments, writer's workshops, and balanced reading systems.

- Vygotsky's view that private speech evolves from audible, self-directed speech is gaining new attention among educators. Self-directed speech mimics the verbal guidance that adults provide as children tackle difficult tasks and is a problem-solving tool. Encouragement of self-directed speech among school-aged children experiencing learning problems facilitates self-control and mastery of new skills.

- During the first year of life, babies can detect similarities and differences among objects, remember past events, and anticipate future ones. They also solve simple problems and begin to speak their first words. By age 2, many motor milestones are met, and language blossoms in terms of vocabulary and grammar.

- Babies whose parents talk often to them later score higher on IQ tests than do children exposed to minimal amounts of parental speech. Critical parent-to-child interactions include affirmation of children's communication efforts, responses to their questions, guidance, and vocabulary diversity.

## R.E.A.L. Sites

**Site name:** Rising Scores on Intelligence Tests

**URL:** http://www.amsci.org/amsci/articles/97articles/neisser.html

**Why is it R.E.A.L.?** This article addresses the issue of rising scores on intelligence tests in America. According to the articles you read in this section, intelligence scores should not change from generation to generation or across one's lifetime. After reading this article, what reasons might you give for this occurrence? What can you conclude about the concept of "intelligence" as we have defined it in the traditional sense? How does Gardner's concept of intelligence fit with the issues raised in this article?

- Increase awareness of social and economic factors that may limit the successes of children, particularly in terms of technological exposure.

- Illustrate how children vary in the ways they learn and, therefore, the need for adjustments in our teaching methods.

- Discuss the educational problems and needs of children who were prenatally exposed to street drugs.

- Provide an overview of the controversies surrounding the diagnosis and treatment of attention deficit disorders.

- Explain dyslexia.

# Problems in Learning

The road to academic success is not a smooth one for every child. For some, the issue is primarily economic. Strong minds are not able to reach their full potential and compete on even grounds with more affluent students because of inadequate school funding. School districts lacking monies to upgrade instructional materials and keep up with technological advancements may unintentionally limit their graduates' future academic and employment opportunities. Relatedly, children living in the poorest of school districts often come from families unable to afford the luxury of a home computer. It may also be that such parents, lacking computer literacy themselves, may not recognize the long-range value of such an investment.

For other children, academic difficulties may arise from early life traumas or learning styles that do not conform well to standard educational practices. Children prenatally exposed to street drugs or alcohol frequently suffer from a host of cognitive and behavioral problems. For instance, research suggests that the brains of "snow babies" may be altered from normal. Typically, these children are not mentally retarded but, instead, demonstrate a range of attention-related problems. They are easily distracted, and their learning is hindered. Additionally, it is not uncommon for these children to be poor and live under stressful conditions. Such life circumstances only further compromise these vulnerable children.

The school difficulties of some children suggest very specific forms of learning problems. Attention deficit disorder (ADD) and attention deficit hyperactivity disorder (ADHD) have been the center of many debates. A growing number of children in the United States are being labeled as ADD or ADHD. Some contend that the increase is due to more refined diagnostic procedures. Others view the increase as a symptom of educators' narrow definition of normality. Also at issue is the prescription of medications to correct these children's behaviors. Dyslexia is a more focused form of learning disability. Current research indicates that dyslexics suffer from a language-processing problem, and brain centers are being explored. Individuals experience great difficulty in segmenting written words into their sound units. The result is poor word identification. For dyslexics, reading is laborious, rote memorization and word retrieval from memory are difficult, and performance on timed tests does not accurately represent their abilities. For children demonstrating problems in learning, relatively minor adjustments in teaching methods or the classroom environment may enable these children to achieve, without reliance on medications or relegation to resource rooms.

## Thinking Beyond the Facts

Though "all men and women are created equal," they may not all be able to enjoy educational equality. In the end, the inequalities of our formal and informal educational experiences may play a large role in the quality of our lives, from employment opportunities to a sense of life satisfaction. After reading the articles in this section on problems in learning, consider the advantages and disadvantages you've experienced compared with those of your classmates. How might the technology in someone's home influence the games played, the quality of the homework prepared, readiness for classroom applications, and expectations regarding college attendance? How might family vacations impact students' awareness of geography, distances, cultures, and customs? Consider how classroom size and attractiveness, ethnic and social class diversity of student bodies, and school location might impact students' learning and achievement motivation. Further, imagine living in circumstances in which economic factors severely limit your options.

Complicating matters is the fact that a portion of students do not enter school on even footing with others, due to neurological differences. What would it be like to be distracted by every sight and sound? Think of the last time you saw the alphabet of an unfamiliar language, and imagine trying to decipher a line of text as if it were English. How would you feel about your abilities? about yourself? For more information on how poverty impacts learning and on specific learning-related problems, visit web sites on attention deficit disorders, hyperactivity, dyslexia, autism, mental retardation, and computer literacy.

## Questions

**Reading 17.** Why do children from low-income homes face future employment disadvantages even if they graduate from high school?

What are the arguments for and against computer-lending programs for low-income families?

**Reading 18.** According to animal studies, how does prenatal cocaine exposure alter the brain?

Why do apparently normal children, who were prenatally exposed to cocaine, have difficulties in regular classrooms?

**Reading 19.** How do experts determine if a child is suffering from Attention Deficit Hyperactivity Disorder?

How might typical classroom appearances and routines contribute to the occurrence of behaviors felt to be incompatible with learning, even among normal children?

**Reading 20.** How does the current explanation of dyslexia differ from popular explanations of the past?

How might course assignments be altered for someone suffering from dyslexia?

Why do children from low-income homes face future employment disadvantages even if they graduate from high school? What are the arguments for and against computer-lending programs for low-income families?

# Computers Should Be Made Available to Children of Low-Income Families

**Robert J. Walker**

During the news show "CNN Today," an eight-year-old child, home from school with his mother due to illness, called in to compete for the daily prize of a CNN coffee mug. The winner of the mug was to be the first caller with the correct answer to three trivia questions. One of the questions was: "What was the 50th state added to the United States in 1959?" The little boy responded very confidently, "Hawaii!," as if to say, "Why would you ask me such an easy question?"

The two commentators hosting the show were amazed. The eight-year-old answered all three questions correctly and won the mug. When asked by one of the hosts whether his mother gave him the answers, the little boy responded, "No, I got them off the computer." It is obvious that this child lives in a home environment where computer technology is used to enhance his academic abilities, and thus has a definite head start on learning. This is not the case for most youngsters in low-income families.

In the area of technology, the U.S. family structure is divided into two societies—one where young children have access to computers and another where they do not. According to a 1993 U.S. Census report, in homes where the family income is less than $20,000, just 15% of the children living in these homes have access to a computer. In most cases, the computer is an old back-and-white terminal at best.

In contrast, 74% of those where the family income is $75,000 or above have computers. When considering race, 43% of the homes of white children have computers, compared to 16% of black and 15% of Hispanic youngsters.

College-educated Asian-American males between the ages of 24 and 54 grossing around $75,000 annual income are the largest group to use computers either at home or at work. Undereducated African-American males between the ages of 19 and 54 making $11–20,000 annually are the largest segment that do not use computers.

Along with providing low-income children with food and clothing, it is important to make sure that they are not at a technological disadvantage. Steps must be taken to ensure they will not be left behind when it comes to computer literacy.

Technology is moving at warp speed, bringing about ways of learning that a few years ago only could be dreamt about.

Many educators are adding computers into their daily curriculum. Students who have computer skills primarily acquired by the use of a home computer will be able to take full advantage of the technological environment. Those who don't have access to a home computer will be left at the mercy of whatever computer time is provided at school.

When a youngster can work on an assignment at home and transfer the material to the school by way of a disk or through an e-mail address, learning becomes fun and exciting. Students who use computers don't perceive that they actually are doing something academically. To them, it is more like playing a video game at the mall.

Students utilizing computers to master basic skills perform better on standardized tests. Through the use of the computer, pupils in the lower grades tend to write more because the keyboard is easier to utilize than pencil or pens. The dropout rate for high school students who use computers regularly at home and school is drastically lower than the general high school population. Students who have computer skills are more likely to attend college than those who do not.

The Apple Classrooms of Tomorrow, a research project sponsored by Apple Computer, Inc., has revealed these key findings:

- Technology acts as a catalyst for fundamental change in the way children learn and teachers teach.

- It revolutionizes the traditional educational methods practiced by teachers today.

- Children become re-energized and much more excited about learning, resulting in significantly improved grades, while dropout and absenteeism rates fall.

- Kids interact and collaborate more when using technology, debunking the myth that it might isolate children and teachers.

Research has shown that youngsters learn best when several of their senses are used. With computer-assisted instruction, three of the five senses are employed. The child touches the computer, hears the sounds made by it, and sees the images on the monitor, virtually all at the same time. Important pre-literacy skills and the principles of cause and effect are being developed when a youngster begins to recognize that a specific letter pressed on the keyboard creates an image on the computer screen. Even slow-to-average children exposed to computers suddenly blossom forth.

The computer is a machine with virtually unlimited capabilities. These can be multiplied by plugging into a network of other computers by way of the Internet, bulletin board systems, or data banks via modem and telephone line. From his or her home, a child can have access to libraries across the world. More than 4,000 data bases exist in the U.S. alone, ranging from general information services such as news, weather, and sports to Web sites such as Library of Congress, Globe-Learn, World War II Archive, African-American History, Mega-Mathematics, and Science Learning Network. Children can log on to many of the major Federal agencies, including the National Science Foundation and the Smithsonian Institution, and gather the latest information on a topic of interest.

For many youngsters in low-income families, the schools are not filling in the technology gap of the home. Children in low-income families tend to live in low-income communities and usually attend schools where there is a limited tax base with no money for computers.

Presently, minorities make up less than 10% of the scientists and engineers in America. This low figure primarily is due to the fact that preparation for most careers in the areas of science and math begins at an early age. Often, because of the high cost of technology, minority children are not properly exposed to it when young.

Traditionally, the academic gap between children in low-income and middle-class families was that of a lack of basic learning materials such as books and manipulatives. These learning materials, for the most part, were inexpensive and relatively easy to provide. However, with the explosion of the technological revolution, the academic gap between low-income and middle-class kids has widened. This academic gap mainly is due to the reality that most low-income families simply are unable financially to purchase the tools necessary to place their children into the technological mainstream.

As technology becomes more and more the heartbeat of education and society, its place in the home is becoming increasingly crucial. More than ever, children, regardless of their families' economic situation, must receive basic skills instruction through the use of computer technology.

## Bringing the Computer Home

The Bringing Learning Home Alliance, a collaborative organization established by Apple Computer; Scholastic, Inc.; the National Geographic Society; The Public Broadcasting Service; and the Computer Learning Foundation, sponsors a family computing workshop to encourage parents to become more involved in their children's education by purchasing a home computer.

Nearly four out of five parents feel that giving their offspring basic computer training will provide them with an educational advantage once they start school. Furthermore, parents believe that the best way for them to encourage their children to use a computer is to buy one and begin utilizing it.

Even though it is apparent that kids will be at a competitive disadvantage if they don't have computer skills, there often is resistance in low-income families. Most simply can not afford the cost of computer technology, and many low-income parents are not computer literate themselves and therefore don't see the great need for purchasing such an expensive piece of equipment.

Critics argue that it is not a matter of money, but priority. If low-income families can afford a $150 pair of brand-name sneakers, designer jeans, CD players, and VCRs, they can purchase a computer. The critics fail to realize that finding the money to purchase these items is a lot easier than coming up with the wherewithal to buy a $2,000 computer, even if it may be possible to do so on an installment plan with a free printer added.

Critics argue further that, if some type of computer loan program were provided for low-income families, they would use the computers merely to play games. Computer enthusiasts counter the critics by making the point that computer games have educational value by teaching logic and vocabulary skills. Charles P. Lecht, president of the

New York consulting firm Lecht Scientific, maintains that "Computers help teach kids to think. Beyond that, they motivate people to think. There is a great difference between intelligence and manipulative capacity. Computers help us to realize that difference."

Probably the most important effect of computer games is that they have brought the computer into millions of homes and convinced millions of people that it is fun, useful, and easy to operate. Individuals from all socioeconomic levels have developed their interest in computers through playing computer games.

Indiana's Buddy Project, which sends computers home to live for two years with 6,000 families throughout the state, has proven that such a loan program can work. Alan Hill, president of the Corporation for Educational Technology, the Indianapolis nonprofit group that administers the Buddy Project states, "We want to equip kids and their parents to become independent, lifelong learners."

"We also want to level the playing field, so that the poor kid's output is as good as the rich kid's," indicates Buddy Project manager Nancy Miller. By logging onto the BuddyNet via modem, children and parents are able to view a list of daily class activities and check on homework assignments.

The education potential of youngsters in the Buddy Project has been enhanced greatly, and parents have become more involved with their children's schoolwork. Teacher Jim Greiner says, "What's also amazing is the parents' response. Half the kids here are on free lunch, and I'd say only a handful of families had computers at home. But 80% or more of the parents answer me on

BuddyNet each night, many of them third-shift factory workers who log on after midnight. Parent conferences are different now. Fifteen minutes is too long—the parents already know how their kids are doing."

Microsoft Corp. founder Bill Gates, along with several business partners, came up with a computer-based strategy to bring school closer to home. The Microsoft Parent-Teacher Connection Server provides parents with local dial-up access to school bulletin boards and e-mail, as well as video conferencing. Gates maintains that "The most important use of information technology is to improve education. His idea is that technology will make it possible for parents, students, and teachers to communicate by way of a global schoolhouse on the Internet. The drawback to this global schoolhouse concept, though, is that it may push poor children even further behind since they do not have the home computers which are a prerequisite.

Kids only have to look at the world around them to see examples of how the computer is used in Americans' daily lives, whether in shopping at the supermarket, ordering fast food, or pumping gas into the family car at the gas station. Supermarkets use computers to keep accurate inventory records and to speed up checkouts; banks to access financial records more quickly and process transactions at a much higher degree of accuracy than can be done by human hands; schools for educational training purposes; and automotive manufacturers in newer cars to make it easier to diagnose a problem and automatically adjust the suspension system for a smoother ride.

The medical profession would be paralyzed without the

use of computers. Virtually every medical test given—from taking a patient's temperature to examining the brain via a CAT scan—are done by some type of computer. A personal computer can send letters, do calculations at the touch of the mouse, diagnose an illness, custom-tailor an insurance program in minutes, test recipes, plan a trip, and file a tax return.

## Workplace of the Future

Most employed Americans earn their living not by producing things, but as "knowledge workers," exchanging various kinds of information. The computer already has changed how most Americans do their jobs.

Youngsters who are denied the opportunity to use technology in their homes not only will suffer academically, but will be limited in the future job market. Whether working on Wall Street or at Wal-Mart, knowing computer technology is a necessity. Regardless of what future occupations today's young children seek—whether in medicine, education, industry, auto mechanics, banking, or food service—those who learn their basic skills at an early age and are comfortable in the use of technology will be at a definite advantage. According to Harvard Business School professor Rosabeth Moss Kanter, "The 'haves' will be able to communicate around the globe. The 'have-nots' will be consigned to the rural backwater of the information society."

Over the past two decades, computers have become an integral part of contemporary life. Today, most businesses use them for marketing, design, financial and statistical analysis, training, and much more. It has become increasingly important that children acquire at least basic computer skills in order to function effectively in the information-driven society and economy.

Computer-related jobs are among the most rapidly growing employment segments in the U.S. Economic studies predict that computer equipment will represent about 40% of all capital expenditures by businesses in the 21st century. A computer-literate workforce will be needed to manufacture, operate, program, and manage new equipment. The most sought-after computer specialists probably will be systems analysts, programmers, and operators. Computer consultants will be necessary to improve the efficiency of systems already in use. Computer security specialists will be in great demand to help protect the integrity of the huge information banks being developed by businesses and governmental agencies.

Other important careers in this rapidly expanding field include computer scientists, to perform research and teach at universities; hardware designers; engineers to work in areas such as microchip and peripheral equipment design; and information-center or database administrators to manage the information collected. Various support careers such as technical writers, computer-based training specialists, and operations managers will be in great demand. Although many support careers don't call for extremely technical backgrounds, they do require a knowledge of computers.

As more small and medium-sized businesses become computerized, there will be a need for employees to be computer-literate. In the 21st century, very few jobs requiring common labor will be available. Virtually all menial tasks will be done by computers, including garbage pickup. Many cities already have shifted to computerized trucks that collect specially designed trash cans from the curbs of residential homes. This eliminates the need for a driver and two persons on the back of the truck to empty the cans manually. The driver, by way of the truck's built-in computer, can do alone what it once took three men to do.

The price of a home computer continues to fall. According to one computer expert, if the price of an automobile had dropped over the years like the price of computers, a Rolls-Royce today would cost around $2.75. Moreover, if automobile technology had developed as rapidly as computer technology, that Rolls would run 3,000,000 miles on a gallon of gas.

Perhaps the day will come when computers will be as affordable as a portable 19" television set. Until that time comes, concerned citizens who have the resources, private industries, and state and Federal agencies must develop and fund programs to ensure that all children will have access to computers in their homes. Laptop computer loan programs at local libraries and youth centers could be established so that kids in low-income families can borrow one for home use in the same manner they can go to the library and borrow books. To some, this may seem a little far-fetched. However, if such programs are not created, children living in low-income families will not have a fair chance of competing in a technological society, and the cost to us all may be far greater than the cost of computers for such a program.

 **Article Review Form at end of book.**

According to animal studies, how does prenatal cocaine exposure alter the brain? Why do apparently normal children, who were prenatally exposed to cocaine, have difficulties in regular classrooms?

# Hope for 'Snow Babies'

## Sharon Begley

*With Mary Hager in Washington*

The epidemic of crack cocaine had just hit the inner cities in the mid-1980s when pediatricians and hospital nursery workers began reporting truly harrowing observations: babies born to women who had used cocaine while pregnant were not like other infants. They were underweight. They trembled. As newborns they were as rigid as plastic dolls. They cried inconsolably, seeming to recoil from hugs or touches and startled at the slightest sound. As they approached school age, it seemed that many could not sit still or focus, even on activities they enjoyed. For schools and for society, warned the press and the legions of anti-drug crusaders, cocaine babies would be a lost generation.

Well, scientists have found this generation. The snow babies, it seems, are neither the emotional and cognitive cripples that many predicted—nor the perfectly normal kids that biological revisionists have lately been claiming. Last week, at a landmark conference in Washington convened by the New York Academy of

Sciences, more than three dozen neurologists, pediatricians and other researchers presented studies suggesting that the effects of cocaine on a fetus are far from simple, let alone predictable. They depend not only on such obvious things as how much of the drug the mother took and when but also on what sort of environment the baby grows up in. Although studies on large numbers of school-age children are only beginning, research on toddlers suggests that "most cocaine-exposed children do very well," says Dr. Barry Kosofsky of Harvard Medical School, co-chair of the conference. "Cocaine is not a sledgehammer to the fetal brain."

But neither is it a prenatal vitamin. Experiments show that rats, rabbits and monkeys exposed to cocaine in utero are profoundly messed up. Their brains develop abnormally. Neurons are too long or too short. "Receptors" to which brain chemicals attach are too many or too few or too sensitive. The animals' behavior reflects these aberrations: they typically act impulsively, have trouble learning and can't block out extraneous sights and sounds when learning a task. The chal-

lenge, obviously, is to figure out why the human and animal data tell such a "on the one hand, on the other hand" story it takes a human octopus to keep it all straight.

One reason cocaine-exposed children do not seem to be faring worse may reflect how human studies are done. To get a clean result, scientists must compare children who are as similar as possible on every measure except the one being studied—cocaine exposure. It is a fact of life, and thus of science, that the women and children who wind up in these studies are not the wealthy Wall Street traders sniffing a line at the end of a hard day. Instead they are poor, and often single, and the home they bring their baby to can be chaotic. These children have so many strikes against them that adding cocaine to the mix may not hurt them much more. Or as Prof. Barry Lester of Brown University puts it, "If you grow up in such a lousy environment, things are so bad already that cocaine exposure doesn't make much difference." That may be the case in a study at Philadelphia's Albert Einstein Medical Center. At the age of 4, cocaine-exposed kids score 79 on

IQ tests; their peers in the impoverished neighborhood score 82. The U.S. average is 90 to 109.

Studies of coke-exposed children may also be looking for the wrong thing. "It is possible that what is being tested are not areas where these children are most vulnerable," says Lester. In tests at Einstein, for instance, cocaine-exposed children figure out the locks and secret compartments in a box holding little toys. And at the University of Illinois, Dr. Ira Chasnoff finds in his study of 170 children that the coke-exposed ones had roughly the same IQ scores at the age of 6 as those whose mothers were clean. But children take IQ tests, and do puzzles for scientists, in quiet rooms with few distractions. All of the animal data suggest that the brain systems most damaged by cocaine are those that control attention and especially, screen out irrelevant sights and sounds. "The children do fine in a quiet room by themselves," says neuroscientist Pat Levitt of the University of Pittsburgh. "But there is no question they have alterations in their brain structure and function which, while not keeping them from learning a task in isolation, could well hurt them in real life."

Real life is the classroom as multimedia madhouse, with posters covering every wall and kiddie art dangling from lights. It is not clear how cocaine-exposed children will fare in such environments. Of the 119 studies on how cocaine affects a child's development, reports Lester, only six have followed the children beyond the age of 3. One is already setting off alarm bells. A pilot study at Wayne State University in Detroit finds that teachers rated 27 cocaine-exposed 6-year-olds as having significantly more trouble paying attention than 75 nonexposed children (the teachers did not know who was who).

There is little debate that distractibility hinders learning. That's why thousands of parents put their hyperactive children on Ritalin. And that's why cocaine-exposed children who seem to be OK now may fare worse as they make their way through school. Dr. Gideon Koren of Toronto's Hospital for Sick Children is following 47 cocaine-exposed children who were adopted as infants. Their new families "can't tell the difference" between these children and others, says Koren. But he can. When the children were 3 years old, their language skills were developing a little more slowly than that of nonexposed children; there were no IQ differences. But at the ages of 5 and 6, an IQ gap of 10 points has opened up. The older the children get, says Koren, "the more likely there will be [cognitive] differences" compared with other kids. "These must be biological differences."

It's too soon to draw final conclusions. Clearly the legions of crack babies have not turned out as badly as was feared, but the damage assessment is continuing. Most likely, the effects of cocaine are real but small. How starkly those effects show up depends, argues Kosofsky, on myriad factors, including the environment in which the child is raised. In Toronto, Koren's cocaine-exposed kids have, at the ages of 5 and 6, lower IQ scores than their otherwise healthy siblings. But their average score of 106 is still more than 20 points higher than typical scores of children raised in disadvantaged homes.

There will be plenty of time for further study. Even though the crisis has left the front pages, every year at least 40,000 babies are born to women who took cocaine while pregnant, according to a 1995 estimate by the National Institute on Drug Abuse. For years these children have been demonized and written off. But as the results of studies of young children show, few are beyond the help that a loving and stress-free home can provide. As last week's conference broke up, scientists who spend their nights tracking neurotransmitters and their days running underfunded clinics for cocaine-exposed kids raised a very different question: is labeling these babies "hopeless and lost" just a handy excuse to avoid helping them and their mothers?

 **Article Review Form at end of book.**

How do experts determine if a child is suffering from Attention Deficit Hyperactivity Disorder? How might typical classroom appearances and routines contribute to the occurrence of behaviors felt to be incompatible with learning, even among normal children?

# Children Who Burn Too Brightly

Are we sacrificing children's creativity for the sake of uniformity?

## David J. Welsh, Ph.D.

The daily procession of children marching to the nurse's office for their lunchtime dose of stimulant medication has become an all-too-familiar sight in school buildings across America. Children identified as exhibiting symptoms of a supposed neurological condition known as "attention deficit hyperactivity disorder" (ADHD) take medicine to improve their concentration and behavior in the classroom. Current estimates suggest over two million school-age children are diagnosed with ADHD, and production amounts of the principal drug used for treatment (methylphenidate or Ritalin) increased 400 percent between 1990 and 1994. If the trends of the past few years continue, 15 percent of the pediatric population could be taking some type of psychostimulant medication by the year 2000. As a psychologist who consults with school systems on a daily basis, I regularly visit buildings where this projection is already a reality.

What has caused such an apparent epidemic of dysfunction among America's children? Answers vary depending on one's philosophical and professional learnings. The gurus of the ADHD movement suggest that genetically based malfunctions in the brain's use of neurotransmitters (chemicals used by the brain to process information) cause certain children to be unusually distractible, highly impulsive, and/or physically overactive. They argue that the growing numbers of children labeled with ADHD simply reflect our growing understanding of the disorder and our increasing sophistication in detecting it. However, research studies have yet to provide either an objective test for ADHD or physical evidence of brain abnormalities.

Could it be that subtler and more complex social forces are at the heart of the ADHD explosion? Because there is no definitive and objective test for ADHD, the diagnosis rests primarily on an adult's description of excessively active, highly impulsive, or extremely distractible behavior. Child care professionals recognize that young children (particularly boys) often exhibit these behavioral characteristics. An observer's determination that certain behaviors are excessive or inappropriate depends very much on the observer's own attitudes, preferences, and personality. For example, Mrs. Steadfast sees impulsivity and distractibility where Mrs. Freespirit sees enthusiasm and divergent thinking. To appreciate the subjective nature of behavior ratings, simply ask yourself if you would want your own psychiatric status evaluated according to the opinions of your coworkers, supervisor, or spouse!

Another factor behind the ADHD explosion may be an underlying assumption that all children should behave within certain carefully defined boundaries. These boundaries may be established by the external demands of the situation (e.g., sitting quietly in small spaces for extended periods of time listening to an adult and/or doing paperwork). Behavior which falls outside these boundaries is deemed abnormal or dysfunctional. In my book, *The Boy Who Burned Too Brightly*, I use the symbol of a flame burning on

*Early Childhood News,* Nov./Dec. 1997. Reprinted with permission.

top of a child's head as a metaphor for a child's personality and temperament. The main character in the book is a young boy with a flame which burns very brightly, somewhat inconsistently, and with unusual colors and designs. To some observers, this unique flame is a source of delight and enchantment. To others it is inappropriate and unwelcome; he burns too brightly. I wonder if sometimes (particularly in group settings) we come to value uniformity and consistency more than individuality and creativity.

Many child care professionals are drawn to their field out of a deep love for children and an appreciation for children's individual differences. We know that each child has his or her own special gifts and talents, personality, and temperament. Billy is a risk-taker. Travis plays it safe. Sally loves to read. Amy would rather draw. Andre responds quickly. Matthew moves in slow motion. Samantha takes things seriously. Alison laughs at life. Although children often share many common cognitive, social, and emotional characteristics related to specific developmental stages, there tends to be more variability than uniformity. Children's individual differences add flavor and texture to our centers, classrooms, and homes and make each small soul a valuable and irreplaceable treasure.

Certainly there are times and places where we may wish someone's flame would burn a little less brightly. Undoubtedly some children have flames which threaten to burn out of control. We must recognize that children's behavior reflects not only their temperament and personality, but also the time and place in which they live. Today's children live in very challenging times. Many must cope with the stress of broken or blended families. Most are exposed to thousands of hours of fast-paced, electronic "entertainment" promoting questionable values and negative role models. Others have to supervise themselves and their siblings in the lonely hours after school before parents arrive home. Too many are victims of abuse or neglect. Some have schedules so crowded with activities that there is little time for spontaneous play and carefree relaxation. All are living in a society which races along at an increasingly chaotic and frenzied pace. For these and a myriad of other environmental reasons, many children may exhibit significant levels of distractibility and restlessness.

Thanks to recent advances in psychopharmacology, we now have a new generation of drugs which are remarkably effective in altering thoughts, feelings, and behaviors. For example, Ritalin often dramatically reduces children's activity levels while in-

creasing their concentration on tasks they might otherwise find dull or boring. It would be a mistake, however, to interpret these changes as evidence of an underlying disorder in need of medical correction. In fact, controlled studies suggest that psychostimulants produce similar effects in most children, even if they do not have an identified disability. It may be that when we see medication-related changes in behavior, we are simply seeing the effects of a powerful drug which alters the way many children respond to their environment. If we medicate them to change their behavior, what have we lost in the bargain? And if we formally label them as disordered, do we alter the way they are perceived by others and by themselves?

In our well-intentioned attempts to ensure that each and every child obtains his or her own maximum level of success, let us not push for uniformity at the price of individuality. Let us not value consistency more than creativity. Let us not view differences as deficits. Instead, let us strive as parents and professionals to view each and every child as a totally unique and irreplaceable creation. May each and every one burn forever brightly!

 **Article Review Form at end of book.**

How does the current explanation of dyslexia differ from popular explanations of the past? How might course assignments be altered for someone suffering from dyslexia?

# Dyslexia

**Sally E. Shaywitz**

One hundred years ago, in November 1896, a doctor in Sussex, England, published the first description of the learning disorder that would come to be known as developmental dyslexia. "Percy F., . . . aged 14, . . . has always been a bright and intelligent boy," wrote W. Pringle Morgan in the *British Medical Journal*, "quick at games, and in no way inferior to others of his age. His great difficulty has been—and is now—his inability to learn to read."

In that brief introduction, Morgan captured the paradox that has intrigued and frustrated scientists for a century since: the profound and persistent difficulties some very bright people face in learning to read. In 1996 as in 1896, reading ability is taken as a proxy for intelligence; most people assume that if someone is smart, motivated and schooled, he or she will learn to read. But the experience of millions of dyslexics like Percy F. has shown that assumption to be false. In dyslexia, the seemingly invariant relation between intelligence and reading ability breaks down.

Early explanations of dyslexia, put forth in the 1920s, held that defects in the visual system were to blame for the reversals of letters and words thought to typify dyslexic reading. Eye training was often prescribed to overcome these alleged visual defects. Subsequent research has shown, however, that children with dyslexia are not unusually prone to reversing letters or words and that the cognitive deficit responsible for the disorder is related to the language system. In particular, dyslexia reflects a deficiency in the processing of the distinctive linguistic units, called phonemes, that make up all spoken and written words. Current linguistic models of reading and dyslexia now provide an explanation of why some very intelligent people have trouble learning to read and performing other language-related tasks.

In the course of our work, my colleagues and I at the Yale Center for the Study of Learning and Attention have evaluated hundreds of children and scores of men and women for reading disabilities. Many are students and faculty at our university's undergraduate, graduate and professional schools.

One of these, a medical student named Gregory, came to see us after undergoing a series of problems in his first-year courses. He was quite discouraged.

Although he had been diagnosed as dyslexic in grade school, Gregory had also been placed in a program for gifted students. His native intelligence, together with extensive support and tutoring, had allowed him to graduate from high school with honors and gain admission to an Ivy League college. In college, Gregory had worked extremely hard and eventually received offers from several top medical schools. Now, however, he was beginning to doubt his own competence. He had no trouble comprehending the intricate relations among physiological systems or the complex mechanisms of disease; indeed, he excelled in those areas requiring reasoning skills. More problematic for him was the simple act of pronouncing long words or novel terms (such as labels used in anatomic descriptions); perhaps his least well-developed skill was rote memorization.

Both Gregory and his professors were perplexed by the inconsistencies in his performance.

How could someone who understood difficult concepts so well have trouble with the smaller and simpler details? Could Gregory's dyslexia—he was still a slow reader—account for his inability to name body parts and tissue types in the face of his excellent reasoning skills?

It could, I explained. Gregory's history fit the clinical picture of dyslexia as it has been traditionally defined: an unexpected difficulty learning to read despite intelligence, motivation and education. Furthermore, I was able to reassure Gregory that scientists now understand the basic nature of dyslexia.

Over the past two decades, a coherent model of dyslexia has emerged that is based on phonological processing. The phonological model is consistent both with the clinical symptoms of dyslexia and with what neuroscientists know about brain organization and function. Investigators from many laboratories, including my colleagues and I at the Yale Center, have had the opportunity to test and refine this model through 10 years of cognitive and, more recently, neurobiological studies.

## The Phonological Model

To understand how the phonological model works, one has first to consider the way in which language is processed in the brain. Researchers conceptualize the language system as a hierarchical series of modules or components, each devoted to a particular aspect of language. At the upper levels of the hierarchy are components involved with semantics (vocabulary or word meaning), syntax (grammatical structure) and discourse (connected sentences). At the lowest level of the hierarchy is the phonological module, which is dedicated to processing the distinctive sound elements that constitute language.

The phoneme, defined as the smallest meaningful segment of language, is the fundamental element of the linguistic system. Different combinations of just 44 phonemes produce every word in the English language. The word "cat," for example, consists of three phonemes: "kuh," "aah," and "tuh." (Linguists indicate these sounds as |k|, |æ| and |t|.) Before words can be identified, understood, stored in memory or retrieved from it, they must first be broken down, or parsed, into their phonetic units by the phonological module of the brain.

In spoken language, this process occurs automatically, at a preconscious level. As Noam Chomsky and, more recently, Steven Pinker of the Massachusetts Institute of Technology have convincingly argued, language is instinctive—all that is necessary is for humans to be exposed to it. A genetically determined phonological module automatically assembles the phonemes into words for the speaker and parses the spoken word back into its underlying phonological components for the listener.

In producing a word, the human speech apparatus—the larynx, palate, tongue and lips—automatically compresses and merges the phonemes. As a result, information from several phonemes is folded into a single unit of sound. Because there is no overt clue to the underlying segmental nature of speech, spoken language appears to be seamless. Hence, an oscilloscope would register the word "cat" as a single burst of sound; only the human language system is capable of distinguishing the three phonemes embedded in the word.

Reading reflects spoken language, as my colleague Alvin M. Liberman of Haskins Laboratories in New Haven, Conn., points out, but it is a much harder skill to master. Why? Although both speaking and reading rely on phonological processing, there is a significant difference: speaking is natural, and reading is not. Reading is an invention and must be learned at a conscious level. The task of the reader is to transform the visual percepts of alphabetic script into linguistic ones—that is, to recode graphemes (letters) into their corresponding phonemes. To accomplish this, the beginning reader must first come to a conscious awareness of the internal phonological structure of spoken words. Then he or she must realize that the orthography—the sequence of letters on the page—represents this phonology. That is precisely what happens when a child learns to read.

In contrast, when a child is dyslexic, a deficit within the language system at the level of the phonological module impairs his or her ability to segment the written word into its underlying phonological components. This explanation of dyslexia is referred to as the phonological model, or sometimes as the phonological deficit hypothesis.

According to this hypothesis, a circumscribed deficit in phonological processing impairs decoding, preventing word identification. This basic deficit in what is essentially a lower-order linguistic function blocks access to higher-order linguistic processes and to gaining meaning from text. Thus, although the language processes involved in comprehension and meaning are intact, they cannot be called into play, because they can be accessed only after a word has been identified. The impact of the phonological deficit is most obvious in reading, but it can also affect speech in predictable ways. Gregory's dilemma with long or novel words, for example, is entirely consistent with the body of evidence that supports a phonological model of dyslexia.

That evidence began accumulating more than two decades ago. One of the earliest experiments, carried out by the late Isabelle Y. Liberman of Haskins Laboratories, showed that young children become aware between four and six years of age of the phonological structure of spoken words. In the experiment, children were asked how many sounds they heard in a series of words. None of the four-year-olds could correctly identify the number of phonemes, but 17 percent of the five-year-olds did, and by age six, 70 percent of the children demonstrated phonological awareness.

By age six, most children have also had at least one full year of schooling, including instruction in reading. The development of phonological awareness, then, parallels the acquisition of reading skills. This correspondence suggested that the two processes are related. These findings also converge with data from the Connecticut Longitudinal Study, a project my colleagues and I began in 1983 with 445 randomly selected kindergartners; the study continues in 1996 when these children are age 19 and out of high school. Testing the youngsters yearly, we found that dyslexia affects a full 20 percent of schoolchildren—a figure that agrees roughly with the proportion of Liberman's six-year-olds who could not identify the phonological structure of words. These data further support a connection between phonological awareness and reading.

During the 1980s, researchers began to address that connection explicitly. The groundbreaking work of Lynette Bradley and Peter E. Bryant of the University of Oxford indicated that a preschooler's phonological aptitude predicts future skills at reading. Bradley and Bryant also found that training in phonological awareness significantly improves a child's ability to read. In these studies, one group of children received training in phonological processing, while another received language training that did not emphasize the sound structure of words. For example, the first group might work on categorizing words by their sound, and the second group would focus on categorizing words according to their meaning. These studies, together with more recent work by Benita A. Blachman of Syracuse University, Joseph E. Torgesen of Florida State University and Barbara Foorman of the University of Houston, clearly demonstrate that phonological training in particular—rather than general language instruction—is responsible for the improvements in reading.

Such findings set the stage for our own study, in the early 1990s, of the cognitive skills of dyslexic and nondyslexic children. Along with Jack M. Fletcher of the University of Texas–Houston and Donald P. Shankweiler and Leonard Katz of Haskins Laboratories, I examined 378 children from seven to nine years old on a battery of tests that assessed both linguistic and nonlinguistic abilities. Our results as well as those of Keith E. Stanovich and Linda S. Siegel of the Ontario Institute for Studies in Education made it clear that phonological deficits are the most significant and consistent cognitive marker of dyslexic children.

One test in particular seemed quite sensitive to dyslexia: the Auditory Analysis Test, which asks a child to segment words into their underlying phonological units and then to delete specific phonemes from the words. For example, the child must say the word "block" without the "buh" sound or say the word "sour" without the "s" sound. This measure was most related to a child's ability to decode single words in standardized tests and was independent of his or her intelligence, vocabulary and reasoning skills. When we gave this and other tests of phonemic awareness to a group of 15-year-olds in our Connecticut Longitudinal Study, the results were the same: even in high school students, phonological awareness was the best predictor of reading ability.

If dyslexia is the result of an insufficiently developed phonological specialization, other consequences of impaired phonological functioning should also be apparent—and they are. Ten years ago the work of Robert B. Katz of Haskins Laboratories documented the problems poor readers have in naming objects shown in pictures. Katz showed that when dyslexics misname objects, the incorrect responses tend to share phonological characteristics with the correct response. Furthermore, the misnaming is not the result of a lack of knowledge. For example, a girl shown a picture of a volcano calls it a tornado. When given the opportunity to elaborate, she demonstrates that she knows what the pictured object is—she can describe the attributes and activities of a volcano in great detail and point to other pictures related to volcanoes. She simply cannot summon the word "volcano."

This finding converges with other evidence in suggesting that whereas the phonological component of the language system is impaired in dyslexia, the higher-level components remain intact. Linguistic processes involved in word meaning, grammar and discourse—what, collectively, underlies comprehension—seem to be fully operational, but their activity is blocked by the deficit in the lower-order function of phonological processing. In one of our studies, Jennifer, a very bright young woman with a reading disability, told us all about the word "apocalypse." She knew its meaning, its connotations and its correct usage; she could not, however, recognize the word on a printed page. Because she could not decode and identify the written word, she could not access her fund of knowledge about its meaning when she came across it in reading.

Of course, many dyslexics, like Gregory, do learn to read and even to excel in academics despite their disability. These so-called compensated dyslexics perform as well as nondyslexics on tests of word accuracy—they have learned how to decode or identify words, thereby gaining entry to the higher levels of the language system. But they do so at a cost. Timed tests reveal that decoding remains very laborious for compensated dyslexics; they are neither automatic nor fluent in their ability to identify words. Many dyslexics have told us how tiring reading is for them, reflecting the enormous resources and energy they must expend on the task. In fact, extreme slowness in making phonologically based decisions is typical of the group of compensated dyslexics we have assembled as part of a new approach to understanding dyslexia: our neuroimaging program.

## The Neurobiology of Reading

The phonological model incorporates a modular scheme of cognitive processing in which each of the component processes used in word identification is carried out by a specific network of brain cells. Until recently, however, researchers have had no firm indication of how that scheme maps onto the actual functional organization of the human brain. Unlike many other functions, reading cannot be studied in animals; indeed, for many years the cerebral localization of all higher cognitive processes could be inferred only from the effects of brain injuries on the people who survived them. Such an approach offered little to illuminate the phenomena my colleagues and I were interested in. What we needed was a way to identify the regions of the brain that are engaged when healthy subjects are reading or trying to read.

Our group became quite excited, then, with the advent in the late 1980s of functional magnetic resonance imaging (fMRI). Using the same scanning machine that has revolutionized clinical imaging, fMRI can measure changes in the metabolic activity of the brain while an individual performs a cognitive task. Hence, it is ideally suited to mapping the brain's response to stimuli such as reading. Because it is noninvasive and uses no radioisotopes, fMRI is also excellent for work involving children.

Since 1994, I have worked with several Yale colleagues to use fMRI in studying the neurobiology of reading. Bennett A. Shaywitz, Kenneth R. Pugh, R. Todd Constable, Robert K. Fulbright, John C. Gore and I have used the technique with more than 200 dyslexic and nondyslexic children and adults. As a result of this program, we can now suggest a tentative neural architecture for reading a printed word. In particular, the identification of letters activates sites in the extrastriate cortex within the occipital lobe; phonological processing takes place within the inferior frontal gyrus; and access to meaning calls on areas within the middle and superior temporal gyri of the brain.

Our investigation has already revealed a surprising difference between men and women in the locus of phonological representation for reading. It turns out that in men phonological processing engages the left inferior frontal gyrus, whereas in women it activates not only the left but the right inferior frontal gyrus as well. These differences in lateralization had been suggested by behavioral studies, but they had never before been demonstrated unequivocally. Indeed, our findings constitute the first concrete proof of gender differences in brain organization for any cognitive function. The fact that women's brains tend to have bilateral representation for phonological processing explains several formerly puzzling observations: why, for example, after a stroke involving the left side of the brain, women are less likely than men to have significant decrements in their language skills, and why women tend more often than men to compensate for dyslexia.

As investigators who have spent our entire professional lives trying to understand dyslexia, we find the identification of brain sites dedicated to phonological processing in reading very exciting—it means that we now have a possible neurobiological "signature" for reading. The isolation of

## The Myths of Dyslexia

**Mirror writing is a symptom of dyslexia.**
In fact, backwards writing and reversals of letters and words are common in the early stages of writing development among dyslexic and nondyslexic children alike. Dyslexic children have problems in naming letters but not in copying letters.

**Eye training is a treatment for dyslexia.**
More than two decades of research have shown that dyslexia reflects a linguistic deficit. There is no evidence that eye training alleviates the disorder.

**More boys than girls are dyslexic.**
Boys' reading disabilities are indeed identified more often than girls', but studies indicate that such identification is biased. The actual prevalence of the disorder is nearly identical in the two sexes.

**Dyslexia can be outgrown.**
Yearly monitoring of phonological skills from first through 12th grade shows that the disability persists into adulthood. Even though many dyslexics learn to read accurately, they continue to read slowly and not automatically.

**Smart people cannot be dyslexic.**
Intelligence is in no way related to phonological processing, as scores of brilliant and accomplished dyslexics—among them William Butler Yeats, Albert Einstein, George Patton, John Irving, Charles Schwab and Nicholas Negroponte—attest.

---

such a signature brings with it the future promise of more precise diagnosis of dyslexia. It is possible, for example, that the neural signature for phonological processing may provide the most sensitive measure of the disorder. Furthermore, the discovery of a biological signature for reading offers an unprecedented opportunity to assess the effects of interventions on the neuroanatomic systems serving the reading process itself.

## Putting It in Context

The phonological model crystallizes exactly what we mean by dyslexia: an encapsulated deficit often surrounded by significant strengths in reasoning, problem solving, concept formation, critical thinking and vocabulary. Indeed, compensated dyslexics such as Gregory may use the "big picture" of theories, models and ideas to help them remember specific details. It is true that when details are not unified by associated ideas or theoretical frameworks—when, for example, Gregory must commit to memory long lists of unfamiliar names—dyslexics can be at a real disadvantage. Even if Gregory succeeds in memorizing such lists, he has trouble producing the names on demand, as he must when he is questioned on rounds by an attending physician. The phonological model predicts, and experimentation has shown, that rote memorization and rapid word retrieval are particularly difficult for dyslexics.

Even when the individual knows the information, needing to retrieve it rapidly and present it orally often results in calling up a related phoneme or incorrectly ordering the retrieved phonemes. Under such circumstances, dyslexics will pepper their speech with many um's, ah's and other hesitations. On the other hand, when not pressured to provide instant responses, the dyslexic can deliver an excellent oral presentation. Similarly, in reading, whereas nonimpaired readers can decode words automatically, individuals such as Gregory frequently need to resort to the use of context to help them identify specific words. This strategy slows them further and is another reason that the provision of extra time is necessary if dyslexics are to show what they actually know. Multiple-choice examinations, too, by their lack of sufficient context, as well as by their wording and response format, excessively penalize dyslexics.

But our experience at the Yale Center suggests that many compensated dyslexics have a distinct advantage over nondyslexics in their ability to reason and conceptualize and that the phonological deficit masks what are often excellent comprehension skills. Many schools and universities now appreciate the circumscribed nature of dyslexia and offer to evaluate the achievement of their dyslexic students with essays and prepared oral presentations rather than tests of rote memorization or multiple choices. Just as researchers have begun to understand the neural substrate of dyslexia, educators are beginning to recognize the practical implications of the disorder. A century after W. Pringle Morgan first described dyslexia in Percy F., society may at last understand the paradox of the disorder.

 **Article Review Form at end of book.**

# WiseGuide Wrap-Up

- Low-income children, especially from families with incomes under $20,000 a year, are less likely to have access to home or school computers than are children from higher-income families. Lack of exposure places these children at a technological disadvantage in the classroom and in future job markets.

- Fortunately, children who were prenatally exposed to cocaine are not displaying the extensive

developmental problems once anticipated. However, all is not normal. These children remain vulnerable to their often impoverished and economically stressful home environments. In classrooms, evidence suggests that these children are highly distractible and may benefit from classroom modifications.

- The number of children diagnosed with attention deficit hyperactivity disorder (ADHD) has increased

dramatically in recent years. Better diagnostic methods and treatments are in part the reasons for the increase. Some, however, are concerned that the increase is also the direct result of narrow definitions of tolerable classroom behavior.

- Dyslexia is now recognized as a deficiency in the processing of the phonemes that make up all written and spoken words.

## R.E.A.L. Sites

This list provides a print preview of typical **coursewise** R.E.A.L. sites. There are over 100 such sites at the **courselinks**™ site. The danger in printing URLs is that web sites can change overnight. As we went to press, these sites were functional using the URLs provided. If you come across one that isn't, please let us know via email to: webmaster@coursewise.com. Use your Passport to access the most current list of R.E.A.L. sites at the **courselinks**™ site.

**Site name:** Disabilities: Attention Deficit Disorder (ADD)

**URL:** http://www.kidsource.com/kidsource/pages/dis.add.html

**Why is it R.E.A.L.?** One of the articles you read presents the issues facing children with ADHD. A very confusing area for both parents and professionals lies in the distinction between groups of children diagnosed with ADHD and those who are gifted. This site provides a link to information comparing the two types of children. Visit the site *ADHD and Children Who Are Gifted* to learn about their differences and similarities. After reading this excellent article, what would you recommend to parents who are concerned about their child's behavior? Are there any distinctive characteristics that distinguish between the two populations? Make a short list of similarities and differences for parents and teachers.

**Site name:** *APA Monitor* Teaching Today's Pupils to Think More Critically

**URL:** http://www.apa.org/monitor/mar97/crit.html

**Why is it R.E.A.L.?** This text article presents the issues surrounding teaching students to think critically. The three types of thinking include critical, creative, and practical. After reading this article, visit the *APA Monitor* web site at http://www.apa.org/monitor/jun97/ei.html and read the article "Can Emotional Intelligence Be Taught in Today's Schools?" How would you use the three types of thinking to solve the problems of teaching emotional intelligence in the schools? Identify the problems involved in developing a program for teaching emotional intelligence.

# section

6

## Learning Objectives

- Increase awareness of the normal stages of language learning.

- Promote understanding of parenting methods that encourage development of effective communication.

- Explain why some children cry more than others.

- Discuss the emergence of gestural communications.

# Language Development

 **WiseGuide Intro**

Language is a uniquely human trait that, on the surface, children appear to master effortlessly. In fact, however, the processes of language expression and comprehension are complicated and require much effort on the part of the child. However, many factors appear to facilitate language acquisition. Most agree that the human brain is wired for the task of learning language. In the womb, the fetus listens to the mother's voice, becoming familiar not with specific words but with the melody of the home language. From birth, infants respond preferentially to voices and are able to distinguish the individual sounds that make up words. At about 6 months, infants begin to play with language sounds. They also quickly focus on those sounds and melodies heard most frequently. Babbling is a universal series of stages through which children pass, and, with each step, their sounds become more and more speechlike. By age 1, most children begin to link their words to meanings. Naming becomes a favorite activity, and from this children develop theories of how to map words to their meanings. By age 2, vocabularies explode, and word-strings of increasing length become the norm. These words are not put together randomly; rather, children seem to be primed for detecting grammatical rules, though not without errors.

Along with this push from nature, environmental stimulation facilitates language development. Caregivers' responses to a variety of early communication efforts appear to be essential to well-developed language skills. Talking to children is important in general. Children raised in silence do not develop normal language patterns. One particularly important characteristic of adult-to-child speech is "parentese." Universally, adults speak parentese in the presence of young children. It is speech that is grammatically simple, repetitive, and clear. It is a singsong type of exaggerated, high-pitched speech. These vocal alternations seem to draw children's attention to the critical features of speech sounds.

The early use of gestures, especially pointing, also seems to be an important aspect of language acquisition. Pointing draws someone else's attention to an event or object of interest. Caregivers' reinforcement of such communication efforts, along with neurological development, may explain the associations found between the onset of pointing and children's level of language comprehension and rate of speech acquisition.

Beginning at birth, babies cry, and some cry more than others. Crying is irritating to our nervous systems and arouses a sense of urgency. Thus, crying is more than a signal of distress. It is the infant's first reliable means of communicating a need. Unfortunately, some infants cry excessively and are difficult to console, despite parents' best efforts. Particularly in the first three months of life, even "futile" efforts to console are better than not responding. What is important is the consistency of the efforts made, which tell the child someone cares and that his or her signals matter. As infants gain control of their bodies and become interested in visually exploring their worlds and manipulating objects, crying typically decreases. This is also a good time to begin reinforcing noncrying behaviors.

## Thinking Beyond the Facts

This section on language development shows that much is known about how children learn to communicate. The human brain is prepared to respond to the sounds that make up all the world's languages, even before birth. Postbirth, the normal home environment provides the stimulation necessary for the discovery of language patterns and means of effective communication. The earliest communication act is the cry. Many parents, however, are unsure of what constitutes a normal amount of crying. Causing as much concern is the issue of what to do about a crying child. Some experts claim that responding to cries only reinforces, crying behavior and "spoils" the child. Others contend that rapid responses to cries teach children that communication efforts matter and that more mature methods of having needs met will develop in time. Who's right? What are your experiences in dealing with a fussy child?

Along with normal language experiences and frustrations, there is also the possibility of something going wrong. Have you known a child showing language delays? What were the causes? Was anything in the environment reinforcing the child's *not* talking? Were illnesses or structural deformities to blame? Since hearing is crucial to language learning, how can parents be sure their children's hearing is normal? What damage might repeated ear infections have on the ear structures and on language development? If the medical community is unsure of appropriate treatment of ear infections, how is a parent to know? For more information on normal language development and common problems, visit web sites on infant sign, crying, colic, otitis media, hearing loss, and deafness.

## ? Questions ?

**Reading 21.** Describe the major features of parentese.

How does parentese seem to promote language learning?

**Reading 22.** Why do adults respond too quickly to the cries of children?

Define a problem crier and the best course of action for dealing with one.

**Reading 23.** Describe the difference between an infant under 6 months of age and one who is over 10 months of age in their responses to the speech sounds of several different languages.

What assumptions do children rely on when learning to connect spoken words to the objects to which they refer?

**Reading 24.** Why do children begin to point?

How is pointing related to language development?

Give some examples of research findings.

Describe the major features of parentese. How does parentese seem to promote language learning?

# New Insights into How Babies Learn Language

## Marcia Barinaga

When it comes to understanding language, it's a phonetic jungle out there. Adult speech is far from uniform, with countless subtle variations on each sound, such as the "a" in "cat" or the "o" in "cot." But somewhere a line must be drawn, separating the cats from the cots. So, as children learn language, they must master which phonetic differences to pay attention to and which to ignore. A paper in this issue of *Science* and one in last week's issue of *Nature* shed some new light on how babies gain this key skill.

Adults in many cultures use a singsong type of exaggerated speech when they speak to babies. This speech, often called "parentese," seems to serve to get the baby's attention and to communicate and elicit emotions. But on page 684, Patricia Kuhl of the University of Washington, Seattle, and her coworkers provide evidence that it may be more than just a tool of endearment. Their analysis of the exaggerated and varied "caricatures" of vowel sounds that mothers use when talking to babies suggests, Kuhl says, that those distortions help

infants learn the key features of the sounds.

But babies then set aside their capacity to make some of these distinctions. Christine Stager and Janet Werker at the University of British Columbia in Vancouver report in the 24 July *Nature* that when infants begin learning words, they neglect some differences between sounds. Presumably, that's because those distinctions won't matter until later, when their vocabulary becomes crowded with similar-sounding words.

Indeed, it appears that at each stage of early language learning, from categorizing sounds to applying those categories as they learn words, infants' brains are honing their efficiency, making rules for what to notice and what to dismiss. "To be experts in a language, we need to learn not only to make relevant distinctions, but to ignore irrelevant variability," says Stanford developmental psychologist Anne Fernald.

Kuhl and others have studied the sound-sorting process that precedes word learning. In 1992, Kuhl's team reported that by 6 months of age, Swedish and American babies learn to catego-

rize vowel sounds, paying attention to distinctions that are meaningful in their native language, such as the difference between "ee" and "ah," while ignoring meaningless variations, such as all the ways a person might say "ee." Work done in the 1980s by Nan Bernstein Ratner at the University of Maryland suggested that English parentese might help babies learn these distinctions. Now Kuhl has probed further by studying the parentese of three different languages—English, Swedish, and Russian—to see if the distorted tones provide cues that may be useful for vowel pronunciation.

Her team's analysis focused on formants, the resonant frequencies that, like notes in a musical chord, make up each vowel sound. If vowel sounds are plotted on a graph, with the frequencies of the two dominant formants represented on the $x$ and $y$ axes, the result is a "vowel triangle," and the sounds "ah," "ee," and "oo" at the corners.

Kuhl's group found that, in all three languages, mothers talking to their babies produced exaggerated versions of vowels, emphasizing the features that distinguish them from each other. This nearly doubled the area of the vowel triangle. "It looks like the mothers are increasing the value of the signal," says Kuhl.

The mothers' speech also provided many examples of each vowel sound. This, Kuhl proposes, may help babies learn the features that make each sound special, and learn to ignore the phonetic variations that fall within a given vowel sound. Indeed, by 20 weeks of age, babies' babbling contains distinct vowel sounds that form their own—albeit higher pitched—vowel triangle.

The work "illustrates a close tie between the input and what the child is doing," says language researcher Peter Jusczyk of Johns Hopkins University. But that falls short of proving that parentese serves an instructive role. "The fact that parents do it doesn't necessarily mean that it is essential for language learning," says Stanford's Fernald. That hypothesis might be tested, she says, with studies across cultures that use different amounts or types of parentese.

Once infants learn the important distinctions between speech sounds in their native language, they appear to bank some of those abilities for later use.

Stager and Werker showed this in a study of infants at 14 months, an age when babies are just beginning to learn words and match them to meanings. They tested to see whether infants who were engaged in word learning would catch small but significant changes in those words.

In earlier studies, Werker and Les Cohen at the University of Texas, Austin, showed that 14-month-olds could learn to associate a particular word with an image, and would notice if the word was changed. Werker and Cohen alternately showed the infants a picture of one nonsense object while playing a tape of the spoken nonsense word "lif" and a picture of another object while playing the word "neem." If, after many repetitions of the object-word pairs, the babies were shown the "lif" object but heard "neem," they studied the object longer, indicating they noticed the name switch.

The current study had the same design, but the names— "bih" and "dih"—differed phonetically by just one sound. Control studies showed that babies could make this distinction when they heard the words on their own. But when the words were linked with objects, the ba-

bies didn't seem to notice the switch. "To our surprise, they are actually listening less carefully" when they are listening for word meaning, says Werker. Werker suggests the babies miss the switch between "bih" and "dih" because—as studies by other teams have shown—their tiny vocabularies don't generally have words that differ by only one sound, so they don't yet need to concentrate on that level of detail. The distinctions they have learned are "almost like reserve capacity," she says.

That makes sense, says Jusczyk; for babies to spend effort on such distinctions would be a waste at that stage of development. "There is only so much you can do at once," he says, and it is important for infants engaged in the daunting task of learning words to disregard information that is not absolutely necessary. Later, when their vocabularies become crowded with words, that reserve capacity to distinguish sounds—a payoff perhaps of parentese—will be essential for navigating in the phonetic jungle.

 **Article Review Form at end of book.**

Why do adults respond too quickly to the cries of children? Define a problem crier and the best course of action for dealing with one.

# Why Is This Baby Crying?

### Eugenie Allen

When Spenser Schott was ten days old, she started to cry more than her parents, Joann and Christopher, thought humanly possible—as much as seven hours a day. When she wasn't eating or sleeping, she was resisting her parents' desperate attempts to calm her.

"It was horrible," recalls Joann. "Spenser would get up in the morning, eat, cry for three hours, nap for a half hour, and then it would start all over again. Sometimes the sound of running water, lots of cuddling, and sheer fatigue from crying would quiet her, but sometimes nothing would. I have so many photos of her screaming!"

Because Spenser was otherwise healthy, the only treatment her pediatrician recommended was continued loving care and the passage of time. "I can't say we enjoyed those days," says Joann. "I was very sad. I wanted to enjoy my first child more." But sure enough, Spenser started to cheer up at around four months, when she was a little more mobile. "By the time she was able to crawl after the things she

wanted, she was a whole new baby," says Joann.

As the Schotts discovered—more thoroughly, perhaps, than many new parents—when a baby cries, the whole family suffers. The moment she stops, suddenly all is well. And if it seems as though she never stops, her parents assume they're doing something terribly wrong.

To their everlasting relief, the Schotts also learned that problem criers are born, not made. Recently, Joann gave birth to Spenser's sister, Caroline, a baby who rarely cries without an obvious reason, and even then it comes as a polite request rather than an angry demand. "They're as different as they could be," says Joann.

Decades of study still can't tell parents why some babies cry more than others or offer a sure-fire cure for problem crying, but out of the research comes one reassuring fact: What matters most isn't whether your efforts to console your child work every time, but whether you consistently make those efforts. Spenser Schott resisted every trick in the book; her sister calms readily and reliably. But both girls got the message early on that someone was

there for them. And for parents, that's the whole point of trying to figure out what's wrong.

## Every Newborn's Cry Is Different

Although a healthy newborn's cry registers at 84 decibels—slightly louder than the sound of traffic at a busy intersection—it's not just the loudness that overwhelms, it's the pitch, or shrillness, of the cry. Evelyn Thoman, director of the Infant Studies Laboratory at the University of Connecticut, says some babies are born with a "velvet cry," while others have wails that sound like "fingernails on a blackboard."

Not only does crying sound alarming, it can look pretty bad, too. A newborn at full tilt may have a red or purple face, a furrowed brow, quivering lips, a squared mouth, and flailing arms and legs. He may gasp and swallow air, adding to his distress. And as if that weren't enough, he may even "cry dry" for several days before his tear ducts start functioning.

Such dramatic displays send many first-time parents fumbling for an off switch. And with about four out of five healthy, full-term

## The Nature of a Cry: Newborn to 3 years

Developmental milestones are never set in stone: Your baby may cry more or less at each stage and may do so earlier or later than other children. Crying is also likely to increase during a growth spurt or emotional stress.

### Birth to 1 Month

In the beginning, crying is a physiological response to pain or discomfort. Baby may be hungry, wet, tired, hot, or cold. He may be in pain from the trauma of birth or have gas or colic.

### 1 to 3 Months

Babies acquire the neurological control to cry spontaneously, but the behavior is still fairly primitive. Average crying time peaks at about three hours a day in six-week-olds and then tapers off. Many cases of colic begin and end now. Most babies also start to smile and gurgle.

### 3 to 4 Months

Baby establishes enough of a routine that you can interpret her cries more confidently. She's also developing emotions. Besides suffering from hunger, a wet diaper, or fatigue, she may cry because she's bored or lonely, frightened or surprised, or because she simply wants attention.

### 4 to 6 Months

Intentional crying gets under way. A baby will cry and put her arms up to be carried, look to you for a response, and cry more if you refuse—or break into a broad grin if you comply.

### 6 to 12 Months

Many happy babies revert to crying now because of separation anxiety—the fear that if Mommy and Daddy leave, they won't return. A related cause of increased crying is the conflict that accompanies the mastery of gross motor skills such as crawling and walking: A baby fears that if *he* leaves Mommy and Daddy, *he* may not return. Daytime partings, bedtime, and middle-of-the-night wakefulness may be especially hard.

### 1 Year

Around this age, your baby may acquire a few important gestures and words that will gradually replace his cry: bottle, teddy bear, night-night. But he'll still wail when he's hurt, sick, or angry, and he might have lingering fears about being separated from you.

### 12 to 18 Months

She may start throwing tantrums at this age, but according to child psychologist Burton White, you can limit them if you catch out-of-control crying and kicking when it first surfaces—most commonly on the changing table, at about ten months. The trick is to change diapers quickly and matter-of-factly, without singing songs or bringing out toys to distract a baby who's going berserk. If a child starts throwing full-fledged tantrums, though, there's little you can do other than avoid situations that provoke them. Once a tantrum is under way, says childcare expert Penelope Leach, "all you can do is wait it out and hope she feels better soon."

### 18 to 24 Months

The big development at this age is whining, which Leach says becomes a habit in children who find it difficult to get attention. To put an end to it, she says, "we need to make it easier and more rewarding for children to speak." That means paying attention to your toddler before she starts to whine, asking older siblings to do the same, and eliminating competing background noise like the television.

### 2 to 3 Years

Now, your child may surprise you with a new sorrowful cry that's equally intense whether he's spilled his milk or lost a pet. This development comes with the child's emerging vulnerability and understanding of loss.

---

newborns, that switch is fairly easy to find. These babies tend to have an obvious need when they cry, and their parents become adept at anticipating and meeting those needs: Baby lets out a squawk whenever you undress her; in response, you keep baths to a minimum and drape a blanket over her when you change her diaper. She prefers being burped upright, over your shoulder, so you accommodate her.

Then there's the other fifth of the infant population. Problem criers—who suffer from extreme fussiness or the mysterious ailment called colic—confound their parents' attempts to soothe them. And while some of these high-needs children stop crying long enough to smile and gurgle, others don't.

While there's no consensus about what determines the kind of crier a baby will be, research shows that except in some cases of severe neglect (when babies actually cry less, not more), parents don't *create* crying types. And, thankfully, a fussy newborn doesn't necessarily become a crabby toddler or preschooler.

## Is Your Baby a Problem Crier?

Ordinary crying is like a phone call, says child psychologist Penelope Leach, author of *Your Baby and Child*. "When the phone rings, we answer it. It stops ringing, and we talk to whoever's on the other end of the line." But in the case of a baby who suffers from extreme fussiness or colic, she explains, "we keep picking up the damn phone, but the noise doesn't stop." Unfortunately, this is one phone call your answering machine can't handle.

How to tell if your baby has either condition—or both? According to Barry Lester, director of the Infant Crying and Behavior Clinic at Brown University School of Medicine, a baby is an excessive crier if he cries for more than three hours a day, three days a week, for three weeks in a row; shows no other symptoms beyond the cry itself; and can usually be comforted. A baby with colic, on the other hand, is definitely an excessive crier, but he displays additional signs of distress: The cry begins suddenly, typically in early evening, with no cranky period beforehand; he acts like he's in severe physical pain, with his legs drawn up to the abdomen, for example, or his arms and legs stiffened; and he is absolutely inconsolable.

In most cases, colic starts at two to four weeks and stops by three months—to the day, say many parents. Extremely fussy babies often improve their outlook when they can do more for themselves—hold a toy, begin to crawl—usually between three and six months.

Both colicky babies and excessive criers may benefit from consolation strategies (see *Consoling Tactics,* this page *). For their parents, Lester prescribes a little perspective: "The parents who can tell themselves that this will pass and that they didn't do anything to cause it do much better than those who can't." Friends, family, or your pediatrician can supply advice or moral support, or you may want to contact Lester's colic clinic (401/453-7640 or 7630), the only one of its kind in the country, for a telephone consultation.

*Does not appear in this publication.

## Soothing Doesn't Mean Quieting

If you've got a crier, don't abandon the effort to console her. Penelope Leach points to recent research in the Netherlands that suggests parents' "futile" efforts are better than nothing: "If you stop doing all the things you've been doing—walking and rubbing and patting and so forth—and leave the baby alone," Leach says, "she cries a great deal more. In other words, even if you're not making her totally happy, you still may be reducing crying from miserable screaming to whining or whimpering—and that's a very big difference."

Of course, no one can offer round-the-clock comfort, so Leach and other experts recommend several stand-ins, starting in the first few weeks with warm, snug swaddling whenever your loving arms aren't available. By the age of two months, a baby can learn self-soothing techniques like sucking a pacifier or her own fingers. By three months, she can find her thumb or stare at a rattle or an interesting pattern. At four months, she can hold the rattle. That's also the age when she'll be comforted by the sound of your voice from across the room, so you can stall her for a few minutes with verbal reassurance. And when she's about six months old, you can offer her books and toys instead of a perch on your hip every time she lets out a whimper.

What's more, says Burton White, director of the Center for Parent Education in Newton, Massachusetts, and author of *Raising a Happy, Unspoiled Child*, it's very important to cuddle your baby when she's *not* upset, so she doesn't think she must cry to get your attention.

## Can Comforting Become Spoiling?

Let's say that one day your angel suddenly cries whenever you put her down. She seems healthy. She's napped, has had her diaper changed, and has been fed and burped. Still, she's protesting, and you have a mountain of work to do. Is this the time to teach her who's boss?

Before the age of three months, experts say, her mind isn't developed enough to learn that lesson, so letting her cry it out won't do much good. Instead of fretting about *why* she's crying, it's better to accept the fact that she *is* crying and try to console her. The experts disagree on what response is appropriate when a baby is older than three months, however, so you'll need to do what seems best for you.

For example, says Dr. Benjamin Spock, the author of *Baby and Child Care* and a contributing editor of *Parenting*, "When a baby is still fretful or colicky after three months, we suspect that the baby is used to getting his way. He seems to have a bossy, angry expression on his face, as if to say, 'You used to carry me around anytime I fretted, why aren't you doing it now?' I think it's good for parents to have the feeling that it's really all right not to always go to such a baby right away."

Unlike Spock, White argues that children don't have the cognitive skills to manipulate their parents until they're about the age of six months—and that they need their parents' attention until then.

Leach, however, insists that children don't know how to blackmail their parents until they're a year old. Instead of worrying about spoiling your infant, she says, "the useful thing is for parents to ask, 'What message do I want my baby to get?' and then act appropriately. 'Don't bother to cry' is a bad message, because crying is a precursor to communication, and we desperately want our children to talk."

With all the effort that goes into getting a baby to *stop* crying, it's easy to overlook the benefits of baby's built-in alarm system.

"Being a parent would be a great deal worse if your baby never cried at all," says Leach. "It's only because you can count on her to cry if there's something wrong that you can ever relax and watch the TV or go to sleep or make love or have dinner or whatever else you're trying to do."

Even after it's served its purpose as a survival tool, crying remains an important emotional outlet. Once you've survived all the preverbal outbursts, you'll have a healthy child to usher through all the other upsets of childhood, adolescence, and beyond.

 **Article Review Form at end of book.**

Describe the difference between an infant under 6 months of age and one who is over 10 months of age in their responses to the speech sounds of several different languages. What assumptions do children rely on when learning to connect spoken words to the objects to which they refer?

# The Language Explosion

## Geoffrey Cowley

*With Donna Foote in Los Angeles*

Barry is a pixie-faced 3-year-old who can't yet draw a circle or stack his blocks in a simple pattern. There is little chance he will ever live independently. He may never learn to tie his own shoes. Yet Barry is as chatty and engaging a person as you could ever hope to meet. He knows his preschool classmates—and their parents—by name. When he wakes his mom in the morning, he strokes her cheek and tells her how beautiful she is. Then he asks her how she slept. Barry has Williams syndrome, a rare congenital disorder caused by abnormalities on chromosome 7. Children with the condition share an array of distinctive traits, including weak hearts, elfin faces and extremely low IQs. But they're unusually sociable, and often display an extraordinary feeling for language. Ask a Williams child to name an animal, says Dr. Ursula Bellugi of the Salk Institute's Laboratory for Cognitive Neuroscience, and you may get a fanciful discourse on yaks, koalas or unicorns.

If we learned language in the same way that we learn to add, subtract or play cards, children like Barry would not get much beyond hello and goodbye. Nor, for that matter, would normal toddlers. As anyone who has struggled through college French can attest, picking up a new language as an adult is as simple as picking up a truck. Yet virtually every kid in the world succeeds at it—and without conscious effort. Children attach meanings to sounds long before they shed their diapers. They launch into grammatical analysis before they can tie their shoes. And by the age of 3, most produce sentences as readily as laughter or tears.

Scholars have bickered for centuries over how kids accomplish this feat, but most now agree that their brains are wired for the task. Like finches or sparrows, which learn to sing as hatchlings or not at all, we're designed to acquire certain kinds of knowledge at particular stages of development. Children surrounded by words almost always become fluent by 3, whatever their general intelligence. And people deprived of language as children rarely

master it as adults, no matter how smart they are or how intensively they're trained. As MIT linguist Steven Pinker observes in his acclaimed 1994 book "The Language Instinct," "Language is not a cultural artifact that we learn the way we learn to tell time or how the federal government works. It is a distinct piece of [our] biological makeup." Whether they emerge speaking Spanish, Czech or Hindi, kids all acquire language on the same general schedule. And as a growing body of research makes clear, they all travel the same remarkable path.

## Sound

The journey toward language starts not in the nursery but in the womb, where the fetus is continually bathed in the sounds of its mother's voice. Babies just 4 days old can distinguish one language from another. French newborns suck more vigorously when they hear French spoken than when they hear Russian—and Russian babies show the opposite preference. At first, they notice only general rhythms and melodies.

But newborns are also sensitive to speech sounds, and they home in quickly on the ones that matter.

Each of the world's approximately 6,000 languages uses a different assortment of phonemes, or distinctive sounds, to build words. As adults, we have a hard time even hearing phonemes from foreign languages. The French don't notice any real difference between the *th* sounds in *thick* and *then*—and to most English speakers, the vowel in the French word *tu* (*ee* through rounded lips) is just another *oo*. Researchers have found that month-old infants register both of those distinctions and countless others from the world's languages. But at 6 and 10 months, they start to narrow their range. They grow oblivious to foreign phonemes while staying attuned to whatever sounds the speakers around them are using.

Acquiring a set of phonemes is a first step toward language, but just a baby step. To start decoding speech, you have to recognize words. And as anyone listening to a foreign conversation quickly discovers, people don't talk one . . . word . . . at . . . a . . . time. Real-life language—even the melodious "parentese" that parents use with infants—consists mainly of nonstopstreamsofsound. So how do babies suss out the boundaries? Long before they recognize words, says Peter Jusczyk, a cognitive scientist at Johns Hopkins University, they get a feel for how their language uses phonemes to launch syllables. By the time they're 7 months old, American babies are well accustomed to hearing *t* joined with *r* (as in *tram*) and *c* with *l* (as in *clam*), but they've been spared combinations like *db, gd, kt, ts* and *ng*, all of which occur in other languages. And once they have an ear for syllables, word boundaries become less mysterious. *Ten / groaning / deadbeats / are / cleaning / a / train on / blacktop /* makes acoustic sense in English, even if you don't know the words. *Te / ngroanin /gdea / dbea / tsare / cleani / nga / traino / nbla / cktop* isn't an option.

As children start to recognize and play with syllables, they also pick up on the metrical patterns among them. French words tend to end with a stressed syllable. The majority of English words— and virtually all of the *mommy-daddy-baby-doggie* diminutives that parents heap on children—have the accented syllable up front. Until they're 6 months old, American babies are no more responsive to words like *bigger* than they are to words like *guitar*. But Jusczyk has found that 6- to 10-month-olds develop a clear bias for words with first-syllable accents. They suck more vigorously when they hear such words, regardless of whether they're read from lists or tucked into streams of normal speech. The implication is that children less than a year old hear speech not as a blur of sound but as a series of distinct but meaningless words.

## Meaning

By their first birthday, most kids start linking words to meanings. Amid their streams of sweet, melodic gibberish, they start to name things—ball, cup, bottle, doggie. And even those who don't speak for a while often gesture to show off their mastery of the nose, eyes, ears and toes. These may seem small steps; after all, most 1-year-olds are surrounded by people who insist on pointing and naming every object in sight. But as Pinker observes, making the right connections is a complicated business. How complicated?

Imagine yourself surrounded by people speaking a strange language. A rabbit runs by, and someone shouts, "*Gavagai!*" What does the word mean? "Rabbit" may seem the obvious inference, but it's just one of countless logical alternatives. *Gavagai* could refer to that particular creature, or it could have a range of broader meanings, from "four-legged plant eater" to "furry thing in motion." How do kids get to the right level of generalization? Why don't they spend their lives trying to figure out what words like "rabbit" mean?

Because, says Stanford psychologist Ellen Markman, they come to the game with innate mental biases. Markman has shown that instead of testing endless hypotheses about each word's meaning, kids start from three basic assumptions. First, they figure that labels refer to whole objects, not parts or qualities. Second, they expect labels to denote classes of things (cups, balls, rabbits) rather than individual items. Third, they assume that anything with a name can have only one. These assumptions don't always lead directly to the right inference ("I'm not a noying," Dennis the Menace once told Mr. Wilson, "I'm a cowboy"). But they vastly simplify word learning. In keeping with the "whole object" assumption, a child won't consider a label for "handle" until she has one for "cup." And thanks to the "one label per object" assumption, a child who has mastered the word *cup* never assumes that *handle* is just another way of saying the same thing. "In that situation," says Markman, "the child accepts the possibility that the new word applies to some feature of the object."

Words accrue slowly at first. But around the age of 18 months,

## How to Talk 'Parentese' to Your Child

People the world over alter their way of speaking when they address infants and toddlers. The effects of "parentese" (originally called "motherese") continue to be hotly debated, but "a number of [its] features are likely to facilitate language learning," says linguist Naomi Baron of The American University. Among them:

Higher **pitch** captures a child's attention. Speaking more slowly, and with careful enunciation, makes it easier for the baby to distinguish individual words; emphasizing or repeating one word ("Isn't that a **huuuuuge** huge doggie?") also helps.

**Short utterances** help the child grasp grammar more readily than Faulknerian monologues. Don't abandon complex sentences entirely, though: toddlers whose parents use many dependent clauses ("because . . ." and "which . . .") learn to do so earlier than the children of parents who do not.

**Repeating** a child's utterances ("That's right! It's a birdie") assures her she's been understood. Recasting what the child says ("Want cookie?" "Would you like a cookie?") expands her repertoire. The only aspect of parentese that may impede language development: substituting proper nouns for **pronouns** ("Does Billy want to swing?"). These are tricky to master (your "you" is my "I"), and toddlers should be exposed to them.

### Red Flags

Even normal children whose ears are filled with parentese may refuse to speak. Some delays can be harmless, but those after the age of 3 may affect how well a child will read, write and even think.

- **0-3 months** Does not turn when you speak or repeat sounds like coos.

- **4-6 months** Does not respond to "no" or changes in tone of voice, look around for sources of sound like a doorbell, or babble in speechlike sounds such as p, b and m.

- **7-12 months** Does not recognize words for common items, turn when you call her name, imitate speech sounds or use sounds other than crying to get your attention.

- **1-2 years** Cannot point to pictures in a book that you name or understand simple questions ("Where is your Teddy?").

- **2-3 years** Can't understand differences in meaning ("up" vs. "down"), follow two requests ("please pick up the bottle and give it to me"), string together two or three words or name common objects.

- **3-4 years** Does not answer simple "who," "what" and "where" questions. Cannot be understood by people outside the family, use four-word sentences or pronounce most phonemes correctly. If delays persist until kindergarten, most pediatricians recommend speech therapy.

---

children's abilities explode. Most start acquiring new words at the phenomenal rate of one every two hours—and for the first time, they start combining them. Children don't all reach these milestones on exactly the same schedule; their development rates can vary by a year or more, and there's no evidence that late talkers end up less fluent than early talkers. But by their second birthdays, most kids have socked away 1,000 to 2,000 words and started tossing around two-word strings such as "no nap," "all wet" or "bottle juice."

## Grammar

Once kids can paste two words together, it's not long before they're generating sentences. Between 24 and 30 months, "no nap" may become "I don't want nap," and "bottle juice" may blossom into "I want juice." When kids hit that stage, their repertoires start expanding exponentially. Between 30 and 36 months, most acquire rules for expressing tense (*walk* versus *walked*) and number (*house* versus *houses*), often overextending them to produce statements like "I bringed home three mouses." They also start using "function words"—the *somes*, *woulds*, *whos*, *hows*, and *afters* that enable us to ask either "Do you like milk?" or "Would you like some milk?"

More fundamentally, they discover that words can have radically different meanings depending on how they're strung together. Even before children start combining words on their own, most know the difference between "Big Bird is tickling Cookie Monster" and "Cookie Monster is tickling Big Bird." That awareness marks the zenith of language development. A chimp can learn to label things, and a high-powered computer can process more information in a minute than any person could handle in a lifetime. But neither a chimp nor a mainframe is any match for a runny-nosed 3-year-old when it comes to reporting who did what to whom. When a chimp with a signboard signals "Me banana you banana you," chances are he wants you to give him one, but the utterance could mean almost anything. Three-year-olds don't talk that way. The reason, most linguists agree, is that natural selection has outfitted the human brain with software for grammatical analysis. As MIT linguist Noam Chomsky realized more than 30 yeas ago, the world's languages all build sentences from noun phrases ("The big dog") and verb phrases ("ate my homework"). And toddlers who have never heard of grammar identify them effortlessly.

To confirm that point, psycholinguists Stephen Crain and Mineharu Nakayama once invited 3-, 4- and 5-year-olds to interview a talking "Star Wars" doll (Jabba the Hutt). With a child at his side, one researcher would pull out a picture and suggest asking Jabba about it. For example: "Ask Jabba if the boy who is unhappy is watching Mickey Mouse." You can't compose the right sentence— "Is the boy who is unhappy watching Mickey Mouse?"— unless you recognize *the-boy-who-is-unhappy* as a single noun phrase. As Chomsky would have predicted, the kids got it right every time.

If children's minds were open to all the possible relationships among words, they would never get very far. No one could memorize 140 million sentences, but a kid who masters 25 common recipes for a noun phrase can pro-duce more than that number from scratch. Too much mental flexibility would confine children, Pinker observes; "innate constraints set them free." Not everyone is blessed with those constraints. Kids with a hereditary condition known as Specific Language Impairment, or SLI, never develop certain aspects of grammar, despite their normal IQs. But those are rare exceptions. Most kids are so primed for grammatical rules that they'll invent them if necessary.

Consider hearing adults who take up American Sign Language so they can share it with their deaf children. They tend to fracture phrases and leave verbs unconjugated. Yet their kids still become fluent, grammatical signers. "Children don't need good teachers to master language," says Elissa Newport, a cognitive scientist at the University of Rochester. "They pick up whatever rules they can find, and sharpen and extend them." That, according to University of Hawaii linguist Derek Bickerton, is why the crude pidgins that crop up in mixed-language communities quickly evolve into fully grammatical creoles. When language lacks a coherent grammar, children create one.

That's not to say language requires no nurture. Children raised in complete silence grow deaf to grammar. "Chelsea," whose correctable hearing problem went untreated until she was 31, eventually learned enough words to hold a job in a vet's office. Yet her expressive powers have never surpassed those of a chimp with a signboard. She says things like "The woman is bus the going" or "I Wanda be drive come." Fortunately, Chelsea is a rare exception. Given even a few words to play with, most kids quickly take flight. "You don't need to have left the Stone Age," Pinker says. "You don't need to be middle class." All you need to be is young.

 **Article Review Form at end of book.**

Why do children begin to point? How is pointing related to language development? Give some examples of research findings.

# Starting Point

## George Butterworth

Tugging on her mother's jacket, a small child too young to talk, points her index finger at a puppy in a pet shop window. A geography teacher points to various countries on a map as he calls out their names. An angry father points at a dent in his new car and asks his teen-age son, "How did that happen?"

Pointing with the index finger, arm extended in the direction of the interesting object, remaining fingers curled under the hand, thumb held down and to the side, is a vital part of human communication. Sometimes, it is accompanied by speech; often not. We point at things we know and at things we have never seen before. Pointing can be a way of telling—making a point—or asking. Always, however, the intention is to draw someone's else's attention to an object or event of interest.

Drawing attention to an object or an interesting event is part of communication for a number of species. A hunting dog signals that it has found prey by standing still and "pointing" with its whole body (from nose to tail) and bent foreleg. Vervet monkeys have several predator-specific alarm calls to warn troop members when danger is near. But unlike finger pointing, most such behavior is restricted to specific situations. Will the dog, for example, point to indicate to its owner the whereabouts of a bone that has gotten wedged under the couch? And just how intentional is the signal? Would the dog point at prey or the vervet give an alarm call even if it had no audience?

Finger pointing is apparently unique to humans. Of course, most animals don't have fingers to point with, but even our fellow apes don't point in their natural state. After extensive interactions with humans, apes sometimes use an extended hand to refer to things, but they practically never extend the index finger separately when making the gesture. In a recent study done at Emory University, David Leavens, William Hopkins, and Kim Bard found that a chimpanzee named Clint sometimes uses a form of index finger pointing to draw his trainer's attention to food that has fallen out of reach. Clint, however, has never pointed for the benefit of other chimps, and even with his trainer, he uses his flat hand more often than his index finger. Is there anything special about finger pointing in humans?

Charles Darwin proposed the principle of antithesis to explain how animals convey information. The aggressive posture of a dog preparing to fight, for example, involves many of the same muscles it uses when it adopts the subdued posture of submission.

The postural antithesis of finger pointing is the pincer grip, in which the tip of the index finger and thumb are in opposition. This contrast in the relative position of thumb and index finger is correlated with a change in the focus of attention. In manual tasks involving the pincer grip—holding a pencil, removing a thumbtack, tying shoelaces—the focus is on the object and the job at hand. Pointing, in contrast, directs the attention of another person toward an object some distance off.

Human babies begin to point at about eleven months. (Before they point or understand pointing, they turn their heads in response to other signals—head and eye movements, for example, or shifts in body orientation—that indicate a change in a parent's focus of interest.)

In the 1920s, Russian psychologist Lev Semeonovitch Vygotsky suggested that babies may learn pointing from their mothers and that the gesture begins as a way to request objects that are out of reach. Fabia Franco, of the University of Padua, and I tested this hypothesis. We observed how babies who had just begun to point behaved when placed in a room with attractive toys just out of reach and with dolls some way off. We found that the babies (seated in highchairs next to their mothers) both reached for and pointed at the nearby toys, whereas the distant dolls elicited only pointing. Infants looked at their mothers, both while pointing and immediately afterward, to check whether they had succeeded in redirecting their attention.

In another study, Franco, Paula Perruchini (a student from the University of Rome), and I found that a baby will also point to redirect the attention of another baby, even though neither can yet speak. This time, mothers were seated behind their babies, out of their sight. Our results convinced us that pointing originates as a declaration of interest and a wish to share the experience of an object, not as a consequence of failing to get ahold of it.

Nobuo Masataka, of the Primate Research Center of Kyoto University, found that while interacting with their mothers, three-month-old human babies extend their index fingers rhythmically and make speechlike cooing sounds at the same time. This gesture, a precursor of pointing, together with the results of other experiments Franco and I conducted, suggests that babies are not taught to point by adults. Mothers validate the gesture through their own reactions, but they do not create it.

A number of studies show that finger pointing is related to both gesture and speech. Paul Morissette, of the University of Montreal, and I found that the age at which a baby first points is a good predictor of its progress in understanding language—as measured by the number of indicative gestures (such as pointing with a flat hand or closed fist, clapping, or waving) in the baby's repertoire five months later and how many animal noises the baby recognizes. Margaret Harris, of the University of London, has shown that babies first point in the same week they begin to understand names for objects, such as cat and ball.

Pointing does not necessarily precede a baby's first word. In one of our studies, Morissette and I found that the average age of pointing was 327 days for girls and 350 days for boys. At approximately the same ages, girls already had a vocabulary of three to four words; boys, one. The rate of speech acquisition, however, is correlated with the onset of pointing. Luigi Camioni, of the University of Rome, has found that the earlier babies begin to point, the more words they know at twenty months of age.

Lida Graupner (a postdoctoral fellow working in my laboratory) and I recently established that as long as an object is in the middle of their field of view, most babies are more likely to point with their right hand than their left. (For objects on the periphery, they point with the hand on the same side of the target.) This preference for the right hand may reflect the relative contributions of the left and right parietal areas of the brain (known to be active when adults pay attention to objects in their right or left visual field) and may suggest connections in the nervous system between areas of the brain that control pointing and those involved in speech perception and production. In right-handed people, the major speech centers are located in the left hemisphere, which is the same side of the brain that controls the right hand.

Graupner, Franco, and I also found that when we added sound to the dolls, so that they spoke to the baby as they moved (saying "Hello, baby" and making squeaky sounds like those of a Walt Disney cartoon character), fifteen-month-old baby girls were more likely than boys of the same age to point with the right hand. Such coordination between seeing, hearing, and right-handed pointing may help them learn that sounds refer to things and may explain the often reported advantage many girls enjoy in acquiring speech.

The frequency and speed with which babies point depend on the complexity of the event they have observed. At La-Trobe University in Australia, Beryl McKenzie and I showed babies a toy clown designed to do three things, separately or in combination: rotate on its axis, travel slowly across the babies' field of vision, and "vanish" behind a screen. The more complicated the combination of movements, the longer it took a baby to point. When we combined all three movements, babies generally didn't start pointing for a full ten seconds after the clown disappeared. After this, however, the babies began pointing, vocalizing excitedly (often imitating the squeaky sounds of the clown), and checking with their mothers. It was as though the babies were pointing into the past, as if to say, "Wow, did you see that?"

Once babies start to point with the index finger, they much prefer this to other indicative gestures in their repertoire, such as extending a flat hand or closed fist. Pointing turns out to be more than a means of reorienting someone else's attention; it is a crucial step on the road to language.

 **Article Review Form at end of book.**

# WiseGuide Wrap-Up

- Parentese, the high-pitched and exaggerated speech directed to the young, seems to facilitate speech. Vowel distortions help infants learn the key feature of language sounds.

- Children cry to communicate basic needs for food, warmth, comfort, and attention. Unfortunately, about 20% of infants are problem criers. Parents' consistent responses to cries are important, more so than their success at soothing or determining the underlying causes.

- Before the age of 10 months, infants can distinguish the sounds of all languages. After this age, they begin to narrow their focus to only the sounds they hear around them.

- By age 1, children begin to link words to their meanings and to name things. Innate mental biases enable children to rapidly figure out what words mean. A similar bias seems responsible for the acquisition of grammar.

- Children begin to use pointing to direct the attention of others by 11 months of age. It is a skill validated by the reactions of others but not taught. Its onset is predictive of children's rate of speech acquisition and preschool vocabulary size.

## R.E.A.L. Sites

This list provides a print preview of typical **coursewise** R.E.A.L. sites. There are over 100 such sites at the **courselinks**™ site. The danger in printing URLs is that web sites can change overnight. As we went to press, these sites were functional using the URLs provided. If you come across one that isn't, please let us know via email to: webmaster@coursewise.com. Use your Passport to access the most current list of R.E.A.L. sites at the **courselinks**™ site.

**Site name:** Measuring Your Child's Speech and Hearing Development

**URL:** http://family.disney.com/Features/family_1997_09/tole/tole97 speech/tole97speech.html

**Why is it R.E.A.L.?** As these readings indicate, parents may begin to wonder if their child is progressing normally with respect to speech and language development. This article describes insights into windows of opportunity for children to develop normal speech and language. Visit this site and compose your own "developmental milestones" chart for normal development. Prepare a list of signs for parents and professionals to look for when evaluating children for possible problems.

**Site name:** Fostering Speech and Language Skills

**URL:** http://family.disney.com/Features/family_1998_05/char/char58 speech/char58speech.html

**Why is it R.E.A.L.?** After reading the articles in this section, you may be wondering what parents and others can do to foster good speech and language skill development. This article provides an overview of normal development and then makes suggestions for how to improve skills. Visit one or two daycare facilities and observe the type of language that caregivers model for the children in the centers. Are they demonstrating any of the characteristics mentioned in the article? Observe the older children in the daycare. Chances are they are engaging in some of the techniques that comprise "parentese," discussed in the articles you read. How do the younger children respond to this type of communication?

# section

**7**

## Learning Objectives

- Present information on the developmental phases of play and its importance in social, emotional, and cognitive growth.

- Provide an overview of normal peer influence during childhood and adolescence.

- Discuss why children need to conform to the styles and behaviors of their peers and why "belonging" is important.

- Examine childhood loneliness—its causes and possible solutions.

# Socialization

**WiseGuide Intro**

In recent years, the importance of playing and interacting with peers, having positive friendships, and being included in social networks has gained recognition and has been shown to influence success in many areas of life. Play behaviors of young children have traditionally been discussed in terms of developmental stages, including solitary, parallel, and group play. The socialization value of pretense play has also received considerable attention. Current findings demonstrate that engagement in pretend play promotes advancements in cognitive, emotional, and language development. Vygotsky specifically connected the emergence of impulse control, rule formulation, and socially cooperative behavior to make-believe play. Early play behaviors have also been linked to social and academic competence in later childhood.

With the transition to early childhood, play behavior becomes increasingly peer-centered. Children begin to develop friendships based on similarities, mutual liking, lack of conflict, and, ultimately, intimacy needs. Typically, as friends become more important and peer interactions increase, parents become concerned with peer influences. Research indicates that the nature of this influence is reciprocal. More important, mutual influence increases the similarity between friends but does not shift behavior or attitudes in either a positive or negative direction. However, early friendships do serve as the beginning links to the larger peer group and, with this, rising pressures to conform.

Understanding the need to conform and "fit in" with peers is an arduous task for parents and educators. With the onset of the preteen years, children begin to separate from the family unit and to establish their place in the larger world. This need to break free from parental and family norms is evidenced in the preteens' desire to follow fads and fashions. In addition, preteens may feel the need to belong to cliques, or small crowds of specific peers. As these pressures to conform and belong grow, so does the need for parental support and continued expression of positive family values.

Children who do not experience the separation from family and integration into the larger peer group are at risk for experiencing loneliness and social isolation. Recent research indicates that children's concepts of loneliness are similar to those of adults. Factors often contributing to feelings of loneliness for children include the loss of friends due to conflicts, moves, deaths, or divorce and frequent rejection by playmates. Children who are isolated and rejected by peers express feelings of social dissatisfaction and loneliness. Such feelings may lead to further deterioration of social relationships and academic performance. Early interventions by teachers, counselors, and parents can do much to alleviate children's social skill deficits and perceptions of loneliness.

## Thinking Beyond the Facts

The importance of play and friendships in the lives of children should be clear after reading the articles in this section on socialization. Play is no longer viewed as simply a free-spirited activity that children enjoy. Rather, it is recognized as an important and primary means through which children learn to socialize, problem solve, communicate effectively, and more. Given the value of play in terms of learning and the eagerness of children to engage in playful activities, why don't teachers use play to teach content-specific lessons? How might lessons in math, social studies, reading, and science be incorporated into play? Do you think a curriculum of play could be effective? For which subjects might it be valuable? for which ages or grades? Where are structured approaches to learning probably more effective than playful ones?

Though preschoolers certainly enjoy peer interactions and form friendships, the impact of friends' attitudes and behaviors becomes most evident by elementary school age. Children begin to distinguish best friends from mere classmates, find comfort in peer groups, and model themselves after peers they admire most. For most, peer acceptance comes easily, and having close friends provides a realm for learning about themselves, others, and the world. But, for a few, peer rejection and feelings of inadequacy, self-doubt, and loneliness are never ending. Have you ever felt left out or rejected by classmates? Could you identify in- and out-groups in your schools? Do you remember acting unkindly toward another child because all your friends did too? Since peer rejection can be devastating for the target child, should teachers and parents intervene? If so, how, without embarrassing the targeted child and fueling further teasing? With respect to peers' influence on attitudes and behaviors, is it the parents' place to reject and select their children's friendship options? How much and in what areas should parents attempt to control friendship matters? Should schools "outlaw" the formation of cliques? For more information on patterns of early friendships, visit web sites on play, pretend, social skill development and training, advice to parents, and gang behaviors.

How do Piaget and Vygotsky differ in their views of the origins of pretend play? Play and pretend are said to enhance development in many areas. Give some examples of this enhancement.

# Vygotsky's Theory
## The importance of make-believe play

**Laura E. Berk**

In most theories of cognition and cognitive development, the social and the cognitive make contact only minimally. Rather than being truly joined and interactive, they are viewed as separate domains of functioning. At best, the social world is a surrounding context for cognitive activity, not an integral part of it. Early childhood educators have a long tradition of regarding what the young child knows as personally rather than socially constructed—a tradition that follows from the massive contributions of Piaget's cognitive-developmental theory to our field.

The ideas of the Russian developmental psychologist Lev Vygotsky, who early in this century forged an innovative theory granting great importance to social and cultural experience in development, have gained increasing visibility over the past decade. In Vygotsky's ([1933] 1978) sociocultural theory, the "mind extends beyond the skin" and is inseparably joined with other minds (Wertsch 1991, p. 90). Social experience shapes the ways of thinking and interpreting the

world available to individuals. And language plays a crucial role in a socially formed mind because it is our primary avenue of communication and mental contact with others, it serves as the major means by which social experience is represented psychologically, and it is an indispensable tool for thought (Vygotsky [1934] 1987). A basic premise of Vygotsky's theory is that all uniquely human, higher forms of mental activity are jointly constructed and transferred to children through dialogues with other people.

Vygotsky's ideas are stimulating a host of new ways to educate young children that emphasize opportunities for discussion and joint problem solving. A central Vygotskian concept that has played a formative role in these efforts is the *zone of proximal development*, which refers to a range of tasks that the child cannot yet handle alone but can accomplish with the help of adults and more skilled peers. As children engage in cooperative dialogues with more mature partners, they internalize the language of these interactions and use it to organize their independent efforts in the same way (Berk 1992). According to so-

ciocultural theory, supportive guidance from adults that creates a *scaffold* for children's learning is essential for their cognitive development. Such communication sensitively adjusts to children's momentary progress, offering the necessary assistance for mastery while prompting children to take over more responsibility for the task as their skill increases (Wood & Middleton 1975; Wood 1989). Furthermore, *cooperative learning*—in which small groups of peers at varying levels of competence share responsibility and resolve differences of opinion as they work toward a common goal—also fosters cognitive maturity (Forman 1987; Tudge 1992).

These Vygotskian ideas about teaching and learning have largely been implemented in academically relevant early childhood contexts, such as literacy, mathematics, and science (Moll 1990; Forman, Minick, & Stone 1993); but a close look at Vygotsky's writings reveals that they recur as major themes in his view of play. Although Vygotsky's works contain only a brief 12-page statement about play, his discussion is provocative, innovative, and ahead of his time. In accord with his emphasis on social experience and language as vital forces in cognitive development, Vygotsky ([1933] 1978) emphasized representational play—the make-believe that blossoms during the preschool years and evolves into the games with rules that dominate middle childhood. Vygotsky accorded fantasy play a prominent place in his theory, granting it the status of a "leading factor in development" (p. 101), as the following frequently quoted remarks reveal:

Play creates a zone of proximal development in the child. In play, the child always behaves beyond his average age, above his daily behavior; in play it is as though he were a head taller than himself. As in the focus of a magnifying glass, play contains all developmental tendencies in a condensed form and is itself a major source of development. (p. 102)

As we discuss Vygotsky's theory and the research stimulated by it, we will see that he situated play squarely within a sociocultural context. Adults and peers scaffold young children's play, nurturing the transition to make-believe and its elaboration throughout the preschool years. Representational play serves as a unique, broadly influential zone of proximal development within which *children advance themselves* to ever-higher levels of psychological functioning. Consequently, Vygotsky's theory has much to say to teachers about the importance of promoting make-believe in preschool and child care programs.

## Development and Significance of Make-Believe Play

Vygotsky began his consideration of the importance of play by suggesting that if we can identify its defining features, we can gain insight into its functions in development. To isolate the distinctiveness of play, Vygotsky explored characteristics regarded by other theorists as central to playful activity and found them wanting. For example, the common assumption that play is pleasurable activity is not specific to play. Many other experiences, such as eating a favorite treat, being granted the undivided attention of a parent, or listening to an exciting story, are at least as gratifying and sometimes more so than is play. Furthermore, certain playful experiences—games that can be won or lost—are not pure fun for the child when they result in disappointing outcomes.

A second way of understanding play is to highlight its symbolic features, as Piaget ([1945] 1951) did in his characterization of make-believe as a means through which children practice representational schemes. Yet symbolism is another feature that is not exclusive to play. Both Piaget and Vygotsky noted that it also characterizes language, artistic, and literacy activities during the preschool years.

Vygotsky concluded that play has two critical features that, when combined, describe its uniqueness and shed light on its role in development. First, all representational play *creates an imaginary situation* that permits the child to grapple with unrealizable desires. Vygotsky pointed out that fantasy play first appears at a time when children must learn to postpone gratification of impulses and accept the fact that certain desires will remain unsatisfied. During the second year, caregivers begin to insist that toddlers delay gratification (e.g., wait for a turn) and acquire socially approved behaviors involving safety, respect for property, self-care (e.g., washing hands), and everyday routines (e.g., putting toys away) (Gralinski & Kopp 1993).

The creation of an imaginary situation in play, however, has often been assumed to be a way in which children attain immediate fulfillment of desires not satisfied in real life. Vygotsky pointed out that this commonly held belief is not correct. A second feature of all representational play is that it *contains rules for behavior* that children must follow to successfully act out the play scene. Games that appear in the late preschool period and flourish during the school years are clearly rule based. Even the simplest imaginative situations created by very young children proceed in accord with social rules, although the rules are not laid down in advance. For example, a child pretending to go to sleep follows the rules of bedtime behavior. Another child, imagining himself to be a father and a doll to be a child, conforms to the rules of parental behavior. Yet a third child playing astronaut observes the rules of shuttle launch and space walk. Vygotsky ([1933] 1978) concluded, "Whenever there is an imaginary situation, there are rules" (p. 95). A child cannot behave in an imaginary situation without rules.

These attributes of play—an imaginary situation governed by rules—provide the key to its role in development. According to Vygotsky, play supports the emergence of two complementary capacities: (a) the ability to separate thought from actions and objects, and (b) the capacity to renounce impulsive action in favor of deliberate, self-regulatory activity.

## Separating Thought from Actions and Objects

In creating an imaginary situation, children learn to act not just in response to external stimuli but also in accord with internal ideas. Infants and very young children, Vygotsky ([1933] 1978) explained, are reactive beings; momentary perceptions trigger their behavior. A baby who sees an attractive toy grabs for it without delay. A toddler runs after a ball that has rolled into the street without considering consequences. "[I]n play, things lose their determining force. *The child sees one thing but acts differently in relation to what he sees. Thus, a condition is reached in which the child begins to act independently of what he sees*" (p. 97).

Just how does imaginative play help children separate thought from the surrounding world and rely on ideas to guide behavior? According to Vygotsky, the object substitutions that characterize make-believe are crucial in this process. When children use a stick to represent a horse or a folded blanket to represent a sleeping baby, their relation to reality is dramatically changed. The stick becomes a pivot for separating the meaning "horse" from a real horse; similarly, the blanket becomes a pivot for distinguishing the meaning "baby" from a real baby. This adjustment in thinking occurs because children change the substitute object's real meaning when they behave toward it in a pretend fashion.

Vygotsky emphasized that young children have difficulty severing thinking—or the meaning of words—from objects; they do so only gradually. Indeed, such research reveals that object substitutions become more flexible as children get older. In early pretense, toddlers use only realistic objects—for example, a toy telephone to talk into or a cup to drink from. Around age 2, children use less realistic toys, such as a block for a telephone receiver. Sometime during the third year, children can imagine objects and events without any direct support from the real world, as when they say to a play partner, "I'm calling Susie on the phone!" while pretending to dial with their hands or without acting out the event at all. By this time, a play symbol no longer has to resemble the object or behavior for which it stands (Bretherton et al. 1984; Corrigan 1987).

According to Vygotsky ([1930] 1990), in helping children separate meaning from objects, the pretending of early childhood serves as vital preparation for the much later development of abstract thought, in which symbols are manipulated and propositions evaluated without referring to the real world. And in detaching meaning from behavior, make-believe also helps teach children to choose deliberately from among alternative courses of action. This capacity to think in a planful, self-regulatory fashion is also strengthened by the rule-based nature of play, as we will see in the following section.

## Renouncing Impulsive Action

Vygotsky pointed out that the imaginative play of children contains an interesting paradox. In play, children do what they most feel like doing, and to an outside observer, the play of preschoolers appears free and spontaneous. Nevertheless, play constantly demands that children act against their immediate impulses because they must subject themselves to the rules of the make-believe context or the game they have chosen to play. According to Vygotsky ([1933] 1978), free play is not really "free"; instead, it requires self-restraint—willingly following social rules. As a result, in play the young child displays many capacities that "will become her basic level of real action and morality" in the future (p. 100). By enacting rules in make-believe, children come to better understand social norms and expectations and strive to behave in ways that uphold them. For example, a child occupying the role of parent in a household scene starts to become dimly aware of parental responsibilities in real situations and gains insight into the rule-governed nature of the parent-child relationship (Haight & Miller 1993).

When we look at the development of play from early to middle childhood, the most obvious way in which it changes is that it increasingly emphasizes rules. The greater stress on the rule-oriented aspect of play over time means that children gradually become more conscious of the goals of their play activities. Vygotsky ([1933] 1978) summarized. "The development from games with an overt imaginary situation and covert rules to games with overt rules and a covert imaginary situation outlines the evolution of children's play" (p. 96). From this perspective, the fantasy play of the preschool years is essential for further development of play in middle childhood—specifically, for movement toward game play, which provides additional instruction in setting goals, regulating one's behavior in pursuit of those goals, and subordinating action to rules rather than to impulse—in short, for becoming a cooperative and productive member of society. Play, in Vygotsky's theory, is the preeminent educational activity of early childhood.

## Impact of Imaginative Play on Development

Was Vygotsky correct in stating that make-believe serves as a zone of proximal development, supporting the emergence and refinement of a wide variety of competencies? A careful examination of his theory reveals that the benefits of play are complex and indirect; they may take years to be realized (Nicolopoulou 1991). Still, considerable support exists for Vygotsky's view that play contributes to the development of a diverse array of capacities in the young child.

Sociodramatic play, the coordinated and reciprocal make-believe with peers that emerges around age 2 1/2 and increases rapidly until age 4 to 5, has been studied thoroughly. Compared to social nonpretend activities (such as drawing or putting together puzzles), during social pretend activities, preschoolers' interactions last longer, show more involvement, draw larger numbers of children into the activity, and are more cooperative (Connolly, Doyle, & Reznick 1988). When we consider these findings from the standpoint of Vygotsky's emphasis on the social origins of cognition, it is not surprising that preschoolers who spend more time at sociodramataic play are advanced in general intellectual development and show an enhanced ability to understand the feelings of others. They are also seen as more socially competent by their teachers (Burns & Brainerd 1979; Connolly & Doyle 1984).

A growing body of research reveals that make-believe play strengthens a variety of specific mental abilities. For example, it promotes memory. In a study in which 4- and 5-year-olds were asked either to remember a set of toys or to play with them, the play condition produced far better recall. Rather than just naming or touching the objects (strategies applied in the "remember" condition), children who played with the toys engaged in many spontaneous organizations and uses of the materials that enabled them to memorize effortlessly (Newman 1990). In this way, play may provide a vital foundation for more sophisticated memory strategies mastered during middle childhood that depend on establishing meaningful relationships among to-be-remembered information. Other research confirms that opportunities to engage in fantasy play promote children's storytelling and story memory (Saltz, Dixon, & Johnson 1977; Pellegrini & Galda 1982).

Language is also greatly enriched by play experiences. As children engage in play talk, they often correct one another's errors, either directly or by demonstrating acceptable ways to speak. For example, in enacting a telephone conversation, one kindergartner said, "Hello, come to my house please." Her play partner quickly countered with appropriate telephone greeting behavior: "No, first you've get to say 'what are you doing'" (Ervin-Tripp 1991, p. 90). Vocabulary expands during make-believe as children introduce new words they have heard during recent experiences. One 4-year-old playing nurse remarked to an agemate, "I'm going to give you a temperature" (p. 90). Although her first use of the term was not correct, active experimentation increases the chances that she will notice more about the context in which "temperature" is applied and move toward correct usage. Furthermore, the linguistic skills required to express different points of view, resolve disputes, and persuade peers to collaborate in play are numerous. Play offers an arena in which all facets of conversational dialogue can be extended.

Make-believe also fosters young children's ability to reason about impossible or absurd situations—a finding highly consistent with Vygotsky's emphasis that fantasy play assists children in separating meanings from the objects for which they stand. A repeated finding in the cognitive development literature is that through much of early and middle childhood, thinking is tied to the here and now—to concrete reality; but under certain conditions, young children attain a "theoretical" mode of reasoning.

Consider the following syllogism: All cats bark. Rex is a cat. Does Rex bark? Researchers had a group of 4- to 6-year-olds act out problems like this with toys. A second group of children were told that the events were taking place on a pretend planet rather than on Earth. A control group merely listened and answered the question. Children in the two "play" conditions gave more theoretical than factual responses and were also able to justify their answers with theoretical ideas—for example, "In the story, cats bark, so we can pretend they bark" (Dias & Harris 1988, 1990). Entering the pretend mode seems to enable children to reason with contrary facts as if they were true—findings that provide striking verification of Vygotsky's ([1933] 1978) assumption that in play, the child is well "beyond his average age, above his daily behavior" (p. 102).

Finally, young children who especially enjoy pretending or who are given encouragement to engage in fantasy play score higher on tests of imagination and creativity. When children use play objects in novel ways, the objects seem to stimulate the discovery of new relationships and enhance children's ability to think flexibly and inventively (Dansky 1980; Pepler & Ross 1981).

In sum, fantasy play contributes to social maturity and the construction of diverse aspects of cognition. For people who have questioned whether play activities, so indigenous and absorbing to children, must be curbed in favor of more "productive" activities or whether play constitutes a powerful zone of proximal development, the findings just reviewed clearly grant play a legitimate and fruitful place in children's lives.

## Scaffolding Children's Make-Believe Play

The Piagetian view, dominant for the past three decades, claims that make-believe emerges spontaneously when children become capable of representational thought. Piaget and his followers assumed that children lack the cognitive competencies to share play symbols with others—both adults and peers—until well into the preschool period (e.g., Fein 1981). Not until recently have researchers seriously addressed the social context of children's play experiences. Their findings challenge the notion that fantasy play is an unprompted phenomenon arising solely from tendencies within the child. Instead, new evidence suggests that make-believe, like other higher mental functions, is the product of social collaboration.

## Adult–Child Play

Twenty-four-month-old Elizabeth is being carried upstairs for a diaper change by her mother.

**Elizabeth:** My going Sherman Dairy. (Sherman Dairy is the family's favorite dessert restaurant.)

**Mother:** You're going to Sherman Dairy?

**Elizabeth:** Yeah.

**Mother:** Is Andrew the cook? (Andrew is a 4-year-old friend who is playing with Elizabeth's sister.)

**Elizabeth:** Yep. (Pause) *My* cook.

**Mother:** (Putting Elizabeth on the changing table and beginning to change her) You're the cook? You can cook with your dishes, right? Do you have some pots and pans?

**Elizabeth:** Yep. (Adapted from Haight & Miller 1993, p. 46)

In the play sequence above, 2-year-old Elizabeth initiates a make-believe scenario in which a trip upstairs for a diaper change is transformed into a journey to buy ice cream. Her mother encourages her to expand the imaginative theme and act it out with toys. The play episode is elaborated and sustained as her mother asks questions that help Elizabeth clarify her intentions and think of new ideas.

Vygotskian-based research on play emphasizes that make-believe is, from its beginnings, a social activity (El'konin 1966; Garvey 1990). In Western industrialized societies, play first appears between caregivers and children; children initially learn pretense and games under the supportive guidance of experts. From these interactions, children acquire the communicative conventions, social skills, and representational capacities that permit them to carry out make-believe on their own.

In the most extensive study of caregiver scaffolding of make-believe, Haight and Miller (1993) followed the development of pretend play at home of nine middle-class children between 1 and 4 years of age. Social make-believe was common across the entire age span, consuming from 68 to 75%

of children's total pretend time. Furthermore, mothers were the children's principal play partners until 3 years of age. By age 4, children played approximately the same amount with their mothers as they did with other children (siblings and peers). Children's pretending with mothers, however, was not caused by a lack of child playmates at the youngest ages. Several investigations reveal that 1- and 2-year-olds who have fairly continuous access to other children prefer to play with their mothers (Dunn & Dale 1984; Miller & Garvey 1984). These findings confirm the Vygotskian view that play with caregivers gradually gives way to play with peers as children's competence increases.

Further evidence that caregivers teach toddlers to pretend stems from Haight and Miller's observation that at 12 months, make-believe was fairly one sided; almost all play episodes were initiated by mothers. From age 2 on, when pretending was better established, mothers and children displayed mutual interest in getting make-believe started; half of pretend episodes were initiated by each. At all ages, mothers typically followed the child's lead and elaborated on the child's contribution. Thus, although pretense was first introduced to 12-month-olds by their mothers, it quickly became a joint activity in which both partners participated actively in an imaginative dialogue and in which the adult gradually released responsibility to the child for creating and guiding the fantasy theme.

Children's object substitutions during make-believe are also largely traceable to episodes in which their mothers showed them how to engage in object renaming or suggested a pretend action to the child (Smolucha 1992). By the time their children are 2 years old, mothers talk more about nonexistent fantasy objects, a change that may prompt children to widen the range of object substitutions in their play (Kavanaugh, Whittington, & Cerbone 1983). Furthermore, many parents and early childhood teachers surround children with toys designed to stimulate pretend themes. By offering an array of objects specialized for make-believe, caregivers communicate to children that pretense is a valued activity and maximize opportunities to collaborate with them in integrating props into fantasy scenes.

## Consequences of Supportive Caregiver-Child Play

In their longitudinal study, Haight and Miller (1993) carefully examined the play themes of mother-child pretense and found that it appeared to serve a variety of functions, including communicating feelings, expressing and working through conflicts, enlivening daily routines, and teaching lessons. These diverse social uses of caregiver-child play suggest that adult support and expansion of preschoolers' make-believe should facilitate all the developmental outcomes of play already discussed, although as yet, no systematic research on the topic exists.

Accumulating evidence does show that children's make-believe play with their mothers is more sustained and complex than is their solitary make-believe play. One- to 3-year-olds engage in more than twice as much make-believe while playing with mothers than while playing alone. In addition, caregiver support leads early make-believe to include more elaborate themes (Dunn &

Wooding 1977; O'Connell & Bretherton 1984; Zukow 1986; Slade 1987; Fiese 1990; Tamis-LeMonda & Bornstein 1991; Haight & Miller 1993; O'Reilly & Bornstein 1993). In line with Vygotsky's zone of proximal development, very young children, for whom make-believe is just emerging, act more competently when playing with a mature partner than they otherwise would. In Haight and Miller's study, suggestive evidence emerged that mother-child play promotes effective child-child play. Children whose mothers ranked high in pretending when their children were 1 year old ranked high in peer play at 4 years. And children of the most enthusiastic and imaginative parents were among the most highly skilled preschool pretenders.

## Critical Features of Adult-Child Play

Although mother-child play has been granted considerable research attention, a search of the literature revealed no studies of teachers' participation in young children's play. Yet evidence on the effect of adult-child play suggests that it is vital for teachers in preschool and child care programs to engage in joint play with children.

Teachers' effective playful involvement with children requires early childhood environments that are developmentally appropriate. Especially important are generous adult-child ratios, a stable staff that relates to children sensitively and responsively, and settings that are richly equipped to offer varied opportunities for make-believe. These factors are critical because they ensure that teachers have the necessary time, rapport, and play props to en-

courage children's imaginative contributions and to scaffold them toward social pretend play with peers.

At the same time, adults walk a fine line in making effective contributions to children's pretense. The power of adult-child play to foster development is undermined by communication that is too overpowering or one sided. Fiese (1990) found that maternal questioning, instructing, and intrusiveness (initiating a new activity unrelated to the child's current pattern of play) led to immature, simple exploratory play in young children. In contrast, turn taking and joint involvement in a shared activity resulted in high levels of pretense. Furthermore, adult intervention that recognizes children's current level of cognitive competence and builds on it is most successful in involving children. Lucariello (1987) reported that when 24- to 29-month-olds were familiar with a play theme suggested by their mother, both partners displayed advanced levels of imaginative activity and constructed the scenario together. When the theme was unfamiliar, the mother took nearly total responsibility for pretense.

## Promoting Social Pretend Play with Peers

At preschool, Jason joins a group of children in the block area for a space shuttle launch. "That can be our control tower," he suggests to Vance, pointing to a corner by a bookshelf.

"Wait, I gotta get it all ready," states Lynette, who is still arranging the astronauts (two dolls and a teddy bear) inside a circle of large blocks, which represent the rocket.

"Countdown!" Jason announces, speaking into a small wooden block, his pretend walkie-talkie.

"Five, six, two, four, one, blastoff!" responds Vance, commander of the control tower.

Lynette makes one of the dolls push a pretend button and reports, "Brrm, brrm, they're going up!" (Berk 1993, p. 311)

When pretending with peers, children make use of the many competencies they acquire through their play with adults. Yet pretend play with peers must also be responsive and cooperative to result in satisfying play experiences and to serve as a zone of proximal development in which children advance their skills and understanding. According to Göncü (1993), social play with peers requires *intersubjectivity*—a process whereby individuals involved in the same activity who begin with different perspectives arrive at a shared understanding. In the play episode just described, the children achieve a high level of intersubjectivity as they coordinate several roles in an elaborate plot and respond in a smooth, complementary fashion to each other's contributions.

The importance of intersubjectivity for peer social play is suggested by the work of several major theorists. Piaget ([1945] 1951) notes that for children to play together, they must collectively construct play symbols. Likewise, Vygotsky ([1933] 1978) claimed that in pretense with peers, children jointly develop rules that guide social activity. And Parten (1932) labeled the most advanced form of peer social participation *cooperative play*, in which children orient toward a common goal by negotiating plans, roles, and divisions of labor.

Recent evidence indicates that intersubjectivity among peer partners increases substantially during the preschool years, as the amount of time children devote to sociodramatic play rises. Between 3 and 4-1/2 years, children engage in more extensions and affirmations of their partners' messages and fewer disagreements, assertions of their own opinions, and irrelevant statements during play (Göncü 1993). Interestingly, preschoolers have much more difficulty establishing a cooperative, shared framework in "closed-end" problem solving, in which they must orient toward a single correct solution to a task (Tudge & Rogoff 1987). Here again is an example of how children's competence during play is advanced compared to other contexts. By middle childhood, the social skills mastered during sociodramatic activities generalize to nonplay activities.

When we look at the features of harmonious child-child play, the relevance of warm, responsive adult communication for encouraging such play becomes even clearer. Even after sociodramatic play is well underway and adults have reduced their play involvement, teachers need to guide children toward effective relations with agemates. Observational evidence indicates that teachers rarely mediate peer interaction except when intense disagreements arise that threaten classroom order or children's safety. When teachers do step in, they almost always use directive strategies, in which they tell children what to do or say (e.g., "Ask Daniel if you can have the fire truck next") or solve the problem for them (e.g., "Jessica was playing with that toy first, so you can have a turn after her") (File 1993, p. 352).

A Vygotskian-based approach to facilitating peer interaction requires that teachers tailor their intervention to children's current capacities and use techniques that help children regulate their own behavior. To implement intervention in this way, teachers must acquire detailed knowledge of individual children's social skills—the type of information teachers typically gather only for the cognitive domain. When intervening, they need to use a range of teaching strategies because (like cognitive development) the support that is appropriate for scaffolding social development varies from child to child and changes with age. At times the adult might model a skill or give the child examples of strategies (e.g., "You could tell Paul, 'I want a turn'"). At other times, she might ask the child to engage in problem solving ("What could you do if you want a turn?") (File 1993, p. 356). In each instance, the teacher selects a level of support that best matches the child's abilities and momentary needs and then pulls back as the child acquires new social skills.

Children can be socialized into sociodramatic play by a variety of expert partners. In a recent comparison of the make-believe play of American and Mexican siblings, Farver (1993) found that American 3-1/2- to 7-year-olds tended to rely on intrusive tactics; they more often instructed, directed, and rejected their younger siblings' contributions. In contrast, Mexican children used more behaviors that gently facilitated—invitations to join, comments on the younger child's actions, suggestions, and positive affect. In this respect, Mexican older siblings were similar to American mothers in their scaffolding of play, a skill that appeared to be fostered by the Mexican culture's assignment of caregiving responsibilities to older brothers and sisters.

These findings suggest that multi-age groupings in early childhood programs offer additional opportunities to promote make-believe and that older siblings from ethnic-minority families may be particularly adept at such scaffolding—indeed, they may be as capable as adults! Because of their limited experience with the caregiving role and their more conflictual relationships with siblings, children from ethnic-majority families may need more assistance in learning how to play effectively with younger peers. In classrooms with a multicultural mix of children, children of ethnic minorities who are skilled at scaffolding can serve as models and scaffolders for agemates, showing them how to engage young children in pretense.

## Conclusion

The vast literature on children's play reveals that its contributions to child development can be looked at from diverse vantage points. Psychoanalytic theorists have highlighted the emotionally integrative function of pretense, pointing out that anxiety-provoking events—such as a visit to the doctor's office or discipline by a parent—are likely to be revisited in the young child's play but with roles reversed so that the child is in command and compensates for unpleasant experiences in real life. Piaget underscored the opportunities that make-believe affords for exercising symbolic schemes. And all theorists recognize that pretense permits children to become familiar with social role possibilities in their culture, proving important insights into the link between self and wider society.

Vygotsky's special emphasis on the imaginative and rule-based nature of play adds an additional perspective to the viewpoints just mentioned—one that highlights the critical role of make-believe in developing reflective thought as well as self-regulatory and socially cooperative behavior. For teachers who have always made sure that play is a central feature of the early childhood curriculum, Vygotsky's theory offers yet another justification for play's prominent place in programs for young children. For other teachers whose concern with academic progress has led them to neglect play, Vygotsky's theory provides a convincing argument for change—a powerful account of why pretense is the ultimate activity for nurturing early childhood capacities that are crucial for academic as well as later-life success.

## References

Berk, L.E. 1992. Children's private speech: An overview of theory and the status of research. In *Private speech: From social interaction to self-regulation*, eds. R.M. Diaz, & L.E. Berk. 17–53. Hillsdale, NJ: Erlbaum.

Berk, L.E. 1993. *Infants, children, and adolescents*. Boston: Allyn & Bacon

Bretherton, I., B. O'Connell, C. Shore, & E. Bates. 1984. The effect of contextual variation on symbolic play: Development from 20 to 28 months. In *Symbolic play and the development of social understanding*, ed. I. Bretherton. 271–98. New York: Academic.

Burns, S.M., & C.J. Brainerd. 1979. Effects of constructive and dramatic play on perspective taking in very young children. *Developmental Psychology* 15: 512–21.

Connolly, J.A., & A.B. Doyle. 1984. Relations of social fantasy play to social competence in preschoolers. *Developmental Psychology* 20: 797–806.

Connolly, J.A., A.B. Doyle, & E. Reznick. 1988. Social pretend play and social interaction in preschoolers. *Journal of Applied Developmental Psychology* 9: 301–13.

Corrigan, R. 1987. A developmental sequence of actor-object pretend play in young children. *Merrill-Palmer Quarterly* 33: 87–106.

Dansky, J.L. 1980. Make-believe: A mediator of the relationship between play and associative fluency. *Child Development* 51: 576–79.

Dias, M.G., & P.L. Harris. 1988. The effect of make-believe play on deductive reasoning. *British Journal of Developmental Psychology* 6: 207–21.

Dias, M.G., & P.L. Harris. 1990. The influence of the imagination of reasoning by young children. *British Journal of Developmental Psychology* 8: 305–18.

Dunn, J., & N. Dale. 1984. I a daddy: 2-year-olds' collaboration in joint pretend with sibling and with mother. In *Symbolic play*, ed. I. Bretherton. 131–58. New York; Academic Press.

Dunn, J., & C. Wooding. 1977. Play in the home and its implications for learning. In *Biology of play*, eds. B. Tizard, & D. Harvey. 45–58. London: Heinemann.

El'konin, D. 1966. Symbolics and its functions in the play of children. *Soviet Education* 8: 35–41.

Ervin-Tripp, S. 1991. Play in language development. In *Play and the social context of development in early care and education*, eds. B. Scales, M. Almy, A Nicolopoulou, & S. Ervin-Tripp. 84–97. New York: Teachers College Press.

Farver, J.M. 1993. Cultural differences in scaffolding pretend play: A comparison of American and Mexican mother-child and sibling-child pairs. In *Parent-child play*, ed. K. MacDonald. 349–66. Albany, NY: State University of New York Press.

Fein, G. 1981. Pretend play: An integrative review. *Child Development* 52: 1095–118.

Fiese, B. 1990. Playful relationships: A contextual analysis of mother-toddler interaction and symbolic play. *Child Development* 61: 1648–56.

File, N. 1993. The teacher as guide of children's competence with peers. *Child & Youth Care Forum* 22: 351–60.

Forman, E.A. 1987. Learning through peer interaction: A Vygotskian perspective. *Genetic Epistemologist* 15: 6–15.

Forman, E.A., N. Minick, & C.A. Stone. 1993. *Contexts for learning*. New York: Oxford University Press.

Garvey, C. 1990. *Play*. Cambridge, MA: Harvard University Press.

Göncü, A. 1993. Development of intersubjectivity in the dyadic play of preschoolers. *Early Childhood Research Quarterly* 8: 99–116.

Gralinski, J.H., & C.B. Kopp. 1993. Everyday rules for behavior: Mothers' requests to young children. *Developmental Psychology* 29: 573–84.

Haight, W.L., & P.J. Miller. 1993. *Pretending at home: Early development in a sociocultural context*. Albany, NY: State University of New York Press.

Kavanaugh, R.D., S. Whittington, & M.J. Cerbone. 1983. Mothers' use of fantasy in speech to young children. *Journal of Child Language* 10: 45–55.

Lucariello, J. 1987. Spinning fantasy: Themes, structure, and the knowledge base. *Child Development* 58: 434–42.

Miller, P., & C. Garvey. 1984. Mother-baby role play: Its origins in social support. In *Symbolic play*, ed. I. Bretherton. 101–30. New York: Academic

Moll, L.C. 1990. *Vygotsky and education*. New York: Cambridge University Press.

Newman, L.S. 1990. Intentional versus unintentional memory in young children: Remembering versus playing. *Journal of Experimental Child Psychology* 50: 243–58.

Nicolopoulou, A. 1991. Play, cognitive development, and the social world. In *Play and the social context of development in early care and education*, eds. B. Scales, M. Almy, A. Nicolopoulou, & S. Ervin-Tripp. 129–42. New York: Teachers College Press.

O'Connell, B., & I. Bretherton. 1984. Toddler's play alone and with mother: The role of maternal guidance. In *Symbolic play*, ed. I. Bretherton 337–68. New York: Academic.

O'Reilly, A.W., & M.H. Borstein. 1993. Caregiver-child interaction in play. In *New directions for child development*, eds. M.H. Bornstein, & A.W. O'Reilly. 55–66. San Francisco: Jossey-Bass.

Parten, M. 1932. Social participation among preschool children. *Journal of Abnormal and Social Psychology* 27: 243–69.

Pellegrini, A.D., & L. Galda. 1982. The effects of thematic-fantasy play training on the development of children's story comprehension. *American Educational Research Journal* 19: 443–52.

Pepler, D.J., & H.S. Ross. 1981. The effect of play on convergent and divergent problem solving. *Child Development* 52: 1202–10.

Piaget, J. [1945] 1951. *Play, dreams, and imitation in childhood*. New York: Norton.

Saltz, E., D. Dixon, & J. Johnson. 1977. Training disadvantaged preschoolers on various fantasy activities: Effects on cognitive functioning and impulse control. *Child Development* 46: 367–80.

Slade, A. 1987. A longitudinal study of maternal involvement and symbolic play during the toddler period. *Child Development* 58: 367–75.

Smolucha, F. 1992. Social origins of private speech in pretend play. In *Private speech: From social interaction to self-regulation*. eds. R.M. Diaz, & L.E. Berk. 123–41. Hillsdale, NJ: Erlbaum.

Tamis-LeMonda, C.S., & M.H. Bornstein. 1991. Individual variation, correspondence, stability, and change in mother and toddler play. *Infant Behavior and Development* 14: 143–62.

Tudge, J.R.H. 1992. Processes and consequences of peer collaboration: A Vygotskian analysis. *Child Development* 63: 1364–79.

Tudge, J.R.H., & B. Rogoff. 1987. Peer influences on cognitive development: Piagetian and Vygotskian perspectives. In *Interaction in human development*, eds. M.H. Bornstein, & J.S. Bruner. 17–40. Hillsdale, NJ: Erlbaum.

Vygotsky, L.S. [1933] 1978. The role of play in development. In *Mind in society*, eds. M. Cole, V. John-Steiner, S. Scribner, & E. Souberman. 92–104. Cambridge, MA: Harvard University Press.

Vygotsky, L.S. [1934] 1987. Thinking and speech. In *The collected works of L.S. Vygotsky: Vol. 1. Problems of general psychology*, eds. R. Rieber & A.S. Carton, trans. N. Minick. 37–285. New York: Plenum.

Vygotsky, L.S. [1930] 1990. Imagination and creativity in childhood. *Soviet Psychology* 28: 84–96.

Wertsch, J.W. 1991. A sociocultural approach to socially shared cognition. In *Perspectives on socially shared cognition*, eds. L.B. Resnick, J. M. Levine, & S.D. Teasley. 85–100. Washington, D.C: American Psychological Association.

Wood, D.J. 1989. Social interaction as tutoring. In *Interaction in human development*, eds. M.H. Bornstein, & J.S. Bruner. 59–80. Hillsdale, NJ: Erlbaum.

Wood, D.J., & D. Middleton. 1975. A study of assisted problem solving. *British Journal of Psychology* 66: 181–91.

Zukow, P.G. 1986. The relationship between interaction with the caregiver and the emergence of play activities during the one-word period. *British Journal of Developmental Psychology* 4: 223–34.

 **Article Review Form at end of book.**

Why do children seem so superficial in their views of what is "cool"?
What does being "cool" mean to an elementary school-aged child?

# Why Cool Rules

## David Laskin

"Amy is cool," my ten-year-old daughter, Emily, informed me the other day. "She wears cool clothes, she likes cool music. If you're friends with her, you're cool."

*Cool.* The very word summoned up a huge dripping chunk of my own hopelessly uncool youth. Groovy, hip, neat, and far out have all come and gone, but cool endures. It's an instant signifier of style that bridges the abyss separating us and our kids. Baggy pants and thumb rings have replaced the bell-bottoms and mood rings of my day, just as No Doubt and the Spice Girls have shouldered aside The Stones and Peter Frampton. But the concept stays the same. Cool is the ultimate aspiration and compliment.

Moreover, cool starts to matter a lot when a kid hits 7 or 8. "That's because just around this age, children are beginning to develop a more mature sense of themselves in a social context," according to Kim Kendall, Ph.D., a Seattle-based clinical psychologist specializing in adolescents. "It's the dawning of a perception of who they are in comparison to others. At this age, children think things like, 'I have blue eyes, red hair, nice clothes—does this mean I'm cool?' Initially, their sense of social identity is based on superficial things. They add more abstract qualities, such as personality and character, later on."

A neighbor of ours, Teri LeClair, has noticed the first glimmerings of that broader social awareness within both her 9-year-old son and 8-year-old daughter. "Both of them are making judgments about where they want to fit, instead of just bebopping along to their own drummer, as they used to do. Alicia definitely wants to hang with the right kids. Cool for her is denim overalls, big shirts, and leggings, along with the same cute little shoulder-length haircut as her buddies. With Zach, the mark of coolness is sports—playing them and dressing like the other kids who play them."

Our kids' pursuit of cool may strike you, as it often strikes me, as shallow and materialistic. But in fact, it signals an important developmental shift away from the relationships children have in their homes and out into the larger arena of the world—a world that is sometimes ruled by peers. "Being cool is a child's way of creating a sense of difference from the family," explains Samuel Osherson, Ph.D., a professor of psychology at Harvard and the author of *The Passions of Fatherhood* (Ballantine). "It's how he consolidates his identity." An awareness of cool can enhance your child's sense of belonging and extend his social skills. It can also prod him into trying out unfamiliar roles and seeing life from new perspectives—"flirting with different versions of the self," says Osherson.

Parents sometimes find the declaration of independence implicit in coolness alarming, even threatening. "I was scared to death when my son wanted those really wide baggy jeans," our friend Teri Jones told us. "I thought it meant he was becoming one of those gangsta-rapper wannabes." But it's essential to separate your child's style from his substance. As Kendall puts it, "When it comes to the big issues—relationships, morality, politics, religion, marriage—children this age continue to look to their parents for guidance."

## "Cool" Matters More Than "Original"

Which means that while you may not be able to control your child's craving for coolness, you still retain a pretty strong influence on him. But try to tread carefully. Remember, all those march-to-the-beat-of-your-own-drummer lectures don't cut the mustard with children this age. Fitting in matters far more than being original. At the same time, most kids don't really want carte blanche to pursue a vision of coolness that winds up being illegal (such as smoking cigarettes), threatening, or ultraweird. Many 10-year-olds talk about how cool nose rings or tattoos are, but most of them wouldn't really want their parents' permission to get one.

In fact, I was surprised to discover as a parent how much coolness has in common with conformism. Back in fifth grade, I always thought the cool kids were the trendsetters, the free spirits—in other words, leaders. In truth, coolness has always had a lot more to do with going along with the herd than with breaking new ground.

"Cool means conveying a certain style, attitude, wit, social adeptness, or appearance, such as when kids become concerned with dressing the 'right' way. This is *not* the same as being a leader," notes Sharon R. Weinstein, M.D., a child and adolescent psychiatrist at Harvard Medical School. "Being socially accepted will generally mean being a follower." Of course, this also means that being labeled as uncool can have a devastating impact on a child's social life, as kids get into the business of defining and monitoring what used to be called "the 'in' crowd."

When you consider how often children switch alliances and barter friendships, it's not surprising that cool is a very slippery concept. The coolest kid in second grade can be washed up by fifth. This spring's cool look evaporates over the summer. Deciding who's cool and who isn't is a mysterious business, in which the standards shift constantly. Everybody seems to just know who the cool kids are. It's something you either have or you don't.

If kids often have a difficult time navigating the shoals of cool, just how are parents supposed to know which way to point the tiller? Some general principles might be in order.

## Don't Try to Understand What's Cool or What Isn't—and Don't Argue about It

Kids are the ultimate arbiters. After all, their peer group is the one that makes up the rules (and constantly changes them). Saying, "I don't think that music is cool, I think it's noise" only guarantees that your child will tune you out. So does pretending to appreciate her styles or sounds if your heart isn't in it; kids have keen radar for this kind of insincerity.

## Help Your Child Fit In

Don't worry that shelling out for the team jacket or the hairstyle that everybody else has will turn your child into a superficial, materialistic status-seeker. As long as what he wants to do or wear doesn't conflict strongly with your values (or wreck your budget), go along with it.

If, despite your efforts to help him belong, your child still complains of being rejected or targeted for teasing by the cool crowd, you may need to consult teachers or other parents to get to the bottom of the problem. "If a child is being picked on, there's usually a reason beyond whether he's cool or not," says Miriam Gutmann, M.D., a psychiatrist on the faculty of the Chicago Center for Family Health. "Kids shun another kid because he makes them uncomfortable or he doesn't respect the social rules."

Sometimes the problem is a relatively straightforward one, such as a hygiene matter that parents can help the child address. At other times, complaints of being rejected signal that a child is depressed or troubled. "Kids slight each other all the time," Gutmann says, "and most of them know how to roll with the punches. That's part of being cool. But if a child is unhappy, he'll take those little digs more to heart. The others will realize that they've got a ready victim." She adds, "When a child has a complaint about being rejected by peers over the course of a month or more, I suggest that parents talk to the school's counselor or social worker, if there is one. If not, consider visiting a child psychologist or psychiatrist."

## Don't Be Afraid to Say No When You Need To

If your child's desires compromise her safety or your limits, you can explain to a 10-year-old, "I don't care how much you want a tattoo. I feel you're too young to make a decision that you'll have to live with for the rest of your life. Besides, I'm not convinced tattooing is safe." Couch your arguments in terms of your child's welfare, *not* your own tastes.

You're also justified in telling a child, "I realize those sneakers are important to you, but I can't in good conscience pay $100 out of my own pocket for them. If you'd like to earn the money yourself, you can spend it as you like."

In addition, you can—and ought to—let her know when her definition of cool conflicts with your values: "If being cool means making fun of other kids just because of the way they dress, I'm not so sure I'd want to be cool."

## Maintain Perspective

Your child's insistence on being cool can be trying, but it's a healthy and inevitable part of growing up. "You wouldn't want a child to skip over it or not be interested," says Kendall. "It's a hurdle all kids need to clear,." And while they're in the air, our job is to remain, well, cool.

 **Article Review Form at end of book.**

Describe what research has shown about how friends influence one another. What are the two theoretical perspectives of peer influence in adolescence? Explain each and the sources of their differences.

# Friendship and Friends' Influence in Adolescence

## Thomas J. Berndt

Friendships have an important influence on adolescents' attitudes, behavior, and development. Theorists do not agree, however, on whether this influence is generally positive or generally negative. One theoretical perspective emphasizes the positive effects of close friendships on the psychological adjustment and social development of adolescents. Theorists who adopt this perspective argue that interactions with friends improve adolescents' social skills and ability to cope with stressful events.[1] A second theoretical perspective emphasizes the negative influence of friends on adolescents' behavior. Theorists who adopt this perspective argue that friends' influence often leads to antisocial or delinquent behavior.[2]

The two perspectives differ not only in their assumptions about the effects of friends' influence, but also in their assumptions about processes or pathways of influence. In the first perspective, the influence of friendships depends on the features of these relationships. For example, friendships that are highly intimate are assumed to enhance adolescents' self-esteem and understanding of other people. In the second perspective, friends' influence depends on the attitudes and behaviors of friends. For example, adolescents whose friends drink beer at parties are assumed to be likely to start drinking beer themselves. Thus, the first pathway of influence focuses on features of friendship and the second focuses on friends' characteristics.

Each perspective contains a kernel of truth, but each provides a one-sided view of the effects of friendships. Theorists who emphasize the positive features of friendship seldom acknowledge that friendships can have negative features, too. Adolescents often have conflicts with friends, and these conflicts can negatively affect adolescents' behavior toward other people. Theorists who emphasize the negative influence of friends' characteristics seldom acknowledge that many adolescents have friends with positive characteristics. These friends are likely to influence behavior positively.

In sum, friends can have positive or negative effects on adolescents via either of the two pathways of influence. In this review, I present evidence for these assertions and argue for more comprehensive and balanced theories of friendship in adolescence.

## Friendship Features

"How can you tell that someone is your best friend?" Open-ended questions like this one were used by several researchers to assess the age changes in conceptions of friendships. The responses of children and adolescents confirmed that they regard several features of friendship as important. They said that friendships involve mutual liking, prosocial behavior (e.g., "we trade tapes with each other"), companionship (e.g., "we go places together"), and a relative lack of conflicts (e.g., "we don't fight with each other"). Many adolescents, but few elementary school children, also referred to intimacy in friendships. Adolescents said, for example, that they "talk about their problems with best friends" and that "a best friend really understands you." These findings are consistent with hypotheses that intimate friendships emerge in adolescence.[1]

Thomas J. Berndt, Friendship and Friends' Influence in Adolescence, *Current Directions in Psychological Science*, Vol. 1, No. 5, pp. 156–159, October 1992. © 1992 American Psychological Society. Reprinted with the permission of Cambridge University Press.

Gradually, researchers shifted from studies of conceptions of friendship to studies of the actual features of friendships. Researchers also devised structured rating scales for assessing the features identified in earlier studies. The new measures made it possible to examine several questions about the nature and effects of friendships.[3]

Recent research has confirmed that intimacy becomes a central feature of friendship in early adolescence. Adolescents usually rate their own friendships as more intimate than do elementary school children. The increase in intimacy may be due partly to adolescents' growing understanding of the thoughts, feelings, and traits of self and others. It may also be due to the fact that adolescents spend more time with their friends than younger children do. Friendships are more significant relationships in adolescence than earlier.

Girls describe their friendships as more intimate than do boys. Some writers have suggested that the sex difference is merely a matter of style: Girls express their intimacy with friends by talking about personal matters, and boys express their intimacy in nonverbal ways. However, scattered evidence suggests that boys' friendships are less intimate because boys trust their friends less than girls do.[4] More boys than girls say that friends might tease them if they talk about something clumsy or foolish that they did. More girls than boys say that they share intimate information with friends because their friends listen and understand them.

This sex difference does not simply reflect a developmental delay for boys. In adulthood, women also tend to have more intimate friendships than men.[5]

Still, the difference should not be exaggerated, because significant differences have not been found on all measures in all studies. Yet when differences are found, females' friendships usually appear more intimate than males' friendships.

Intimacy is closely related to other features of friendship. Adolescents' ratings of the intimacy of their friendships are correlated with their ratings of the friends' loyalty, generosity, and helpfulness. In short, friendships that are highly intimate tend to have many other positive features. Such friendships are comparable to the supportive social relationships that help adults cope with stressful life events.[6]

We might ask, then, if intimate and supportive friendships have equally positive effects on adolescents' adjustment and coping. In several studies, adolescents with more supportive friendships had higher self-esteem, less often suffered from depression or other emotional disorders, and were better adjusted to school than subjects with less supportive friendships.[7] These data are consistent with theories about the benefits of friendship, but come from correlational studies and so are open to alternative interpretations. Most important is the possibility that self-esteem and other indicators of adjustment contribute to the formation of supportive friendships rather than vice versa.

Longitudinal studies help to answer questions about causal direction, but longitudinal studies of adolescents' friendships are rare. The available data suggest that supportive friendships have significant but modest effects on some aspects of behavior and adjustment. Supportive friendships are not a panacea: They do not ap-

pear to have as powerful or as general an influence on adolescents as some theorists have suggested. Additional research is needed to identify the specific aspects of behavior and development that are most strongly affected by variations in positive features of friendship.

Equally important for future research is greater attention to the negative features of friendship. Adolescents interviewed about their conceptions of friendship commented on conflicts with friends, but many researchers ignored these comments. Many measures of friendship focus exclusively on positive or supportive features. This is a serious omission, because recent studies suggest that conflicts with friends can contribute to negative interactions with other peers and with adults.[8] With friends, adolescents may develop an aggressive interaction style that they then display with other interaction partners. Theories that emphasize the positive effects of supportive friendships need to be expanded to account for the negative effects of troubled friendships. Researchers need to measure both the positive and the negative features of friendships. New research with both types of measures should provide a more complete picture of friendship effects via the first pathway of influence.

## Friends' Characteristics

You and your friends found a sheet of paper that your teacher must have lost. On the paper are the questions and answers for a test that you are going to have tomorrow. Your friends all plan to study from it, and they want you to go along with them. You don't think you should, but they tell you to do it anyway. What would you really do: study from the paper or not study from it?

Many researchers have used hypothetical dilemmas like this one to measure friends' influence on adolescents. In this dilemma, friends supposedly put pressure on an adolescent to engage in antisocial behavior, cheating on a test. Adolescents' responses to similar dilemmas are assumed to show the degree of adolescents' antisocial conformity to friends. Research with these dilemmas has provided the most direct support for theories of friends' negative influence.[2]

However, research with other methods has shown that the hypothetical dilemmas are based on faulty assumptions about the processes and outcomes of friends' influence in adolescence.[7] Some researches observed friends' interactions in school, summer camps, and other settings. Other researches recorded friends' discussions, in experimental settings, as they tried to reach a consensus on various decisions. Both types of research suggest that the studies of conformity dilemmas—and popular writings about peer pressure—seriously distort reality.

In natural settings, influence among friends is a mutual process. Adolescents influence their friends as well as being influenced by them. Mutual influence is most obvious during interactions between a pair of friends. When two friends talk together, each has chances to influence the other. Even when friends interact in a group, decisions are usually made by consensus after group discussion. Groups rarely divide into a majority that favors one decision and one person who favors another. Therefore, models of group decision making describe friends' influence better than do models of individuals conforming to a majority.

In natural settings, influence seldom results from coercive pressure by friends. Friends' influence often depends on positive reinforcement. For example, friends express their approval of certain opinions and not others. Adolescents who are engaged in a discussion also listen to the reasons that friends give for their opinions. The influence of reasoning, or informational influence, may be as important in adolescents' groups as it is in adults' groups.[9] In addition, friends' influence does not always result from explicit attempts to influence. Adolescents admire and respect their friends, so they may agree with friends simply because they trust the friends' judgment.

Of course, friends sometimes do try to put pressure on adolescents. Adolescents also know that they risk disapproval or ridicule if they advocate opinions different from the opinions of most of their friends. In extremely cohesive groups, like some urban gangs, adolescents may even be threatened with physical harm if they do not go along with important group decisions, such as to attack another gang. But such situations and such groups are uncommon. Few friendship groups are as highly organized as an urban gang. Most adolescents simply choose new friends if they constantly disagree with the decisions of their old friends. The freedom of adolescents to end friendships limits their friends' use of coercive pressure as an influence technique.

Research on adolescents' responses to antisocial dilemmas is also misleading because it implies that friends usually pressure adolescents to engage in antisocial behavior. Experimental studies of friends' discussions suggest a different conclusion. So do longitudinal studies in which friends' influence is judged from changes over time in the attitudes or behavior of adolescents and their friends.[7] These studies show that the direction of friends' influence depends on the friends' characteristics. For example, if an adolescent's friends do not care about doing well in school, the adolescent's motivation to achieve in school may decrease over time. By contrast, if an adolescent's friends have good grades in school, the adolescent's grades may improve.

Viewed from a different perspective, the usual outcome of the mutual influence among friends is an increase over time in the friends' similarity. Often, the increased similarity reflects a true compromise: Friends who differ in their attitudes or behaviors adopt a position intermediate between their initial positions. Some adolescents, however, are more influential than their friends. Other adolescents are more susceptible to influence than their friends. The sources of these individual differences need further exploration.

Finally, longitudinal studies suggest that the power of friends' influence is often overestimated.[10] In one study, friends' influence on adolescents' educational aspirations was nonsignificant. In another study, friends' influence on adolescents' alcohol use was nonsignificant. These findings are unusual, but even the statistically significant effects that are found are often small.

The conclusion that friends have only a small influence on adolescents is so contrary to the conventional wisdom that its validity might be questioned. Many studies seem to support the assertion of popular writers that friends have a strong influence on adolescents, but these studies often have serious flaws.[7] Researchers have frequently used adolescents' reports on their friends' behavior as measures of the friends' actual behavior. Then the researchers have estimated the friends' influence from correlations for the similarity between adolescents' self-reports and their reports on friends. Yet recent studies have shown that adolescents' reports on their friends involve considerable projection: Adolescents assume their friends' behavior is more like their own than it actually is.

Another flaw in many studies is the estimation of friends' influence from correlations for friends' similarity at a single time. However, influence is not the only contributor to friends' similarity. Adolescents also select friends who are already similar to themselves. On some characteristics (e.g., ethnicity), friends' similarity is due entirely to selection rather than to influence. To distinguish between selection and influence as sources of friends' similarity, longitudinal studies are needed. Recent longitudinal studies suggest that friends' influence on adolescents is relatively weak.

However, weak effects should not be interpreted as null effects. Underestimating the influence of friends would be as serious a mistake as overestimating it. At all ages, human beings are influenced by individuals with whom they have formed close relationships. Adolescents have close relationships with friends and, therefore, are influenced by friends. Friends influence adolescents' attitudes toward school and the broader social world. Friends influence adolescents' behavior in school and out of school. This influence is not a social problem

unique to adolescence, but one instance of a universal phenomenon. To understand friends' influence better, theorists need to abandon the simplistic hypothesis of peer pressure toward antisocial behavior and consider the multiple processes of friends' influence and the varied effects of these processes.

## Conclusion

Current thinking about adolescents' friendships is dominated by two theoretical perspectives that are incomplete and one-sided. One perspective emphasizes the benefit of friendships with certain positive features, such as intimacy. Intimacy is a more central feature of friendships in adolescence than in childhood. Intimate friendships have positive effects on adolescents, but these friendships seem to affect only some aspects of psychological adjustment. Moreover, some adolescents have friendships with many negative features, such as a high rate of conflicts. These conflicts often spill over and negatively affect other relationships. Adults concerned about adolescents' friendships should not only try to enhance the positive features of close friendships, but also try to reduce their negative features.

The second theoretical perspective emphasizes the negative influence of friends whose attitudes and behaviors are undesirable. Adolescents are influenced by their friends' attitudes and behaviors, but adolescents also influence their friends. Over time, this mutual influence increases the similarity between adolescents

Acknowledgments—The author's research was supported by grants from the Spencer Foundation, the National Science Foundation, and the National Institute of Mental Health.

and their friends. Friends' influence does not generally lead to shifts either toward more desirable or toward less desirable attitudes and behaviors. These findings imply that adults concerned about negative influences of friends should try not to reduce friends' influence but to channel that influence in a positive direction.

## Notes

1. T.J. Berndt, Obtaining support from friends in childhood and adolescence, in *Children's Social Networks and Social Supports*, D. Belle, Ed. (Wiley, New York, 1989); R.L. Selman and L.H. Schultz, *Making a Friend in Youth: Developmental Theory and Pair Therapy* (University of Chicago Press, Chicago, 1990); J. Youniss and J. Smollar, *Adolescent Relations With Mothers, Fathers, and Friends* (University of Chicago Press, Chicago, 1985).
2. U. Bronfenbrenner, *Two Worlds of Childhood* (Russell Sage Foundation, New York, 1970); L. Steinberg and S.B. Silverberg, The vicissitudes of autonomy in early adolescence, *Child Development*, 57, 841–851 (1986).
3. T.J. Berndt, Children's comments about their friendships, in *Minnesota Symposium on Child Psychology: Vol. 18. Cognitive Perspectives on Children's Social Behavioral Development*, M. Perlmutter, Ed. (Erlbaum, Hillsdale, NJ, 1986); R.C. Savin-Williams and T.J. Berndt, Friendships and peer relations during adolescence, in *At the Threshold: The Developing Adolescent*, S.S. Feldman and G. Elliott, Eds. (Harvard University Press, Cambridge, MA, 1990).
4. T.J. Berndt, Intimacy and competition in the friendships of adolescent boys and girls, in *Gender Roles Through the Life Span*, M.R. Stevenson, Ed. (University of Wisconsin Press, Madison, in press).
5. W.K. Rawlins, *Friendship Matters: Communication, Dialectics, and the Life Course* (Aldine de Gruyter, Hawthorne, NY, 1992); M.S. Clark and H.T. Reis, Interpersonal processes in close relationships, *Annual Review of Psychology*, 39, 609–672 (1988).

6. S. Cohen and T.A. Wills, Stress, social support, and the buffering hypothesis, *Psychological Bulletin, 98,* 310–357 (1985); H.O.F. Veiel and U. Baumann, *The Meaning and Measurement of Social Support* (Hemisphere, New York, 1992).

7. T.J. Berndt and R.C. Savin-Williams, Variations in friendships and peer-group relationships in adolescence, in *Handbook of Clinical Research and Practice With Adolescents*, P. Tolan and B. Cohler, Eds. (Wiley, New York, in press).

8. T.J. Berndt and K. Keefe, *How friends influence adolescents' adjustment to school*, paper presented at the biennial meeting of the Society for Research in Child Development, Seattle (April 1991); see also W.W. Hartup, Conflict and friendship relations, in *Conflict in Child and Adolescent Development*, C.U. Shantz and W.W. Hartup, Eds. (Cambridge University Press, Cambridge, England, in press).

9. T.J. Berndt, A.E. Laychak, and K. Park, Friends' influence on adolescents' academic achievement motivation: An experimental study, *Journal of Educational Psychology, 82,* 664–670 (1990).

10. J.M. Cohen, Sources of peer group homogeneity, *Sociology of Education, 50,* 227–241 (1977); D.B. Kandel and K. Andrews, Processes of adolescent socialization by parents and peers, *International Journal of the Addictions, 22,* 319–342 (1987).

 **Article Review Form at end of book.**

Why is belonging to a clique desired by preteens and of benefit? What should parents do and not do if their child is rejected by a clique?

# The Age of Cliques

If your child isn't in with the "in" crowd, here's how to help.

## Karen Levine

"In fifth grade, we had this very strong clique. We did everything together," says Ariana Kanwit, now an eighth-grader. "Then in sixth, the other girls decided to kind of kick me out. They stopped calling. They passed notes about me and spread lies. It ruined my whole school year, and it turned out that the person who started the whole thing was actually my best friend. I found other friends, but I spent a lot of time crying."

Ariana's story has a happy ending—sort of. "This year I got back in my clique," she reports. "I'm not sure how it happened, but I like it a lot."

You may wonder why she would even *want* to be accepted by such a group, but adults easily forget how intense and volatile social life can be for kids this age—and how thoroughly dominated it is by cliques. At some point between the fifth and eighth grades, your child is almost certain to experience the ecstasy of being accepted by a clique, the agony of being banished, and (often) the relief of being reembraced.

What makes cliques so powerful? It helps to think of them in terms of a preteen's social development. The middle-school years mark your child's transition out of an insulated family life and into the world of peers. She naturally feels far less sure of her footing on this new and constantly shifting grounds—and, just to make matters even more complicated, she may well be grappling with the body changes of puberty, which can have a deeply unsettling effect on her sense of who she is.

## Belonging to a Group Is a Way of Being "Normal"

"The peak of conformity comes at around age 13," explains David Anderegg, Ph.D., a psychologist in Lenox, Massachusetts. "At this age, there's nothing more important to a kid than being just like everyone else—normal. In general, not until high school do kids become more concerned with expressing their individuality."

With all these factors in play, it's only natural that a child would surround herself with a coterie of friends whose very existence confirms her "okayness."

But if cliques help preteens feel safer and more powerful, membership can come at a cost: Insiders often treat outsiders in ways that seem inexcusably cruel. As sixth-grader Isaac Warshaw puts it, "My crowd in school is pretty funny, but sometimes when they're being funny, they're really being mean. They'll call a kid a name and all the other kids will laugh, just because they want to be part of the group."

Are the members of the clique oblivious to the feelings of the one being teased? "They don't think about that," Isaac says. "It's hard to tell kids not to make fun of someone. They'll say, 'What's with you? This kid's nothing but a loser.'"

Often the most difficult question for a parent is: How can you help when your child is rejected by a clique? A child this age simply isn't ready to hear you give advice, no matter how sound, about accepting or even taking pride in being different from other kids. Once your child is more at ease with her social world, she'll be more receptive to your message.

## Let Your Child Belong

In the meantime, the greatest service you can do for your child is to help him learn to be part of the group, rather than giving him reasons he shouldn't. Anderegg tells the story of a sixth-grader who was being mercilessly teased because he wore sweatpants. "They were regarded as babyish, and the cool thing to do was to wear jeans. The boy's parents placed a high value on individuality, and they felt that their son should have the right to wear them without being teased. In fact, what he really wanted was to fit in with his peers. His parents gave him a great deal of moral support, but it would have been more helpful if they'd gone out and bought him some jeans."

One way you *shouldn't* try to help your child, however, is by fighting her battles for her. When her daughter, Lara, was going through a miserable year of exclusion from a clique she had belonged to, Anne Rosen wanted very much to intercede. "We considered bringing it up with the parents of the girls who were being cruel. But Lara begged us not to, because it would have been humiliating for her. She wanted to tough it out. So we tried to be loving and support her without trying to fix things."

At the beginning of the next school year, Lara was admitted to the clique once again. It's highly doubtful that the kids in her crowd would have shown her the same respect if they'd seen her as someone incapable of standing up for herself.

## Don't Pressure a Child to Be Part of the Group

Standing on the sidelines can be excruciating for many parents, especially when a child's struggle with the ins and outs of cliques triggers painful memories and emotions from their own childhoods. Some parents are so eager to see their children accepted that they unwittingly add to the social pressure ("I'm sure you must have done something to get them upset" or "Why don't you throw a party for everyone over at our house?"). Other parents, who see themselves as outsiders, undermine their child's wish to be part of the group ("These kids don't sound like they're good enough for you"). Try to avoid becoming so involved in your preteen's social life that you make it harder for him to resolve his own issues.

And remember that there are factors in your child's rejection by a clique that are beyond his or anyone else's control. In their desire to conform, children often hone in on details that make certain kids different—weight, for example, or a last name that lends itself to an insulting variation. Then there's puberty. Notes Anderegg, "Boys who are slow to mature physically and girls who mature early are most likely to be targeted by cliques." (However, boys who experience puberty early are likely to be popular.) Anderegg adds that problems connected to a child's developmental pace are temporary and usually resolve themselves.

Still, your preteen isn't likely to find much solace in such explanations. He's hurting right now, and it seems to him as if he's going to be persecuted forever. What he needs to hear from you, often, is that you love and value him. No long conversations are necessary; you can simply acknowledge his feelings by saying something like, "The way they spoke to you really stinks" or "I'm really sorry that you're going through all this." You might say, "When I was in fifth grade, my best friend turned on me and I was devastated. I felt like I was without a friend in the whole world."

It's also valuable to remind your child that difficult times do eventually end. You can tell him, "I know it feels as if you've been abandoned forever, but it really will pass. You could even become friends with those kids again." Don't expect that your preteen will show much gratitude for the comforting words; he may even snap at you and tell you that you don't understand him. Just remember that despite appearances to the contrary, you still have an enormous amount of influence over the way your child views himself.

That's just as true if your child happens to be one of the mean-spirited insiders. It's important to let kids this age know that you disapprove of hurtful behavior. The key is to convey your values without resorting to an angry, preachy tone; once you get on the soapbox, your message is virtually guaranteed to go in one ear and out the other. Instead, talk about your own feelings clearly and directly, rather than making accusations. Say to your child, "I really don't like the idea of a tight little group of friends making outsiders feel miserable," or "In our family we care a great deal about other people's feelings, and I expect you to treat people just as kindly as Dad and I do."

Isaac Warshaw's mother, Patricia McKeon, put just the right spin on her message. "I've pointed out to Isaac that *all* kids his age are vulnerable to teasing, and that if you can stick up for a friend when other kids are saying unkind things, then that friend might stick up for you later. By mentioning those things, I feel I've done my job. But what he does with that information has to be his own decision."

 **Article Review Form at end of book.**

How can teachers help children who are rejected by their peers find social acceptance? Describe the typical behaviors and feelings of a child identified as lonely.

# Lonely Children

**Janis R. Bullock**

Emily's parents have recently divorced and Emily has moved to a new home and neighborhood. She has been attending her new preschool for a month, yet she is still withdrawn, appears sad, and shows little interest in her surroundings. When children approach her, she has downcast eyes and rarely responds. Some children no longer seek her out.

Daniel approached his teacher with tears in his eyes. When the teacher inquires about him, Daniel shares with her that his favorite cat has been hit by a car. Together they talk about the incident and his feelings. Two months later Daniel continues to talk about "Annie" with sadness.

Several children in Sarah's first grade class are talking about going to a birthday party the following weekend. When one child asks Sarah if she will be going, she answers in a quiet voice, "No, I wasn't invited." She later confides in the teacher that she doesn't have any friends and that no one likes her.

Although these children's circumstances are different, they all are experiencing loneliness to some degree. Yet, research and intervention in educational settings focusing on children who are lonely—for reasons other than missing their parents (separation anxiety)—are a fairly recent phenomenon. Lately, there has been considerable research regarding children's loneliness due to poor peer relations. Teachers are learning more about the issue. One explanation for the earlier lack of attention to this topic is the belief that most young children do not experience feelings of loneliness. This is an inaccurate assumption— many children report feeling lonely (Asher, Parkhurst, Hymel, & Williams, 1990). Research suggests that very young children understand the concept of loneliness and often feel what Weiss (1973) calls "the loneliness of social isolation." Teachers who work closely with children and families are realizing that there are many reasons for children to feel lonely, and they are realizing the consequences of loneliness and beginning to express their concerns.

People who spend time observing children realize that children who feel lonely often experience poor peer relationships. Because they are relatively friend-less, these children express more loneliness than their nonrejected or socially isolated peers. Interestingly, these findings are consistent across many studies as well as across the age range from kindergarten to first grade through middle school (Cassidy & Asher, 1992). Furthermore, Hymel et al. (1983) found measurements of children's loneliness fairly consistent over a one-year period, which suggest that children's loneliness is long-lived. Lonely children experience feelings of sadness, malaise, boredom, and alienation. They often feel excluded, which can be damaging to their self-esteem. Early childhood experiences that contribute to loneliness may lead to loneliness during adulthood. We should approach loneliness in children with the same sensitivity and understanding that we use in responding to lonely adults. Lonely children miss out on many opportunities to interact with their peers. Given the benefits of peer interactions and friendships, this should raise many concerns for teachers who work with young children. It is critical for teachers to realize that peer relations matter to children, and that lonely children place as much importance on them as do other children.

Reprinted with permission from the National Association for the Education of Young Children.

Although young children do experience feelings of loneliness, researchers (Cassidy & Asher, 1992) have only recently investigated children's *knowledge* of this concept. In a study on kindergarten and first grade children's knowledge of loneliness, children responded appropriately to a series of questions regarding what loneliness is ("being sad and alone"), where it comes from ("nobody to play with"), and what one might do to overcome feelings of loneliness ("find a friend"). These studies suggest that children's concepts of loneliness have meaning for them, are similar to those shared by adults, and can be reliably assessed.

Several significant factors contribute to feelings of loneliness in children. Some of these may be the death of a parent or other significant person; the divorce of parents; conflict within the home or at school; moving to a new school or neighborhood; losing a friend; losing an object, possession, or pet; or routinely being rejected by playmates. How children respond to such losses varies considerably and is partially determined by how they interpret the situation. What is important is the child's reactions and feelings associated with the loss that has brought on the feelings of loneliness.

## What Can Teachers Do?

A sensitive, supportive teacher will attempt to assess each child's situation and understand the importance of the feelings associated with the loss or social problem. Participating in careful observation of children is a necessary first step in order to gain insights. While observing a child who appears lonely, teachers can focus on the following:

Does the child appear timid, anxious, unsure of self, or sad?

Does the child show a lack of interest in the surroundings?

Does the child seem to be rejected by playmates?

Does the child avoid other children by choice?

Does the child appear to lack social skills that might prevent him from initiating or maintaining interactions?

Does the child have the necessary social skills but seem reluctant or unwilling to use them?

Does the child's apparent loneliness seem to be a consistent pattern over time or is it a recent phenomenon?

When assessing children it's important to be sensitive to and aware of their developmental abilities. For example, it has been suggested that young children who play alone may be at increased risk for later problems, both socially and cognitively. Many preschool and kindergarten children, however, engage in nonsocial activities that are highly predictive of competence. The "parallel-constructive" behaviors identified by Rubin (1982) are commonly found in preschool and elementary classrooms. Children may be engaged in a variety of block, art, or literacy activities, for example, yet may not be interacting with others. Teachers will need to observe children over a period of time, document their behavior, and watch their interactions with peers in order to determine whether they show signs of loneliness or are happily and productively self-employed.

Because loneliness can be related to a variety of causes, teachers will need to consider the many approaches that can be adapted to the individual needs of the child. Teachers can think about what kinds of classroom activities may be helpful to a child who is feeling lonely. Sensory activities, such as clay, art, or water play, can be calming and soothing to children. Some children may more easily be able to express their feelings through manipulation and drawing. Arranging the dramatic play area with props may help some children act out or express their feelings and experience a sense of control. Crisis-oriented books—referred to as bibliotherapy (Jalongo, 1983)—may help a child in coping with a personal crisis such as parental divorce, loss of an object or friend, or death of a pet or significant person. Sharing carefully selected literature with children may assist in facilitating emotional health. Children who are able to express and articulate their concerns may want to talk about their unhappiness.

Children who are rejected outright by their peers express the greatest degree of loneliness and social dissatisfaction (Asher et al., 1990). Children are rejected for many reasons and teachers will need to assess the circumstances that seem to lead to the rejection. Is the child acting aggressively toward others? Does the child have difficulty entering ongoing play and adapting to the situation? Does the child have difficulty communicating needs and desires? Once the problem is identified, teachers can assist the child in changing the situation. The teacher can point out the effects of the child's behavior on others, show her how to adapt to the on-going play, or help her clearly communicate feelings and desires. In many cases the teacher can succeed in helping the child feel better.

Children who are socially isolated also report feelings of loneliness, although to a lesser extent than do rejected children. Although these children may not be rejected by their peers they rarely interact with them. The inability to interact with peers is often due to a lack of social skills. These children may also be extremely shy, inhibited, anxious, and lacking in self-confidence. If children lack certain skills, the teacher can focus on giving feedback, suggestions, and ideas that the child can implement. Children who possess adequate social skills but are reluctant to use them can be given opportunities for doing so by being paired with younger children. This experience give the older child occasions to practice skills and boost self-confidence (Furman, Rahe, & Hartup, 1979).

Suggesting to a parent the possibility of inviting a peer over to the child's home may be a good idea; if the parent follows through, in this simpler social situation, the child may be able to form a friendship. Developing relationships with parents and working with them is crucial in order to determine whether the child's feelings of loneliness are associated with the home environment. When teachers become aware of children who are experiencing loneliness due to a family crisis, they can lend their support in a variety of ways. By expressing concern to the child the teacher can convey a sense of caring. Spending extra time listening can be reassuring and helpful to some children. Teachers can make

contact with parents, discuss their observations of the child, and share what they are doing in the classroom that might also be continued at home. In addition teachers can ask parents for their recommendations about what might make the child feel more comfortable at school. Teachers also can share relevant resources with parents, such as literature or information about parent discussion groups that might be available in the community.

In more extreme cases where a child's loneliness seems chronic, teachers may want to suggest referral of the child for counseling. A situation may arise where a child does not respond to techniques possible in a group setting; the teacher sees little change over time. A parent may be pushing a teacher to work harder with the child or asking for additional suggestions on what to do to help the child at home. The teacher may feel unqualified to give further advice. In fact, it is unethical for teachers to act as therapists or parent educators if this expertise is not part of their training. Teachers will need to acknowledge the parent's concern and suggest other resources. A professional teacher will need to take time to compile resources or make referrals. Information might include a variety of services, such as mental health clinics; child, family, and marriage counselors; psychologists; and developmental screening clinics.

## Summary

Observation is the key to detecting feelings of loneliness in children. Loneliness may be the result of a loss of someone or something important, a problem at home, or a continual sense of being an out-

sider among peers. Children may be able to express their feelings of sadness or isolation through sensory activities, drawing and painting, literature, and conversation. Teachers can show children who lack social skills how to merge into play and better communicate with peers. As teachers, parents, researchers, and other professionals who work with families learn about the immediate and long-term consequences associated with loneliness in children, additional intervention strategies can be articulated.

## References

Asher, S.R., Parkhurst, J.T., Hymel, S., & Williams, G.A. (1990). Peer rejection and loneliness in childhood. In S.R. Asher & J.D. Cole (Eds.) *Peer rejection in childhood* (pp. 253–273). New York: Cambridge University Press.

Cassidy, J., & Asher, S.K. (1992). Loneliness and peer relations in young children. *Child Development, 63*(2), 350–365.

Furman, W., Rahe, D., & Hartup, W.W. (1979). Rehabilitation of socially withdrawn preschool children through mixed-age and same-age socialization. *Child Development 50*(4), 915–922.

Hymel, S., Freigang, R., Franke, S., Both, L., Bream, L., & Borys, S. (1983, June). *Children's attributions for social situations: Variations as a function of social status and self-perception variables*. Paper presented at the annual meeting of the Canadian Psychological Association, Winnipeg, Manitoba.

Jalongo, M.R. (1983). Using crisis-oriented books with young children. *Young Children, 38*(5), 29–36.

Rubin, K.H. (1982). Nonsocial play in preschoolers: Necessary evil? *Child Development, 53*(3), 651–657.

Weiss, R.S. (1973). *Loneliness: The experience of emotional and social isolation*. Cambridge: MIT Press.

## For Further Reading

Bullock, J.R. (1988). Encouraging the development of social competence in young children. *Early Child Development and Care, 37*, 47–54.

Bullock, J.R. (1991). Supporting the development of socially rejected children. *Early Child Development and Care, 66*, 15–23.

Bullock, J.R. (1993). Children's loneliness and their relationships with family and peers. *Family Relations, 42*(1), 46–49.

Hazen, N., Black, B., & Fleming-Johnson, F. (1984). Social acceptance: Strategies children use and how teachers can help children learn them. *Young Children, 39*(6), 26–36.

Kemple, K.M. (1991). Preschool children's peer acceptance and social interaction. *Young Children, 46*(5), 47–54.

Pellegrini, A.D., & Glickman, C.D. (1990). Measuring kindergartners' social competence. *Young Children, 45*(4), 40–44.

Rogers, D.L., & Ross, D.D. (1986). Encouraging positive social interaction among young children. *Young Children, 41*(3), 12–17.

 **Article Review Form at end of book.**

# WiseGuide Wrap-Up

- Vygotsky's view of play as a medium through which children experiment with social roles and learn the cultural rules of conduct and self-control is gaining attention. Play, and especially pretend play, is recognized as an activity that promotes the development of many cognitive, social, and language skills.

- Children's pretend play gradually becomes more sophisticated and socially complex over time and with the guidance of adults. Pretend play begins in the context of parent-toddler interactions. Initially, parents take the lead but quickly allow their children to create and guide play. Parent-child pretend promotes competence in peer play and stimulates more complex forms of imaginative play and problem solving.

- By age 7–8, being like everyone else becomes socially important. At this age, children are capable of making social comparisons, but based only on superficial aspects such as appearance.

- There are two major perspectives on friendship influence. One is that having close friends has a positive effect on psychological adjustment and social development. Research from this perspective shows that teens with supportive friends suffer less often from depression, have higher self-esteem, and are better adjusted to school than adolescents without close friendships. The other perspective emphasizes the negative influences of adolescent friendships on behaviors and attitudes as a result of peer pressure.

- Children entering middle school also enter the world of cliques. As children grapple with self-identity issues and puberty, conformity peaks. Cliques provide preteens with feelings of safety, power, and belonging. Unfortunately, being part of the in-group often gives children the license to ridicule out-group peers.

- Children, like adults, experience loneliness. The causes of poor relationships and peer rejection are many, but they often appear related to home-based stressors, such as parental divorce, frequent display of aggressive behaviors, and immature social skills.

## R.E.A.L. Sites

This list provides a print preview of typical **coursewise** R.E.A.L. sites. There are over 100 such sites at the **courselinks**™ site. The danger in printing URLs is that web sites can change overnight. As we went to press, these sites were functional using the URLs provided. If you come across one that isn't, please let us know via email to: webmaster@coursewise.com. Use your Passport to access the most current list of R.E.A.L. sites at the **courselinks**™ site.

**Site name:** Beating Peer Pressure

**URL:** http://family.disney.com/Features/family_1997_05/hudv/hudv57peer/hudv57peer.html

**Why is it R.E.A.L.?** This site presents issues relating to and suggestions for dealing with peer pressure in children from ages 10 to 20. The article suggests that participation in school activities and exercise may help build confidence as a defense against peer pressure. It also reports that the need to be thin is extremely important for female teens. How does the information in this article support your own experiences with the "teen years"? Visit with several teenagers in your area and ask their opinion on the peer pressure issues. What types of activities do peers pressure them to perform? Your readings indicate that peer pressure is mutual. Do you agree? Why or why not?

**Site name:** Abused Children Have More Conflicts with Friends

**URL:** http://www.apa.org/monitor/jun97/friends.html

**Why is it R.E.A.L.?** The articles in this section argue that certain features are characteristic of friendships at different ages. The article at this site discusses the research from three articles on the nature of the friendships of abused children. How are they different from those of nonabused children? What implications do these types of friendships have for children in their adult years? How might teachers and others intervene to nurture more rewarding friendships for abused children?

# section 8

## Learning Objectives

- Provide an overview of normative American family life.

- Describe the impact of father involvement in the raising of children.

- Present an overview of results from a survey on the discipline methods that families today prefer.

- Discuss sibling relationships and their impact on development.

- Summarize current research on the influence of media violence and recommendations for countering the negative effects.

# Family Issues

 **WiseGuide Intro**

The roles and responsibilities of family members have changed as a function of numerous modern-day factors, such as home lives that vary widely from the traditional ideal, mixed messages concerning parenting styles, and media influences. Areas of major interest include the role of fathers, new discipline methods, sibling relationships, and televised violence.

Interactions between fathers and their children have received much attention. The time fathers spend with their children has increased drastically since the 1960s for many reasons. Fathers are now involved in the birth process, participate in many activities as primary caregiver, and engage in more meal preparation and housework than ever before. However, the percentage of time fathers spend with offspring still lags far behind that of mothers. In most homes, mothers assume the primary roles of playmate, comforter, nursemaid, nurturer, and disciplinarian. The skillfulness of mothers in performing these many family tasks is not inborn. The gender-typed behaviors of mothers and fathers is a matter of socialization and cultural norms. Despite the parenting inequities, children of involved fathers experience enriched interactions, the byproduct of which seems to be promotion of cognitive functioning, social skill development, and a willingness to take risks.

An area of great debate among experts, parents, and grandparents centers on discipline techniques. Long gone are the days of using physical punishment and spanking as primary methods of discipline. Newer discipline techniques emphasize the use of time-out procedures, inductive reasoning, ignoring, and loss of privileges. Parents today report that their own parents were stricter with them, and they reject many of the punishment tactics of the past. A climate of nonviolence appears to be the new norm for disciplining children, with spanking held out only for rare instances.

Perhaps making it possible to rely less on physical force to control children are trends toward smaller families. In contrast to previous generations, most children today will grow up with only one sibling, as an only child, or in a blended family. Given these family trends, research addressing questions about the nature and benefits of sibling relationships has reemerged. After all, sibling relationships are the longest social partnerships of our lives, enduring longer than friendships, marriages, and our parents. Sibling relationships may shape how we feel about ourselves, how we understand and feel about others, and even how much we achieve in our lifetimes. The debate continues on the advantages and disadvantages of being an only child versus being one of several children.

In today's world, one of the greatest factors influencing our development is exposure to television. Television has become a regular baby-sitter, and even playmate, for many children. A major concern of professionals and parents alike is the influence of the countless hours of exposure to media violence. Specific concerns surround the manner in

**Reading 30.** How do the parenting styles of mothers and fathers differ?

How can women encourage men to become more involved in family care without nagging?

**Reading 31.** What are some commonalities and differences between today's parents' methods of discipline and the discipline tactics of the previous generation?

How has discipline changed for the better and worse in the past 20 years? Describe some of the changes.

**Reading 32.** How is the finding that siblings tend to be more different than alike explained? Provide two perspectives.

What are the truths and myths about being an only child?

**Reading 33.** Why is the context in which violence is portrayed considered a risk factor?

How does violence portrayed in adults' and children's programming differ?

which violence is presented, the punishment of perpetrators, and the consequences of violent acts. Recommendations for negating the influence of violent programming include parental supervision, mutual watching of programs, and awareness of the risks that different kinds of violence pose.

## Thinking Beyond the Facts

Many of us probably think first of our mothers when asked about who most influenced our early development. However, it should be clear from the articles in this section on family issues that many forces act together to influence the direction of our development. It is no longer acceptable for fathers to simply bring home a paycheck and dole out punishments. More and more, fathers are expected to nurture, teach, and play with their children. How involved was your father with the children? Which of your traits do you think are directly related to interactions you had or did not have with your father? Do your experiences and outcomes match research findings on father-child interactions? As a parent, what might you do differently or encourage your spouse to do differently with your offspring? Consider not only how parents interact with children but also how spouses treat one another in terms of sharing family- and home-related tasks. What is your definition of family fairness? Would you be comfortable carrying out tasks traditionally viewed as the domain of the opposite sex?

Fathers and mothers alike must deal with unacceptable child behaviors. What are your views of discipline and punishment? How much power to control their children should parents exert? If a child feels his or her parents are too restrictive or opposes their methods of punishment, should the child be able to take legal action to stop them? In your opinion, were your parents too strict or too lenient with you? Will you follow in their footsteps when it comes to dealing with your own children? Were any of your siblings treated preferentially or more harshly than others? What impact do you think such differential treatment had on family interactions and individual outcomes? How about television viewing and access to the World Wide Web? Should parents restrict the amount of TV watched and, if so, until what age? Are v-chips an infringement on children's rights? Are parent-imposed limits on chat room or web site access fair? Consider examining more about these family issues by visiting web sites on time-outs, spanking, parenting issues, television ratings, violence, and educational programming.

How do the parenting styles of mothers and fathers differ? How can women encourage men to become more involved in family care without nagging?

# Make Room for Daddy

## David Ruben

**Scene one:** The telephone rings. My seven-year-old daughter, Hallie, answers. It's one of her classmates, calling to arrange a play date. "My mom's not home," I hear her say. "My dad's here, but he doesn't know about this stuff."

**Scene two:** With her fork poised mid-air, Hallie looks up from her dinner—we're the only ones left at the table, her mother and younger sister having already trundled off to the bath—and fixes me with one of her I've-just-been-struck-by-the-most-interesting-notion stares.

"It's funny that Mom's the one who usually cooks our dinner, picks out our clothes, and makes our lunches," she offers amiably. "It's like she's in charge of the house or something."

Ouch. Double ouch.

Here I am, convinced I'm a new, improved breed of dad—involved with my kids, shouldering my share of family burdens and chores, helping to reinvent traditional fatherhood from the wing tips up—and my own daughter is talking like I'm *dispensable* or something.

Hurriedly, I scan a mental checklist: When my wife was pregnant, did I miss a single birthing class? When she delivered, wasn't I right there by her side, holding her hand, feeding her ice chips? When my daughters were babies, didn't I dutifully change their diapers, sterilize their bottles, crawl out of bed for 3:00 a.m. feedings?

And these days, I'm the family's chief breakfast cook and off-to-school chauffeur. I schlepp to PTA meetings and soccer games. I've learned to twist my daughter's tresses into passable ponytails (no mean feat). I know my kids' favorite books and best tickle spots. You don't need to tell *me* that Baby Bop is the most annoying creature on the planet. OK, I still can't tell Mary Kate from Ashley. But I'm working on it.

Why, then, do I have the feeling that if my family had an "essential personnel only" emergency, I'd get the day off?

I reflect some more—this time with an unflinching eye—and a different picture begins to emerge. Granted, I'm more involved in childrearing and household tasks than my own father was. But my wife still does the li-

oness' share of laundry, grocery shopping, and bed making. And no matter how much time I spend with the kids, most of parenthood's heavy lifting—the constant planning, organizing, and managing of family matters—falls largely to her. If my daughter thinks of my wife as the family maestro and me as second fiddle, well, maybe that's because it's true.

Our arrangement is hardly unique: Most of our friends seem to have the same setup. As a rule, it seems, the steady, almost imperceptible heartbeats of family life pulse to a distinctly maternal rhythm.

These roles persist despite the surge of mothers into the workforce over several decades, despite more than a quarter century of feminist agitation for more equitably shared parenting responsibilities, and despite the revelation that most working mothers come home and work a "second shift."

And they endure in spite of the fact that the media has declared involved fatherhood de rigueur, in spite of the avalanche of daddy-celebrating tomes, and in spite of Hollywood's infatuation with the boor-redeemed-by-fatherhood

## You've Come a Long Way, Daddy. . . But Not Far Enough

**+** The time fathers spent with their children grew by a third between the 1960s and the 1980s. And, according to 1992 estimates, fathers spend more than six hours a day with their kids on weekends.

**+** On average, men's contributions to meal preparation, housecleaning, and laundry or ironing have nearly doubled since 1970.

**+** Fathers were credited as the primary caregivers by a surprising 23 percent of employed mothers of children under five, according to a 1991 survey of 13,000 families conducted by the federally funded Population Reference Bureau.

**+** In 1973, barely a quarter of fathers were present at the delivery of their children; today, over three quarters are there for their children's birth.

**−** Fathers spend only about two fifths as much time with their children as mothers do, according to three independently conducted surveys.

**−** The average wife devotes about three times as many hours to indoor housework as the average husband does.

**−** Researchers have found no single childrearing task for which fathers bear primary responsibility.

**−** Almost nine in ten women in a 1994 survey said that taking care of the family is mainly their responsibility.

---

theme. (*Kramer vs. Kramer, She's Having a Baby, Nine Months*).

All of which makes me wonder: What's hype and what's reality? Just how far have fathers really come?

## Close, But No Cigar

I'm not the only one who's wondering: Fatherhood is a hot topic among researchers as well. And after consulting with a bevy of them, I can safely conclude that fatherhood in America has evolved for the better. But there is plenty of room for improvement (see "You've Come a Long Way, Daddy. . . " and "But Not Far Enough").

"Today's fathers are increasingly likely to be nurturing family men," says Scott Coltrane, a sociologist at the University of California at Riverside. "But women continue to do most of the family work."

That said, most studies on the subject of family roles don't even begin to address what may be the greatest imbalance of all: the fact that women still perform most of the planning, delegating, arranging, and supervising—of everything from laundry to emotions—to keep the family running. When my wife is away from home, for example, I'll take center stage quite competently. But even in her absence, she's still running the show: Like so many wives, she leaves me lists ("Pick up Tess at 3:00 p.m. Remember to pack a snack for Hallie"). And though my pride may be wounded, I still consult the list religiously.

It's the difference between help and leadership, cooperation and command. Robert Griswold, a historian who specializes in family studies at the University of Oklahoma, explains it this way: "If the mother says, 'Go out and get a new pair of shoes for our daughter,' the well-intentioned father will do it. But he probably hasn't ever taken it upon himself to look in her closet to see whether or not she needs new shoes."

Mention Griswold's shoe-buying example to Michael Kimmel, a sociologist at the State University of New York at Stony Brook, and he throws in a footwear quip of his own: "There used to be a joke in the fifties that fathers didn't know the color of their children's eyes," Kimmel says. "Today we do. But we still don't know their shoe size."

All in all, a pretty apt summation of fatherhood in the nineties.

## More Than Just Another Body

Sometimes when I'm feeling deeply philosophical—or don't want to miss the fourth quarter of the big game to help with dinner—I wonder, why fight tradition? Mothers have shouldered most of the family load for decades, centuries, maybe eons. Why not just let sleeping gender roles lie?

One obvious answer: The world has changed. My wife has a job. So do more than half of all mothers with young children. We dads aren't doing more because we're more conscientious or evolved than our forefathers. We're doing more because someone has to pick up the slack—not to mention the children, the take-out, and the quart of milk.

But there's a more profound reason for fathers to become more fully engaged: There's too much at stake for them *not* to. Studies show that involved dads contribute to myriad positive quali-

## Helping Fathers Get Into the Act

Many dads who want to become involved in their children's lives aren't always quite sure what they're supposed to do—especially in the early days of parenthood, when they're faced with a crying, wriggling baby. A father may need encouragement from Mom before he feels comfortable in his new role. Let him know that you consider parenthood a joint endeavor and that you value his participation.

- Attend childbirth classes together and arrange for your partner to be present for the baby's birth.
- Welcome Dad into the nursing relationship. He can play a pivotal role by bringing the baby to you, helping position her, getting you a drink of water, encouraging your efforts, and settling the baby after feedings.
- Give your partner plenty of opportunities to soothe a crying newborn, entertain a bored baby, or

lull a drowsy infant to sleep. Instead of worrying whether he's doing things right, think about whether he's doing the right things. A loving father's sincere attempt to care for his baby is far more important than whether the diaper gets put on backward occasionally.

- Encourage Dad to take over the evening routine. Wrapping up the day with a play-filled bath followed by a cozy storytime can be one of the most intimate moments in fathering.
- Take turns visiting the pediatrician. Conversations with the doctor can bolster a father's knowledge and confidence about nutrition, development, safety, and even behavior and discipline.
- Ask Dad to share responsibility for routine childcare chores, such as buying and wrapping a birthday present, packing a lunch, giving medicine, or taking a child for a haircut.

Special moments with children usually aren't the result of scheduled, structured events. They're a result of the sheer quantity of time spent together, often doing ordinary, mundane things.

- Have your child's father participate at school by going to parent-teacher conferences, helping with homework assignments, or attending PTA meetings.
- Urge your partner to read to your child, even when it's not bedtime. Long after children are able to read by themselves, they still enjoy hearing a good book.
- Encourage Dad to get even more physical. Shared athletic activity doesn't have to involve competitive sports. What child wouldn't relish the chance to go fishing, shoot baskets, jog, bike, skate, wrestle, or simply walk the dog with his father?

Marianne Neifert, M.D.

---

ties in their children, from self-confidence, social poise, and initiative to empathy, cooperation, and a certain resistance in both boys and girls to gender stereotypes. (Young children with supportive dads, for instance, tend to have less traditional views about dual-earner couples and parents sharing childcare.)

Dad's influence extends well beyond the development of social skills. Studies indicate that the early involvement of fathers tends to challenge and boost the cognitive development of babies as young as a year old. Such fatherly input has staying power: "Research suggests that the care fathers provide is a significant factor in their children's later success and happiness," says John Snarey, a professor of human development at Emory University, whose book *How Fathers Care for the Next Generation* chronicles four decades of father-

hood. According to one section of his study, the more accessible dads are to their children, the more likely those youngsters are to enjoy a relatively peaceful and conflict-free adolescence.

## The Daddy Difference

Snarey's work also shows that fathers often play a key role in the development of athletic and overall physical confidence in girls and intellectual and academic skills in boys.

"By giving their children what they may not be getting elsewhere—throwing a ball with a daughter or discussing a book with a son—fathers help to produce balanced adults," Snarey says. "Support in unconventional areas is what dads provide." In other words, Snarey adds, "fathers and mothers are not interchangeable. Kids get something

from their dads that's different from what they get from their moms."

That difference becomes especially evident during play—one of the most common forms of father-child interaction. From the outset, research shows, fathers tend to play more energetically and physically with their children than do mothers. (In fact, several studies have found that babies and young children often prefer Dad over Mom when it comes to playtime.) Fathers rough-house. They play tag. They tickle. They are lively, unpredictable, exciting. They goof around more and encourage more risk taking: "Go for it. Let's see how far you can jump off the couch," a dad might dare.

Mothers, on the other hand, tend to be more protective around their kids. Their play tends to be more restrained and often involves objects like blocks or dolls.

## How Fathers Pitch In

Do moms and dads shoulder childrearing responsibilities equally? *Parenting* asked subscribers to American Online and found that the answer was yes—but a qualified yes. About 1,500 respondents told us that mothers and fathers do share some childrearing chores. But when it comes to time-consuming tasks like going to the dentist or cooking, moms are more likely to step up to the plate.

**Who changes the diapers?**

| | |
|---|---|
| 48% | Both do equally |
| 40% | Mostly Mom |
| 3% | Mostly Dad |
| 9% | Neither |

**. . . plays with the kids?**

| | |
|---|---|
| 71% | Both do equally |
| 18% | Mostly Mom |
| 10% | Mostly Dad |
| 1% | Neither |

**. . . comforts a crying child?**

| | |
|---|---|
| 49% | Mostly Mom |
| 47% | Both do equally |
| 3% | Mostly Dad |
| 1% | Neither |

**. . . dresses the kids?**

| | |
|---|---|
| 62% | Mostly Mom |
| 30% | Both do equally |
| 4% | Mostly Dad |
| 4% | Neither |

**. . . plans and prepares dinner?**

| | |
|---|---|
| 68% | Mostly Mom |
| 19% | Both do equally |
| 11% | Mostly Dad |
| 2% | Neither |

**. . . disciplines the children?**

| | |
|---|---|
| 60% | Both do equally |
| 22% | Mostly Mom |
| 10% | Mostly Dad |
| 8% | Neither |

**. . . takes the kids to the dentist?**

| | |
|---|---|
| 69% | Mostly Mom |
| 27% | Both do equally |
| 4% | Mostly Dad |

**. . . stays home when a child is sick?**

| | |
|---|---|
| 74% | Mostly Mom |
| 16% | Both do equally |
| 5% | Mostly Dad |
| 5% | Neither |

**Who responded:** About 70 percent of respondents were mothers (45 percent were stay-at-home moms, 44 percent worked outside the home, 11 percent ran a home business); 30 percent were fathers (7 percent were stay-at-home dads, 12 percent worked outside the home, 81 percent had a home business); 51 percent had one child, 32 percent had two, 17 percent had three or more.

"A working-hard-at-playing quality sets fathers apart from mothers," Snarey says.

Neither approach is necessarily better than the other, according to experts. "Each parent's style teaches a child different things about the world," says Mitch Golant, a Los Angeles psychologist who studies family dynamics. "Mother's approach informs him that the world can be cuddly, safe, nurturing, and supportive. Father's way lets him know that life can be all of that, but that it can also be jostling, unsettling, surprising, and fun."

## Inherent or Acquired?

But do mothers and father really come by their different roles "naturally" or are they learned? Many researchers aren't so sure.

"Parenting roles are mostly a social and cultural function," says sociologist Coltrane. "They're not biologically set in stone." Therefore, he adds, there's no reason men can't learn to be more nurturing, no reason they can't take on more household responsibilities. "I think what most mothers do isn't instinct, it's practice. After all, there are plenty of single

dads who don't lack for family-management capabilities."

Yet fifty-fifty sharing may be an unrealistic goal, Coltrane says. "After all, there's no getting around the fact that mothers are the ones who ovulate, lactate, and carry babies for nine months. Gender isn't going to go away. But if men did even one third of the childcare, it would be a great leap forward."

## Stepping Up to the Plate

So what's holding fathers back? Our own resistance to change is the most obvious answer. Pitching in may ultimately pay off down the road, but let's face it, in the short run, it can be a royal pain. If traditional dads missed the boat on emotional intimacy, at least they got to read the paper or tip a few cold ones with the boys, no questions asked, no guilt conferred.

But there's also no denying that some mothers are ambivalent about sharing the household power and control—a phenomenon that some observers have dubbed, "the glass ceiling for men."

"Women aren't always so generous about letting go," Coltrane says. "In some cases, men are far more eager to take on the cooking and childcare tasks than women are to share them." Besides, sometimes monarchy is easier than democracy: In a busy, dual-career family, both spouses may find it more efficient to have a single administrator than to share the power.

And then there's that informal social networking and community-building at which women seem to be so much more gifted than men. My wife meets more parents and arranges more play dates in a single drop-off at nursery school than I manage over an entire year.

Add to this phenomenon the fact that in most families the man earns more money and is therefore the logical candidate to work more and parent less. "If women made one dollar for every 70 cents that men made," says Coltrane, "I think that family roles and responsibilities would change quite quickly."

But Coltrane and other "new fatherhood" advocates remain optimistic. After all, they point out, fatherhood has already undergone massive changes. And it will almost certainly continue to evolve. In what direction and at what speed, however, is ultimately up to fathers themselves.

"The question used to be, can men do it?" Coltrane says.

"Well, we've pretty much found out that they can. Now, the real question is, *will* they?"

I honestly don't know. But I think I'll get up right now and go check my daughters' closets. They may need some new shoes.

 **Article Review Form at end of book.**

What are some commonalities and differences between today's parents' methods of discipline and the discipline tactics of the previous generation? How has discipline changed for the better and worse in the past 20 years? Describe some of the changes.

# Discipline
## The new rules

**Mary Conners**

You do it filled with doubt. You do it with regret. You do it with a stomach-churning sense of inadequacy. No child-rearing task saps your confidence like disciplining does, according to the results of the latest *Parents* poll, "How Do You Discipline?" (June 1997). But despite your misgivings, you're trying harder and doing better than you realize—better, perhaps, than any preceding generation.

Judging by the more than 4,000 responses to our poll, today's parents are hardly wimps. Nor are they the harsh dictators that their own parents often were. The majority of respondents, 61 percent, believe their parents were stricter than they are, and many are rejecting the punishments of the past. Instead, our readers are seeking new skills and strategies—in essence, stocking their own disciplinary tool kits.

Parents today understand that discipline is more like a socket wrench than a hammer; one size does not fit all situations. Different kids and different circumstances all call for different techniques. Parents recognize that instilling discipline in a child calls

### Crimes and Punishment

| Here's what the majority rules as the best responses: | | |
|---|---|---|
| **Tells a lie** | Warning or reprimand | 53% |
| **Refuses to eat** | Ignore the behavior | 62% |
| **Won't go to bed** | Warning or reprimand | 56% |
| **Ignores request to do chores** | Take away privilege or toy | 42% |
| **Talks back to/defies parent** | Time-out | 40% |
| **Ignores/tunes out parent** | Warning or reprimand | 45% |
| **Disrespectful to another adult** | Warning or reprimand | 51% |
| **Endangers self** | Warning or reprimand | 48% |
| **Deliberately destructive** | Time-out | 36% |
| **Hits someone** | Time-out | 57% |
| **Swears** | Warning or reprimand | 44% |
| **Steals** | Take away privilege or toy | 38% |

for discipline on their own part, especially the resolve not to succumb to anger—what one respondent aptly describes as "an adult temper tantrum."

### Spanking Takes a Backseat

How much have our readers departed from their parents? Consider this remarkable snapshot: The majority of respondents, 68 percent, report that they were spanked as children. More than a third of those spanked, 36 percent, say they were "hit hard enough to hurt" at least once a week. And

while 72 percent of respondents believe that spanking is an acceptable form of discipline, an even bigger number, 75 percent, say they do not spank their own children. Of the readers who report they were regularly spanked as children, 27 percent now consider spanking wrong under any circumstances.

Sarah Boldt, of Stoddard, Wisconsin, shrugs off the spankings that she received growing up in a single-parent household. "My mother raised five children alone. She was just very busy," says the 35-year-old mother of two school-age kids. But five years ago, Boldt stopped spanking. Today she and her husband, Ronald, are firm believes in time-outs. "You don't have to hit kids to make them understand right from wrong," she declares. "Before, I simply did not know of other alternatives that would be as effective. Now I do."

For some respondents, the spanking they received as kids were motivation enough to find a better way: "I lived in a household where spanking got completely out of control," recalls Vicky DeCoster, 35, of Omaha, Nebraska, the mother of a 3-year-old. "I have read my diary entries from back then, and they consisted of things like 'Mommy beat me today because I did not wash my hands before I opened the refrigerator door.' We have a chance to change our generation's attitude toward violence. No one needs to be like their parents."

The "anything but spanking" sentiments of the majority of our respondents, nearly all married, middle-class mothers, mirror a wider cultural shift. "There's a big trend away from wanting to spank your child," says Irwin A. Hyman, Ed.D., professor of school psychology at Temple University and author of *The Case Against Spanking* (Jossey-Bass Publishers). "People think and read more about child-rearing now. They are more aware of alternative punishments, and are much more aware of the connection between spanking and child abuse."

## Parents Have New Roles, But Few Role Models

No matter what methods they use, many readers doubt their effectiveness at disciplining. While 92 percent of respondents are con-

fident in their ability to teach right from wrong, only 52 percent feel that way about disciplining (see Discipline Doubts, page 140). Thirteen percent confess they have little or no confidence—a far higher percentage of pessimism than expressed for any other child-rearing skill they were asked about.

And it doesn't get any better with age. While levels of confidence in most other skills tend to be higher in older moms, only 13 percent of respondents over age 31 expressed total confidence in their ability to discipline, compared with 17 percent of those 25 and under.

Why all the insecurity? For one thing, our readers view discipline as a high-stakes endeavor. Virtually all respondents agree that lax discipline of children leads to problems in American society, notably crime and disrespect for others. Yet many new parents lack the resources and role models they need to discipline effectively today. "The only training we have as parents is the fact that we all have parents ourselves. A lot of people are aware that that's simply not enough," says Nancy Samalin, a contributing editor of *Parents* and the author of *Loving Your Child Is Not Enough* (Penguin).

Jane Nelsen, Ed. D., author of *Positive Discipline* (Ballantine Books), points to the dramatic changes in our society in the last few decades—particularly the changing roles of women. Years ago, many children had a ready model for submissiveness right in their own homes—their moms. "Children don't behave like they used to in the old days—but then again, neither do their mothers," Nelsen points out. "Children need to learn new ways of cooperation."

## Consistency Is the No. 1 Challenge

The two biggest challenges our readers face in disciplining their children are consistency (17 percent) and anger (15 percent). Regrettably, anger also plays a major, unhappy role in the type of punishment meted out. While nearly half of the respondents believe the main reason to spank is to let a child know what's unacceptable, the next largest group, 26 percent, admit that "losing my temper" is the impetus (see "Blowing Up," page 70*).

"I hate to spank, since I was spanked a lot as a kid," writes Joyce VanderVere, 40, the mother of a 5- and 6-year-old in Muskegon, Michigan. "But I work third shift and get four or five hours of sleep a day, so my temper is easily ignited. I really have to concentrate to keep it together."

Jennifer Singletary, of Southfield, Michigan, uses a variety of tactics to discipline her four boys, ages 1 to 10. Whether she's imposing time-outs, taking away privileges, or even spanking, Singletary, 32, believes that consistency is key: "I have friends who are not consistent with any form of discipline. Their kids are going to test the limits, and they know there's no line." When she feels herself getting angry, she tells her children that she needs a time-out—and they know to back off.

Writes Norma Andes, 40, a mother of two in Norfolk, Virginia, "I want to teach my 4-year-old internal control, so he decides to do what is right, versus external control, so he behaves just to avoid being hit. It takes longer and is messier to teach, and involves my dealing with my own anger instead of venting it on him."

*Does not appear in this publication.

## Moms Punish More Often Than Dads

While our readers are unsure of their discipline decisions, they are not alone in making or enforcing them. Forty-two percent feel that they and their spouse are equally successful at making their children understand the reasons for the discipline. All is not equal, however. Sixty-six percent of moms, whether or not they work outside the home, say they punish more frequently than does their spouse.

Parents faithfully follow our country's credo—United We Stand, Divided We Fall—in their private lives. More than half of respondents (57 percent) say they only disagree with their spouse about discipline once a month or less. Fifty-two percent report that they discuss discipline issues with their spouse at least weekly. and many try to hold those conversations away from little ears. But whenever parents disagree, the majority of them (54 percent) believe it results in less effective disciplining.

### Discipline Doubts

| When you rated your confidence in six crucial child-rearing skills, discipline came in dead last. Here's a breakdown of what you feel you can handle well. | |
| --- | --- |
| Teach my child right from wrong | 92% |
| Teach my child the importance of education | 90% |
| Teach my child to be compassionate | 87% |
| Teach my child to behave responsibly | 82% |
| Teach my child to get along with others | 81% |
| Discipline my child effectively | 52% |

### Discipline Now and Then

Reasoning and time-outs are in, nagging and threats are on their way out. Here's how you handle your kids' bad behavior—and what you remember your parents doing. At least once a week. . .

| . . . you discipline with: | | . . . they disciplined with: | |
| --- | --- | --- | --- |
| 88% | Reprimands | 81% | Reprimands |
| 78% | Reasoning | 69% | Yelling |
| 61% | Yelling | 56% | Nagging |
| 56% | Ignoring behavior | 53% | Threatening |
| 50% | Time-out | 44% | Reasoning |
| 44% | Taking away toy or privilege | 38% | A slap on the hand or swat on the rear |
| 40% | Threatening | 37% | Taking away toy or privilege |
| 31% | Nagging | 34% | Ignoring the behavior |
| 25% | Giving in | 24% | Hitting hard enough to hurt |
| 17% | Bribing | 21% | Giving in |
| 16% | Swat on the rear end | 11% | Bribing |
| 12% | Slap on the hand | 10% | Time-out |
| 4% | Giving extra chores | | |
| 3% | Hitting hard enough to hurt | | |

"I'm more apt to try reasoning, but my husband threatens with spanking. I never dispute his disciplining, and vice versa, in front of the kids, but afterward we butt heads once in a while," writes Joyce VanderVere.

"If one of us is disciplining and the other disagrees, we let the person doing the disciplining follow through. But then we talk about it as soon as possible, and try to come up with how we will deal with this behavior in the future," writes Mary Kay Healy, 32, mother of a preschooler and a toddler, in Hebron, Connecticut.

Parents also make a point of discussing discipline issues with their caregivers. More than half (55 percent) of the respondents with childcare providers give them explicit discipline instructions. Several readers give special credit to caregivers and teachers for expanding their horizons. "I feel very lucky to have such a partner in my daughter's upbringing," writes one mom.

Of all the tools that our readers use, verbal reprimands or warnings are the most popular (88 percent of respondents use them at least a few times a week). Fifty percent use time-outs at least once a week. But today's parents try to approach each discipline situation as unique (see Crimes and Punishment, page 138). What's the best way to handle a child who won't eat? Ignore him (62 percent). A child who lies? Give a warning or reprimand (53 percent). Some parents even use spanking selectively, for a child who endangers himself (26 percent), for instance, or is deliberately destructive (20 percent).

### Searching for Solutions

Numbers, of course, tell only part of the story. Your generous letters—dashed off during naptime, typed on business letterhead, scrawled on note paper from the Disneyland Hotel—show the importance you place on learning new ways to discipline.

Karen Westin, of Holts Summit, Missouri, points to books, classes, and seminars by parent educators. "The positive techniques advocated by these folks have significantly cut down on my yelling, which I hate, and my frustration," writes the 36-year-old mother of two small children.

Others, like 36-year-old Michelle Hotton, of Alberta, Canada, have sought counseling to help them break from the past. "Now my husband and I have no problem telling our parents that they are never to hit our children," writes Hotton, the mother of a 5- and 1-year-old, who recalls her father beating her with a belt.

Today, discipline with her own daughter "is not easy," Hotton writes, nor is she a perfect parent. "My biggest problem is yelling," she admits. For all its flaws, though, she feels her way is better than the old way. "I have learned that it's okay to apologize to a child and admit you're wrong," she concludes, "something that my parents would not do."

 **Article Review Form at end of book.**

How is the finding that siblings tend to be more different than alike explained? Provide two perspectives. What are the truths and myths about being an only child?

# The Secret World of Siblings

### Erica E. Goode

*They have not been together like this for years, the three of them standing on the close-cropped grass. New England lawns and steeples spread out below the golf course. He is glad to see his older brothers, has always been glad to have "someone to look up to, to do things with." Yet he also knows the silences between them, the places he dares not step, even though they are all grown men now. They move across the greens, trading small talk, joking. But at the 13th hole, he swings at the ball, duffs it and his brothers begin to needle him. "I should be better than this," he thinks. Impatiently, he swings again, misses, then angrily grabs the club and breaks it in half across his knee. Recalling this outburst later, he explains, simply: "They were beating me again."*

As an old man, Leo Tolstoy once opined that the simplest relationships in life are those between brother and sister. He must have been delirious at the time. Even lesser mortals, lacking Tolstoy's acute eye and literary skill, recognize the power of the word *sibling* to reduce normally competent, ra-

tional human beings to raw bundles of anger, love, hurt, longing and disappointment—often in a matter of minutes. Perhaps they have heard two elderly sisters dig at each other's sore spots with astounding accuracy, much as they did in junior high. Or have seen a woman corner her older brother at a family reunion, finally venting 30 years of pent-up resentment. Or watched remorse and yearning play across a man's face as he speaks of the older brother whose friendship was chased away long ago, amid dinner table taunts of "Porky Pig, Porky Pig, oink, oink, oink!"

Sibling relationships—and 80 percent of Americans have at least one—outlast marriages, survive the death of parents, resurface after quarrels that would sink any friendship. They flourish in a thousand incarnations of closeness and distance, warmth, loyalty and distrust. Asked to describe them, more than a few people stammer and hesitate, tripped up by memory and sudden bursts of unexpected emotion.

Traditionally, experts have viewed siblings as "very minor actors on the stage of human de-

velopment," says Stephen Bank, Wesleyan University psychologist and co-author of *The Sibling Bond*. But a rapidly expanding body of research is showing that what goes on in the playroom or in the kitchen while dinner is being cooked exerts a profound influence on how children grow, a contribution that approaches, if it may not quite equal, that of parenting. Sibling relationships shape how people feel about themselves, how they understand and feel about others, even how much they achieve. And more often than not, such ties represent the lingering thumbprint of childhood upon adult life, affecting the way people interact with those closest to them, with friends and coworkers, neighbors and spouses—a topic explored by an increasing number of popular books, including *Mom Loved You Best*, the most recent offering by Dr. William and Mada Hapworth and Joan Heilman.

## Shifting Landscape

In a 1990s world of shifting social realities, of working couples, disintegrating marriages, "blended" households, disappearing grandparents and families spread across a continent, this belated validation of the importance of sibling influences probably comes none too soon. More and more children are stepping in to change diapers, cook meals and help with younger siblings' homework in the hours when parents are still at the office. Baby boomers, edging into middle age, find themselves squaring off once again with brothers and sisters over the care of dying parents or the division of inheritance. And in a generation where late marriages and fewer children are the norm, old age may become for many a time when siblings—not devoted sons and daughters—sit by the bedside.

*It is something that happened so long ago, so silly and unimportant now that she is 26 and a researcher at a large, downtown office and her younger brother is her best friend, really, so close that she talks to him at least once a week. Yet as she begins to speak, she is suddenly a 5-year-old again on Christmas morning, running into the living room in her red flannel pajamas, her straight blond hair in a ponytail. He hasn't even wrapped it, the little, yellow-flowered plastic purse. Racing to the tree, he brings it to her, thrusts it at her— "Here's your present, Jenny!"—smiling that stupid, adoring, little brother smile. She takes the purse and hurls it across the room. "I don't want your stupid present," she yells. A small crime, long ago forgiven. Yet she says: "I still feel tremendously guilty about it."*

Sigmund Freud, perhaps guided by his own childhood feelings of rivalry, conceived of siblingship as a story of unremitting jealousy and competition. Yet, observational studies of young children, many of them the groundbreaking work of Pennsyl-vania State University psychologist Judy Dunn and her

colleagues, suggest that while rivalry between brothers and sisters is common, to see only hostility in sibling relations is to miss the main show. The arrival of a younger sibling may cause distress to an older child accustomed to parents' exclusive attention, but it also stirs enormous interest, presenting both children with the opportunity to learn crucial social and cognitive skills; how to comfort and empathize with another person, how to make jokes, resolve arguments, even how to irritate.

The lessons in this life tutorial take as many forms as there are children and parents. In some families, a natural attachment seems to form early between older and younger children. Toddlers as young as 14 months miss older siblings when they are absent, and babies separated briefly from their mothers will often accept comfort from an older sibling and go back to playing happily. As the younger child grows, becoming a potential playmate, confidant and sparring partner, older children begin to pay more attention. But even young children monitor their siblings' behavior closely, showing a surprisingly sophisticated grasp of their actions and emotional states.

## Parental Signals

To some extent, parents set the emotional tone of early sibling interactions. Dunn's work indicates, for example, that children whose mothers encourage them to view a newborn brother or sister as a human being, with needs, wants and feelings, are friendlier to the new arrival over the next year, an affection that is later reciprocated by the younger child. The quality of parents' established relationships with older siblings can also influence how a new younger brother or sister is received. In an-

other of Dunn's studies, first-born daughters who enjoyed a playful, intense relationship with their mothers treated newborn siblings with more hostility, and a year later the younger children were more hostile in return. In contrast, older daughters with more contentious relationships with their mothers greeted the newcomer enthusiastically—perhaps relieved to have an ally. Fourteen months later, these older sisters were more likely to imitate and play with their younger siblings and less apt to hit them or steal their toys.

In troubled homes, where a parent is seriously ill, depressed or emotionally unavailable, siblings often grow closer than they might in a happier environment, offering each other solace and protection. This is not always the case, however. When parents are on the brink of separation or have already divorced and remarried, says University of Virginia psychologist E. Mavis Hetherington, rivalry between brothers and sisters frequently increases, as they struggle to hold on to their parents' affection in the face of the breakup. If anything, it is sisters who are likely to draw together in a divorcing family, while brothers resist forming tighter bonds. Says Hetherington: "Males tend to go it alone and not to use support very well."

Much of what transpires between brothers and sisters, of course, takes places when parents are not around. "Very often the parent doesn't see the subtlety or the full cycle of siblings interactions," says University of Hartford psychologist Michael Kahn. Left to their own devices, children tease, wrestle and play make-believe. They are the ones eager to help pilot the pirate ship or play storekeeper to the sibling's impatient customer. And none of this pretend play, researchers find, is wasted. Toddlers who engage regularly in make-believe with older siblings later show a precocious grasp of others' behavior. Says Dunn: "They turn out to be the real stars at understanding people."

Obviously, some degree of rivalry and squabbling between siblings is natural. Yet in extreme cases, verbal or physical abuse at the hands of an older brother or sister can leave scars that last well into adulthood. Experts like Wesleyan University's Bank distinguish between hostility that takes the form of humiliation or betrayal and more benign forms of conflict. From the child's perspective, the impact of even normal sibling antagonism may depend in part on who's coming out ahead. In one study, for example, children showed higher self-esteem when they "delivered" more teasing, insults and other negative behaviors to their siblings than they received. Nor is even intense rivalry necessarily destructive. Says University of Texas psychologist Duane Buhrmester: "You may not be happy about a brother or sister who is kind of pushing you along, but you may also get somewhere in life."

*They are two sides of an equation written 30 yeas ago: Michèle, with her raven-black hair, precisely made-up lips, restrained smile; Arin, two years older, her easy laugh filling the restaurant, the sleeves of her gray turtleneck pulled over her hands.*

*This is what Arin thinks about Michèle: "I have always resented her, and she has always looked up to me. When we were younger, she used to copy me, which would drive me crazy. We have nothing in common except our family history—isn't that terrible? I like her spirit of generosity, her direction and ambition. I dislike her rapid conversation and her idiotic*

*friends. But the reality is that we are very close, and we always will be."*

*This is what Michèle sees: "Arin was my ideal. I wanted to be like her, to look like her. I think I drove her crazy. Once, I gave her a necklace I thought was very beautiful. I never saw her wear it. I think it wasn't good enough, precious enough. We are so different—I wish that we could be more like friends. But, as we get older, we accept each other more."*

It is something every brother or sister eventually marvels at, a conundrum that novelists have played upon in a thousand different ways: There are two children. They grow up in the same house, share the same parents, experience many of the same events. Yet they are stubbornly, astonishingly different.

A growing number of studies in the relatively new field of behavioral genetics are finding confirmation for this popular observation. Children raised in the same family, such studies find, are only very slightly more similar to each other on a variety of personality dimensions than they are, say, to Bill Clinton or to the neighbor's son. In cognitive abilities, too, siblings appear more different than alike. And the extent to which siblings *do* resemble one another in these traits is largely the result of the genes they share—a conclusion drawn from twin studies, comparisons of biological siblings raised apart and biological children and adopted siblings raised together.

## Contrasts

Heredity also contributes to the *differences* between siblings. About 30 percent of the dissimilarity between brothers and sisters on many personality dimensions can be accounted for by differing ge-

netic endowments from parents. But that still leaves 70 percent that *cannot* be attributed to genetic causes, and it is this unexplained portion of contrasting traits that scientists find so intriguing. If two children who grow up in the same family are vastly different, and genetics accounts for only a minor part of these differences, what else is going on?

The answer may be that brothers and sisters don't really share the same family at all. Rather, each child grows up in a unique family, one shaped by the way he perceives other people and events, by the chance happenings he alone experiences, and by how other people—parents, siblings, and teachers—perceive and act toward him. And while for decades experts in child development have focused on the things that children in the same family share—social class, child-rearing attitudes and parents' marital satisfaction, for example—what really seem to matter are those things that are not shared. As Judy Dunn and Pennsylvania State behavioral geneticist Robert Plomin write in *Separate Lives: Why Siblings Are So Different,* "Environmental factors important to development are those that two children in the same family experience differently."

Asked to account for children's disparate experiences, most people invoke the age-old logic of birth order. "I'm the middle child, so I'm cooler headed," they will say, or "Firstborns are high achievers." Scientists, too, beginning with Sir Francis Galton in the 19th century, have sought in birth order a way to characterize how children diverge in personality, IQ or life success. But in recent years, many researchers have backed away from this notion, asserting that when family size, number of siblings and social class are taken into account, the explanatory power of birth ranking becomes negligible. Says one psychologist: "You wouldn't want to make a decision about your child based on it."

At least one researcher, however, argues that birth order does exert a strong influence on development, particularly on attitudes toward authority. Massachusetts Institute of Technology historian Frank Sulloway, who has just completed a 20-year analysis of 4,000 scientists from Copernicus through the 20th century, finds that those with older siblings were significantly more likely to have contributed to or supported radical scientific revolutions, such as Darwin's theory of evolution. Firstborn scientists, in contrast, were more apt to champion conservative scientific ideas. "Later-borns are consistently more open-minded, more intellectually flexible and therefore more radical," says Sulloway, adding that later-borns also tend to be more agreeable and less competitive.

## Hearthside Inequities

Perhaps most compelling for scientists who study sibling relationships are the ways in which parents treat their children differently and the inequalities children perceive in their parents' behavior. Research suggests that disparate treatment by parents can have a lasting effect, even into adulthood. Children who receive more affection from fathers than their siblings do, for example, appear to aim their sights higher in terms of education and professional goals, according to a study by University of Southern California psychologist Laura Baker. Seven-year-olds treated by their mothers in a less affectionate, more controlling way than their brothers or

sisters are apt to be more anxious and depressed. And adolescents who say their parents favor a sibling over themselves are more likely to report angry and depressed feelings.

Parental favoritism spills into sibling relationships, too, sometimes breeding the hostility made famous by the Smothers Brothers in their classic 1960s routine, "Mom always loved you best." In families where parents are more punitive and restrictive toward one child, for instance, that child is more likely to act in an aggressive, rivalrous and unfriendly manner toward a brother or sister, according to work by Hetherington. Surprisingly, it may not matter who is favored. Children in one study were more antagonistic toward siblings even when *they* were the ones receiving preferential treatment.

Many parents, of course, go to great lengths to distribute their love and attention equally. Yet even the most consciously egalitarian parenting may be seen as unequal by children of different ages. A mother may treat her 4-year-old boy with the same care and attention she lavished on her older son when he was 4. But from the 7-year-old's perspective, it may look like his younger brother is getting a better deal. Nor is there much agreement among family members on how evenhandedly love is apportioned: Adolescents report favoritism when their mothers and fathers insist that none exists. Some parents express surprise that their children feel unequally treated, while at the same time they describe how one child is more demanding, another needs more discipline. And siblings almost never agree in their assessments of who, exactly, Mom loves bests.

## Nature vs. Nurture

Further complicating the equation is the contribution of heredity to temperament, each child presenting a different challenge from the moment of birth. Plomin, part of a research team led by George Washington University psychiatrist David Reiss that is studying sibling pairs in 700 families nationwide, views the differences between siblings as emerging from a complex interaction of nature and nurture. In this scheme, a more aggressive and active child, for example, might engage in more conflict with parents and later become a problem child at school. A quieter, more timid child might receive gentler parenting and later be deemed an easy student.

*In China, long ago, it was just the two of them, making dolls out of straw together in the internment camp, putting on their Sunday clothes to go to church with their mother. She mostly ignored her younger sister, or goaded her relentlessly for being so quiet. By the time they were separated—her sister sailing alone at 13 for the United States—there was already a wall between them, a prelude to the stiff Christmas cards they exchange, the rebuffed phone calls, the impersonal gifts that arrive in the mail.*

*Now, when the phone rings, she is wishing hard for a guardian angel, for someone to take away the pain that throbs beneath the surgical bandage on her chest, keeping her curled under the blue and white cotton coverlet. She picks up the receiver, recognizes her sister's voice instantly, is surprised, grateful, cautious all at once. How could it be otherwise after so many years? It is the longest they have spoken in 50 years. And across the telephone wire, something is shifting, melting in the small talk about children, the wishes for speedy recovery. "I think we both realized that life can be very short," she says. Her pain, too, is dulling now, moving away as she listens to her sister's voice. She begins to say a small prayer of thanks.*

For a period that seems to stretch forever in the timelessness of childhood, there is only the family, only the others who are un-chosen partners, their affection, confidences, attacks and betrayals defining the circumference of a limited world. But eventually, the boundaries expand, friends and schoolmates taking the place of brothers and sisters, highways and airports leading to other lives, to office parties and neighborhood meetings, to other, newer families.

## Adult Bonds

Rivalry between siblings wanes after adolescence, or at least adults are less apt to admit competitive feelings. Strong friendships also become less intense, diluted by geography, by marriage, by the concerns of raising children and pursuing independent careers. In national polls, 65 percent of Americans say they would like to see their siblings more often than the typical "two or three times a year." And University of Indianapolis psychologist Victoria Bedford finds, in her work, that men and women of child-rearing age often show longing toward siblings, especially those close in age and of the same sex. Yet for some people, the detachment of adulthood brings relief, an escape from bonds that are largely unwanted but never entirely go away. Says one woman about her brothers and sisters: "Our values are different, our politics diametrically opposed. I don't feel very connected, but there's still a pressure to keep up the tie, a kind of guilt that I don't have a deeper sense of kinship."

## Only Children: Cracking the Myth of the Pampered, Lonely Misfit

Child-rearing experts may have neglected the psychology of sibling ties, but they have never been hesitant to warn parents about the perils of siring a single child. Children unlucky enough to grow up without brothers or sisters, the professional wisdom held, were bound to be self-centered, unhappy, anxious, demanding, pampered and generally maladjusted to the larger social world. "Being an only child is a disease in itself," psychologist G. Stanley Hall concluded at the turn of the century.

Recent research paints a kinder picture of the only child—a welcome revision at a time when single-child families are increasing. The absence of siblings, psychologists find, does not doom children to a life of neurosis or social handicap. Day care, preschool and other modern child-care solutions go far in combatting an only child's isolation and in mitigating the willfulness and self-absorption that might come from being the sole focus of parental attention. And while only children may miss out on some positive aspects of growing up around brothers and sisters, they also escape potentially negative experiences, such as unequal parenting or severe aggression by an older sibling. Says University of Texas at Austin social psychologist Toni Falbo: "The view of only children as selfish and lonely is a gross exaggeration of reality."

Indeed, Falbo goes so far as to argue that only children are often better off—at least in some respects—than those with brothers and sisters. Reviewing over 200 studies conducted sine 1925, she and her colleague Denise Polit conclude that only children equal firstborns in intelligence and achievement, and score higher than both firstborns and later-borns with siblings on measures of maturity and leadership. Other researchers dispute these findings, however. Comparing only children with firstborns over their life span, for example, University of California at Berkeley psychologist B.G. Rosenberg found that only children—particularly females—scored lower on intelligence tests than did firstborns with a sibling.

Rosenberg distinguishes between three types of only children. "Normal, well-adjusted" onlies, he says, are assertive, poised and gregarious. "Impulsive, acting out" only children adhere more to the old stereotype, their scores on personality tests indicating they are thin-skinned, self-indulgent and self-dramatizing. The third group resembles the firstborn children of larger families, scoring as dependable, productive and fastidious.

Perhaps the only real disadvantage to being an only child comes not in childhood but much later in life. Faced with the emotional and financial burdens of caring for aging parents, those without siblings have no one to help out. But as Falbo points out, even in large families such burdens are rarely distributed equally.

How closely sibling ties are maintained and nurtured varies with cultural and ethnic expectations. In one survey, for example, 54 percent of low-income blacks reported receiving help from a brother or sister, in comparison with 44 percent of low-income Hispanics and 36 percent of low-income whites. Siblings in large families are also more likely to give and receive support, as are those who live in close geographical proximity to one another. Sex differences are also substantial. In middle and later life, sisters are much more likely than brothers to keep up close relationships.

So important, in fact, is the role that sisters play in cementing family ties that some families all but fall apart without them. They are the ones who often play the major role in caring for aging parents and who make sure family members stay in touch after parents die. And in later life, says Purdue University psychologist

Victor Cicirelli, sisters can provide a crucial source of reassurance and emotional security for their male counterparts. In one study, elderly men with sisters reported greater feelings of happiness and less worry about their life circumstances.

## Warmth or Tolerance?

Given the mixed emotions many adults express about sibling ties, it is striking that in national surveys the vast majority—more than 80 percent—deem their relationships with siblings to be "warm and affectionate." Yet this statistic may simply reflect the fact that ambivalence is tolerated more easily at a distance, warmth and affection less difficult to muster for a few days a year than on a daily basis. Nor are drastic breaches between siblings—months or years of silence, with no attempt at rapprochement—unheard of. One man, asked by a researcher about his brother, shouted, "Don't mention that son of a bitch to me!" and slammed the door in the psychologist's face.

Sibling feuds often echo much earlier squabbles and are sparked by similar collisions over shared responsibility or resources—who is doing more for an ailing parent, how inheritance should be divided. Few are long lasting, and those that are probably reflect more severe emotional disturbance. Yet harmonious or antagonistic patterns established in childhood make themselves felt in many adults' lives. Says psychologist Kahn: "This is not just kid stuff that people outgrow." One woman, for example, competes bitterly with a slightly older co-worker, just as she did with an older brother growing up. Another suspects that her sister married a particular man in part to impress her. A scientist realizes that he argues with his wife in exactly the same way he used to spar with an older brother.

For most people, a time comes when it makes sense to rework and reshape such "frozen images" of childhood—to borrow psychologist Bank's term—into designs more accommodating to adult reality, letting go of ancient injuries, repairing damaged fences. In a world of increasingly tenuous family connections, such renegotiation may be well worth the effort. Says author Judith Viorst, who has written of sibling ties: "There is no one else on Earth with whom you share so much personal history."

 **Article Review Form at end of book.**

Why is the context in which violence is portrayed considered a risk factor? How does violence portrayed in adults' and children's programming differ?

# The National Television Violence Study

## Key findings and recommendations

Preventing violence involves identifying the combination of factors that contribute to it, from biological and psychological causes to broader social and cultural ones. Among these, television violence has been recognized as a significant factor contributing to violent and aggressive antisocial behavior by an overwhelming majority of the scientific community.

However, it is also recognized that televised violence does not have a uniform effect on viewers. The outcome of media violence depends both on the nature of the depiction and the sociological and psychological makeup of the audience. In some cases, the same portrayal of violence may have different effects on different audiences. For example, graphically portrayed violence may elicit fear in some viewers and aggression in others. Family role models, social and economic status, educational level, peer influences, and the availability of weapons can each significantly alter the likelihood of a particular reaction to viewing televised violence.

The context in which violence is portrayed may modify the contributions to viewer behaviors and attitudes. Violence may be performed by heroic characters or villains. It may be rewarded or it may be punished. Violence may occur without much victim pain and suffering or it may cause tremendous physical anguish. It may be shown close-up on the screen or at a distance.

This study is the most comprehensive scientific assessment yet conducted of the context in which violence is depicted on television, based on some 2,500 hours of programming randomly selected from 23 television channels between 6 A.M. to 11 P.M. over a 20-week period. Television content was analyzed at three distinct levels: (1) how characters interact with one another when violence occurs (violent interaction); (2) how violent interactions are grouped together (violent scene); and (3) how violence is presented in the context of the overall program.

Violence is defined as any overt depiction of the use of physical force—or the credible threat of such force—intended to physically harm an animate being or group of beings. Violence also includes certain depictions of physically harmful consequences against an animate being or group that occur as a result of unseen violent means.

### Key Findings

- *The context in which most violence is presented on television poses risks for viewers.* The majority of programs analyzed in this study contain some violence. But more important than the prevalence of violence is the contextual pattern in which most of it is shown. The risks of viewing the most common depictions of televised violence include learning to behave violently, becoming more desensitized to the harmful consequences of violence, and becoming more fearful of being attacked. The contextual patterns noted below are found consistently across most channels, program types, and times of day. Thus, there are substantial risks of harmful effects of viewing violence throughout the television environment.

- *Perpetrators go unpunished in 73% of all violent scenes.* This pattern is highly consistent across different types of programs and channels. The portrayal of rewards and punishments is probably the most important of all contextual factors for viewers as they interpret the meaning of what they see on television. When violence is presented without punishment, viewers are more likely to learn the lesson that violence is successful.

- *The negative consequences of violence are not often portrayed in violent programming.* Most violent portrayals do not show the victim experiencing any serious physical harm or pain at the time the violence occurs. For example, 47% of all violent interactions show no harm to victims and 58% show no pain. Even less frequent is the depiction of any long-term consequences of violence. In fact, only 16% of all programs portray the long-term negative repercussions of violence, such as psychological, financial, or emotional harm.

- *One out of four violent interactions on television (25%) involves the use of a handgun.* Depictions of violence with guns and other conventional weapons can instigate or trigger aggressive thoughts and behaviors.

- *Only 4% of violent programs emphasize an antiviolence theme.* Very few violent programs place emphasis on condemning the use of violence or on presenting alternatives to using violence to solve problems. This pattern is consistent across different types of programs and channels.

- *On the positive side, television violence is usually not explicit or graphic.* Most violence is presented without any close-up focus on aggressive behaviors and without showing any blood and gore. In particular, less than 3% of violent scenes feature close-ups on the violence and only 15% of scenes contain blood and gore. Explicit or graphic violence contributes to desensitization and can enhance fear.

- *There are some notable differences in the presentation of violence across television channels.* Public broadcasting presents violent programs least often (18%) and those violent depictions that appear pose the least risk of harmful effects. Premium cable channels present the highest percentage of violent programs (85%) and those depictions often pose a greater risk of harm than do most violent portrayals. Broadcast networks present violent programs less frequently (44%) than the industry norm (57%), but when violence is included its contextual features are just as problematic as those on most other channels.

- *There are also some important differences in the presentation of violence across types of television programs.* Movies are more likely to present violence in realistic settings (85%) and to include blood and gore in violent scenes (28%) than other program types. The contextual pattern of violence in children's programming also poses concern. Children's programs are the least likely of all genres to show the long-term negative consequences of violence (5%), and they frequently portray violence in a humorous context (67%).

## Recommendations

These recommendations are based both on the findings of this study and extensive research upon which this study is based.

### For the Television Community

- Produce more programs that avoid violence. When violence does occur, keep the number of incidents low, show more negative consequences, provide nonviolent alternatives to solving problems, and consider emphasizing antiviolence themes.

- Increase portrayals of powerful nonviolent heroes and attractive characters.

- Programs with high levels of violence, including reality programs, should be scheduled in late-evening hours when children are less likely to be watching.

- Increase the number of program advisories and content codes. In doing so, however, use caution in language so that such messages do not serve as magnets to children.

- Provide information about advisories and the nature of violent content to viewers in programming guides.

- Limit the time devoted to sponsor, station, or network identification during public service announcements (PSAs) so that it does not compete with the message.

## For Policy and Public Interest Leaders

- Recognize that context is an essential aspect of television violence and that the basis of any policy proposal should consider the types of violent depictions that pose the greatest concern.

- Consider the feasibility of technology that would allow parents to restrict access to inappropriate content.

- Test antiviolence PSAs, including the credibility of spokespersons, with target audiences prior to production. Provide target audiences with specific and realistic actions for resolving conflicts peacefully.

- When possible, link antiviolence PSAs to school-based or community efforts and target young audiences, 8 to 13 years old, who may be more responsive to such messages.

## For Parents

- Watch television with your child. In this study, children whose parents were routinely involved with their child's viewing were more likely to avoid inappropriate programming.

- Encourage critical evaluation of television content.

- Consider a child's developmental level when making viewing decisions.

- Be aware of the potential risks associated with viewing television violence: the learning of aggressive attitudes and behaviors, fear, desensitization or loss of sympathy toward victims of violence.

- Recognize that different kinds of violent programs pose different risks.

 **Article Review Form at end of book.**

# WiseGuide Wrap-Up

- As more women with young children enter the workforce, fathers are being forced to participate more in caregiver and homemaker roles. However, even when their wives are employed, most men do not share in home- and family-based responsibilities at the same level as women. Women still perform most of the planning, delegating, arranging, and supervising of nearly every family task. In essence, employed women work a "second shift."

- Studies indicate that father involvement in childrearing tends to challenge and boost children's cognitive development, plays a role in children's later success and happiness, and is associated with a relatively peaceful and conflict-free adolescence. Further, among girls, father involvement plays a key role in the development of athletic and overall physical confidence. It is also associated with intellectual and academic skillfulness of boys.

- Parents of today are not following in the footsteps of their own parents when it comes to raising children. According to survey results, today's parents feel they are less strict with their own children, refrain from spanking, and rely more often on reasoning and time-out, as compared to parents a generation ago.

- Eighty percent of Americans have at least one sibling. Having a sibling impacts every aspect of family life and plays a role in how people feel about themselves and come to understand others. Sibling rivalry, parental favoritism, birth order, and mutual support are some of the aspects of sibling relationships receiving new attention.

- Children are exposed to violence through the media on a daily basis. Its impact depends strongly on the context in which the violence is depicted and the characteristics of the young viewers. Overall, the most commonly noted risks of violence exposure include learning of violent behaviors, becoming desensitized to harmful consequences, and becoming fearful of being attacked.

## R.E.A.L. Sites

This list provides a print preview of typical **coursewise** R.E.A.L. sites. There are over 100 such sites at the **courselinks**™ site. The danger in printing URLs is that web sites can change overnight. As we went to press, these sites were functional using the URLs provided. If you come across one that isn't, please let us know via email to: webmaster@coursewise.com. Use your Passport to access the most current list of R.E.A.L. sites at the **courselinks**™ site.

**Site name:** Goodkids

**URL:** http://www.flash.net/~goodkids/

**Why is it R.E.A.L.?** As you read these suggestions for parenting techniques for producing good kids, make a checklist of the types of techniques that your parents employed. Did they set realistic consequences, use inductive reasoning, employ consistent demands? How do you think your self-discipline tools relate to the way your parents disciplined you? You may also want to visit a daycare and observe the types of discipline the teachers use. Are they utilizing techniques that will promote healthier individuals? If not, what could they do differently?

**Site name:** Children and Television Violence

**URL:** http://helping.apa.org/kidtvviol.html

**Why is it R.E.A.L.?** This article summarizes several research articles addressing the effects of television violence on children. After reading this article, select three to five television shows at random during prime-time television hours. Watch each show and record the number of verbal and physical acts of violence committed during the show. How many acts were committed by males, females, adults, children, people of different races? How were the acts punished? How did the other people react to the acts of violence? What does the portrayal of consequences of violent acts in the media teach children about being violent in America?

# section 9

## Family Stressors

### Learning Objectives

- Provide an overview of events, problems, and decisions that American families regularly face and their effects on children.

- Specifically discuss problems in American daycare policies and the needs of working families.

- Illustrate the benefits to employees and employers of corporate-level child care supportive attitudes and measures.

- Provide an overview of findings regarding the effects of parental divorce on children of varying ages.

- Examine the effects of gay parenting on children.

- Discuss the negative effect of homelessness on children.

Many of the stresses on today's families are related to changing family structure, including working mothers, divorce, same-sex partnering, and poverty. Child care is a particularly controversial issue resulting from the employment of mothers. The majority of women with infants and young children are employed outside of the home. The primary reason is financial necessity. Despite this necessity, arguments about the positive and negative effects of child care on children continues. With welfare reform, emphasis has shifted somewhat to questions of adequacy. How can the needs of all employed families be met? Can affordable child care be of high quality? Affordable child care encourages mothers to work and promotes gender equality, but many worry that long hours in the care of non relatives may negatively impact children's behaviors, health, and attachments. However, most well-controlled research indicates that child care of widely varying quality has only a small effect on children's development.

Given that child care is a national issue, some companies have responded with attempts to provide quality corporate-sponsored child care for their employees. The benefits of this arrangement may be seen in the reactions of families and workplace profits. With children cared for on the premises, absenteeism, parental stress, and length of maternity leaves are reduced. In addition, stability in the workplace and staff recruitment improve. Parents and children also benefit from closer proximity when crises or illness arises.

The need for quality and convenient child care is also the byproduct of the rise in single-parent households, due largely to divorce. Divorce has negative effects on the social, emotional, and academic achievement of children. Depending on their children's ages, parents can expect a variety of reactions, from regression to immature behaviors and academic difficulties to fantasies of parental reconciliation. Children's quests for answers to their questions about their disrupted families and lives need honest responses, tempered with respect for their levels of understanding.

Family structure further departs from the traditional ideal when the cohabitation of same-sex partners is considered. Children of gay parents are subjected to a wide variety of issues not present in more traditional homes. Daily, these children face questions, jeers, criticism, and glances form homophobic adults and peers. Fortunately, many find support at home in close, understanding parent–child relationships and attitudes tolerant of diversity. Despite the stresses associated with having gay parents, these children appear to be no more at risk for maladjustment than children from heterosexual homes.

Though experiencing parental divorce or gay parenting may be stressful, the family structure breaks down much more when economic hardship results in the loss of one's home. The number of homeless children in America is growing at an alarming rate. Homeless children suffer from delays in cognition, language, and visual-motor development and from psychological problems. Homelessness is a major symptom of extreme poverty and represents a dangerous collapse of the ability to sustain family stability. Correcting this problem will require that multiple agencies and disciplines intensively coordinate their efforts.

## Thinking Beyond the Facts

Women with young children are entering the workforce in record numbers. For some, employment is a financial necessity. However, many are also choosing employment over full-time parenthood, as family size shrinks and as college degrees permit entrance into desirable occupations. Debates over the appropriate care of children while parents work have been heated. How do you feel about nonmaternal care of infants, toddlers, and young children? What risks and benefits do you feel child care poses? Do your views match what researchers have found? Examine the differences and think about sources of bias in your own views, as well as in the research process. Also consider the issue of quality care. What elements would you look for during a visit to a child care center or provider's home? Which should be mandatory and regulated by government agencies? Supporters of maternal employment suggest that as a nation we should provide quality child care for all citizens. How do you feel? Would the availability of low-cost, quality child care enrich children's lives or foster parental neglect? Would it force those who want to be homemakers into the workforce or equalize opportunities for everyone? The same types of questions might be posed, given supportive policies toward same-sex unions and parenthood. Would legalization of the same-sex marriages be supportive of the rights of all families, or would it promote deviance? Would policies accepting of gay adoptive parents pose a threat to adoptive children, or would openness and familiarity encourage tolerance?

If we look to the past, can a pattern be seen, and which perspective is correct? At one time, divorce was associated with family dysfunction and shame. Today, divorce is commonplace. Though children of divorce undoubtedly suffer, questions continue over which is worse — the toll of divorce or the consequences of prolonged exposure to family dysfunction. Thus, on the one hand, simplification of divorce laws and reduced legal costs helped fuel divorce rates. On the other hand, these same changes enabled people involved in problematic and even dangerous relationships to find peace. What are your views of the risks and benefits of divorce? How do you feel about more liberal attitudes and policies on child care, father custody, same-sex marriages, and gay parenting and adoption? Visit web sites on gay and lesbian issues, divorce, daycare, homelessness, and single parents for more information.

## Questions

**Reading 34.** If affordability and availability are the major issues in child care, what do you think we, as a society, should do? Should tax dollars be used to supply child care only to the poor, or should all children be eligible for publicly supported child care? Support your view.

What are the major reasons that mothers of young children work outside the home?

**Reading 35.** What are the benefits to an employee when child care is provided on the grounds or nearby?

Define quality child care. Do you think other aspects should be added? Explain.

**Reading 36.** What are some common initial reactions of children to their parents' divorce?

What are some suggestions for helping children adjust to parental divorce?

**Reading 37.** What has research shown to be the positive and negative effects of having gay parents?

How does having gay parents affect offsprings' sexuality and sexual identity?

**Reading 38.** What might be the long-term effect on society of the negative aspirations of homeless children regarding schooling and future employment?

What factors seem most associated with families entering the ranks of the homeless?

If affordability and availability are the major issues in child care, what do you think we, as a society, should do? Should tax dollars be used to supply child care only to the poor, or should all children be eligible for publicly supported child care? Support your view. What are the major reasons why mothers of young children work outside the home?

# American Child Care Today

## Sandra Scarr

*University of Virginia and KinderCare Learning Centers, Inc.*

Care of American children by anyone other than their own mothers needs to have a name. Even care of children by their own fathers is counted by the U.S. Labor Department as "other relative care." Cultural anxiety about nonmaternal child care is revealed in every aspect of research, practices, and policies that are reviewed in this article.

Terms for the care of children by people other than mothers include *child care, family day care, home care, center care, nanny care, babysitting, preschool education, after-school care,* and others. *Day care* is probably the most frequently used term, although early childhood professionals prefer the term *child care,* because "we take care of *children* not *days*" (M. Guddemi, personal communication, July 6, 1996). Different terms relate to the age of the child (infant, toddler, preschool or school age), the setting (e.g., home versus center), and the primary purpose (babysitting, when the focus is on working mothers' needs, versus preschool education, when the focus is on benefits to the child).

The term *child care* is used throughout this article to include all varieties of nonmaternal care of children who reside with their parent(s) or close family members; it excludes foster care and institutional care.

The assumption of all the nomenclature is that child care provided by anyone other than the child's mother deserves special notice, because it is a nonnormative event that needs definition. In fact, shared child care is the normative experience for contemporary American children, the vast majority of whose mothers are employed. More than half the mothers of infants under 12 months of age are in the labor force; three quarters of school-age children's mothers are working (Behrman, 1996).

## History of Child Care

Nonmaternal shared child care is, in fact, normative for the human young, both historically and worldwide: "Nonparental care is a universal practice with a long history, not a dangerous innovation representing a major deviation from species-typical and species-appropriate patterns of child care" (Lamb, in press). Exclusive maternal care of infants and young children is a cultural

myth of an idealized 1950s, not a reality anywhere in the world either now or in earlier times. Child care has always been shared, usually among female relatives. Until recently, most American children of working parents were cared for by other female relatives, but high rates of female employment have reduced that source of babysitters. What has changed over time and varies cross-nationally is the degree to which child care is bought in the marketplace rather than shared among female relatives.

Today, more American children are cared for by paid providers than by relatives. Relatives have, presumably, some emotional commitment to the health and safety of relatives' offspring; therefore, quality of care was seldom raised as an issue of concern. The predominance of nonrelative care in the last decade has alerted consumers, governments, and the research community to the possibly damaging effects of poor quality care on children's development; the zeitgeist called for critical appraisal of nonmaternal care (Scarr, 1985).

In agricultural societies, infants are typically left in the care of siblings, grandmothers, or female neighbors, who are also caring for their own children. In industrialized societies, mothers' employment outside the home has necessitated nonmaternal care of various types. Demand for child care is driven entirely by the economic need for women in the labor force (Lamb, Sternberg, Hwang, & Broberg, 1992), although occasional subgroups, such as upper-class mothers with heavy social schedules, may use extensive nonmaternal child care (Lamb, in press). Tracing historical changes in maternal employment provides a guide to the demand for and use of nonmaternal child care.

## Employment Moved Out of the Home and Into the Workplace

Prior to the Industrial Revolution, and in nonindustrial parts of the world today, women are both economically productive workers and primary child caregivers. When employment moved outside the home and into the factory and office, men followed work into new settings, and women generally remained at home, without a direct economic role.

In a correlated development, mothers' roles as knowledgeable caregivers began to be stressed. In the late 19th and early 20th centuries, child rearing was no longer a natural species response but a role that required extensive education and knowledge. Children began to have tender psyches that required maternal attention to develop well. Mothers were given an important emotional role in the home that complemented fathers' economic productivity (Kagan, 1980; Scarr, 1984).

Prior to World War II, few women remained in the labor force after childbearing. The need for industrial workers during the war brought many mothers into factories and offices to replace men away at war. Mothers' employment was culturally sanctioned and supported by the government provision of child-care centers attached to war factories. Mothers, as Rosie the Riveter, took on the many paid work roles that had previously been denied them.

After the war, government and cultural supports for mothers' employment were withdrawn, child-care centers were closed and mothers were told to go home to make way in the workplace for returning veterans. The birthrate soared and new suburbs were built as federally sponsored highway programs fueled a boom in housing outside of cities. All of this was a direct result of government policy that held as ideal a two-parent family with a working father and a nonworking mother, ensconced in single-family dwelling.

Erroneous predictions about an economic recession after the war, which became instead an economic boom fueled by unfulfilled consumer demand for cars, refrigerators, and housing, left many jobs open to women. Many mothers did not follow official advice to go home, and female employment has grown steadily since. Goods and services that used to be homemade (e.g., clothing, canned goods, and cleaning) came to be increasingly purchased, requiring additional family income. As the divorce rate and single motherhood soared, more mothers needed jobs to support their families. Today most mothers are employed.

In 1995, 62% of mothers with children under six years were employed. This rate was up more than 2% from 1994 and nearly 5% from 1993. Among mothers with children under two years, 58% were working in March 1995, up 4% from 1993 (1996 Green Book, as cited in Hofferth, 1996). The ideal of a nonemployed mother remained strong, however. One legacy for working mothers of the baby-boom generation and beyond is guilt about their employment.

## Purposes of Child Care

Three major, often conflicting, purposes for child care created the child-care dilemma we as a society suffer today (Scarr & Weinberg, 1986; Stoney & Greenberg, 1996). First, child care supports maternal employment, which for individual families and for the economy has become a necessity. It is assumed that U.S. working families will pay for their own child-care services. Second, child care serves children's development, which can be enhanced by high-quality early childhood programs, whether or not children's mothers are employed. Again, families are expected to pay for early childhood programs, unless they are poor. Third, child care has been used throughout this century to intervene with economically disadvantaged and ethnic minority children to socialize them to the cultural mainstream. Poor and immigrant children could be fed, immunized, given English language experience, behaviorally trained, given an orderly schedule, and so forth (Scarr & Weinberg, 1986; Stoney & Greenberg, 1996). Taxpayers have paid for these services to the poor.

The roots of child care are in the welfare and reform movements of the 19th century. Day nurseries, which evolved into the child-care centers of today, began in Boston in the 1840s to care for the children of widows and working wives of seamen, two groups of women who had to work outside the home. Reformers, such as Jane Addams, founded day nurseries to care for poor and immigrant children, whose mothers had to work (Scarr & Weinberg, 1986). Preteen school-age children required adult supervision to be safely occupied and kept out of trouble. The primary purpose of day nurseries was to keep children safe and fed while their poor mothers worked. Other benefits, such as early education, were secondary.

By contrast, kindergartens and nursery schools began in the early 20th century to enhance the social development of middle- and upper-class children. For a few hours a week, the children could play with others and experience an enriched learning environment under the tutelage of trained early childhood teachers. Nursery school existed to serve the developmental needs of middle- and upper-class children, whose mothers were not employed (Scarr & Weinberg, 1986).

By the late 1960s, educators and child development researchers recognized the value of nursery schools for poor children, who needed the stimulation and learning opportunities that such early childhood settings afforded children from affluent families. Head Start was designed, in large part, to enhance the learning of poor and minority children—to provide the same kinds of early childhood opportunities that middle-class children had enjoyed for decades. Because many of their mothers were supported by welfare, Head Start could involve mothers in early childhood programs and serve children's developmental needs. As part-day, part-year programs, Head Start did not serve the child-care needs of working mothers.

These three purposes for child care set quite different priorities for the services to be offered and have different assumptions about who will pay for them.

Thus, disputes continue about whose goals are to be served by child-care services, who shall pay for them, and what form child care should take. Conflicting advocacy for (a) high-quantity, low-cost caregiving, versus (b) high-quality, high-cost, child-centered preschool education, versus (c) intervention and compensation for poor children continues to compete for attention in debates about American child care.

## Varieties of Child-Care Arrangements

When the focus is on early childhood education, whether for higher or lower income children, the setting is usually a center or preschool. When the focus is on care while parents work, the setting is often a home. In fact, these distinctions have blurred in recent years, as more and more children move from homes to center-based programs, where they receive both extended care and early education.

### Family Day Care Versus Center Care

Family day-care providers care for children in their own homes. The providers' own children are often included in the mix of children, which can include infants through school-age children who come before and after school. Most family day-care homes accommodate 6 or fewer children and have one caregiver. Some larger homes care for 6 to 20 children and employ aides to assist the family day-care providers. States generally regulate larger homes. Family day-care homes are for-profit independent providers.

Child-care centers provide group care for children from infancy to school age in age-segregated groups, with smaller ratios of children at younger ages to adults. Facilities vary from church

basements to purpose-built centers with specialized spaces and equipment. The most notable differences between homes and centers are educational curricula and staff training, which centers are required to provide and homes are not. Parents prefer center-based care for preschool children and home care for infants and toddlers.

### Licensed Versus Unlicensed Care

In all states, child-care centers must be licensed by a state department of social services or its equivalent.[1] Licensure includes regulations on health and safety, ratios of children to adults, group sizes, staff training, and often required play materials. Regular inspections are done semiannually or annually or more frequently if problems have been noted.

Family homes that care for more than six children are usually required to be licensed, although regulations vary considerably from state to state. Most family day-care providers care for fewer than six children and are therefore exempt from any state regulation or inspection. Availability of federal food subsidies to licensed homes, however, has encouraged more family day-care homes to seek licensure or registration. Family day-care homes are rarely visited by state regulators.

### Nonprofit Versus For-Profit Centers

In the United States, child-care centers are sponsored by churches, nonprofit community groups, public schools, Head Start, employers, for-profit independent providers, and corporations. Public schools and Head Start serve older preschool children only, whereas other centers usually include younger children

[1]In 11 states, church-sponsored child care is exempt from all but health and safety licensure.

as well. Only about half of all centers, however, provide infant care, because the required low ratios of infants to providers make infant care prohibitively expensive.

The mix of public provision and private enterprise in U.S. child care reflects the ambivalence Americans feel about whether child care should be primarily a publicly supported service for children or a business expense for working families (partially offset by tax credits). Should tax dollars be used to supply child care only to poor children, or should all children be eligible for publicly supported child care? Should family day care and privately owned centers profit from the child-care business, or should child care be a nonprofit service (as in Hawaii) like primary education?

## Where Are Children Today?

In 1995, there were nearly 21 million children under the age of five years who were not yet enrolled in school. Of these, about 40% were cared for regularly by parents, 21% by other relatives, 31% in child-care centers, 14% in family day-care homes, and 4% by sitters in the child's home. These figures total more than 100% because 9% of children have more than one regular care arrangement, such as enrollment in a part-time preschool program and parental care at home during other hours (Hofferth, 1996). The distribution of center sponsorship is shown Figure 1.

Over the last 30 years, children have been shifted gradually from home to center-based care. In 1965, only 6% of children were cared for in centers; by 1995, 31% were. Use of family day care and care by parents, other relatives, and sitters all declined. Figure 2 shows historical trends in use of different forms of child care. By

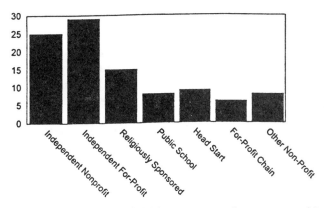

**Figure 1.** Administrative auspices of child-care centers (by percentage) in the United States, 1990 (Willer et al., 1991).

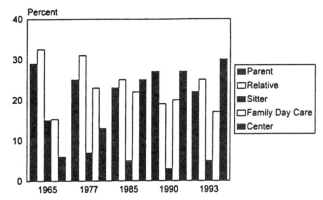

**Figure 2.** Primary care for youngest preschool child of employed mothers, 1965–1993 (Hofferth, 1996).

1990, in families with employed mothers (three fifths of families with young children), only 37% of infants and 32% of children from one to two years of age were cared for primarily by parents. Of three- to four-year-olds, only 25% were primarily in parental care, and 37% were in child-care centers (Hofferth, 1996).

In surveys by *Working Mother* magazine in 1995 and 1996, readers expressed strong preferences for center-based care over home care, whether by relatives or not. Child safety and parental control over the arrangement were prominent reasons for the preference. Home care is unsupervised and usually unlicensed. Television exposés of abuse and neglect in day-care homes have appeared regularly

over the last decade. Relatives do no always abide by parents' child-rearing preferences, such as toilet-training techniques and feeding routines. Paid help is more dependable and controllable. Child-care centers are open even if one caregiver is ill or on vacation (Mason & Kuhlthau, as cited in Mason & Duberstein, 1992).

Relative care is, in general, less costly than other care (Hofferth, 1996). About half of relative care involves payment, but the rates tend to be lower than market rates. Although 23% of parents express a preference for relative care, 77% of mothers prefer another kind of child care (Mason & Kuhlthau, as cited in Mason & Duberstein, 1992). Economic factors play the major role in use of relative care. The more preschool children in the family, the more likely relatives will supply the care, because market discounts for multichild families do not substantially reduce the total cost of child care. The higher the family income, the less likely parents are to choose relative care (Blau & Robbins, 1990).

Older preschool children are more likely than infants and toddlers to be enrolled in center care, but from 1965 to 1995, the use of center care for infants and toddlers grew exponentially, from about 3% in 1965 to 23% in 1993. Parental care of infants and toddlers declined dramatically across that period. School-age care has lagged behind the need for this service and enjoys little public support.

Children from more affluent families and those from families on welfare are most likely to be enrolled in centers rather than cared for in homes. Families with an annual income of more than $50,000 can afford center-based programs; those below the poverty line receive subsidies for child care and enroll their children without charge in Head Start. Working families with annual income below $25,000 but above the poverty line are the least likely to be able to afford and to use center-based child care.

Nearly 10% of mothers work nonstandard hours; they have fewer choices of child-care arrangements. Only 3% of centers and about 17% of family day-care homes provide evening and weekend care (Hofferth, 1996). In two-parent families, children of evening-shift and weekend workers may be cared for by the other parent or by another relative in the case of single-parent families. Father care is a seldom recognized choice that minimizes costs of child care in a dual-income family.

Presser's data from Detroit suggest that child-care preferences often determine whether mothers work shifts other than 9-to-5. Fully one third of dual-income families have one parent working nonstandard hours to offset child-care costs (Presser, 1992b). When mothers work nights and weekends, and when they have more than one preschool child, fathers are more likely to supply some of the child care. As child-care costs rise, parents are more likely to arrange schedules to provide the care themselves (Mason & Duberstein, 1992).

Much has been said about the shortage of child-care spaces in this country (Hofferth, 1992). With annual increases in the percentage and numbers of working mothers (soon to increase dramatically with welfare reform), the child-care supply is not growing sufficiently to meet the demand for the care of infants and toddlers, of mildly sick children, or of children whose parents work nonstandard hours. Infant and toddler care are scarce nationally; because of low ratio requirements of children to staff, infant and toddler care are very expensive and therefore in particularly short supply. Preschool and after-school care are less costly and more readily available. It is also difficult to find suitable care for disabled children. Even with the Americans With Disabilities Act to encourage nondiscrimination, few facilities can provide competent care for disabled children, particularly those with severe behavior disorders and multiple physical handicaps.

The primary problem is that the market for child care is poorly funded, both by limited parental incomes and by low state subsidies. The price of child care cannot be set high enough in many communities to encourage invest-

ment in new facilities or quality programs. Low-income communities have a smaller child-care supply than more affluent ones because of parents' inability to pay for care.

## Child-Care Regulations

The 50 states and the District of Columbia display amazing differences in the regulations they have developed to affect cost and quality of child care. Ratios of children to adults in some states (e.g., Maryland, Massachusetts) are less than half of those approved in other states (e.g., Ohio, Texas). Permissible ratios for children under 12 months of age range from 3 to 8 per caregiver. For children ages 12 to 35 months, the range among states is from 4 to 13 children per caregiver! Teacher training requirements vary from none (e.g., Georgia, Alabama to college degrees or advanced credentials (e.g., Illinois, New Jersey). Group sizes permitted for younger children vary from 4 or 6 children, to 20 children, to legally unlimited numbers.

There is a significant cultural and economic gradient from North to South, whereby parents and state regulators in the Northern tier of states demand better quality preschool and child-care programs and are willing to pay more for lower ratios and more highly trained staff. However, in some Northern states with very low ratios and high training requirements, few parents can afford center-based care. Massachusetts, for example, has less than one third the number of child-care center spaces per capita than Texas, a high-ratio, low-training state, has. Low ratios and teacher training requirements raise the cost of center care to such levels that the vast majority of parents in Massachusetts are forced to use unregulated family day care. By contrast, parents in Texas have the highest provision of center-based programs in the country. The trade-off of quantity and quality in center-based care is a recurring dilemma.

# A Labor Force Perspective on Child-Care Research

Despite national ambivalence about maternal employment, the U.S. economy could not function without women employees and entrepreneurs. Today, 48% of workers are women. It is inconceivable that the 80% of these women who are mothers could stay home. Seldom do developmental psychologists consider the economic legitimacy of child care to serve the goal of maternal employment.

There are two major reasons for maternal employment: (a) economic well-being of the family and (b) gender equality (Scarr, 1996). "Child care policies in many countries have been designed at least in part to promote female employment and to equalize potential employment opportunities of men and women" (Lamb, in press).

First and foremost, mothers (and fathers) are employed because their families need or want the income to enhance their standard of living. In today's economy, it is most often a necessity to have two employed parents to support a family with children. Two thirds of mothers are working to keep their families out of poverty(Scarr, Phillips, & McCartney, 1990). With welfare reform, this proportion will increase.

The second reason for maternal employment—to promote economic, social, and political gender equality—is a more complicated issue. The major reason for discrepancies in men's and women's work compensation and career achievements is that family responsibilities fall more heavily on women, especially when there are small children in the home (Scarr, 1996). Most mothers do not maintain full-time employment or have the same commitment to careers that childless women have or that men have, whether they are fathers or not. Unequal child-care responsibilities lead mothers to be less invested in career development and less motivated to maintain continuous, full-time employment. As several commentators have noted, there cannot be gender equality in the work force until men take more responsibility for child care. According to Supreme Court Justice Ruth Bader Ginsburg, "Women will not be truly liberated until men take equal care of children. If I had an affirmative action plan to design, it would be to give men every incentive to be concerned about the rearing of children" ("Justice Ginsburg Takes on," 1995, p. A4).

Although mothers in the Western industrialized world have increased their economic activity, the gendered division of responsibility and work involved in child-care provision is still the norm in families with young children. When tested for anxiety about leaving their children in child care, fathers expressed more anxiety than mothers, but when asked to rate how their wives felt about leaving children in care, fathers greatly exaggerated their wives' worries about employment and child care (Deater-Deckard, Scarr, McCartney, & Eisenberg, 1994). By inference, fathers think it is the mother's job to worry more about child care, even today. Men's collective choice of nonparticipation in child care helps to maintain men's privilege position in society and in relation to the market and the state (Leira, 1992; Presser, 1992a).

## Child Care and Other Family Supports

One often hears liberal policy analysts yearn for the federal government to provide more family-friendly policies that make balancing work and family life less stressful. Corporations vie each year to be on the *Working Mother* magazine list of the top 100 most family-friendly companies. The world's role models of countries with the most family-friendly policies are the Nordic countries.

Family-friendly government policies in the Nordic countries (Sweden, Norway, Finland, Denmark, and Iceland) help mothers to balance work and family life by granting paid, job-guaranteed maternity and parental leaves, child allowances to supplement family income, an part-time work for mothers when their children are young. Although parental leave and part-time employment opportunities can be used by either fathers or mothers, mothers take more than 95% of the leave time and make up virtually all of the part-time workers.

The collective effect of these family-friendly policies is to increase gender inequality to such an extent that Swedish women earn only half of men's wages (in the United States, women earn 77% of men's wages; "Women's Figures," 1997) and hold virtually none of the top jobs in corporations or universities (Cherlin, 1992; Leira, 1992; Scarr, 1996).

Government policies that support maternal absences from the labor force, such as paid parental leaves and child allowances, make balancing work and family life easier for mothers of young children, but they have long-term deleterious consequences for mothers' careers (Scarr, 1996). Although many admire the Swedish system of extensive supports for working parents, including part-time work opportunities when children are young, Cherlin (1992) cited some of the disadvantages:

Note that you cannot make Partner in a Stockholm law firm working six hours a day. The cost of the system is that its solutions may impede the ability of well-educated mothers to rise up the managerial and professional hierarchies. . . . That still leaves the problem that women . . . may lose experience and continuity in the labor force and the associated promotions and wage increases. (p. 213)

In the United States, where there are few family supports, mothers are more often employed full-time even when their children are infants, thus maintaining more continuous labor force participation, which leads to career advancement, higher incomes, retirement benefits, and other markers of gender equality. Most mothers want to be employed for a variety of reasons. Women's labor force participation is associated with higher family income, greater personal satisfaction, and more social support. However, the double burdens of home and family also lead to role overload and excessive work hours for young mothers in the United States (Scarr, Phillips, & McCartney, 1989). Although working mothers experience greater time stress and role strain (Staines & Pleck, 1983), they express greater satisfaction with their multiple roles than stay-at-home mothers (Scarr, Phillips, & McCartney, 1989).

Significant problems with child-care arrangements and high child-care costs discourage moth-ers' labor force participation and can lead to depression and marital problems (Ross & Mirowsky, 1988; White & Keith, 1990). If child-care costs were more reasonable, national surveys show that 10–20% more mothers would return to the labor force after giving birth (Mason & Duberstein, 1992). Child-care problems impair women's long-term earning prospects by limiting their participation in the labor force (Cherlin, 1992; Collins & Hofferth, 1996; Mason & Duberstein, 1992; Scarr, 1996).

Income inequalities between men and women are largely explained by the lower labor force participation of mothers in their childbearing years. In 1995, childless women in their 20s and 30s earned 98% of men's wages ("Women's Figures," 1997). In addition, women are less likely than men to be given advanced training opportunities, promotions, and managerial responsibility because they are perceived to have less commitment to careers (Scarr, 1996). Subsidized child care is the one family-friendly government policy that supports gender equality and women's career achievements.

## Welfare Reform, or Why Shouldn't Poor Mothers Work Too?

The idea that mothers should be paid to stay at home with children arose during the 1930s, when widows and a few divorcees needed support to rear their children at least to school age. Aid to Families With Dependent Children (AFDC) was the last in a series of programs that was initiated to accomplish this goal. Support levels were generally low, so that a mother and her children could live at the poverty level, but they were provided with medical insurance, food stamps, often housing and clothing allowances, and social services. Gradually, over the past 50 years, welfare (AFDC) recipients came to be identified with never-married minority women and poor White women who had children in their teens and early 20s and were never employed.

As the majority of middle-class mothers entered the labor force in the 1980s, there was a sea-change in thinking about AFDC. By the early 1990s, the majority of middle-class mothers of infants and young children were employed: two thirds when their children were under six years of age and three quarters by the time their children were school age, with most of these mothers working full-time. Married mothers were working at the same rate as single mothers (Scarr, Phillips & McCartney, 1989). Public empathy for mothers supported by AFDC to stay home with their children evaporated. Why should the taxes of working mothers go to support poor mothers to enjoy the privilege of staying home with their children? Reform of the welfare system rose to the top of the political agenda and was passed in 1996. Welfare will no longer be an open-ended, lifetime entitlement. It will provide time-limited support in emergencies, but mothers of children over three years of age can expect to be employed. Child-care assistance for low-income mothers is the key to welfare reform, because single low-income mothers cannot pay market rates for child care.

## "Workfare Means Day Care"

Child care is the essential ingredient in welfare reform and mothers' employment, as indicated by the above heading taken from a recent *Time* magazine article (1996). State by state, policies are being developed to provide child care to permit poor mothers to work. The major intent is to care for children while their mothers are employed, but what quality of care will be afforded be the states? There are no necessary quality assurances, beyond basic health and safety, in the provision of child care that allows mothers to work. Only when one is concerned about the children's development do other qualities of the child-care experience matter.

## The Quality/Cost/ Affordability Dilemma

Child-care is critical to working parents' well-being (Mason & Duberstein, 1992). The availability and affordability of child care of acceptable quality directly affect parents' ability to manage both work and family life. Location, hours of operation, and flexibility (with respect to rules, mildly ill children, and the like) are major factors in the perceived availability of child care. Many parents find their choices quite limited (Galinsky, 1992).

Cost in relation to family income is the major affordability issue (Scarr, 1992b). As in any market-driven service, quality depends on what consumers are willing and able to pay for child care, which economists refer to as the *cost per quality unit of care* (Mason & Duberstein, 1992; Morris & Helburn, 1996). Consumers who are able to pay a high price will find someone willing to provide the service. Low-income families struggle to find acceptable quality care at a price they can afford, although they pay a higher percentage of their income for child care (23% versus 6% in high-income families). The trade-off of cost and quality of services is a major dilemma in American child care (Morris & Helburn, 1996).

Accessibility and cost of child care per quality unit are overriding issues in evaluating the impact of child care on parents (Prosser & McGroder, 1992). Ease of access, measured in travel time to a child-care center, directly affects how likely a mother is to stay in the labor force (Collins & Hofferth, 1996). Middle- and upper income mothers are much more likely to keep their jobs if they use formal child-care arrangements (day-care centers) than if they have informal or no stable arrangements. Labor force participation among low-income mothers is more sensitive to the availability of relatives to care for children, because they cannot afford to pay market rates for child care (Collins & Hofferth, 1996).

## Absenteeism and Productivity Effects

Mothers with secure child care are absent from work and tardy less often and are more productive in the workplace.

When child care arrangements break down, employed parents are more likely to be absent, to be late, to report being unable to concentrate on the job, to have higher levels of stress and more stress-related health problems, and to report lower parental and marital satisfaction. (Galinsky, 1992, p. 167)

Breakdowns in child-care arrangements are frequent and stressful; in a Portland, Oregon study, 36% of fathers and 46% of mothers who used out-of-home care reported child-care-related stress. Leading causes of child-care breakdown are child illness and a provider who quits (Galinsky, 1992). The greater the number of child-care arrangements, the more likely they are to break down and the greater the parental stress. Stable, reliable,

child care of acceptable quality is clearly related to mothers returning to work and staying in the labor force; this is especially true of middle- and high-income mothers (Collins & Hofferth, 1996; Phillips, 1992).

## A Child Development Perspective on Child-Care Research

### Three Waves of Research

The ecology of child-care research has undergone some important changes in the past two decades. Three waves of child-care research have been identified (Belsky, 1984; Clarke-Stewart, 1988; McCartney & Marshall, 1989). In the 1970s, the first wave compared maternal care with any kind of nonmaternal care, without assessment of the quality of either setting in which the care took place. The implicit research question was "How much damage is done to infants and young children by working mothers?" There was no consideration of whether variation in child development depended on variation in kind and quality of care, at home or in other child-care settings.

The second wave examined the quality and variety of child-care settings and introduced the idea that children's responses to child care may be individually different. In the 1980s, many child-care studies actually observed child care in process, evaluated quality of care, and assessed children individually.

The third wave of research included not only proximal influences on the child but distal influences as well. McCartney and Marshall (1989) suggested the inclusion of three systems to describe a true ecological study of the child-care experience: first, variation of child-care quality and type; second, family characteristics; and third, individual differences among children. Although considerable attention has been devoted to evaluating child-care settings, characteristics of parents and family settings have seldom been integrated into child-care research.

A special note should be made on child-care-as-intervention with children from low-income and disadvantaged families. The best studied interventions, such as the Carolina Abecedarian Project (Ramey, Bryant, Sparling, & Wasik, 1985), used child care to enrich poor children's lives with positive results both concurrently and into primary school. Children with poor learning opportunities at home and without sufficient emotional support are particularly benefited by early childhood programs (McCartney, Scarr, Phillips, & Grajeck, 1985), and the more intensive the intervention, the better the results (Ramey & Ramey, 1992).

## Dimensions of Quality

There is an extraordinary international consensus among child-care researchers and practitioners about what quality child care is: It is warm, supportive interactions with adults in a safe, healthy, and stimulating environment, where early education and trusting relationships combine to support individual children's physical, emotional, social, and intellectual development (Bredekamp, 1989).

Although quality of care is a multifaceted concept, the most commonly used measures of center quality are remarkably similar in the dimensions of quality they stress and in their measurement

characteristics (Scarr, Eisenberg, & Deater-Deckard, 1994). Determinations of child-care quality are based on a number of criteria, but the most commonly agreed on are health and safety requirements, responsive and warm interaction between staff and children, developmentally appropriate curricula, limited group size, age-appropriate caregiver:child ratios, adequate indoor and outdoor space, and adequate staff training in either early childhood education or child development (Bredekamp, 1989; Kontos & Fiene, 1987). Caregivers with specific training in child care and child development provide more sensitive and responsive care than do those without such training. In sum, the quality of child care is affected by lower ratios, smaller group sizes, and better qualified teachers (Cost, Quality, and Child Outcomes Study Team, 1995; Scarr, Eisenberg, & Deater-Deckard, 1994; Whitebook, Howes, & Phillips, 1991).

Staff turnover is another common measure of the quality of care. High turnover means that children have fewer opportunities to develop stable, affectionate relationships with caregivers. Stability of care appears to be especially important for infants and toddlers who display more appropriate social behaviors in stable than in unstable care arrangements. (Howes & Stewart, 1987; Suwalsky, Zaslow, Klein, & Rabinovich, 1986). Recently, a tri-state study has shown that quality of care is more closely related to teacher wages than to other structural center-care variables (Phillips, Mekos, Scarr, McCartney, & Abbott-Shim, in press; Scarr, Eisenberg, & Deater-Deckard, 1994).

## Variations in Quality of Care

Few experienced observers would doubt that center quality in the United States varies from excellent to dreadful and is, on average, mediocre (Cost, Quality, and Child Outcomes Study Team, 1995; Hofferth, Brayfield, Deich, & Holcomb, 1991; National Institute of Child Health and Human Development [NICHD] Early Child Care Research Network, 1996; Scarr, Phillips, McCartney, & Abbott-Shim, 1993). Quality in child-care centers is measured, by observation and interview, in units that are regulated (such as ratios of teachers to children, group sizes, and teacher training) and in dimensions that are process-oriented (such as adult–child interactions and developmentally appropriate activities; Phillips, 1987). In European studies, child-care quality also varies but not as dramatically as in the United States (Lamb, Sternberg, Hwang, & Broberg, 1992).

Family day-care homes have seldom been studied, and those that have been sampled may not be representative of the enormous number of unlicensed, unregulated homes. Studies of family day care have found quality to be highly variable (Galinsky, Howes, Kontos, & Shinn, 1994). In the recent NICHD study (NICHD Early Child Care Research Network, 1996), day-care home quality was, on average, fair to good but again highly variable.

Poor quality child care has been reported to put children's development at risk for poorer language and cognitive scores and lower ratings of social and emotional adjustment (for reviews, see Lamb, in press; Scarr & Eisenberg, 1993). Studies of center quality and child outcomes, which controlled statistically for family background differences, have found that overall quality has small but reliable effects on language and cognitive development (Goelman & Pence, 1987; McCartney, 1984; Wasik, Ramey, Bryant, & Sparling, 1990), social competence, and social adjustment (McCartney et al., 1997). Parents and caregivers rated children as more considerate, sociable, intelligent, and task-oriented when caregivers engaged in more positive verbal interactions with the children.[2] Other studies have found that children with involved and responsive caregivers display more exploratory behaviors, are more positive (Clarke-Stewart, Gruber, & Fitzgerald, 1994; Holloway & Reichhart-Erickson, 1989), and display better peer relations (Howes, Phillips, & Whitebook, 1992) than children with uninvolved, unresponsive caregivers. The inferences from these findings are not straightforward, however.

Predictably, quality of care selected by parents has been found to be correlated with parents' personal characteristics (Bolger & Scarr, 1995), thereby complicating interpretations of any effects of child care per se. The confound of family and child-care characteristics leads to overestimation of child-care effects that result instead from family differences. For example, children from families with single employed mothers and low incomes were more likely to be found in lower quality care (Howes & Olenick, 1986). Children in high-quality care had parents who were more involved and inter-

[2]Paradoxically, in one study, children's social adjustment was positively related to poorer quality care, but this finding has not been replicated and is probably sample-specific (Phillips, McCartney, & Scarr, 1987).

ested in compliance than parents of children in lower quality care, and behavioral differences were evident in the center. Parents who use more punitive forms of discipline and hold more authoritarian attitudes toward children were found to choose lower quality care for their children (Bolger & Scarr, 1995; Scarr et al., 1993).

In a recent large study, less sensitive mothers who value work more chose poorer quality child care in the infants' first six months, enrolled their infants in centers at earlier ages for more hours per week, and were more likely to have insecurely attached infants (NICHD Early Child Care Research Network, in press). Of course, variations in parents' interactions with their children and in parents' personality, intelligence, and attitudes determine the characteristics that will be transmitted to children genetically as well as environmentally (Scarr, 1992a; 1993). How can these confounds be sorted out?

Many studies statistically covary out measured family characteristics from associations between child care and child outcomes and look at residual associations. When family and child-care qualities are truly confounded, however, it is impossible to covary out all family effects, because one has only a limited set of measures of the families—typically parents' education, income, and occupation, and some personality, cognitive, or attitudinal test scores. Parents who differ on any one of these measures are very likely to differ on many other unmeasured traits that affect associations between child care and child outcomes. Thus, the small, statistically reliable associations that have been found between child-care quality and child outcomes are exceedingly difficult to interpret.

## Nonmaternal Care

Nonmaternal infant care has been the most controversial issue in the entire child-care research field, but it may soon be laid to rest. Throughout the 1980s and early 1990s, dramatic claims were made about the damaging effects of early entry into "day care" (not defined or measured) on infants' attachments to their mothers (Belsky, 1986, 1988, 1992; Belsky & Rovine, 1988). Reanalysis of data on day care versus "home-reared" infants revealed a slight difference in rates of insecure attachments as measured by the Strange Situation: 37% versus 29% (Clarke-Stewart, 1988, 1989; Lamb, Sternberg, & Prodromidis, 1992). Other measures of attachment showed no relationship to age at entry or amount of infant child care.

Arguments swirled in the public press and developmental literature about whether the results applied only to boys; to infants with insensitive mothers; to infants who experience more than 20, 30, or 35 hours of nonmaternal care a week; or to infants who experience poor quality care (Phillips, McCartney, Scarr, & Howes, 1987). Working mothers were tormented with doubt and guilt (Bowman, 1992). Finally, the NICHD Early Child Care Research Study (NICHD Early Child Care Research Network, in press) of more than 1,000 infants has shown no relationship between age at entry or amount of infant care and attachments as measured by the Strange Situation (for a full review, see Lamb, in press). Naturally, less sensitive, less well-adjusted mothers were much more likely to have insecurely attached infants (NICHD Early Child Care Research Network, in press). Several interaction effects suggested that higher quality care may help to offset poor mothering. Let us hope that is the end of the early child-care controversy.

## Lack of Long-Term Effects

Researchers have explored the possible long-term effects of day-care experiences in different qualities of care for children from different kinds of backgrounds. Children from low-income families are definitely benefited by quality child care, which has been used as an intervention strategy (Field, 1991; Ramey et al., 1985; Ramey & Ramey, 1992). Poor children who experience high-quality infant and preschool care show better school achievement and socialized behaviors in later years than similar children without child-care experience or with experience in lower quality care. For poor children, quality child care offers learning opportunities and social and emotional supports that many would not experience at home.

For children from middle- and upper income families, the long-term picture is far less clear. With a few exceptions that can be explained by the confounding of family with child-care characteristics in the United States, research results show that the impact on development from poorer versus better care within a broad range of safe environments is small and temporary. Given the learning opportunities and social and emotional supports that their homes generally offer, child care is not a unique or lasting experience for these children.

Long-term effects of day-care quality were reported in longitudinal studies by Vandell, Henderson, and Wilson (1988) and by Howes (1988). The former researchers reported that children who attended better quality day-care centers in the preschool period were better liked by their peers and exhibited more empathy and social competence at age eight than children from poorer quality preschool centers. Howes found that after controlling for the effects of some family characteristics, good school skills and few behavior problems were predicted by high-quality care for both boys and girls. However, age at entry and amount of day care were not related to later academic achievement or to social behaviors, so that one suspects that family effects, confounded with child-care quality (Bolger & Scarr, 1995), accounted for the long-term results.

In contrast to the U.S. findings, the results of two longitudinal studies conducted in Sweden indicated that early age of entry into day care was associated with better school performance and positive teacher ratings from childhood to early adulthood (Andersson, 1989; Hartmann, 1995). Of the many differences in family background that could be only partially controlled, early entrants into child care had better educated mothers who returned to work earlier than less achieving mothers. Again, one suspects that unmeasured family effects account for the long-term positive effects of child care in the Swedish study, as they did for negative effects in the U.S. studies.

A more thorough Swedish study (Broberg, Hwang, & Chace, 1993) reported no long-term effects of differences in child-care environments on children's adjustments or achievements at eight to nine years of age. It should be noted, however, that Sweden's uniformly high-quality child-care centers (Hennessy & Melhuish, 1991) do not really test for the effects of poor child care on later development.

No effects of quality of preschool care on school-age development were also reported in a Dutch retrospective study (Goosens, Ottenhoff, & Koops, 1991). However, there was very little variance in the measure of quality in this study, which may account for that finding.

## Four Studies of Long-Term Impact of Varied Child-Care Quality

**Study 1.** In a large U.S. study of highly varied child-care centers (McCartney et al., 1997; Scarr et al., 1993), 720 young children (ages 12 to 60 months) who were enrolled in 120 child-care centers in three states were evaluated for social adjustment. Quality of care in the centers and family characteristics were used to predict differences in parents' and teachers' ratings of children's adjustment and observations of social behaviors.

Both structural (e.g., staff to child ratios, teachers' wages, education, training) and process (interactions, programs) measures were used to evaluate quality of care in the centers. Family structural characteristics (e.g., income, educational levels, race, number of children) and processes (e.g., parenting stress, work–family interference, parental attitudes, separation anxieties) represented family effects. Children's own characteristics of age, gender, and child-care history were also used to predict adjustment and social behavior. Thus, center-care quality, family, and child characteristics were jointly used to predict children's social adjustment and social behaviors.

Results showed substantial effects of child and family characteristics on both teachers' and parents' ratings of children's adjustment and social behaviors and very small, but statistically reliable, effects of quality of child care on social adjustment ratings. In a four-year follow-up study of 141 children, Deater-Deckard, Pinkerton, and Scarr (1996) reported no long-term effects of differences in quality of preschool child care on these school-age children's social, emotional, or behavioral adjustment.

**Study 2.** A study of day-care centers in Bermuda (McCartney, 1984; McCartney et al., 1985; Phillips, McCartney, & Scarr, 1987) emphasized the importance of quality care for infants, toddlers, and preschool children. The major question addressed longitudinally was whether or not the effects of differences in quality of child care in the preschool years continue to be seen at ages five through nine years.

In a follow-up study (Chin-Quee & Scarr, 1994), teacher ratings of social competence and academic achievement were obtained from 127 of the children at ages five, six, seven, and eight years. In hierarchical and simultaneous regressions, family background characteristics, not child-care amounts or qualities, were found to be predictive of social competence and academic achievement in the primary grades. By the school-age years, the effects of infant and preschool child-care experiences were no longer influential in children's development, but family background continued to be important.

**Study 3.** In another longitudinal study in Bermuda (Scarr, Lande, & McCartney, 1989), the child-care experiences of 117 children, who had been assessed for cognitive and social development at two and four years of age, were examined for long-term effects. At

24 months of age, children in center-based care, where the ratio of infants to caregivers was 8:1, had poorer cognitive and language development than children in family day care or at home with their mothers (who did not differ from each other). These results persisted after controlling for maternal education, IQ, income, and occupational status. However, at 42 to 48 months, no differences were found between children in center care and other children.

**Study 4.** In Bermuda, an islandwide screening, assessment, and treatment program was implemented to help children with developmental problems (Scarr, McCartney, Miller, Hauenstein, & Ricciuti, 1994). Child-care histories were also ascertained. Two samples were studied: a population sample of 1,100 Bermudian children and a smaller subsample of children, most of whom were determined to be at risk for developmental problems.

To assess the effects of maternal employment (Scarr & Thompson, 1994), infants with mothers who worked 20 or more hours a week were compared with infants with mothers who worked less than 20 hours a week. To assess the effects of entry into nonmaternal care before the age of one, infants who were placed in regular nonmaternal care before the age of one were compared with infants who did not experience regular nonmaternal care before the age of one. Teacher ratings of social competence and academic achievement were obtained for the children at ages five, six, seven, and eight years.

Results revealed that family background variables frequently predicted child social competence and academic achievement measures in both samples. After controlling for family characteristics,

no differences in school-age outcomes were found between children whose mothers worked 20 or more hours a week when they were infants and children with mothers who worked less than 20 hours a week in either sample. In addition, age of entry into nonmaternal care before the age of one did not significantly predict any child outcome measures.

## Conclusions

In studies in Sweden and Holland, in a large study of child-care centers in the United States, and in three separate studies in Bermuda, differences in child-care experience, both qualitative and quantitative, did not have persistent effects on children's development. In these studies, child-care centers in Bermuda and the United States included both good- and poor-quality care, whereas centers in Sweden and Holland included only good-quality care. Research to date on quality differences does not show a major impact on the development of children from ordinary homes. These results may differ for the children from socioeconomically disadvantaged homes, for whom quality child-care programs may supply missing elements in their lives.

## Public Policy and the Quality/Cost Trade-Off

### Quality/Cost/Affordability Trade-Off

In general, higher quality child care costs more than lower quality care. Fifty to seventy percent of the cost is in staff salaries, and higher quality centers spend proportionately more on labor (Morris & Helburn, 1996). For example, center-based child care costs twice as much in Massachusetts, which has among the most demanding regulations in the United States, as in Georgia, which has more lenient regulations. In a study of 120 centers in three states, centers in Massachusetts had higher quality care, on average, than those in Georgia, but comparisons of costs of living and incomes showed that families in Massachusetts are economically disadvantaged by the high cost of child care (Hancock, Eisenberg, & Scarr, 1993). Whereas the 1990 median family income for Georgia parents who used center-based care was $50,000, in Massachusetts the median income of families who could afford center care was nearly $80,000. Massachusetts families with an annual income of less than about $60,000 were unable to afford state-regulated quality care.

The more stringent the child-care regulations, the less licensed child care will be available and the more families will be forced to use unregulated care for their children. When regulations become so stringent that most families are priced out of the regulated child-care market, one has to wonder about the wisdom of having such expensive regulations.

Unfortunately, regulations have only tangential effects on the actual quality of care. States cannot legislate warm, sensitive interactions or rich learning opportunities provided by talented teachers. Aside from safety and health considerations, which can be effectively regulated, observed quality of child care is correlated only .30 to .40 with regulated variables, such as ratios and teacher qualifications (Scarr, Eisenberg, & Deater-Deckard, 1994). Therefore regulations directly produce higher costs but only indirectly improve quality of care.

In addition, parents may not agree that quality defined by professionals is what they want or are willing to pay for in the child care they choose (Cost, Quality, and Child Outcomes Study Team, 1995; Haskins, 1992). Whereas early childhood professionals value discovery learning and hands-on experience, many working class and more traditional parents prefer structured learning and direct instruction for their preschool children. Individual attention to each child requires more staff than a classroom organized for group instruction. Lower ratios equal higher staff costs, which some parents are not willing to support, especially if the program is not what they want anyway.

States should examine the cost:benefit ratio of their regulations and their impact on making child care affordable, available, and of sufficient quality to support good child development without driving most families into the underground market of unregulated care. Surely, we all expect state regulations to protect children and to assure them a supportive environment in child care. That is the minimum governmental responsibility. Given the wide variation in regulations among the states, however, it should be possible to examine the benefits of greater and lesser costs of child care.

## Equity in Child Care

In the United Stated, a two-tier system is evolving—a higher quality one for both affluent families and the poor, who get public support for child care, and a lower quality one for middle- and lower income working families, who cannot pay for high-quality care (Maynard & McGinnis, 1992; Whitebook et al., 1991). In my opinion and in that of many other child advocates, public support for child care should make quality services available to all children of working families.

To make this dream a reality, we must spend tax moneys efficiently. Government-provided services are the least cost-effective means to provide quality child care. Compare Head Start expenditures per child with those of a typical child-care center with excellent early educational programs. Head Start spends approximately $5,000 per child annually for part-day (typically three to four hours), part-year (public school calendar) programs.[3] For exactly the same amount of money, the government could give poor parents vouchers to purchase quality child care and education in full-day, full-year child-care programs (Cost, Quality, and Child Outcomes Study Team, 1995). Another benefit of vouchers is the reduction in socioeconomic segregation, which results from programs that only poor children may attend. In most nonprofit and for profit centers, between 5% and 40% of the children are on child-care assistance, whereas in Head Start center, nearly 100% of the children are on child-care assistance.

Edward Zigler (Zigler & Finn-Stevenson, 1996) has proposed that public schools, well-entrenched institutions in all communities, be used to implement child-care services for preschool children (not infants or toddlers). With varying mixes of federal, state, local, and private funding, including parental fees, Zigler has prompted more than 400 schools to incorporate child care in their educational programs. Public schools can be one mechanism to increase the child-care supply for older children, but critics complain

[3]Costs of medical, dental, and social service programs are additional.

that most schools need to focus exclusively on improving their existing educational programs, which international surveys show to be of poor quality.

States are currently setting child-care reimbursement rates under the new welfare reform legislation. If they are pressured to serve more children, their rates will be too low to give poor parents access to quality care. If they set rates high enough to give poor parents access to quality care, they may not be able to serve all eligible families. Inadequate funding drives states to make Solomonic choices.

## Whither Child Care in America?

Repeatedly, international research results have shown only small concurrent effects of child care on children's development and no evidence for long-term effects, unless the children are seriously disadvantaged. Observations about the small effects on children of differences in quality of care can be enhanced beyond their practical importance by liberal politicians and child advocates, who may demand high-quality child care regardless of cost. Conservatives, however, will ask the logically obvious question: What is the minimal expense for child care that will allow mothers to work and not do permanent damage to children? Conservative politicians will find the research results conveniently permissive of mediocre quality. Mediocre is not the same as deleterious, unsafe, and abusive care, however, and there is some of that in the United States that must be eliminated. Government standards that prevent terrible care are essential for our nation's well-being.

Debates about welfare reform, working mothers, and child care reflect broad societal conflicts about women, families, and children.

- Is child care in America primarily meant to serve the needs of working parents, with little regard for the education of preschoolers, especially disadvantaged children?

- Will nonwelfare working families have to pay for the child care they need, discouraging many women from entering the labor force, or will the public decide that, like primary education, child care is a public service that deserves broad taxpayer support?

- Will regulations on licensed care be made so expensive that most parents will be priced out of the center-care market and forced to use unregulated care in homes? Or, will state regulations be so lax that American child care will be little better than custodial warehousing?

In summary, I hope the United States will decide that child care is both an essential service for working families and an important service to America's children, especially to the poorest among them. Governments have the responsibility to make child care affordable for all working parents and to regulate child care to assure that children are afforded opportunities to develop emotionally, socially, and intellectually. Regardless of who their parents are, children are the next generation for all of us.

---

## References

Andersson, B. E. (1989). Effects of public day care—A longitudinal study. *Child Development, 60*, 857–866.

Behrman, R. E. (Ed.). (1996). Financing child care. *The Future of Children, 6*(2).

Belsky, J. (1984). Two waves of day care research: Developmental effects and conditions of quality. In R. C. Ainslie (Ed.), *The child and the day care setting* (pp. 24–42). New York: Praeger.

Belsky, J. (1986). Infant day care: A cause for concern? *Zero to Three, 6*, 1–9.

Belesky, J. (1988). The "effects" of infant day care reconsidered. *Early Childhood Research Quarterly, 3*, 235–272.

Belsky, J. (1992). Consequences of child care for children's development: A deconstructionist view. In A. Booth (Ed.), *Child care in the 1990s: Trends and consequences* (pp. 83–94). Hillsdale, NJ: Erlbaum.

Belsky, J., & Rovine, M. J. (1988). Nonmaternal care in the first year of life and the infant–parent attachment. *Child Development, 59*, 157–167.

Blau, D. M., & Robbins, P. K. (1990, April). *Child care demand and labor supply of young mothers over time.* Paper presented at the annual meeting of the Population Association of America, Toronto, Ontario, Canada.

Bolger, K. E., & Scarr, S. (1995). Not so far from home: How family characteristics predict child care quality. *Early Development and Parenting, 4*(3), 103–112.

Bowman, B. (1992). Child development and its implications for day care. In A. Booth (Ed.), *Child care in the 1990s: Trends and consequences* (pp. 95–100). Hillsdale, NJ: Erlbaum.

Bredekamp, S. (1989, November). *Measuring quality through a national accreditation system for early childhood programs.* Paper presented at the annual meeting of the American Educational Research Association, San Francisco, CA.

Broberg, A. G., Hwang, C. P., & Chace, S. V. (1993, March). *Effects of day care on elementary school performance and adjustment.* Paper presented at the biennial meetings of the Society for Research in Child Development, New Orleans, LA.

Cherlin, A. (1992). Infant care and full-time employment. In A. Booth (Ed.), *Child care in the 1990s: Trends and consequences* (pp. 209–214). Hillsdale, NJ: Erlbaum.

Chin-Quee, D., & Scarr, S. (1994). Lack of longitudinal effects of infant and preschool child care on school-age children's social and intellectual development. *Early Development and Parenting, 3*(2), 103–112.

Clarke-Stewart, A. (1988). The "effects" of infant day care reconsidered: Risks for parents, children, and researchers. *Early Childhood Research Quarterly, 3,* 293–318.

Clarke-Stewart K. A. (1989). Infant day care: Maligned or malignant? *American Psychologist, 44,* 266–273.

Clarke-Stewart, K. A., Gruber, C. P., & Fitzgerald, L. M. (1994). *Children at home and in day care.* Hillsdale, NJ: Erlbaum.

Collins, N., & Hofferth, S. (1996, May). *Child care and employment turnover.* Paper presented at the annual meeting of the Population Association of America, New Orleans, LA.

Cost, Quality, and Child Outcomes Study Team. (1995). *Cost, quality, and child outcomes in child care centers* (Public Report, 2nd ed.). Denver: University of Colorado at Denver, Economics Department.

Deater-Deckard, K., Pinkerton, R., & Scarr, S. (1996). Child care quality and children's behavioral adjustment: A four-year longitudinal study. *Journal of Child Psychology & Psychiatry, 37*(8), 937–948.

Deater-Deckard, K., Scarr, S., McCartney, K., & Eisenberg, M. (1994). Paternal separation anxiety: Relationships with parenting stress, child-rearing attitudes, and maternal anxieties. *Psychological Science, 5*(6), 341–346.

Field, T. (1991). Quality infant day-care and grade school behavior and performance. *Child Development, 62,* 863–870.

Galinsky, E. (1992). The impact of child care on parents. In A. Booth (Ed.), *Child care in the 1990s: Trends and consequences* (pp. 159–171). Hillsdale, NJ: Erlbaum.

Galinsky, E., Howes, C., Kontos, S., & Shinn, M. (1994). *The study of children in family child care and relative care.* New York: Families and Work Institute.

Goelman, H., & Pence, A. R. (1987). Effects of child care, family and individual characteristics on children's language development: The Victoria Day Care Research Project. In D. Phillips (Ed.), *Quality in child care: What does research tell us? Research monographs of the National Association for the Education of Young Children* (pp. 43–56). Washington, DC: National Association for the Education of Young Children.

Goosens, F. A., Ottenhoff, G., & Koops, W. (1991). Day care and social outcomes in middle childhood: A retrospective study. *Journal of Reproductive and Infant Psychology, 9,* 137–150.

Hancock, T., Eisenberg, M., & Scarr, S. (1993, March). *Cost of child care and families' standard of living.* Paper presented at the biennial meetings of the Society for Research in Child Development, New Orleans, LA.

Hartmann, E. (1995). *Long-term effects of day care and maternal teaching on educational competence, independence and autonomy in young adulthood.* Unpublished manuscript, University of Oslo, Oslo, Norway.

Haskins, R. (1992). Is anything more important than day-care quality? In A. Booth (Ed.), *Child care in the 1990s: Trends and consequences* (pp. 101–115). Hillsdale, NJ: Erlbaum.

Hennessy, E., & Melhuish, E. C. (1991). Early day care and the development of school-age children: A review. *Journal of Reproductive and Infant Psychology, 9,* 117–136.

Hofferth, S. (1992). The demand for and supply of child care in the 1990s. In A. Booth (Ed.), *Child care in the 1990s: Trends and consequences* (pp. 3–25). Hillsdale, NJ: Erlbaum.

Hofferth, S. (1996). Child care in the United States today. *The Future of Children, 6*(2), 41–61.

Hofferth, S., Brayfield, A., Deich, S., & Holcomb, P. (1991). *National child care survey 1990.* Washington, DC: The Urban Institute.

Holloway, S. D., & Reichhart-Erickson, M. (1989). Child care quality, family structure, and maternal expectations: Relationship to pre-school children's peer relations. *Journal of Applied Developmental Psychology, 4,* 99–107.

Howes, C. (1988). Relations between early child care and schooling. *Developmental Psychology, 24,* 53–57.

Howes, C., & Olenick, M. (1986). Family and child care influences on toddlers' compliance. *Child Development, 57,* 202–216.

Howes, C., Phillips, D. A., & Whitebook, M. (1992). Thresholds of quality: Implications for the social development of children in center-based child care. *Child Development, 63,* 449–460.

Howes, C., & Stewart, P. (1987). Child's play with adults, toys, and peers: An examination of family and child-care influences. *Developmental Psychology, 23,* 423–430.

Justice Ginsburg takes on affirmative action. (1995, April 17). *The Washington Post,* p. A4.

Kagan, J. (1980). Perspectives on continuity. In O. G. Brim & J. Kagan (Eds.), *Constancy and change in human development* (pp. 1–15). Cambridge, MA: Harvard University Press.

Kontos, S., & Fiene, R. (1987). Child care quality, family background, and children's development. *Early Childhood Research Quarterly, 6,* 249–262.

Lamb, M. (in press). Nonparental child care: Context, quality, correlates, and consequences. In W. Damon (Series Ed.) & I. E. Sigel & K. A. Renniger (Vol. Eds.), *Handbook of child psychology: Child psychology in practice* (4th ed.). New York: Wiley.

Lamb, M., Sternberg, K. J., Hwang, P., & Broberg, A. (Eds.). (1992). *Child care in context.* Hillsdale, NJ: Erlbaum.

Lamb, M., Sternberg, K. J., & Prodromidis, M. (1992). The effects of day care on infant–mother attachment: A re-analysis of the data. *Infant Behavior and Development, 15,* 71–83.

Leira, A. (1992). *Welfare states and working mothers.* Cambridge, England: Cambridge University Press.

Mason, K., & Duberstein, L. (1992). Consequences of child care for parents' well-being. In A. Booth (Ed.), *Child care in the 1990s: Trends and consequences* (pp. 127–158). Hillsdale, NJ: Erlbaum.

Maynard, R., & McGinnis, E. (1992). Policies to enhance access to high-quality child care. In A. Booth (Ed.), *Child care in the 1990s: Trends and consequences* (pp. 189–208). Hillsdale, NJ: Erlbaum.

McCartney, K. (1984). The effects of quality of day care environment upon children's language development. *Developmental Psychology, 20,* 244–260.

McCartney, K., & Marshall, N. (1989). The development of child care research. *Newsletter of the Division of Children, Youth, and Family Services, 12*(4), 14–15.

McCartney, K., Scarr, S., Phillips, D., & Grajek, S. (1985). Day care as intervention: Comparisons of varying quality programs. *Journal of Applied Developmental Psychology, 6,* 247–260.

McCartney, K., Scarr, S., Rocheleau, A., Phillips, D., Eisenberg, M., Keefe, N., Rosenthal, S., & Abbot-Shim, M. (1997). Social development in the context of typical center-based child care. *Merrill-Palmer Quarterly, 43*(3), 426–450.

Morris, J., & Helburn, S. (1996, July). How centers spend money on quality. *Child Care Information Exchange,* 75–79.

National Institute of Child Health and Human Development Early Child Research Network. (1996). Characteristics of infant child care: Factors contributing to positive caregiving. *Early Childhood Research Quarterly, 11,* 269–306.

National Institute of Child Health and Human Development Early Child Care Research Network. (in press). The effects of infant child care on infant–mother attachment security: Results of the NICHD Study of Early Child Care. *Child Development.*

Phillips, D. (Ed.). (1987). *Quality in child care: What does research tell us? Research monographs of the National Association for the Education of Young Children.* Washington, DC: National Association for the Education of Young Children.

Phillips, D. (1992). Child care and parental well-being: Bringing quality of care into the picture. In A. Booth (Ed.), *Child care in the 1990s: Trends and consequences* (pp. 172–179). Hillsdale, NJ: Erlbaum.

Phillips, D., McCartney, K., & Scarr, S. (1987). Child care quality and children's social development. *Developmental Psychology, 23,* 537–543.

Phillips, D., McCartney, K., Scarr, S., & Howes, C. (1987). Selective review of infant day care research: A cause for concern. *Zero to Three, 7,* 18–21.

Phillips, D., Mekos, D., Scarr, S., McCartney, K., & Abbot-Shim, M. (in press). Paths to quality in child care: Structural and contextual influences in classroom environments. *Early Childhood Research Quarterly.*

Presser, H. (1992a). Child care and parental well-being: A needed focus on gender trade-offs. In A. Booth (Ed.), *Child care in the 1990s: Trends and consequences* (pp. 180–185). Hillsdale, NJ: Erlbaum.

Presser, H. (1992b). Child-care supply and demand: What do we really know? In A. Booth (Ed.), *Child care in the 1990s: Trends and consequences* (pp. 26–32). Hillsdale, NJ: Erlbaum.

Prosser, W., & McGroder, S. (1992). The supply and demand for child care: Measurement and analytic issues. In A. Booth (Ed.), *Child care in the 1990s: Trends and consequences* (pp. 42–55). Hillsdale, NJ: Erlbaum.

Ramey, C., Bryant, D., Sparling, J., & Wasik, B. (1985). Project CARE: A comparison of two early intervention strategies to prevent retarded development. *Topics in Early Childhood Special Education, 5*(2), 12–25.

Ramey, C. & Ramey, S. (1992). Early educational intervention with disadvantaged children—to what effect? *Applied and Preventive Psychology, 1,* 131–140.

Ross, C. E., & Mirowsky, J. (1988). Child care and emotional adjustment to wives' employment. *Journal of Health and Social Behavior, 29,* 127–138.

Scarr, S. (1984). Mother care/other care. New York: Basic Books.

Scarr, S. (1985). Constructing psychology: Making facts and fables for our times. *American Psychologist, 40,* 499–512.

Scarr, S. (1992a). Developmental theories for the 1990s: Development and individual differences. *Child Development, 63,* 1–19.

Scarr, S. (1992b). Keep our eyes on the prize: Family and child care policy in the United States, as it should be. In A. Booth (Ed.), *Child care in the 1990s: Trends and consequences* (pp. 215–222). Hillsdale, NJ: Erlbaum.

Scarr, S. (1983). Biological and cultural diversity: The legacy of Darwin for development. *Child Development, 64,* 1333–1353.

Scarr, S. (1996). Family policy dilemmas in contemporary nation-states: Are women benefited by family-friendly governments? In S. Gustavsson & L. Lewin (Eds.), *The future of the nation state: Essays on cultural pluralism and political integration* (pp. 107–129). London: Routledge.

Scarr, S., & Eisenberg, M. (1993). Child care research: Issues, perspectives, and results. *Annual Review of Psychology, 44,* 613–644.

Scarr, S., Eisenberg, M., & Deater-Deckard, K. (1994). Measurement of quality on child care centers. *Early Childhood Research Quarterly, 9,* 131–151.

Scarr, S., Lande, J., & McCartney, K. (1989). Child care and the family: Cooperation and interaction. In J. Lande, S. Scarr, & N. Guzenhauser (Eds.), *Caring for children: Challenge to America* (pp. 21–40). Hillsdale, NJ: Erlbaum.

Scarr, S., McCartney, K., Miller, S., Hauenstein, E., & Ricciuti, A. (1994). Evaluation of an islandwide screening, assessment and treatment program. *Early Development and Parenting, 3*(4), 199–210.

Scarr, S., Phillips, D., & McCartney, K. (1989). Working mothers and their families. *Ameican Psychologist, 44,* 1402–1409.

Scarr, S., Phillips, D., & McCartney, K. (1990). Facts, fantasies, and the future of child care in the United States. *Psychological Science, 1,* 26–35.

Scarr, S., Phillips, D., McCartney, K. & Abbott-Shim, M. (1993). Quality of child care as an aspect of family and child care policy in the United States. *Pediatrics, 91*(1), 182–188.

Scarr, S., & Thompson, W. (1994). Effects of maternal employment and nonmaternal infant care on development at two and four years. *Early Development and Parenting, 3*(2), 113–123.

Scarr, S., & Weinberg, R. A. (1986). The early childhood enterprise: Care and education of the young. *American Psychologist, 41,* 1140–1146.

Staines, G. L., & Pleck, J. H. (1983). *The impact of work schedules on the family.* Ann Arbor, MI: Institute for Social Research, Survey Research Center.

Stoney, L., & Greenberg, M. H. (1996). The financing of child care: Current and emerging trends. *The Future of Children, 6,* 83–102.

Suwalsky, J., Zaslow, M., Klein, R., & Rabinovich, B. (1986, August). *Continuity of substitute care in relation to infant–mother attachment.* Paper presented at the 94th annual Convention of the American Psychological Association, Washington DC.

Vandell, D. L., Henderson, V. K., & Wilson, K. S. (1988). A longitudinal study of children with day-care experiences of varying quality. *Child Development, 59,* 1286–1292.

Wasik, B. H., Ramey, C. T., Bryant, D. M., & Sparling, J. J. (1990). A longitudinal study of two early intervention strategies: Project CARE. *Child Development, 61,* 1682–1696.

White, L., & Keith, B. (1990). The effect of shift work on the quality and stability of marital relations. *Journal of Marriage and the Family, 52,* 453–462.

Whitebook, M., Howes, C., & Phillips, D. (1991). *Who cares? Child care teachers and the quality of care in America.* Final report of the National Child Care Staffing Study. Oakland CA: Center on Child Care Staffing.

Willer, B., Hofferth, S., Kisker, E. E., et al. (1991). *The demand and supply of child care in 1990.* Washington DC: National Association for the Education of Young People.

Women's figures. (1997, January 15). *Wall Street Journal,* p. A15.

Workfare means day care. (1996, December 23). *Time,* 38–40.

Zigler, E. F., & Finn-Stevenson, M. (1996). Funding child care and public education. *The Future of Children, 6,* 104–121.

 **Article Review Form at end of book.**

What are the benefits to an employee when child care is provided on the grounds or nearby? Define quality child care. Do you think other aspects should be added? Explain.

# Corporate-Sponsored Child Care

## Benefits for children, families, and employers

**Rebecca Oekerman**

*Texas Tech University, Lubbock, Texas; and Grace Lutheran Early Childhood Program*

## Introduction

By the year 2000, it is expected that 81% of all mothers with preschool and school-age children will be working outside the home (Committee for Economic Development, 1993). While these mothers are at work, their children, 7 million of whom will be 5 years old or less, will need to be cared for in the best manner possible (Children's Defense Fund, 1996). The care options, as they do today, will vary from arrangements with family members to participation in family group homes, to attendance at a child care facility. As these options vary, costs will too.

Correspondence should be directed to Rebecca Oekerman, 3608 Oakridge Drive, Midland, Texas 79707.

It has been shown that contemporary child care can consume one-fourth of a single parent's income (U.S. Census Bureau, 1994).

In actual dollars, the cost per child may reach nearly $5,000 annually with "quality" care costing up to 10% more (Cost, Quality, & Child Outcomes Study, 1995). Hilliard (1985) described quality care as that which:

- is well-planned and organized,
- encourages parental involvement,
- safeguards the health and safety of children,
- occurs within adequate physical space,
- provides ample equipment for learning, and
- is staffed by individuals trained in child development and teaching methods appropriate for use with young children.

Yet, at any price, child care will continue to be difficult to locate and maintain. The National Child Care Survey reported that in 1990, 15% of all employed mothers missed work due to child care problems (Hofferth, Bayfield, Deich, & Holcomb, 1991). Business sources report that these absences cost the workplace $3 billion annually ("Employers Join," 1991). In response to this issue and others (e.g., productivity) the business community has become increasingly involved in providing care for employees' children.

## Employers' Responses to Child Care Needs

In 1982, approximately 600 employers provided some type of child care assistance. By 1990, that number had increased to over 5000 and represented 13% of all employers with more than 100 employees (Sher & Fried, 1994). Corporate America had definitely begun to see the benefits associated with child care as a cost of doing business.

In responding to the needs of their employees, businesses began to devise creative ways to make child care available, affordable, and accessible. Options have grown and now range from direct care to referring parents to agencies whose specific function is to monitor care available locally (see Table I).

## Benefits to Employers Who Assist with Child Care

For their efforts, corporate America has realized numerous benefits. The consequences of assisting parent employees with child care include: less on-the-job employee stress, stability in the workforce, a reduction in absenteeism and tardiness, shortening of the length of maternity leaves, and improved morale and work performance (Friedman, 1991; Ransom, Asehbacher, & Burud, 1989; Waxman, 1991).

Another important but in anticipated benefit for companies has been the efficacious hiring of new employees (*Chain Store Age Executive,* 1985; Friedman, 1991; Ransom et al., 1989). Publicity about a company's involvement with child care for employees has in some cases resulted in prospective employees initiating contact with the business thus saving recruitment expenditures.

As a result of such "bottom line" issues, many businesses have concluded that "providing child care isn't just the nice thing to do— it's the strategically smart thing to do" (Sherer, 1993, p. 50). Moreover, corporate America can take pride in a visible demonstration of employer commitment and bask in the good will their policies have engendered with their employees and their standing in the commu-

| Table I | Child Care Options: Ways Businesses Help |
| --- | --- |
| Direct care | Businesses provide on-site or nearby care centers for daily care, after-school programs, and summer camps. |
| Indirect care | Companies contract with existing centers which provide care for employees' children. |
| | Businesses contribute monetarily to care facilities or finance the upgrading of private home-care providers in return for preferential treatment. |
| Temporary care | Businesses arrange care for emergency care including care for sick children. |
| Pre-paid care | Companies institute special accounts into which employees contribute pre-tax income to be used toward child care. |
| Referral care | Employers contract with referral services that maintain up-to-date information on child care available in the area. |

Sources: Bjorklund, 1994; *Chain Store Age Executive,* 1985; Harper, Densmore, & Motwani, 1993; Segal, 1992.

nity as a whole (Fernandez, 1990; Sher & Fried, 1994).

## Parents Benefit from Corporate Assisted Care

Parent-employees have also realized the benefits of reliable child-care. When utilizing onsite care facility, parents have their children physically close and are readily accessible should emergencies arise. For those parents with older children, a reduction has also been seen in the "3 o'clock syndrome," a heightened anxiety level generated by the fact that many of the employees' children are unsupervised after school is dismissed. Providing care for school-age children has resulted in less worry on the parent's part and allowed for more concentration and productivity (Friedman, 1986).

Consequently, two of the three components of corporate America's commitment to child care, employers, and their employees appear to be benefitting from this arrangement. Yet, for the children being cared for by corporate America, no list of benefits has yet to be empirically formu-

lated. In fact, the actual children involved are mentioned only indirectly if at all, by these businesses.

## Benefits for Children in Corporate Child Care

It is assumed that most companies have a commitment to quality in the child care in ways similar to the exemplary program sponsored by American Savings and Loan Association of Stockton, California. Honored in 1986 by the California Association for the Education of Young Children, this company was recognized for its corporation's dedication to quality care and education (Popejoy, 1986). However, it is possible for a business to view the provision of child care purely as "a requirement for continuity and productivity of work" (Galen & McNamee, 1995), instead of an investment in the future of children.

In an effort to ensure that the care provided is the best they can afford, some workplaces, including the branches of the United States military, are beginning to rely on early childhood accreditation to monitor quality. Corporations may actively encourage (or require) the facilities they sponsor to achieve this standing (Zellman, Johansen, & Van Winkle, 1994), believing that "accreditation is a form of insurance" (Howes & Galinsky, 1996, p. 59). Yet, according to Whitebook (1996), "accredited programs (are) expensive for parents" and "although many programs that have achieved National Association for the Education of Young Children (NAEYC) accreditation are good, an even larger number are only adequate"(p. 43).

Even Bredekamp (1993) who has worked with NAEYC accreditation since its inception has conceded that little research has been conducted to determine whether accreditation actually results in better outcomes for children. One study that did investigate the accreditation process in a corporate setting was undertaken in conjunction with the Johnson and Johnson Child Development Center. Researchers asserted that, "Having a child-centered, physically beautiful environment; the best teaching materials; teachers with excellent credentials . . . and recommended professional standards on ratios and group sizes was necessary but not sufficient to ensure that children were developing well" (Howes & Galinsky, 1996, pp. 58–59).

The desire for corporate-sponsored care will only continue to escalate. And as more companies get involved, it intensifies the responsibility of early childhood advocates to see that the business community is not the main beneficiary in this collaboration. Clearly it is time for those most concerned with the care and education of young children to target corporate America's child care efforts for more study.

Queries that beg to be answered include the logical question of whether research on child care in general is applicable to corporate care. It is assumed that this is the case but perhaps care sponsored by business contains elements not visible in other types of care.

- Do business-minded representatives of sponsoring entities exert influences over the way centers are operated?

- Might these pressures contradict what directors and teachers know is appropriate child care?

- Is child care one of the first benefits to be curtailed when financial difficulties assail businesses and, if so, what does this do to the continuity of care so essential for young children's development?

- Should accreditation rightly be viewed by corporations as a form of insurance against inappropriate caregiving?

Then there are the questions about the impact of corporate-sponsored care on parent-child relationships, including:

- Do children benefit from having their parents visit their classrooms, especially if the visits can only be on an irregular basis?

- Could these frequent contacts breed insecurity in children, especially in toddlers who are in the separation-individuation process?

- Are children who know that their parents are readily available to them, particularly those enrolled in on-site care centers, more securely attached?

These are just a few of the questions that research may someday answer. More will inevitably spring from them or be otherwise posed until, ultimately, early childhood educators know what the benefits of corporate-sponsored child care are for young children.

## Conclusions

Although the list of benefits accrued by businesses sponsoring child care looks impressive, the benefits to the children participating in these efforts should become the focal point. Yes, businesses must be concerned with the "bottom line," yet, when families entrust their children into the hands of corporate America's caregiving they must be assured that the care provided will be beneficial to all the family members involved. Research (e.g., Study Team, 1995; Whitebook, Howes, & Phillips, 1989) has provided suggestions for ways to evaluate the care being provided for young children (see Table II). Corporate-sponsored child care arrangements would do well to include these factors into making their care centers into places where business executives and parents meet to ensure the optimal development of every child.

## References

Bjorklind, B. (1994). County government and local business collaborate for quality child care. *Young Children, 49*(4), 82–83.

Bredekamp, S. (April, 1993). *Lesson on Quality from National Accreditation*. Paper presented at the Meeting of the America Educational Research Association, Atlanta, GA.

Children's Defense Fund (1996). *The state of America's children*. Washington DC: Author.

Committee for Economic Development (1993). *Why child care matters: Preparing children for a more productive America*. New York: Author.

Corporate child care: Making an impact on productivity (1985). *Chain Store Age Executive, 61*(7), 13.

Cost, Quality, and Child Outcomes Study Team (1995). *Cost, quality and child outcomes in child care centers, public report* (2nd ed.). Denver, CO: Economics Department, University of Colorado at Denver.

| Table II | Guidelines for Assessing the Quality of Corporate-Sponsored Child Care |
|---|---|

1. Are staff members, including the center director well-qualified and trained in child development and early childhood education?

2. What has the turnover rate been for staff members within the past year?

3. Does the facility ensure an optimal adult-child ratio for each group of children?

4. Is the physical space sufficient for the number of children using it?

5. Do the staff members give warmth and support to all children, regardless of ethnicity, gender, disabilities or socioeconomic status?

6. Is children's learning enhanced through meaningful, appropriately challenging, hands-on activities?

7. Does the facility encourage parental involvement in all aspects of the operation of its program?

8. Has the center done a self-evaluation to compare itself with professionally recognized standards of child care?

9. With whom does the decision-making authority lie in matters relating directly to the care and education of children?

10. What type of commitment has the sponsoring entity made to providing and maintaining child care?

Employers join for emergency child care: Flexible child care programs favored by working parents (1991). *Employee Benefit Plan Review, 46*(2), 12.

Employers respond to two-career families (1985). *Chain Store Age Executive, 61*(7), 11–13.

Fernandez, H. C. (1990). "Family sensitive" policies can attract employees to human service organizations. *Administration in Social Work, 14*(3), 47–67.

Friedman, D. E. (1986). Child care for employees' kids. *Harvard Business Review, 64*(2), 28–30.

Friedman, D. E. (1991). *Linking work–family issues to the bottom line.*

Galen, M., & McNamee, M. (Feb. 20, 1995). Child care "r" not us. *Business Week*, pp. 38–39.

Harper, E., Densmore, M., & Motwani, J. (1993). New realities in the corporate workplace: Child care in the nineties. *SAM Advanced Management Journal, 58*(3), 4–8.

Hilliard, A. G. (1985). What is quality child care? In B. M. Caldwell and A. G. Hilliard (Eds.), *What is quality child care?*(pp. 17–32). Washington, DC: NAEYC.

Hofferth, S., Bayfield, A., Deich, S., & Holcomb, P. (1991). *National Child Care Survey 1990.* Washington, DC: NAEYC.

Howes, C., & Galinsky, E. (1996). Accreditation of Johnson and Johnson's child development center. In S. Bredekamp and B. A. Willer (Eds.), *NAEYC Accreditation: A decade of learning and the years ahead* (pp. 47–60). Washington, DC: NAEYC.

Popejoy, W. J. (1996). The need for corporate child care is growing. *Bottomline, 3*(12), 52–56.

Ransom, C., Aschbacher, P., & Burud, S. (1989). The return in the child-care investment. *Personal Administrator, 34*(10), 54–58.

Segal, T. (Sept. 28, 1992). Family care: Tips for companies that are trying to help. *Business Week*, pp. 36, 38.

Sher, M. L., & Fried, M. (1994). *Child care options.* Phoenix, AZ: Oryx.

Sherer, J. L. (1993). No longer a luxury. *Hospitals and Health Networks, 67*(6), 50–54.

U.S. Census Bureau (1994). Who's minding the kids? Child care arrangements: Fall 1991. In *Current Population Reports.* Washington, DC: U.S. Government Printing Office.

Waxman, P. (1991). Children in the world of adults: On-site child care. *Young Children, 46*(5), 16–21.

Whitebook, M. (1996). NAEYC accreditation as an indicator of program quality: What research tells us. In S. Bredekamp and B. A. Willer (Eds.), *NAEYC accreditation: A decade of learning and the years ahead* (pp. 31–46). Washington, DC: NAEYC.

Whitebook, M., Howes, C., & Phillips, D. A. (1989). *Who cares? Child care teachers and the quality of care in America. Executive summary of the National Child Care Staffing Study.* Oakland, CA: Child Care Employee Project.

Zellman, G. L., Johansen, A. S., & Van Winkle, J. (1994). *Examining the effects of accreditation on military child development center operations and outcomes.* Santa Monica, CA: Rand.

**Article Review Form at end of book.**

What are some common initial reactions of children to their parents' divorce? What are some suggestions for helping children adjust to parental divorce?

# Parenting Q & A
# Divorce

**Q:** What is the prevailing wisdom regarding telling a seven-year-old and a four-year-old the reasons for getting divorced?

**A:** Divorce and its aftermath are never easy for parents or children. And while divorce is a common experience—approximately one in three U.S. children have experienced a divorce, according to the American Academy of Pediatrics—it is not a "normal" childhood experience.

Children react differently to a divorce depending on their age, sex, temperament and development, but you can be sure there will be some reaction.

Toddlers and preschoolers won't understand the cause of divorce and how it affects them, but they are likely to feel a sense of loss. They may exhibit separation anxiety, become clingy, get angry and have temper tantrums, or regress to behavior they've moved beyond, such as thumb-sucking or wanting a bottle.

School-age children may feel an overwhelming sense of sadness, loss, rejection or guilt. They also may cry easily, have trouble concentrating, develop headaches or stomachaches, take out anger on one or both parents, or have a strong desire for parents to reconcile.

The older the child, the more likely that he or she may ask for the reasons behind the divorce. Kids are perceptive to the feelings of their parents, so it is important to be honest with them. It is also important to avoid badmouthing your former spouse even when there are obvious problems in the marriage, such as alcoholism. Focus on reassuring the children that both parents love them and will always love and support them.

Some questions to expect include:

- Was it my fault?
- Can I still see my grandparents?
- Where am I going to live?
- Will we ever be a family again?
- Why can't we stay together?
- Did you ever love each other?

As the children get older, make sure they know they can ask questions and receive honest answers. Answers need not be detailed to the point of making the parent uneasy but should make the child feel comfortable in trying to understand a difficult situation.

Almost all children hope that their parents will get back together. Don't belittle this hope. Instead, say something like, "I know you'd like that very much, but it won't happen. Mommy and Daddy don't love each other anymore, but we both will always love you."

## Helping Children Adjust

Here are some strategies to help your children make the adjustment:

Talk openly with your children and offer basic, non-threatening information about what's going on. Do not talk to them until you have made the decision to separate. Children will only be frightened and confused to hear that you are thinking of getting divorced but aren't sure yet.

Explain to the children that the divorce is not their fault. It is not unusual for children to think that they did something to make one of the parents leave.

Reassure them that both parents still, and always will, love them.

Reprinted with permission from The Boston Parents' Paper and Parenting Q & A (www.parenting-qa.com).

Encourage the children to express their feelings. One way to do this is to acknowledge their feelings. When they ask you for their other parent, you could say, "You really wish Daddy were here. You miss him a lot." Such validation tends to open up dialogue. A new partner can do this kind of acknowledging as well.

Recognize, rather than minimize, their anger about the divorce. Allow them to feel angry and express their anger in acceptable ways.

Answer their questions as honestly as possible and use language that they can understand. You may have to repeat yourself many times before your children fully understand that their other parent is not coming back. A four-year-old may understand this fact, but may not be ready to accept it. This is normal.

Don't ignore discipline during the adjustment period. Children find comfort in routines and having things stay the same. You may even care to emphasize that by saying, "We still don't use those words (hit our sister, ignore our chores, go to bed late, etc.) in this house."

Encourage the other parent and relatives to follow this advice, too.

Avoid criticizing your former spouse in front of the children. Remember, no matter how good the divorce may be for you, it rarely appears that way to your children. If you are too obvious in your distaste, then your children may start to worry that if you hate your former spouse that much, you may start hating them, too.

 **Article Review Form at end of book.**

What has research shown to be the positive and negative effects of having gay parents? How does having gay parents affect offsprings' sexuality and sexual identity?

# Kids with Gay Parents

**Joseph P. Shapiro
with Stephen Gregory**

Alex Tinker knows what people say about kids like him, kids with gay or lesbian parents: You'll probably turn gay yourself. Your life is going to be a mess. But the 13-year-old is doing just fine as he steps onto the stage along with 260 other Oregon seventh graders being honored for scoring higher on the Scholastic Assessment Test than most high school seniors. As the students' names are called, Alex stands on a chair and points happily to his two proud moms. "Not to brag or anything," he says later, "but if you compared me with an average kid in a normal household, I probably get better grades; I'm probably more athletic; I'm probably equally mentally healthy."

At the heart of the debate over legalizing same-sex marriage lies the well-being of children like Alex. The Senate is expected to vote this week on the "Defense of Marriage Act" that would allow states to refuse to recognize gay marriages even if they are legal elsewhere—a measure adopted by the House and supported by President Clinton. Gay marriages may soon be sanctioned by Hawaiian courts, and 15 states already have adopted statutes barring recognition of gay unions. Critics argue gay marriages would devalue the institution of marriage and give special rights to homosexuals. But their bottom-line objection is that lesbians and gay men cannot be fit parents. Says Robert Maginnis of the Family Research Council: "Both a mom and dad are essential to a balanced upbringing."

Yet many thousands of homosexuals already are living in virtual marriages and parenting children. There are no good estimates of the number of children of gays and lesbians, but researchers are discovering that most children of homosexual parents share Alex Tinker's confident self-assessment. According to a recent American Psychological Association survey of more than 40 research studies on gay parenting, such children are likely to be just as well adjusted as the progeny of traditional unions. The samples in many surveys are small, but the studies show that the children play with the same guns and dolls as do other boys and girls, have similar IQs, develop typical friendships, have a normal sense of well-being and are no more likely to be confused about their sexual identity than kids with straight parents.

What does have an impact on the lives of children whose parents are homosexual is society's reaction. Many are as closeted as their parents. Sons and daughters of gay parents met in July at the sixth annual meeting of the Children of Lesbians and Gays Everywhere (COLAGE), a 2,000 member support and education group. The most popular seminar: knowing whom and when to tell Mom or Dad is gay. At last year's conference in Los Angeles, Maya Jaffe met a classmate from her Maryland high school. Neither knew the other had a gay parent.

In past generations, the children of homosexual parents were likely to be the product of a heterosexual marriage. Typically, the mother or father later came out as gay and the parents divorced. Today, there's a second wave of children of gay parents, many of whom are adopted or who are the natural sons and daughters of lesbian moms.

## Special Delivery

Visiting Alex Tinker's family is like taking an archaeological dig through the layers of such families. Alex, a likable, straight-A student, is the youngest of three siblings living with Bonnie Tinker and her partner of 19 years, Sara Graham. Alex knows that his family is unusual, to say nothing about his conception. In 1982, a family friend bicycled an oyster jar of his own sperm over to Bonnie's house. She administered the insemination herself. Alex considers Bonnie and Sara his parents. But the father occasionally take Alex–along with his own children–hiking or bicycling.

Though the circumstances of his life may seem complicated to outsiders, to Alex they're rather ordinary. Alex loves basketball, watergun fights and, he notes, most everything typical to any 13-year-old boy. While he has been selective in whom he tells about his family, he reports only rare cases of teasing. "I don't think there's anything wrong with being raised differently," he says.

Growing up was more difficult for Alex's older step-siblings. Josh, 28, is Sara's son from an earlier marriage. And Connie, 25 was the legal ward of Bonnie's previous lesbian partner. Josh and Connie's generation had more problems, notes University of Virginia psychology professor Charlotte Patterson, because they "were the pioneers" when homosexuality was less accepted.

It can be an especially hard adjustment for kids who start out living in what they think is a typical heterosexual family to discover suddenly that Mom or Dad is gay. That's similar to what happened to Josh. His father died when he was 10. A few years later, he was sharing his Portland home, a converted blacksmith's shop that his late father had remodeled, with his mother and her new partner, Bonnie, who worked at a battered-women's shelter, and Connie. Josh kept his lesbian mother's existence a secret from his friends; Bonnie avoided parent-teacher conferences and Josh's sports events to protect him. "I couldn't understand it. It was out of the norm," Josh says now. "They weren't my family. Basically, I just hated them."

## No Visitation?

A recent brush with what the family considers homophobia made them closer. Josh says his marriage fell apart over his wife's discomfort with her lesbian in-law's. Josh's wife, the first person he ever told about his gay mother, demanded that there be no contact between their baby daughter and her gay grandmothers. After the divorce, his ex-wife went to court in an unsuccessful attempt to prohibit her daughter from visiting Josh at Sara and Bonnie's house last Christmas. The rancorous battle over visitation "opened my eyes up," says Josh, to the prejudice his mother faced. "I'm older now and more mature," he says. "I don't look at people for their sexual orientation. My mom's lifestyle is her lifestyle. You have to respect that." As for his mother's partner and his step-siblings: "I consider them family now. I'd do anything for them."

Among the toughest and most universal unpleasantries kids in these families face is teasing from classmates. Kate Asmus lost track of the many confrontations with taunting West Hartford, Conn., classmates, which left her burning with tears or anger while the school janitor scrubbed "Kate's a lesbo, your moms recruit" and other graffiti from her locker. Once Kate, then in the eighth grade, ignored the slurs, the harassment stopped. One study found that virtually all children of gay parents report being subjected to unwanted teasing but that nearly all children of traditional families report being bothered by teasing at some time as well.

Despite such occasional ugliness, perhaps most striking about the children of gay parents is how little they say having a homosexual parent truly upsets their lives. "I've never lost a friend because my dad is gay," says Nathaniel Selig, 18. Even his girlfriend, Tara Kelley, and her politically conservative parents are OK about it. Tara's mother, an interior decorator, has worked with gay men.

The rhythm of their lives, such teens say, is like that of any of their peers. Asmus, now 18 and starting a college filmmaking program, notes that her two lesbian mothers "make me do my homework, give me the car when I need it, complain about bills" — just like her friend's parents. "They are my Cleavers; they're my Ward and June, " she says. For Nathaniel Selig, the key is that father John Selig is Dad first: "He's not my *gay* dad. He's my dad." Still, father and son tastes are distinct in the cluttered apartment they shared until Nathaniel recently left for college: It was filled with Nathaniel's soccer trophies and Dallas Cowboys memorabilia and John's gay-pride paraphernalia, rainbow flags and streamers. As for his own sexuality, Nathaniel, who proudly declares his virginity, says: "I don't think I could be taught to love a guy the way that I could love a girl. It's just not me."

## Sketchy Studies

No issue is more controversial then whether gay parents produce gay children. Northwestern University psychology professor Michael Bailey, who has studied the genetics of homosexuality, says that the sketchy studies that do exist "are finding rates on the order of 10 percent of the offspring" of gay parents who turn out gay themselves, higher than the "generally accepted range between 1 and 4 percent" of the population that gays constitute.

But just because gay parents have a higher percentage of gay offspring doesn't mean that their parenting styles are responsible. If homosexuality is largely genetic—as Bailey's own ground-breaking studies of twins suggest—then it makes sense that homosexuality would run in families. Alex Tinker has an aunt, one of Bonnie's sisters, who is also a lesbian. And if being gay is at times a choice—as some homosexuals say—then it also is logical that kids with positive gay role models would be more likely to see homosexuality as an OK choice. After years of bad relationships with men—"they're bossy and controlling"—Connie Tinker started dating women. Her lesbian mothers, however, always had encouraged her dating of men.

For gay parents, having a gay child can be jarring—since it plays into antigay arguments that they "proselytize" their homosexuality. Dan Cherubin knows. He founded Second Generation, a support group for the gay children of gay parents. Cherubin was shocked when, marching in New York's gay-pride parades, his group was greeted with chilliness and even hostility by other gay marchers.

Several studies suggest offspring of gays and lesbians are rarely confused about their own sexual identity. If anything, says Maya Jaffe, 17, having a gay parent may make teens even more secure about their heterosexuality. "I'm more sure about my sexuality than my friends," says Jaffe, who lives with her two moms in Rockville, Md., "because I know it would be OK if I am a lesbian. But I'm not."

And having gay parents also may foster empathy and tolerance. That is clear from Jaffe's eclectic mix of friends, which includes mostly straight kids but also gay ones (one boy came out to her before telling anyone else he is gay), and friends across race and class lines.

One specter, however, haunts some children of homosexuals: AIDS. For Stefan Lynch, 24 watching his father die five year ago was particularly lonely. The father talked about it little, already feeling guilty abut "abandoning me when I was a teenager," recalls Lynch. And Lynch, now director of COLAGE, hid his own hard times at school from his dad, feeling "he had enough on his shoulders." In some families, AIDS strikes more than once. Breauna Dixon, 7, wrote a picture book abut her father's death that is used in AIDS support groups. Breauna now lives with her father's partner—who became her guardian—and the man's new live-in partner (her third "dad"), who has HIV.

Custody decisions for Breauna would have been easier if her dads could have married. Many gay couples find that, without the sanction of law, they spend thousands of dollars for lawyers to draft papers that make clear who can make life-and-death guardianship decisions for their children. Often gay couples will keep multiple sets of these papers—at home, in the car or with them at all times—in case of emergency.

For Connie Tinker, there was a cost to such uncertain legal status. Connie's mother, Bonnie, is a lesbian activist in Oregon—but it wasn't always that way. It was Bonnie's former partner who was Connie's legal guardian. And although Bonnie has reared Connie from the time her daughter was an infant, Bonnie at first kept her own name off the guardianship papers. Bonnie, who now runs a gay-parenting network, feared Connie would be put into foster care if social workers discovered she has lesbian parents. (Courts often deny custody to gay parents. Last month, a Florida court upheld the transfer of 12-year-old Cassie Ward from her lesbian mother to her father, despite the fact that he had served eight years in prison for killing his first wife.) Once, when Connie was 7, police took her into custody, mistaking her for a 13-year-old they wanted to arrest. Despite her terror and anger, Bonnie felt she could not complain. Not until Connie turned 18—and it was no longer a judge's decision—did Bonnie formally adopt her.

Because of such problems, Connie's mothers say they would welcome the chance to get a marriage license at city hall. But even if Bonnie and Sara one day marry, their youngest son, Alex Tinker, doubts it would change his life. His moms are already in what, to him, feels like marriage and family. "It's kind of like finding a new species of life," says Alex, who hopes to go to MIT to study engineering. "It's always existed before, but now it's in the books."

 **Article Review Form at end of book.**

What might be the long-term effect on society of the negative aspirations of homeless children regarding schooling and future employment? What factors seem most associated with families entering the ranks of the homeless?

# Homeless Children in the United States

## Mark of a nation at risk

### Ann S. Masten

One of the most disturbing images to emerge in public consciousness during the past decade is that of the homeless child. Public concern grew as stories of homeless families filled the media. Books like *Rachel and Her Children,* by Jonathan Kozol, roused the conscience of the nation. Clearly, emergency shelters and welfare hotels like New York City's Martinique, so vividly depicted by Kozol, were not fertile ground for child development.

Various attempts have been made to estimate the magnitude of the problem of homeless Americans, but, as the 1990 U.S. Census takers found, counting the homeless presents a host of definitional and methodological issues. Consequently, estimates varied. Nonetheless, data converged on three conclusions: (1) the number of homeless Americans increased during the 1980s, (2) the problem was significant (even by conserva-

tive estimates), and (3) the number of homeless families with children was increasing both in absolute terms and as a percentage of the total homeless population.

The estimate published in 1988 by the Institute of Medicine of the National Academy of Sciences represented a midrange figure: Nationwide, it was estimated that 100,000 children were homeless on any given night, excluding minors on their own. For 1989, the U.S. Conference of Mayors reported that 36% of the homeless population in their 27-city survey consisted of families and more than half of the family members were children. Approximately 25% of all the homeless Americans in this survey were minors.

Congress responded to the surge of homelessness by enacting in 1987 the Stewart B. McKinney Homeless Assistance Act. Homeless persons were defined as those who lack a "fixed, regular, and adequate night-time residence" or who reside in emer-

gency shelters and other places not intended to be homes. This legislation had the goal of coordinating government efforts and providing funds to meet the needs of the homeless. This law also stated the policy of Congress that each state ensure the access of each homeless child to a free and appropriate education.

Concerned scientists also responded to the alarming phenomenon of homeless children. Psychiatrist Ellen Bassuk and her colleagues were the first to publish much-needed data on the mental health problems of homeless mothers and their children. Their studies, suggesting significant developmental delays and psychological problems among homeless children in Massachusetts, influenced the McKinney legislation. Response by other investigators soon followed. The purpose of this review is to highlight the issues and findings emerging from research on the health, education,

Ann S. Masten, Homeless Children in the United States: Mark of a Nation at Risk, *Current Directions in a Psychological Science,* Vol. 1, No. 2, pp. 41–44, April 1992. © 1992 American Psychological Society. Reprinted with the permission of Cambridge University Press.

and psychological status of homeless children.

The focus of this review is children and adolescents living with their families. Minors on their own, "runaway" and "throwaway" children, are a distinctly different group of homeless individuals. Very little research has been done with unaccompanied minors, although limited data suggest high rates of mental illness, substance abuse, posttraumatic stress, suicidal behavior, trouble with the law, and histories of abuse among these adolescents, particularly among "street kids."[1]

## Homeless Families: Who Are They?

Surveys of homeless families suggest that young families headed by mothers who are poor and unskilled have been particularly vulnerable to the macroeconomic and social trends that have led to the recent increase of homelessness among families. Nationwide, the majority of homeless families are headed by single mothers. These mothers tend to be young, and the age distribution of their children is correspondingly skewed, with more infants and preschoolers than school-age children.

The ethnic composition of homeless families appears to reflect in large part the ethnicity of very poor families in a given region. Among urban families, ethnic minorities are overrepresented in the homeless population. Beyond minority status, little is known about cultural factors that may influence shelter utilization. The prevalence and acceptability of "doubling up" families in a single apartment or of seeking public assistance may vary among communities and among cultural groups.

Income levels are very low among homeless families. Many depend on welfare supports that result in incomes well below the federal poverty level. Others, fleeing or abandoned by the family breadwinner, have no current income.

The immediate "cause" of living in an emergency shelter is typically a financial crisis characterized by too little money and no affordable alternative housing. However, pathways to this predicament appear to be diverse. Some families are migrating from one place to another, seeking a better job or life. In others, relationship conflicts have resulted in leaving a residence by choice or by force. In still others, economic hardships have gradually eroded family resources or came overnight when a parent lost a job, a building was condemned, or the rent went up. Many low-income families live from check to check and have no savings to buffer the costs of losing a job or moving, for whatever reason. Once lost, housing can be difficult to regain in a tight housing market, and up-front costs such as security deposits may be difficult to meet. There is a strong consensus among researchers as well as advocates that during the 1980s the growing shortage of low-income housing, the recessionary economic forces early in the decade, and the falling value of economic assistance to poor families combined to squeeze more families into the ranks of the homeless.

Personal problems may also contribute to economic hardship or the necessity of moving. Deinstitutionalization and severe mental illness do not appear to be salient causal factors for family homelessness. Unwise choices, substance abuse, or mental health problems may play a role. Bad luck also may be a significant factor differentiating homeless families from other very poor, vulnerable families who retain housing. Systematic research on the risk factors and processes leading to homelessness remains very limited.

## The Stresses of Homelessness for Children

Concerns about homeless children stem in large part from the deprivations and adversities associated in the public mind with the image of "homelessness." Journalistic accounts of life in a welfare hotel like the Martinique would alarm any reasonable person about risks to the children. More systematic, if less dramatic, studies of shelter life and the experiences that precede homelessness substantiate public concern. In a study of families residing in a Minneapolis shelter, homeless children had experienced significantly more stressful life events out of their control over the past year than a very similar comparison group of poor children living at home.[2] Events such as illness, injury or arrest of a parent, or separation of parents may have been causally related to the outcome of homelessness, although this could not be determined in the study.

By the time they arrive in a shelter, children may have experienced many chronic adversities and traumatic events. More immediately, children may have gone hungry and lost friends, possessions, and the security of familiar places and people at home, at school, or in the neighborhood. Children perceive the strain of frightened parents who do not know what is going to happen. Shelters, which may provide for basic needs of housing, food, and clothing, can be very stressful for parents and children. Locations are usually undesirable, particularly with respect to children playing outside. Moreover, necessary shelter rules may strain a child and family life. For example, it is typical for no visitors to be allowed and for children, including adolescents, to be required to be accompanied at all times by a parent. Some shelters separate fathers and adolescent males from the rest of their families. Children also may be humiliated by other children at school or on the bus knowing where they live. Health care, education, and other services may be difficult to access.

Based on demographic data and the circumstances of many homeless families, it is reasonable to predict that homeless children are at considerable risk for health problems and developmental delays, as well as academic, emotional, and behavioral problems. A small but growing number of studies corroborates the high-risk status of homeless children.

## Health

The elevated rate of health problems in homeless children has been documented with data from 16 cities participating in the National Health Care for the Homeless Program initiated by the Robert Wood Johnson Foundation, the Pew Memorial Trust, and the U.S. Conference of Mayors.[3] Compared with normative samples of urban children coming in for health care, homeless children had two to four times the rates of respiratory infections, skin problems, nutritional deficiencies, gastrointestinal disorders, and chronic illnesses. Several studies have found immunization delays to be more common among homeless children than among other poor children. A study in New York found much higher rates of a total lack of prenatal care

among homeless women than poor, housed women.[4] Not surprisingly, rates of low birth weight and infant mortality were higher as well. These health problems could impair current functioning and compromise future development, particularly in the context of continuing poverty and inadequate health care.

## Education

Homeless children miss more school, have repeated a grade more often, and receive fewer special educational services than other school-age children. Before advocates and the McKinney legislation focused national attention on the educational deprivation of homeless children, many of these children were effectively denied access to education by barriers such as residency requirements, lack of immunization or school records, and transportation. Although the 1987 McKinney Act required states to ensure that homeless children had access to public education, barriers remain.

Several studies have found significant learning delays in homeless children at all grade levels, including preschool. In a recent pilot study conducted in a Minneapolis shelter, the 8- to 12-year-old children ($N = 20$) were an average of 14 months behind their age levels on a standardized individual achievement test, significantly below national norms for this test.

## Development and Mental Health

Controlled studies of the cognitive, social, and emotional development or well-being of homeless children are few in number. Particularly little is known about the socioemotional status of

homeless infants. Results are consistent in finding delays in development, but differences between homeless and other poor children are not found consistently. Studies of preschoolers indicate cognitive, social, and visual-motor delays in development. Language delays are particularly prominent. Two controlled studies of preschoolers found elevated rates of behavior problems among homeless compared with poor, housed comparison groups.[5,6] Similar results have been found using the same instrument for homeless school-age children in Boston,[7] Los Angeles,[8] Minneapolis,[2] and Philadelphia.[6] The Minneapolis study, for example, included 159 children ages 8 to 17 who lived in the largest shelter in the region. Homeless children and adolescents had significantly more behvioral and emotional problems than the general population, particularly for antisocial problems. The proportion of children with Total Problem scores in the clinical range on the Child Behavior Checklist was twice the normative rate. Although scores for homeless children tended to be higher than scores for the very low-income comparison group, the similarities among very poor children, whether housed or homeless, were more compelling than the differences.

Several findings in the Minneapolis study suggested other effects on these children. Compared with poor, housed children, more homeless children expected they might live in a shelter as adults. Fewer homeless children and adolescents reported having a close friend, and they had spent less time with friends over the past week. Compared with other Minneapolis elementary school children, homeless children had substantially lower job aspirations for the future. These differences may reflect the subtle but lasting tolls of long-term deprivation, as well as recent experiences.

There were other ways in which poor children, regardless of housing status, appeared to be more alike than different. Poor, housed boys, like homeless children, had low job aspirations. A comparison of 8- to 12-year-olds showed both the homeless and the housed poor had higher levels of fear than a control group of urban schoolchildren. Fears of deprivation, for example, such as fears of hunger and having no place to live, were salient in both groups of poor children.

## Implications

Studies of homeless families strongly suggest that homeless status is a powerful marker of high cumulative vulnerability and risk for child development. The most alarming implication of the data, however, is that homeless children represent the plight of millions of American children being reared in poverty.[9] Homeless families typically arise from a vulnerable population of extremely poor families. Although the crisis of homelessness itself appears to add to the risks for problems in health, education, and development, the differences between homeless and other very poor children often are not so great as the differences between poor children and the general population.

Homeless children appear to represent the ominous tip of the iceberg of poverty threatening the course of this nation's future. Policies and programs to assist homeless families or prevent homelessness among families must address this problem in the larger context of poverty. Clearly, multiple strategies at many levels of intervention will be required to improve the odds for good developmental outcomes in these children.

Shifting the odds for favorable child development among the nation's poorest children will take time, even if this task becomes the top priority of every relevant national, state, and local agency in the country. The problem of homeless children is not going to disappear in the near future. Therefore, more immediate efforts to intervene on behalf of these children are needed.

Research indicates that many homeless children need direct health, educational, and mental health services. Access to available resources is a key problem. Schools and preschool programs may be able to play a critically important role as the access point to both family services and psychological support for children. Schools have diverse opportunities to help meet many of the basic needs of homeless children, including food and health care, stability, relationships with competent peers and adults, and extracurricular activities that build self-efficacy. Schools, however, cannot be expected to assist homeless and other highly mobile, disadvantaged children without added resources.

Researchers have an important role to play in providing information to guide policy and evaluate programs. Although a number of studies have been conducted and more are under way, there are major gaps in the knowledge base. Little is known about the processes leading to or out of homelessness or the factors that ameliorate risk and facilitate better outcomes for children and their families. Most studies include heterogeneous samples of homeless families that differ markedly in background and current status on many dimensions that may be crucial for understanding causes and outcomes and for developing strategies to reduce the risks of becoming homeless or ameliorate its effects on parents and children. There is also a great need for information on the welfare of unaccompanied minors and how homeless runaways and abandoned children differ from or resemble homeless adolescents who stay with their families.

In addition, there is a profound shortage of normative data on the development of ethnic minority children and of appropriately standardized measures for use with low-income or minority children. Normative data on the development of ethnically and socioeconomically diverse populations of children would provide the context for understanding developmental problems among homeless and other high-risk populations.

Finally, it is clear that isolated efforts, whether in the domain of research, policy, or intervention, limited to one place, one discipline, or one perspective, are inadequate to meaningfully address the complex problem of homeless children. Coordinated, multifaceted efforts are required at each level in each domain of inquiry and action. Helping homeless children and preventing homelessness may also depend on national acceptance of the idea that poor children belong to all of us. Certainly, their development will affect all of our futures.

## Notes

1. M.J. Robertson, *Characteristics and circumstances of homeless adolescents in Hollywood*, paper presented at the annual meeting of the American Psychological Association, Boston (August 1990).
2. A.S. Masten, D. Miliotis, S.A. Graham-Bermann, M. Ramirez, and J. Neemann, *Children in homeless families: Risks to mental health and development*, manuscript submitted for publication (1991).
3. J.D. Wright, Homelessness is not healthy for children and other living things, in *Homeless Children: The Watchers and the Waiters*, N.A. Boxhill, Ed. (Haworth Press, New York, 1990).
4. W. Chavkin, A. Kristal, C. Seabron, and P.E. Guigli, The reproductive experience of women livig in hotels for the homeless in New York City, *New York State Journal of Medicine, 87,* 10–13(1987).
5. J. Molnar, W.R. Rath, T.P. Klein, C. Lowe, and A.H. Hartmann, *Ill Fares the Land: The Consequences of Homelessness and Chronic Poverty for Children and Families in New York City*(Bank Street College of Education, New York, 1991).
6. L. Rescorla, R. Parker, and P. Stolley, Ability, achievement, and adjustment in homeless children, *American Journal of Orthopsychiatry, 61,* 210–220 (1991).
7. E.L. Bassuk and L. Rosenberg, Psychosocial characteristics of homeless children and children with homes, *Pediatrics, 85,* 257–261 (1990).
8. D.L. Wood, R. B. Valdez, T. Hayashi, and A. Shen, Health of homeless children and housed, poor children, *Pediatrics, 86,* 858–866 (1990).
9. C.M. Johnson, L. Miranda, A. Sherman, and J.D. Weill, *Child Poverty in America* (Children's Defense Fund, Washington, DC, 1991).

## Recommended Reading

Institute of Medicine. (1988). *Homelessness, Health, and Human needs* (National Academy Press, Washington, DC).
Rafferty, Y., and Shinn, M. (1991). The impact of homelessness on children. *American Psychologists, 46,* 1170–1179.

Acknowledgments—Support for the author's research on homeless children, partially described in this article, was provided by a McKnight Professorship and a Graduate school Grant-in-Aid award from the University of Minnesota.

 **Article Review Form at end of book.**

# WiseGuide Wrap-Up

- Nonmaternal child care is the norm for children worldwide and historically. Exclusive maternal care of infants and young children is a cultural myth of an idealized 1950s. The primary change in child care arrangements of today is not the absence of mothers providing the care but a shift from relative care to nonrelative babysitters. Of child care options available, center-based care is currently the most preferred arrangement.

- Child care serves three major purposes. It supports maternal employment. It serves child development needs by providing high-quality early childhood programs. It is also a means of socializing economically disadvantaged and ethnic minority children into the cultural mainstream.

- Child care supply and quality of services are currently inadequate. Particularly lacking are infant and toddler programs, consistency of regulations, and supports to allow for affordable quality care. Such issues are all the more pressing when gender equality in the workplace and home are considered and with the start of welfare reform.

- Corporate-sponsored child care may be one means of supporting maternal employment. The provision of child care services at or near the workplace reduces parental worries and allows for rapid responses in emergencies. At the same time, such supports translate into more productive and satisfied employees and can be useful recruitment incentives.

- One in three American children face parental divorce. Reactions vary in accordance with child's age, sex, developmental status, and temperament. It's not unusual for children facing the stress of divorce to express negative emotions, to ask many difficult questions, and to show regression in behaviors and poor school performance. Honest answers, reassurance, acknowledgment of feelings, and discipline consistecy can facilitate childrens' adjustment to the changes associated with divorce.

- Most people are opposed to same-sex marriages and question the adequacy of gay parents. However, studies indicate that children of gay and heterosexual parents are equally likely to be well adjusted, to play with masculine and feminine toys, and to develop health, sexual identities. One of the toughest issues for children of gay parents to face is the teasing from classmates when their parents' sexual orientation becomes public.

- The number of homeless families with young children is increasing. Lacking stable homes and economic security, these children suffer from repeated illnesses, developmental delays, and psychological problems that adversely affect their learning.

## R.E.A.L. Sites

This list provides a print preview of typical **coursewise** R.E.A.L. sites. There are over 100 such sites at the **courselinks**™ site. The danger in printing URLs is that web sites can change overnight. As we went to press, these sites were functional using the URLs provided. If you come across one that isn't, please let us know via email to: webmaster@coursewise.com. Use your Passport to access the most current list of R.E.A.L. sites at the **courselinks**™ site.

**Site Name:** Divorce

**URL:** httn://www.studyweb.com/family/famdiv.htm

**Why is it R.E.A.L.?** This site links to articles and sites regarding divorce and its impact on the family. Visit this site and connect to the Demographics and Family Composition site. Compare the birth, marriage, and divorce rates of U.S. women with women from other countries. Why do you think these rates differ from country to country? What cultural expectations may influence these behaviors?

**Site Name:** America's Homeless Children: Will Their Future Be Different?

**URL:** http://nch.ari.net/edsurvey97/

**Why is it R.E.A.L.?** This text article is a summary of the survey of homeless education programs in July 1997. It includes state and local profiles, tables, recommendations, and conclusions regarding the plight of homeless children in America. Visit this web site and investigate the plight of homeless children in your state. What kinds of programs are available in your local area? Make a list of all the agencies and task forces currently addressing this serious problem for America's children.

# section 10

## Children's Health

### Learning Objectives

- Provide an overview of common and risk-related health concerns.

- Examine the long-term effects of unhealthy eating behaviors, including malnutrition, overeating, and dieting.

- Provide information on possible interventions to improve children's eating habits.

The health and well-being of children have improved drastically over the past two decades. Improvements in modern medicine have all but eliminated childhood diseases such as polio, smallpox, and measles. As a result, most serious illnesses of childhood involve respiratory problems such as bronchiolitis, wheezing, ear infections, and asthma. Yet, one of the most misunderstood disorders may still be Sudden Infant Death Syndrome (SIDS). The unknown causes of this disease have spurred the use of "preventative" treatments. The best advice to parents on keeping their children healthy is to establish a strong relationship with a pediatrician.

An ongoing relationship with a pediatrician is also the best means by which parents can monitor and feel confident in the growth and development of their children. Parents often have health-related concerns, such as the safety of immunizations, whether growth rates are normal, or if a child is too active or sedentary. In our weight-conscious society, a major concern is the appropriateness of a child's weight. While interventions to reduce fat content of diets and increase activity levels may be effective early in development, often these same weight concerns persist into childhood and adolescence. The concern for excessive weight gain in childhood has resulted in over 40% of 9- and 10-year-old girls trying to lose weight, whether they need to or not. Concern about body image are surfacing much earlier than in previous generations. When weight concerns turn into an obsession with thinness, a red flag is raised for the potential development of anorexia nervosa or bulimia. The age of onset for these disorders continues to drop. Most researchers and physicians agree that stress on healthful diets and lifestyles must replace obsessions with weight.

While a portion of our youth are starving themselves by "choice," another group is going hungry because of poverty. Malnutrition and undernutrition trigger an array of health problems that can become chronic if not corrected. Recent studies indicate that, even among severely malnourished infants, establishment of a healthy diet by age 3 will allow for normal brain growth. Undernourishment, though not associated with brain abnormality, is related to poor cognitive functioning. Undernourished children lack the energy and motivation to learn and experience developmental delays due to lowered expectations from adults, minimal desire to explore the environment, and illness. The lowered aspirations and performance of these children as adults further promote poverty, underachievement, and poor health.

### Thinking Beyond the Facts

The United States is viewed as an affluent nation, filled with citizens able to purchase nearly anything desired and health care options that are topped by no one. Though true for many, there is a significant and growing number of families who have difficulty meeting even the basic needs of their children. Obtaining quality health services and providing a balanced diet are expensive. We also are a nation with many habits and fads that are contrary to healthy living. Americans continue to overeat and then diet, smoke, use drugs, and do not get enough exercise, despite knowledge of the health risks. Children lacking health care are frequently ill and may unknowingly spread harmful diseases to others. Hungry children lack the energy to learn from even the most well-designed interventions. Overweight and out-of-shape children are at risk for costly diseases later in life. Similarly, children who starve themselves in an effort to meet thinness ideals create a host of bodily disorders. What do you think are some of our nation's attitudes that enable us to establish state-of-the-art medical services alongside poor health and lifestyle choices? Why do you think attempts at promoting attitudes of prevention and health care education have not been widely successful in the United States? How does our "for-profit" health care system create inequities in health-related services? What might be the positive and negative consequences of a shift to socialized health care? For more information on children's health care needs and problems, visit web sites on immunizations, childhood diseases, dieting and eating disorders, nutrition, and obesity.

Discuss the controversy over treating otitis media with antibiotics.
What is crib death? How might it be prevented?

# You've Come a Long Way, Baby

**Russell Watson and Brad Stone**

Vicki and Arthur Wohlfeiler of Beachwood, Ohio, had two children, the younger one 11, when their daughter Carly was born in the spring of 1994. Carly turns 3 this June, and already she has given the Wohlfeilers a broader perspective on child rearing; they have now done it in the 1970s, '80s and '90s. A lot has changed. There are new medicines—the Wohlfeilers are particularly grateful for over-the-counter ibuprofen—and toys are generally safer. It's much easier now to raise a health baby, they say. Some changes have made the job more difficult; health insurance, for one, is maddeningly more complicated. "It's a trade-off," says Vicki, 46. "But it's generally easier, especially since, this time, we know what to expect."

Everyone goes into child rearing with a medicine chest full of folk wisdom: Feed a cold, starve a fever. Don't give your baby a bath when she has a cold. Teething can cause a high fever; aspirin is a good way to bring it down. Today pediatricians would quarrel with those bromides—and even with some of the advice they themselves may have dispensed a decade ago, for few areas of medicine have changed as drastically as pediatrics. Here is a look at some of the new thinking that affects the health of every child.

## The Immunization Push

The most important thing parents can do is make sure their children are properly vaccinated. But getting the right shots, in the right sequence, at the right time isn't always easy, because the immunization cookbook keeps changing. Currently, the American Academy of Pediatrics (AAP) recommends that, in the first 18 months of life, children receive 10 vaccines, some in multiple doses, some in combination with others. Many are familiar: measles, mumps, rubella, polio, diphtheria, tetanus and hepatitis. Among the newer vaccines is *Haemophilus influenzae* b, known as "Hib," which immunizes against bacteria that can cause several dangerous ailments, including meningitis; it was approved for infants under 1 year of age only in 1990. And just last year, the Food and Drug Administration approved a new toxoid against pertussis (whooping cough)that has fewer side effects than the previous one.

One of the more controversial immunizations is the two-year-old vaccine for chickenpox. Some parents argue that because the disease is a normal and relatively harmless affliction of childhood, their kids should be spared this particular needle. But the AAP recommends the vaccine for all children between 12 and 18 months who have not already had chickenpox. The disease is more severe if it occurs after puberty, often turning into pneumonia. And at any age a poxy child is trouble for parents. "It's more of an economic issue," says Dr. Harry R. Lubell, a pediatrician in Sleepy Hollow, N.Y. "With two parents working, they're going to lose a week of work for each child who gets chickenpox."

Overall, American children are better protected by vaccines than ever. According to the federal Centers for Disease Control and Prevention (CDC), 75 percent of children between 19 and 35 months are up to date on their shots, compared with only 55 percent five years ago. And new vaccines are on the way. "I fully expect we'll have vaccines for all common ailments in 10 years' time," says Lubell.

## Babies Don't Break, But Some Symptoms Are Cause for Real Alarm

You've just been handed your seven-pound bundle of joy and your first reaction is: Help! How do I keep from breaking it? Take heart. Babies may not bounce, but neither do they get a fatal infection if they suck a dirty thumb. Here are the top 10 conditions that parents of 0-to-3s should look out for:

1. It isn't called **the common cold** for nothing. In their first two years, most children will have eight to 10 colds, complete with runny nose, sneezing, decreased appetite, cough and sore throat. Most toddler colds aren't serious. But in infants under 6 months, colds can develop into bronchiolitis(see worry No. 2), croup(a distinctive barky cough)or pneumonia. If the baby is irritable, feverish, coughing, breathing rapidly or uninterested in eating, her cold could be developing into something worse. Parents should call the pediatrician.

2. "All that wheezes is not asthma," says Dr. Joseph Zanga of the American Academy of Pediatrics. In infants, **wheezing,** accompanied by rapid breathing, is more often a symptom of bronchiolitis, a viral infection of the lungs' small breathing passages. Treatment includes saline drops in the nose and a nasal aspirator. Parents should keep the home free of cigarette smoke and use clean humidifiers (dry air aggravates nasal passages and sore throats). Severe cases, where babies turn blue around the lips and fingertips from lack of oxygen, may require hospitalization.

3. Two thirds of all children will have at least one **ear infection** ("acute otitis media") by their second birthday. Most pediatricians prescribe antibiotics; left untreated, infections can lead to scarring and hearing loss. But recently, questions have been raised about whether antibiotics fight ear infections any better than the body's natural immune system does.(page 44).*

4. High temperatures make kids miserable and parents nervous. But **fevers** are the body's natural defense against infection, so some pediatricians let them run their course. Others prescribe acetaminophen. (Aspirin is out because of its link to Reye's syndrome—a rare but serious illness that can damage the brain and liver.) Because newborn's immature immune systems make them more susceptible to unusual infections, their fevers should be monitored closely: temperatures above 100.3 need immediate medical attention. "We hop on it very quickly," says Dr. Alan Woolf of Children's Hospital in Boston. In toddlers, fevers that reach 103 or linger for more than a day or two also concern docs.

5. The most common cause of **vomiting** in young children is a stomach or intestinal infection. But vomiting can also be a symptom of a more serious illness like pneumonia, meningitis or appendicitis. Danger signs include severe abdominal pain, repeated vomiting that lasts more than 24 hours and blood or bile. Most vomiting will cease on its own, but doctors recommend extra fluids to prevent dehydration.

6. Symptoms of **dehydration** include a parched, dry mouth, less urination, irritability and listlessness. Children should be given small amounts of "rehydrating" liquids—electrolyte solutions that contain a balance of salt, sugar and minerals. Liquids should be administered slowly—first teaspoons, gradually tablespoons. Dehydration is dangerous because it can lead to kidney failure, shock and even death: severe cases may require hospitalization for intravenous rehydration.

7. **Diarrhea** generally goes away by itself within a few days. "Except for a somewhat sore bottom, the infant will be fine," says the AAP's Zanga. Sweet liquids like juices and Jell-O should be avoided: sugar aggravates diarrhea. Give small amounts of liquid to prevent dehydration.

8. Diaper **rash,** usually caused by wet diapers that stay on too long, is easy to identify because of where it appears. Impetigo, a **skin infection** characterized by pimply, crusty, itchy sores, is common in 2- and 3-year-olds. Rashes and skin irritations are seldom dangerous unless accompanied by other symptoms, especially a high fever. "That's a child I want to see immediately," says Woolf, because it can indicate a more serious bacterial infection.

9. When a baby or toddler **falls** from a height much greater than a bed, watch for repeated vomiting, clumsiness or dizziness. Any could indicate a brain injury and require immediate medical attention.

10. Parents often worry that their child is growing too fast or too slow or taking too long to walk or talk. But many delays simply reflect a child's unique developmental schedule. "There isn't a single age that a child has to develop a particular trait," says Dr. Ron Kleinman of Massachusetts General Hospital. "There's a range for all of us."

Claudia Kalb in Boston

*Does not appear in this publication.

## The Age of Asthma

But for now, kids still get sick. The leading chronic illness among American children is asthma. It af-fects about 4.8 million youngsters under the age of 18, and the number of cases has risen nearly 80 percent in the last 15 years, calculates the American Lung Association.

The reason isn't entirely clear. The cause may be environmental—air pollution, tobacco smoke, allergens in poorly ventilated homes, even cockroach droppings—or it may be that more kids are in day care, where they are exposed to other kids' germs.

Asthma restricts breathing by clogging the airways; an attack can be treated with inhalers that dilate the bronchial passages. Asthma cannot be prevented entirely, but its effects can be diminished in several ways. Cleaning up children's surroundings—rugs vacuumed, bedding laundered—and the air they breathe (no tobacco smoke) is an obvious step. As long as they manage the disease properly, parents don't have to treat asthmatic children like babies all their lives. "People should realize that asthma is common, and children don't have to live sedentary lives because of it," says Dr. Richard Evans of Children's Memorial Hospital in Chicago.

## Fighting Crib Death

Sudden infant death syndrome (SIDS), the dreaded "crib death," kills about 3,000 babies a year, 95 percent in the first six months of life. The cause of SIDS isn't known. Some kids have a slightly higher risk than others. They include premature babies and those with breathing problems arising from the way their brains regulate respiration. Researchers also think some crib deaths may be caused by placing babies face down on blankets or other soft bedding.

Several methods have been suggested for reducing the risk of SIDS. The most promising is to lay babies on their sides or backs. The AAP began to recommend that five years ago, and between 1993 and 1995 the number of crib deaths dropped 30 percent. Researchers also recommend breast-feeding, which helps fight respiratory ailments and allergies. Parents also should keep their babies away from tobacco smoke, which can clog breathing passages.

Other precautions are more controversial. Electronic monitors can warn of changes in breathing and heart rate, but they also produce frequent false alarms. Some researchers suggest that mothers should sleep with their babies, arguing that the mother will be more alert to any crisis, while her presence alone may help to rouse a child who has stopped breathing. Other researchers oppose the practice, citing the danger of rolling over on the baby.

## Heading Off Trouble

Doctors are more aware than ever of the need for preventive measures. That's partly because of the move to cost-conscious managed care. But in addition to saving money, prevention produces healthier babies. Parents still have a lot to learn. Though most know good hygiene is essential, few wash hands—their own or their children's—as often as they should. Many germs spread more readily by hand than through the air.

The best thing parents can do to ensure preventive care is to maintain a strong relationship with a pediatrician—which isn't easy in underserved poor areas or when health-insurance or managed-care arrangements mandate a change of doctors. The AAP calls the ideal pediatric practice a "medical home," a 24-hour-a-day service to which parents can comfortably turn, by telephone if not in person, whenever they need help. "The closer the relationship parents have with a pediatrician, the more potential there is for children to stay healthy," says the AAP's Dr. Thomas Tonniges.

Early diagnosis is one benefit. "If hearing loss is detected in a child between the ages of 4 and 6 months, the outcome is significantly improved," says Tonniges. "A dislocated hip can be identified in a newborn and treated conservatively with a sling. But wait until the child is walking, and he may need surgery." Without a primary physician, parents of sick kids all too often end up in hospital emergency rooms, where they generally encounter long waits, high costs—and a doctor who has never seen their child before. With all the recent advances in medical science and those still to come, today's toddlers have unequaled prospects for long-term health. But their parents have to know how to make the system work for them.

 **Article Review Form at end of book.**

What are the recommended methods of gently helping a young child slim down? What are some of the effects of being a chubby child?

# The Case against Baby Fat

## Laura Nathanson, M.D.

Tammy's mother and I are giggling at Tammy, who is a card. Here for her yearly checkup, the 3-year-old has conned me out of my shoes and my stethoscope and is conducting a satirical rendition of "The Mad Pediatrician" on her dolls. She is adorable. She is also chubby.

Many pediatricians would say to Tammy's mom, "Don't worry, it's just baby fat." After all, nobody wants a little child to feel bad about her body. Everybody wants parents to feel 100 percent love, pride, and approval toward their children. Nobody wants to sow the seeds of worry about weight that could lead to eating disorders later on.

But I've learned through the years that this hands-off approach can produce the very problem it is designed to avoid. Childhood is the only time when weight gain can be slowed, allowing a youngster to "grow" into a healthy weight for her height. Sometimes that happens, and it's easier and much more effective than trying to lose weight later. But parents can't assume it will occur naturally and not act.

These days, the typical American child tends to eat more calories, especially fat calories, than she needs relative to the amount of exercise she gets. Some children maintain a normal weight because their bodies naturally burn off the extra calories as waste. Others, like Tammy, become chubby.

A youngster who weighs more than she should can have a rough time. I'd hate to see Tammy in, say, third grade, being mocked or rejected by her classmates, unable to run without panting and sweating, and unable to keep up on the playground. I'd hate to see her parents becoming more and more anxious, nagging and worrying her. I'd hate to have Tammy grow up angry and self-conscious, feeling as if her weight is the most important thing about her. That's a real setup for an eating disorder.

## It Isn't Always Obvious That a Child Is Overweight

For reasons we don't understand, extra weight in a girl triggers early puberty. Instead of entering adolescence at age 10, a chubby girl may start as early as age 8 and begin menstruating by fourth or fifth grade. Contrary to popular myth, a girl who weighs more than she should doesn't lose her "baby fat" during this time: A female's hormones are programmed to encourage weight gain at this stage of life. Emotionally, the double whammy of being first in the class to enter puberty and gaining even more weight can be devastating.

Parents of children like Tammy usually have three important questions for the pediatrician: How can I tell if my child is overweight and how long it will take her to grow into those extra pounds? Does an inherited metabolism doom a child to a lifetime of being overweight? How can I help my overly chubby youngster slow down her rate of gain?

Because chubbiness is so common, a youngster who weighs more than she should has come to look normal to her parents, and even her pediatrician. In fact, it's not unusual for the parents of a normal-weight youngster to worry that their child is too skinny! That's because a normal child doesn't typically gain pounds as fat between ages 2 and about 10, but as muscle and bone. No wonder normal-weight kids seem to be "all skin and bones".

Since eyeballing a child is an unreliable gauge of chubbiness, ask your doctor to confirm any suspicions you—or he—may have by consulting a pediatric growth chart. If I think a child is chubby, I consult the chart that looks at how much a child weighs in relation to her height; this is known as the weight-by-height chart. If I see a child whose weight is above the 75th percentile of children who are the same sex and height, and progressing toward the 90th percentile, I am very concerned that the child's weight will get out of hand. And a child who weighs more than 95 percent of her peers of the same sex and height is considered obese.

## Slowing Down Weight Gain Can Actually Be Fun

Tammy is 38 inches tall—about average for a 3-year-old girl—and weights 40 pounds. A normal weight for her height is 32 pounds, which means she is "off the chart," above the 95th percentile, of weight for height. Forty pounds would be her "ideal" weight if she were about 43 inches tall.

If Tammy continues to put on pounds at her present rate, the chart predicts that at age 10 she will be 4 feet 7 inches tall and weigh 105 pounds; her normal-weight girl-friends of the same height will weigh about 70 pounds. The extra 35 pounds means that Tammy will be 50 percent over-weight—well above the obese line.

On the other hand, if we can slow down Tammy's weight gain as she grows, she should reach a comparatively normal weight by second or third grade. If we could keep her from gaining *any* pounds—an unhealthy and un-kind goal—Tammy would reach the right height for her present weight by age 5.

## Simple Changes Make a Difference

The key to helping a chubby child slow her weight gain is to not make her feel deprived. Happily, lots of kids' favorite foods come in low-fat versions. You can also make simple substitutions without sacrificing flavor. Get your child involved in making healthy food choices by letting her help you shop or prepare meals. Don't assume that just because something is lower in calories, your child can eat more of it. And be sure to let her indulge a little on special occasions, such as birthday parties and holidays.

| Instead of | Serve |
| --- | --- |
| french toast | pancakes |
| scrambled egg | poached egg |
| banana | kiwi fruit |
| ice cream | ice pop |
| pudding | gelatin |
| chocolate-chip cookies | graham crackers |
| processed American cheese | part-skim mozzarella |
| grilled cheese cooked in butter | "grilled" low-fat cheese sandwich, melted in toaster oven |
| bologna slice | turkey slice |
| beef hot dogs | chicken franks |
| meat loaf | lean hamburger patty |
| lasagna | macaroni and low-fat cheese |
| spaghetti and meatballs | spaghetti and turkey meatballs |
| apple juice | flavored seltzer |

This will require some thought and commitment. Tammy has inherited a metabolism that doesn't burn up extra calories as waste. She also has trouble telling when she has eaten enough, and she enjoys eating, even when she's not hungry. Yes, genetics matter. When one or both birth parents are obese, the child may inherit the predisposition to be overweight. In Tammy's case, her mother has a weight problem. But this legacy doesn't mean that Tammy is doomed to a lifetime of being over-weight; it simply requires vigilance over pessimism. We need to re-think her lifestyle, helping her cut back on extra calories and increasing her activity level.

But is all has to be fun. Tammy needs to feel absolutely adorable—and normal—while this happens. Nobody is going to mention her weight to her, look at her critically, or utter words or sighs that make her feel as if she's somehow a disappointment.

First, Tammy's parents and I tackle the amount of exercise she gets. We don't assume that she's naturally active just because she's a little kid. Instead, we'll see to it that she participates in a half hour of sweaty outdoor physical activity at least twice a day. To make sure this happens, her parents—or perhaps a reliable teenager they hire—will teach her and help her practice basic sports skills now and as she grows, including how to throw and catch a ball, jump rope, bicycle, and roller-skate.

## Food Shouldn't Be Used As a Reward or Punishment

Second, we change Tammy's eating habits. She starts to drink water, not apple juice, for thirst. We replace her cheese, yogurt, and 2 percent milk with nonfat dairy products and limit her to 16 ounces a day. Then there's the matter of ketchup: Tammy loves the stuff. Perhaps she's truly addicted to it. "She even put it on a peanut-butter sandwich one time instead of jelly," says her mother. While ketchup is low in fat, it has 16 calories per tablespoon, so piling it on really adds up. Telling her it's not healthy causes fuss and tears, but this is easier to do at age 3 than it will be at age 7.

Her father, who does the cooking, promises that there'll be a dish Tammy likes at each meal. But if it's fat- or calorie-rich, he'll prepare enough for only one generous helping per person. It's easier to say, "There isn't any more," than, "You can't have seconds." He'll make sure the rest of the meal offers plenty of tasty, low-fat foods, like fruits and vegetables. Dessert is sweet and fun to eat, but healthy and low in fat and calories: a cut-up apple with a raisin face, an oatmeal cookie, or some gelatin.

Tammy's grandparents promise to show their love with extra attention, not cookies, candy, and rich desserts. Tammy must not go hungry, however. She must have choices to make, but among foods that are good for her. We won't let her choose between an apple and a Ding Dong and then be angry when she picks the latter. The pantry and refrigerator contain lots of healthy low-fat and low-sugar snacks.

Finally, we pay attention to the food cues in Tammy's life that tempt her to eat when she's not hungry. Her parents limit her television watching to one hour a day, so that commercials for chocolate-covered sugar bombs won't seduce her. Her day-care provider gives snacks only when Tammy is hungry, not as a ritual. There are no more handouts, such as crackers or treats, for her to munch on all day long.

All the adults vow to put food in its proper place. Using it as a reward or bribe or withholding it as a punishment will just backfire. Because the food served at a social occasion represents ceremony and celebration, it's not wise to control what Tammy eats at birthday parties or holiday meals. Singling her out would make her feel as though she were being punished, and cause her to focus even more on food.

Most important, we'll nourish Tammy's good feelings about herself and make sure she has lots of opportunities to gain skills and friends. The more adorable and competent and powerful she feels, the less she'll rely on eating for a sense of self. Helping Tammy will be a great deal of fun, but quite a challenge. I myself am very tempted to offer her—oh, say, a Twinkie—just for the return of my stethoscope. And my left shoe.

 **Article Review Form at end of book.**

What does a healthy diet consist of? What are the long-term benefits of implementing nutritional programs in our schools?

# Malnutrition, Poverty and Intellectual Development

**J. Larry Brown
and Ernesto Pollitt**

The prevalence of malnutrition in children is staggering. Globally, nearly 195 million children younger than five years are undernourished. Malnutrition is most obvious in the developing countries, where the condition often takes severe forms; images of emaciated bodies in famine-struck or war-torn regions are tragically familiar. Yet milder forms are more common, especially in developed nations. Indeed, in 1992 an estimated 12 million American children consumed diets that were significantly below the recommended allowances of nutrients established by the National Academy of Sciences.

Undernutrition triggers an array of health problems in children, many of which can become chronic. It can lead to extreme weight loss, stunted growth, weakened resistance to infection and, in the worst cases, early death. The effects can be particularly devastating in the first few years of life, when the body is growing rapidly and the need for calories and nutrients is greatest.

Inadequate nutrition can also disrupt cognition—although in different ways than were previously assumed. At one time, underfeeding in childhood was thought to hinder mental development solely by producing permanent, structural damage to the brain. More recent work, however, indicates that malnutrition can impair the intellect by other means as well. Furthermore, even in cases where the brain's hardware is damaged, some of the injury may be reversible. These new findings have important implications for policies aimed at bolstering achievement among underprivileged children.

Scientists first investigated the link between malnutrition and mental performance early in this century, but the subject did not attract serious attention until decades later. In the 1960s increasing evidence of undernutrition in industrial nations, including the U.S., along with continuing concern about severe malnutrition in developing countries, prompted researchers to examine the lasting effects of food deprivation. A number of studies in Latin America, Africa and the U.S. reported that on intelligence tests children with a history of malnutrition attained lower scores than children of similar social and economic status who were properly nourished. These surveys had various experimental limitations that made them inconclusive, but later research has firmly established that undernutrition in early life can limit long-term intellectual development.

## Worry over Brain Damage

For many years, scientists considered the connection between nutrition and intellectual development to be straightforward. They assumed that poor nutrition was primarily a worry from conception to age two, when the brain grows to roughly 80 percent of its adult size. In this critical period, any degree of malnutrition was thought to halt the normal development of the brain and thereby to inflict severe, lasting damage.

Gradually, though, investigators recognized that the main-effect model, as we have termed this view, was too simplistic. For instance, the emphasis on the first two years of life proved somewhat misguided. Brain growth in that period is not always terminated irreversibly in undernourished children. Rather it may be put on hold temporarily; if diet improves by age three or so, growth of the brain may continue at close to a normal pace. Conversely, injury to the brain can occur even when a child suffers malnutrition after the first two years of life—a sign that providing adequate nutrition throughout childhood is important to cognitive development. Focusing exclusively on the first two years of life is thus inadequate.

Furthermore, although severe underfeeding in infancy can certainly lead to irreparable cognitive deficits, as the main-effect model predicts, the model cannot fully account for intellectual impairment stemming from more moderate malnutrition. This flaw became apparent in the 1960s, when researchers showed that mildly undernourished children from middle- or upper-income families (whose nutrient deficits stemmed from medical conditions) did not suffer the same intellectual troubles as did mildly underfed children in impoverished communities. If poor nutrition impaired cognition only by structurally altering the brain, the two groups should have performed alike. Something else had to be at work as well. In other words, factors such as income, education and other aspects of the environment could apparently protect children against the harmful effects of a poor diet or could exacerbate the insult of malnutrition.

## No Energy to Learn

In the 1970s research by David A. Levitsky and Richard H. Barnes of Cornell University helped to clarify how malnutrition might hinder cognitive development in ways other than injuring the brain. Levitsky and Barnes studied rodents to examine the effects of malnutrition. Levitsky concluded that the malnourished animals performed less well on tests of mental ability, such as maze running, not because they suffered brain damage but mostly because, lacking energy, they essentially withdrew from contact with their peers and the objects in their environment. In addition, mothers coddled the less mobile infants, further hindering their growth and independence.

By extrapolation, the findings implied that cognitive disability in undernourished children might stem in part from reduced interaction with other people and with their surroundings. This fundamental shift in understanding produced increased optimism about the prospects for remediation; if decreased social interaction was partly at fault for cognitive impairment, then social and intellectual remediation could presumably help make up for deficits in the youngsters' experiences.

Although the new ideas were compelling, scientists did not have much human evidence to buttress the changing views. A recent study by one of us (Pollitt) and several collaborators adds strong support to the notion that malnutrition affects intellectual development in part by compromising many different aspects of a child's development. The research also provides added insight into how poor diet and economic adversities during childhood combine to impede intellectual

functioning later in life. Pollitt's collaborators included Reynaldo Martorell of Emory University, Kathleen S. Gorman of the University of Vermont, Patrice L. Engle of California Polytechnic State University and Juan A. Rivera of the Institute of Nutrition of Central America and Panama.

The project was an extensive follow-up of Guatemalan children who were studied by other scientists many years earlier. In 1969 the Institute of Nutrition of Central America and Panama, with the help of various U.S. government agencies and private foundations, began a massive effort to examine the value of nutritional supplements in preventing the health problems of malnutrition. For eight years, residents of four villages in Guatemala received one of two nutritional supplements. When this phase of the study was being planned, researchers felt that protein was the most important nutrient missing from diets in developing countries. Therefore, project workers looked specifically at how children would respond to added protein in their diets. The mothers and children in two of the villages received a high-protein supplement called Atole (the Guatemalan name for a hot maize gruel). Inhabitants of the other two villages—who constituted the control group—received Fresco, a sweet, fruit-flavored drink, which contained no protein. Both supplements provided vitamins and mineral as well as calories; Fresco provided a third the calories of Atole.

When the study began, all pregnant women, and all children under the age of seven in the villages, were invited to participate. During the course of the study, children under seven who moved into the villages and women who became pregnant were also asked to join the project. More than 2,000 children and mothers participated between 1969 and 1977. Regular medical exams of the children revealed that both supplements improved the health of the participants, but Atole performed more impressively. For instance, in all four villages, the rate of infant mortality decreased. But in the villages that received Atole, infant mortality decreased 69 percent, whereas in villages receiving Fresco, the rate went down by just 24 percent. Also, only Atole improved growth rates in children under three.

## Gains in Guatemala

In the follow-up study, carried out in 1988 and 1989, Pollitt and his colleagues visited the villages to assess how these early nutritional supplements affected intellectual development over the long term. More than 70 percent of the original participants—by then, ranging in age from 11 to 27 years old—agreed to take part in the follow-up. In particular, the team's analysis concentrated on the group of roughly 600 people who were exposed to Atole or Fresco both prenatally and for at least two years after birth. These adolescents and young adults took literacy, vocabulary and reading comprehension tests, a general knowledge exam, an arithmetic test and a standard nonverbal intelligence test. The researchers then determined how education and economic status (measured by house quality, father's occupation and mother's education) correlated with test scores.

The subjects who received Atole in early life performed significantly better on most tests of cognition than those who received Fresco. The strongest effects of Atole were observed among those at the low end of the social and economic ladder: these children performed as well as the more privileged children in their villages [*see box on these two pages**]. Atole thus served as a kind of social equalizer, helping children from low-income families achieve at the same level as their slightly more economically advantaged peers within the village. But the children of this study all lived in extreme poverty and did not perform at the same level as, say, a child from a middle-income household in a more prosperous area of Guatemala. Hence, adequate nutrition by itself could not fully compensate for the negative effects of poverty on intellectual growth.

In addition, Atole appeared to have increased the advantage of education. With every additional year of schooling, the differences in achievement between the adolescents who received Atole and those who consumed Fresco increased. This result indicates that poor nutrition can essentially negate some typical benefits of education. In separate but related studies, Pollitt and his collaborators, working in Peru, and Sally Grantham-McGregor of the University of the West Indies, working in Jamaica, have demonstrated that learning capabilities are affected by how recently one has eaten. So breakfast every day before school is indeed important, particularly among children at risk for undernutrition.

The better long-term effects in the Atole group can largely be explained by the differences in the children's motor skills, physical growth, and social and emotional development. The youngsters who received

*Does not appear in this publication.

Fresco in their early life suffered more physical disadvantages—a slower rate of growth and a slower rate of recovery from infection, for example—compared with those who received Atole. Because development was hindered, these children also learned to crawl and walk slightly later on average than the infants who received Atole. Pollitt and his colleagues speculate that for the infants who took Fresco, this limitation delayed the acquisition of the cognitive skills that children develop when they explore their social and physical environment.

Furthermore, because these undernourished toddlers remained small for their age, adults might have tended to treat them as if they were younger than their actual age. Such a response would very likely slow cognitive development, if the toddlers were not challenged—to talk, for instance—in the same way that other children their age were. Children who consumed Atole, in contrast, avoided malnutrition, grew up faster and were presumably exposed to more challenges in their social environment. Of course, the results do not rule out the possibility that the Fresco recipients may have suffered some degree of brain damage that impeded their later functioning. The findings, however, imply that additional factors, such as the child's social environment, played a major role as well.

The results in Guatemala are also consistent with the prevailing understanding of the interactions between poor nutrition, poverty and education. Nutritional supplements combat the effects of poverty, but only somewhat. A well-nourished child may be better able to explore the environment, but an impoverished community may offer little to investigate. And although schools can provide much of the stimulation children need, early malnutrition can undermine the overall value of education. Most important, this study demonstrates that poor nutrition in early childhood can continue to hinder intellectual performance into adulthood.

Because the early planners of the Guatemalan study chose to examine protein, these results emphasize protein's importance to intellectual growth. The supplements also included calories, vitamins and minerals; consequently, their role should be taken into account, but the arrangement of this particular study makes isolating the effects difficult.

Other work links essential vitamins and minerals to mental ability. For example, in one study in West Java, Pollitt and his colleagues showed a close association between iron-deficiency anemia (the most common consequence of malnutrition) and poor mental and motor skills in children. The researchers gave iron supplements to babies between 12 and 18 months old who were suffering from iron-deficiency anemia. The mineral significantly improved the infants' scores on mental and motor skills tests. Sadly, children with iron-deficiency anemia are more susceptible to lead poisoning, which produces its own set of

neurological disorders that interfere with proper cognition. Consequently, poor children face a double jeopardy: they are more likely to be anemic and more likely to live where lead poisoning is widespread.

## Correcting and Preventing Impairment

Studies such as the one in Guatemala have prompted many scholars including one of us (Brown), to suggest that when the social and economic aspects of a child's environment cannot be easily changed, providing adequate nutrition during infancy and later will at least lessen the cognitive deficits engendered by poverty. Nutritional supplements cannot by themselves reverse the long-term adverse effects of earlier undernutrition, however. The ideal would be to provide additional support, such as tutoring, opportunities to develop new social skills and guidance from an involved parent or another concerned adult. Recent studies have shown that enriched education programs for children in economically impoverished communities can often ameliorate some of the problems associated with previous malnutrition.

To have the best chance at being useful, such intervention should be comprehensive and sustained. Most undernourished

children face persistent challenges that can exacerbate the effects of underfeeding. They frequently live in areas with substandard schools and with little or no medical care. Their parents are often unemployed or work for very low wages. And the children may suffer from illnesses that sap energy needed for the tasks of learning.

On balance, it seems clear that prevention of malnutrition among young children remains the best policy—not only on moral grounds but on economic ones as well. The U.S., for example, invests billions of dollars in education, yet much of this money goes to waste when children appear at the school door intellectually crippled from undernutrition. The immediate expense of nutrition programs and broader interventions should be considered a critical investment in the future. Malnutrition alters educational preparedness and, later, workforce productivity, making it an unacceptable risk for its victims as well as for a nation's strength and competitiveness. Steps taken today to combat malnutrition and its intellectual effects can go a long way toward improving the quality of life—and productivity—of large segments of a population and thus of society as a whole.

 **Article Review Form at end of book.**

# WiseGuide Wrap-Up

- Parents should be familiar with the major symptoms of common childhood illnesses. Familiarity will enable parents to make appropriate judgments regarding the need for medical attention. Much attention is currently being given to immunizations, the treatment of asthma, prevention of crib deaths, and the appropriate treatment of ear infections.

- The importance of a balanced diet begins in early childhood. Chubbiness is no longer thought of as cute and as something outgrown. Being overweight in childhood is associated with many health and social problems. Gently guiding the overweight child toward a low-fat and nutritionally balanced diet and a lifestyle that includes regular exercise is important.

- Dieting among young girls is occurring earlier. By 9–10 years of age, 40% of children report they are trying to lose weight by restricting food intake. Eating disorders typically emerge after the onset of puberty and may severely damage children's bodily systems.

- Studies suggest that infants' brains are amazingly resilient and are able to rebound following early life malnutrition.

- Current research indicates that poor nutrition impairs cognitive performance, not by causing brain abnormalities but because undernourished children lack energy essential for attending to information. Undernourished children receive less attention from caregivers, achieve developmental milestones later, and explore their environments less then do well-nourished children. These early learning deficits hinder learning in school and throughout life.

## R.E.A.L. Sites

This list provides a print preview of typical **coursewise** R.E.A.L. sites. There are over 100 such sites at the **courselinks**™ site. The danger in printing URLs is that web sites can change overnight. As we went to press, these sites were functional using the URLs provided. If you come across one that isn't, please let us know via email to: webmaster@coursewise.com. Use your Passport to access the most current list of R.E.A.L. sites at the **courselinks**™ site.

**Site name:** Something Fishy—Eating Disorders
**URL:** http://www.something-fishy.com/ed.htm
**Why is it R.E.A.L.?** This web site is a comprehensive listing of information regarding eating disorders in childhood and adolescence. It includes facts about, definitions of, and signs and symptoms of all major eating disorders and links to articles and further research information. Visit this site and complete the self-test for eating disorders. Most college females diet during their years at school. How does your attitude about your weight and food measure up? Use the answer key to determine your likelihood of developing an eating disorder.

**Site name:** Bandaids and Blackboards
**URL:** http://funrsc.fairfield.edu
**Why is it R.E.A.L.?** This website provides a child's perspective on what it is like to grow up with chronic illnesses. Visit this site and review the perspectives on chronic illness from a child's, a teen's, and a parent's perspective. Compare the issues for each group and think about how they differ. What does a child feel that a parent should be aware of in order to help the child cope? What issues would you include in a parenting class for parents of a chronically ill child? Are there any issues that would apply to coping with everyday child illness?

**Site name:** KidsHealth.org: Children's Health and Parenting Information
**URL:** http://www.kidshealth.org/index2.html
**Why is it R.E.A.L.?** Kidshealth provides information on growth, food, fitness, nutrition, childhood infections, immunizations, and medical and surgical procedures. Visit this site and read stories from real children regarding their illnesses. Often the perspective presented in textbooks is that of an adult. How do you think the child's point of view differs from the adult perspective? How would this information be helpful in dealing with children with serious illnesses?

# section

# 11

## Learning Objectives

- Present information on factors that influence the course of normal identity.

- Discuss the socialization experiences of our sons and daughters.

- Compare the sexual behaviors of adults and children, with discussions of normal childhood sexuality.

- Examine situations that interfere with the development of healthy self-concepts.

- Discuss problems existing within foster care and adoption services.

# Issues in Identity

 **WiseGuide Intro**

The phrases "she's so much like her mother" and "he is his father's son" are heard often. Some researchers suggest that family similarities are largely genetic. Others contend that the behaviors modeled by same-sex parents and reinforced when imitated promote gender and family resemblances. While the debate continues over the relative importance of nature and nurture in the development of our "maleness" or "femaleness," most agree that the answer lies in their interaction. However, regardless of which side "wins," success in our society may depend on developing traits that combine the best of both genders. For our sons and daughters to flourish in modern times, they need to acquire the behaviors and attitudes that open doors to opportunities, not only those fitting their given sex.

One aspect of normal development is the establishment of a healthy sexual identity. Parents and teachers are often confused by the wide array of sexual behaviors that young children exhibit. When sexual behaviors are observed, caregivers need to distinguish normal acts stemming from curiosity from those that are abnormal. Children's sexual behaviors are characterized by curiosity and play, spontaneity and openness, and sensuality and excitement. Without shame or shock, caregivers need to respond to children's questions in ways that provide accurate information, promote the development of appropriate sexual behaviors and comfort with sexuality, and prevent the occurrence of potentially harmful actions.

The continuum of sexual normality must be expanded somewhat as children leave the innocence of the preschool years behind. At relatively young ages, some children experience feelings and desires different from the norm. Gay youths often report having experienced the first feelings of being "different" long before the onset of puberty. Unfortunately, few supports or informational resources exist for these children due to societal attitudes that fail to accept homosexuality. Without positive role models, attitudes of acceptance, and resources to consult, these youths often feel depressed and lonely and suffer from low self-esteem and identity confusion. Reforms, including policies demanding tolerance and programs for teachers, parents, and peers regarding issues faced by gay youths, must be incorporated into our schools to ensure the success of all students.

Children who are without parents also face uncertainties in their quest to develop a sense of identity. Estimates suggest that there are 100,000 children living in foster homes across the United States. Many are of minority status and older. While the demand for infants by adoptive couples far exceeds the supply, there is an abundance of older children waiting for families. The earlier the adoption process occurs, the higher the probability of positive outcomes. Children who grow up in foster homes or experience repeated failed placements may lack the sense of security necessary to develop healthy identities and self-mastery. They may also lack lasting friendships and stable support systems. Laws protecting parental rights, overburdened case workers, poorly coordinated registries, and the like only prohibit the adoption of many children. Reform and modernization must be demanded for the sake of these children and the adults who become frustrated in their attempts to provide homes.

## Thinking Beyond the Facts

Through socialization forces, children learn about culturally accepted roles, behaviors, and attitudes. This process begins early in life, with the biological sex of a child imposing distinct opportunities and limits. A child's age influences what is culturally tolerated, particularly in the area of sexuality. Most Americans are uncomfortable with children's expressions of sexuality and unsure of how to respond, especially if viewed as deviating from the norm. Family background further influences socialization experiences and our views about a child's worth. Learned biases leave many feeling ambivalent about welfare and homeless children, older foster children, and children whose parents are criminals. Stories abound about welfare dependency cycles within families, high rates of mental illness and violent acting-out among those in long-term foster care, and criminal mindsets running in families. What are your hidden fears and biases? Should we, as a nation, promote androgyny or sex differences in our children? Are supportive attitudes toward sexual diversity dangerous? Should we suppress the normal sexual curiosities of our children early or encourage "healthy" expression? Are our fears of the impact of negative family experiences justified, or are they largely based on the media's exaggeration of rare events? How open and tolerant should our attitudes be toward healthy individual identities? To read more about factors impacting the development of identities, see web sites on homosexuality, childhood sexuality, adoption and foster care, and gender differences.

How is the parenting of boys different from the parenting of girls?
What are some recommendations for "taming boys"?

# Raising Sons, Raising Daughters

## Leslie Bennetts

Before I had children, it seemed so simple: Aside from the obvious anatomical differences, what distinguished one sex from another was largely the product of socialization. Sure, boys and girls behave differently—but that was because we treat them that way from birth.

When my oldest friend had twins, I watched in amazement as she, her parents and her in-laws hovered around the cribs, looking down at two indistinguishable infants. "What a big husky guy!" they said admiringly to the one wrapped in blue. "You look like a football player!" Then, "What a beautiful little creature! Look how graceful she is," they cooed to the baby in pink.

Several years later, I watched the twins play at an outdoor barbecue. The boy had grown into a rough-and-tumble fellow who spent the afternoon running, yelling, tackling other boys and rolling around on the ground, gleefully oblivious to the mud. His sister, a coquette with ribbons in her long wavy hair and an immaculate ruffled dress, spent the day sashaying around the lawn, making charming conversation.

Well, of course the twins' behavior conformed to stereotypes, I thought—they'd had those social roles reinforced from the moment they emerged from the womb.

Then I had my own children, and all my steadfast convictions went out the window. As the last of my friends to become a mother, I inherited a vast assortment of hand-me-downs—not just clothes and books, but also toys that ran the gamut from baby dolls to tow trucks. The perfect unisex laboratory, I thought—no sex-role stereotyping in this house!

## Girly Girls and Boys' Boys

My daughter proved to be a spirited, independent child who asserted herself without hesitation. Yet in other ways she quickly became a classic girly girl. As a writer who works at home, I wear comfortable pants 365 days a year—but by the time Emily was two, she insisted on wearing a dress every day, preferably one decorated with ruffles or rhinestones, the gaudier the better. And despite the ecumenical array of toys available to her, she simply ignored the cars and trucks, the plastic hammers and building blocks. Every time a birthday rolled around, so did the demands every good feminist mother dreads: "I want Glitter Beach Barbie!" "I want Cut and Style Barbie!" "I want nail polish!" "I want makeup!" Maybe she'll grow out of it, I thought, trying to quell my dismay.

Then my son arrived. Not only was he fascinated with all the toys his sister had rejected—his favorite was the battery-operated steering wheel she had never touched—he specialized in taking objects apart and trying to put them back together. Although his pacifist parents don't permit toy guns or other weapons, Nicky amasses an arsenal with whatever raw material is at hand. He can't take a walk in the park without turning every stick into an instrument of aggression. He doesn't actually hit anything; he just derives immense pleasure from brandishing it in the air and making threatening noises.

As for presents, Nicky obsesses about toys my husband and I would never buy. After examining an original edition of

*Winnie-the-Pooh,* he seized upon a drawing of Christopher Robin with a pop-gun and mounted a passionate campaign for one of his own. Forget about *Power Rangers;* if even *Winnie-the-Pooh* inspires warlike fantasies, what's a parent to do?

## Does Nature Beat Nurture?

Gender difference is a hot topic these days, as experts who study the genetics of sexual development rethink the old nature-versus-nurture question. Most agree that the key to an individual's development lies in the interaction between the two forces. Yet many mysteries remain. There are clearly sex-based characteristics; scientists have found both physical and cognitive differences in the brains of males and females, according to a recent *Yale Children's Health Letter.* And just this past March, in a story that made headlines, the *Archives of Pediatric and Adolescent Medicine* offered support for the argument that biology is destiny. The journal published a follow-up study of a baby boy who, after his penis was accidentally cut off during a botched circumcision in the 1960s, had a vagina surgically created, received female hormones and was supposedly raised successfully as a girl. For years, the case was cited in scientific literature as proof that we are all born gender-neutral and that sex roles are learned.

But in fact, as the 1997 study revealed, the child had been desperately unhappy and maladjusted as a girl, routinely ripping off dresses and even trying to urinate while standing up. At age fourteen—upon learning her medical history for the first time—the child decided to undergo a second sex-change surgery and revert to being male. Today, he is a happily married man with three adopted children.

## Doing Right by Our Daughters

But while it seems clear that there are inborn gender differences, most parents can also agree that minimizing the most egregious of those differences will ultimately enrich the lives of both sexes.

Over the last two or three decades, most parents have, in fact, made dramatic changes in the way they raise girls. "They are far likelier to encourage them to take work seriously, to aspire to a profession that interests them, to be financially and psychologically independent, not to view themselves solely as future wives and mothers," observes Myriam Miedzian, Ph.D., the author of *Boys Will Be Boys: Breaking the Link Between Masculinity and Violence* (Anchor, 1992).

Unfortunately, even the feistiest little girls often falter as they mature. *Meeting at the Crossroads,* a landmark study by Carol Gilligan, Ph.D., of Harvard and Lyn Mikel Brown, Ed.D., of Colby College, in Waterville, Maine, found that even girls growing up amid privilege suffer a traumatic loss of confidence as they approach puberty. At the age of eleven or twelve, formerly self-confident girls begin to repress emotions, grow afraid to voice opinions and become paralyzed at the prospect of even minor conflict; already they have so thoroughly internalized our society's dictates about "good girls" that they put their own needs last.

The reasons why are likely to be found in their mothers. "Before women can encourage confidence, outspokenness and a sense of personal authority in their girls, they have to model that behavior themselves," says Lyn Mikel Brown. "And that's not easy, because

### Emboldening Your Girls

1. Encourage physical activity, and don't express disapproval if she gets messy. "Sports are important because they give girls a sense of being connected to their bodies and feeling powerful," says Lyn Mikel Brown. "Anorexia and bulimia are about dissociation from your body."

2. Help her to become a critical consumer. When you're watching television, discuss the subtext in the ads. Talk about the pressures our culture imposes on women and girls; help her deconstruct the messages about thinness, female attractiveness and feminine roles. Such conversations should start early; Brown notes with dismay that her ten-month-old daughter received a children's book that depicts a ladybug sweeping the floor while a bow-tie-wearing frog sits in an armchair reading the newspaper.

3. Distinguish between polite behavior and stereotypically "feminine" behavior. Don't encourage her to be silent, passive or always nice at the expense of her own needs and opinions. Help her to understand that she can be courteous and respectful of others even when she has a conflict with them.

4. Examine your own behavior and attitudes. "I hear over and over again, 'How can we help girls?', but women don't often enough ask, 'How can we deal with these issues within ourselves?'" says Brown. "It's deeper than knowing the right ways to act. It's about changing the way you think—changing your own comfort level about moving out of traditionally feminine roles."

we've all been raised in a culture where there are power differences between men and women. But girls are watching, particularly around the ages of ten, eleven and twelve; that's a pivotal time, when they either suffer a drop in self-esteem or they hold onto their voices. Those who do the latter, our research has shown, are girls who have mothers or other women in their lives who exhibit strength and courage."

At that age, notes Brown, "girls start to really notice unfairness and power differences: 'Why does Daddy always get his way?' 'How come all the school principals are men?'"

In the face of such deeply entrenched inequities, what can a lone parent do? "One answer is conversation—about how the world is changing, and how your daughter might participate in that change," says Brown. "Parents have to be aware of how their schools work. Are the teachers up-to-date on the research on gender equity and gender bias? Is there a sexual harassment policy? If girls see their parents actively involved in their lives, they learn that they're taken seriously."

## What We're Saying to Sons

But when it comes to boys, we have not made corresponding changes in our child rearing. While it's true that most boys today know their way around a kitchen a little better than their fathers did, "what hasn't changed," says Miedzian, "is that people are still raising boys in accordance with what I call 'the masculine mystique': being tough, being dominant, lacking empathy. There's a reluctance to encourage caring and sensitivity. Parents are

## Taming Your Boys

1. Carefully monitor their exposure to popular entertainment. "The evidence is overwhelming that entertainment has a major influence on children," says Myriam Miedzian. "Do everything you can to control it. Don't kid yourself into thinking that this is not a big deal. Get some sort of parental-control device."

2. Make sure you're aware of what they're learning in their sports programs. "Meet the coach and make sure he is not encouraging or allowing the boys to use derogatory terms about girls: Insulting a boy by calling him a 'girl' or a 'wuss' is common," Miedzian says. "Be especially careful about sports that revolve around physical assault; if possible, steer your son to some other sport."

3. "If you son is exhibiting kind, sensitive, empathetic behavior, applaud it," Miedzian says. "Rid yourself of the idea that it has anything to do with being gay."

4. Expect your son to perform the same household tasks as your daughter. Ask him to baby-sit and set the table; ask her to do yard work. "If you don't, your son will grow up thinking guys just mow the lawn and women do all the housework," warns Miedzian.

afraid those qualities will make boys soft. Underlying it all is the fear of homosexuality. That's the source of a lot of parental decisions, like not letting boys play with dolls unless they're violent action figures."

"If you treated boys and girls exactly the same, you'd still get more aggressive boys than girls—and obviously we don't treat them the same," says James Garbarino, Ph.D., a child psychologist and director of the Family Life Development Center at Cornell University, in Ithaca, New York.

"There's more tolerance of aggression in boys, whereas there should be less, because boys are more vulnerable to it. We need to tame our boys and embolden our girls, but we tend to do the exact opposite."

That process, Miedzian maintains, requires a thorough understanding of the effects of popular culture. "Boys today are surrounded by entertainment with incredibly violent heroes; films and television are not only more pervasive than they were forty years ago, they're more violent," she says. "Video games, too, are extra-ordinarily violent. These forms of entertainment lead to desensitization and lack of empathy."

Also, because many adult women are naive about what Miedzian calls "male culture," they often underestimate the degree to which certain sports, such as football, glorify violence. "Some coaches tell their players to 'take out' a player from the opposing team," she notes. "'Taking out' a player means injuring him so badly he can no longer play." The fact that many fathers see nothing wrong with this kind of talk further compounds the problem.

How can we encourage empathy in our sons? Parents can start by confronting their own double standards. Miedzian cites one study in which small boys and girls were put in a room with their parents and a large assortment of dolls. When the girls played nicely with a doll, the parents would say things like, "What a nice mommy you are!"

"Hardly any of the parents said anything like that to the boys," Miedzian reports. "Yet here was a golden opportunity to encourage boys from an early age.

You could say, 'You'll be such a good daddy someday!' Boys need to develop nurturing qualities. We are finally beginning to embolden our girls, but we are not sensitizing our boys."

## The Best of Both Worlds

For better or worse, the traits our culture encourages in boys—independence, self-reliance, strength, competitiveness—happen to be those most linked to success. It is therefore crucial that girls acquire them—just as boys must cultivate such virtues as kindness and sensitivity. Ultimately, though, it is a mistake to segregate human characteristics as either "male" or "female," no matter how much biology steers us in that direction. To do so deprives both sexes of the opportunity to realize their true potential. "It's about having a range of options for all good qualities," agrees Brown. "I don't think we want girls to become boys or boys to become girls. We want both to become full human beings."

 **Article Review Form at end of book.**

When should parents be concerned about their young child's sexual behaviors? Compare adult and child sexual behaviors. How should parents approach children's sexual behaviors and questions?

# Becoming Sexual

## Differences between child and adult sexuality

**Fred Rothbaum,**
**Avery Grauer,**
**and David J. Rubin**

Parents and teachers sometimes see behaviors in three- to five-year-old children that suggest complete innocence and disinterest regarding sexuality, and at other times they observe behaviors that seem blatantly sexual. Caregivers often wonder how to distinguish normal,[1] healthy behaviors from those that are not. To ascertain the range of children's sexually oriented behaviors with a view toward helping parents and teachers address them, we interviewed and observed parents and teachers of children ages three to five, observed the children at home and in the classroom, and reviewed related studies.

We learned that children's normal sexual behaviors comprise an extraordinarily broad spectrum, which can foster uncertainty and anxiety for caregivers contending with those behaviors. We believe

1. Normality has both a statistical and an evaluative meaning and we are relying more on the latter. In most cases statistical normality alone is insufficient in drawing conclusions about whether a behavior is problematic.

that parents' and teachers' anxieties about children's sexuality and concerns about its normality stem largely from misunderstanding how it differs from that of adults and attributing to it adult meanings.

Most of the caregivers with whom we talked realize that language, peer play, and other critical aspects of human functioning develop stages from infancy through adulthood. Yet many of these caregivers seemed surprised to learn that sexuality follows a similar course. Research and anecdotal evidence clearly indicate that children's sexual behavior often does not have the same meaning and is not accompanied by the same thoughts and feelings as manifestly similar adult behavior. We believe that the meaning of children's behavior can be distinguished from that of adults along three dimensions: curiosity and play versus knowing and consequential behavior; spontaneity and openness versus self-consciousness and privacy; and sensuality and excitement versus passion and eroticism. By recognizing and understanding these dimensions, caregivers can learn to defuse their own tensions regarding children's sexual behaviors—even those as diverse yet normal as the three described at the opening of

the article.* (Based on these dimensions, we provide some guidelines at the end of this article for dealing with children's sexual behavior.)

We recognize that many adults are deeply concerned about sexual abuse and child behaviors that might indicate abuse. Our decision to focus on normal sexual behaviors stems from the belief that such behaviors have adaptive and educational roles in children's lives. We believe also that a fuller understanding of normal child sexuality is critical to an understanding of that which is abnormal. In the final section we briefly address behaviors that we see as abnormal and problematic.

## Children's Behaviors That Appear Sexual

### Curiosity and Play

Just as children are curious about adult roles such as firefighter and teacher, they are also curious and playful about sexuality.[2] Adults,

*Not included in this publication.

2. Most of the literature dealing with children's curiosity about sexuality focuses on the development of children's understanding of reproduction. We do not address reproduction here because it is treated extensively elsewhere. For readers interested in this topic, see the list of further readings.

too, are interested in the body, but their knowledge about sexuality and its consequences gives a distinctly different character to their behavior. Children's interest in sexuality centers on the body and its functions and is manifest through direct physical exploration and use of language.

Our interviews and observations yielded abundant examples of children's direct physical exploration. One mother described finding her four-year-old son and a five-year-old neighbor (also a boy) in the bathroom playing doctor and inspecting each other's "private parts." Another mother told of her four-year-old daughter asking her to play the villain while the child played a princess and her father a prince (a classic enactment of Freud's Electra complex). The daughter included in her play the element of jealousy, making her behavior seem even more adultlike. Another child flirtatiously asked his mother to play "cereal girl" while he played "sugar boy."

These examples of exploratory play are consistent with research findings that sex play, such as looking at and touching others' genitals, or games, such as seeing who can urinate farthest, are prevalent prior to adolescence (Gagnon & Simon 1973).

The adultlike quality of some children's comments and behaviors can confuse care-givers into thinking the children's behavior is truly adult. One mother related how her four-year-old son climbed into his parents' bed after his father had left, removed his pants, and said, "I won't be needing these anymore." Yet there are often clues that a child is simply practicing a small part of a much larger adult role. For example, the child who removed his pants seemed to regard this as the culmination rather than the beginning of the act of "seducing" his mother. There was no indication that the child was concerned with any ensuing "sexual" contact.

Similarly, while children's behaviors can be very purposeful, their purposes often differ from those of adults. For example, parents provided considerable evidence of children's attempts to touch a father's penis or a mother's breast. Such acts often involve determined curiosity, attempts at humor, and limit testing—but not erotic fulfillment. Occasionally, such touching may simply be absentminded.

Parents and teachers also reported numerous instances of children experimenting with language related to the body, and particularly to the private parts, going to the bathroom, and sexuality. Terms such as *poo poo, pee pee, wee wee, fart, penis, vagina, butt, teat,* and creative combinations of these words, such as *butt-face* and *penis-breath* elicit squeals of delight and hilarity among children. This is eminently normal behavior, deriving in part from children's attraction to the forbidden. Because parts of the body are imbued with special meaning and are generally inaccessible for exploration, children are all the more fascinated with them.[3]

## Spontaneity and Openness

A second way in which the sexual behavior of children differs from that of adults is that children are

3. Children have a very limited understanding of the distinction between play and reality. They are sometimes fearful that their curiosity and play will spill over into reality and have dangerous consequences. If adults become alarmed, children are likely to assume that their behavior is indeed serious—without understanding why. Adults need to reassure children that their sexual behavior is playful. In so doing, caregivers can help children separate their curiosity and play from the knowing, consequential sexual behavior of mature adults.

much less self-conscious and insistent about privacy. Children enjoy being naked. One mother echoed the sentiments of many parents when recounting how her three-year-old daughter "enjoys running out of bathroom naked after a bath or after using the potty. I think she feels free."

Most young children are aware that running around naked is generally taboo, but they typically have little understanding of the rationale behind this prohibition. They know enough to delight in the violation of this rule but not enough to experience adultlike shame. (Fox 1980; Finkelhor 1981).

Parents and teachers also noted children's lack of modesty regarding more blatant sexual behaviors. A father told of his three-year-old son who self-pleasures in the bathtub, when having his diapers changed, and at other "times of opportunity." Parents reported that their three-year-olds are unabashed about self-pleasuring, sometimes calling attention to themselves with such comments as, "Look, Mommy, my penis is getting bigger" and "We are the vagina girls." These comments and behaviors do not always occur in the bathroom or bedroom. For instance, one parent reported that her four-year-old daughter sucks her forefinger and touches her vagina while watching television in the family room.

Teachers noted a clear progression in children's need for privacy regarding self-stimulation behaviors. Such behaviors are more apparent in three-year-olds, who are constantly being watched, than in five-year-olds (Friedrich et al. 1991). For older children, the behaviors seem more likely to occur while playing in groups in "secretive" spaces such as bathrooms and small, enclosed places. One child care setting designed its bathrooms to accommodate children's increasing self-awareness: the five-year-olds' bathroom, as compared to the three-year-olds', is farther from the classroom and more protected from view.

Children are inconsistent in their privacy needs. For example, a young girl using a restaurant bathroom insisted that her mother hold the door open, even though restaurant patrons could see the girl straddling the toilet. Later, when leaving the restaurant, the mother tried to lift her daughter's dress slightly to help her put on her boots, but the little girl protested "because everyone would see my knees."

## Sensuality and Excitement

Most of the behaviors discussed so far lack the passionate, erotic quality that adults tend to associate with sexuality. Even when these qualities seem to be present, closer examination typically indicates otherwise. For example, a six-year-old boy saw a beautiful nurse and commented, "She's a major babe," with all the inflection an adult male might use. In the overwhelming majority of examples of such behavior, the child is engaging in the accoutrements of sexuality and romance (for example, gift giving, declarations of love, sadness at absence) rather than passionate physical displays (such as prolonged kissing, erotic touching, or genital contact). Children go through the motions, but their actions only superficially resemble those of adults; they lack deeper erotic resonance.

Young children's eroticism, when it occurs, is typically a matter of self-stimulation. For example, a father of a four-year-old boy spoke of how, while watching television, his son would lie on top of his stuffed puppy dog and rub his penis against it. A small percentage of children are habitual masturbators, regularly and energetically manipulating their genitals to the point of great excitement and eventual relaxation—not unlike an orgasm (Kinsey, Pomeroy, & Martin 1948). But masturbation with arousal and orgasm is probably the exception (Gunderson, Melias, & Skar 1981). More often, masturbation has a soothing, sedating effect for young children and does not seem to be associated with orgasm. As compared to older children, young children have less awareness of a connection between erotic pleasure and their self-stimulation and thus engage in less purposive efforts to induce the pleasure. Young children have far less understanding of and experience with eroticism than adults. Child behavior that appears erotic to adults is more likely experienced as simple sensuality or excitement by children.

Contributing to simple sensuality and excitement, as opposed to passion and eroticism, are cognitive limitations. Eroticism is more than a physical sensation; it is an awareness and understanding of these sensations. As Dr. Ruth is fond of saying, sexuality is more a matter of what is between the ears than what is between the legs. One eight-year-old boy complained to his mom that his penis was painfully hard. To offer reassurance, the mother said, "When you get older, you will actually enjoy it." The boy responded in disbelief, "What am I going to do, play baseball with it?"

Similarly, most demonstrations of physical affection initiated by children—hugging, kissing, and other sensual touching or stroking—owe more to at-

## Suggestions for Caregivers When Responding to Children's Sexual Behavior

Understanding the ways in which children's sexuality differs from adults' should help in implementing these principles for responding to children's sexual behavior.

- Adopt an attitude that is respectful, matter-of-fact, and lighthearted.
- Be conservative in responding to the children's actions and liberal in responding to their words and requests for information.
- Take your cue from the children: If they don't seem worried or concerned, then in most cases you should not either.

tachment needs than to Eros. In adulthood, too, physical contact can mix attachment motives with sexual motives; but for young children, attachment needs are primary.

Last, from a biological and evolutionary perspective, it is unlikely that children have the same drive to engage in mating behavior as older, fertile adolescents and adults (Kendrick & Trost 1987). For boys and girls alike, progress in the mating sequence and feelings of eroticism and passion depend in part on testosterone levels, which are low prior to adolescence. Biology limits sexuality for preschoolers, who are not ready to assume the roles and responsibilities accompanying the consummation of relationships.

## A Model for Viewing Children's Sexuality

Caregivers too often see only the superficial similarities between the sexual behaviors of children and adults and mistakenly equate them. We believe this confusion is responsible for much of caregivers' anxiety about childhood sexuality.

Children's play involving sexual roles and relationships is universal (Ford & Beach 1951). In all societies children ages three to five are learning gender-related roles and relationships; they practice "going to work," being a parent, talking on the phone, and other important aspects of adult life. Children's work is to play the roles of adults as a means of learning more about the adoption of those roles. Through play children also develop the larger scripts they will need to experience adult sexuality (Gagnon & Simon 1973). Indeed, crosscultural studies indicate that practicing coital positions and motions is common in societies that allow it (Money & Lamacz 1989).

Childhood coital practice occurs even in our own society. One mother reported that her four-year-old son asked her to lie down on the couch and to close her eyes. When she asked him why, he responded, "You'll see." He then mounted her, mimicking the behavior of an adult male during intercourse. When later asked about his behavior, he said, "I just wanted to see what it was like to be on you." The parents had no knowledge of their son observing intercourse.

Is this normal behavior? What guidelines should we use to decide? At first glance the behavior seems precocious and worrisome. Based on the three dimensions described above, however, this incident, we believe, falls within the normal realm. First, there are compelling elements of curiosity and play in this child's behavior. He said he wanted to see what it was like to lie on his mother. His demeanor and actions are playful, as opposed to tense, compulsive, or

forceful. Second, the behavior is unselfconsciously spontaneous and open, probably because the child had little understanding of the psychological or physical implications of his actions. While there is an element of privacy involved in asking the mother to close her eyes, there is more of a gamelike quality to this request than a sense of self-awareness or secrecy. Even if the child sensed he was engaging in a forbidden activity, his method of obtaining privacy is more typical of younger than older children (for example, he made no demand for secrecy). Finally, there is no indication that his behavior is linked to genital arousal or eroticism, and there is no evidence of his having an awareness of intercourse.

When children say "I hate you," we are prone to read sophisticated adult meanings into their simple statement of anger. The misunderstanding arises because we view the child's behavior through an adult lens. Similarly, when children exhibit behavior the least bit sexual, we tend to assume they have mastered the larger sexual repertoire. In both cases we overlook developmental differences that distinguish children from adults, and we thereby address issues that, for the children, do not exist.

## Recommendations for Dealing with Children's Developing Sexuality

We provide here three general guidelines for addressing children's sexual behavior.

### Which Behaviors Are Problematic?

If a child's sexual behaviors are frequent, persist despite efforts to redirect them, and become a preoc-

cupation, then they are abnormal and problematic. This rule-of-thumb applies to behaviors ranging from sexual language to masturbation. In instances involving two or more children or the use of force, or if there is several years' age difference between the children or a notable difference in size, then sexual behaviors are abnormal and problematic. Penetration of any bodily orifice with a foreign object constitutes abnormal and problematic behavior. In addition to these "hard" signs, it is useful to know that adaptive sexuality is typically accompanied by pleasure and spontaneity, while maladaptive sexuality is typically accompanied by anger and tension.

### When to Set Limits?

Adults should set firm limits where clear-cut problematic behaviors, such as those just described, are involved. But there are many sexual behaviors that are not clear-cut: a child repeatedly caressing and kissing a teacher's face; a child saying to another, "Suck my dick"; a child passing a note that reads, "I want to sex you"; a seven-year-old boy getting on top of a four-year-old girl and making moves suggestive of intercourse (both children are fully clothed); a child getting under a mother's nightgown "because I love to play house in there"; a child taking a bath and asking his parent, "Would you pour water on my penis? It feels good."

In responding to these and other sexual behaviors, we believe it is best to err on the side of setting limits. Children's positive attitudes about and future enjoyment of sexuality are not likely to be endangered if restraints are placed on their behaviors. For example, it is helpful for a caregiver to say to a child, "I don't want you to touch my breast because that is my private space." As long as caregivers sensitively and thoughtfully redirect the child's activities and adopt a respectful, matter-of-fact, light-hearted attitude, there is little possibility of a downside to the imposition of limits. On the upside, the caregiver is steering the child away from activities that can be problematic in certain situations and behaviors that, over time, can become extreme.

## How to Talk to Children about Sexual Matters?

There is extensive literature on how to talk to children about adult love, intercourse, and reproduction. Many of the principles identified in that literature pertain to talking with children about their sexually relevant behavior. We have articulated five basic principles.

1. **Keep it simple.** An overload of information or emotion is harder to digest than a few well-chosen words. This brings to mind the classic joke about the child who asks, "Where did I come from?" After the parent stumbles through an awkward explanation of the birth process, the confused child says, "Oh, I thought I came from Pittsburgh." Another example involves a mother who works for Planned Parenthood who talks about condoms in her lectures about safe sex. One day her four-year-old daughter asked, "Mommy, what's a condom?" The mother wondered how far she should go in explaining intercourse and, indeed, where she should begin. Remembering to keep it simple, she showed her daughter a condom; the daughter said "Oh" and walked away. The child had

gotten the answer she wanted and was satisfied with that level of knowledge.

2. **Listen carefully to the child.** The less you say, the more energy you can devote to listening and observing the child—which is how you can be most helpful. Consider carefully the actions of children and their peers before reacting. For instance, a preschooler who says, "Suck my dick" has not necessarily been sexually abused; more likely the child has an adolescent sibling. Children's use of sexual words can make it seem as if they know more than they do. Language play is normal and common, and awareness of that type of play makes setting limits and reacting positively that much easier.

3. **Give the child basic facts before analyzing her feelings.** Children need to know what is going on before they can figure out how they feel. Adults often make the mistake of probing children's feelings, which young children have great difficulty understanding and articulating, while failing to impart rudimentary information or address the child's misconceptions. When the child asked her mother, "What's a condom?" the mother would have done her child a disservice if she had launched into a discussion about the social and psychological significance of birth control; the child was requesting only basic information about a physical object. As for caregivers concerned that facts will make children less innocent and more knowing, we point out the gulf that exists between children and adults in comprehension

and reasoning (Gordon, Schroeder, & Abrams 1990). Children's understanding is limited regardless of how much information they are given.

4. **Talk with other adults about your own feelings before talking with the child about his feelings.** The more you clarify your own feelings, desires, and anxieties, the better able you are to separate them from your child's. Coming to terms with your own feelings makes it easier to respond to the child and help him understand his own actions and thoughts.

5. **Approach topics when the opportunities naturally occur.** When a child comments about or otherwise responds to nudity, a door closed for privacy, a racy joke, an R-rated movie, a pregnant woman, or the like, parents and teachers should seize the moment and begin a dialogue with the child. Too often we ignore these natural opportunities and arbitrarily create occasions for dialogue. When children's interest is already engaged, they are most likely to share and explore their ideas.

## Conclusion

Most caregivers have two seemingly conflicting agendas: (a) to foster children's feelings of comfort about sexuality and discussing sexual matters and (b) to facilitate the development of limits regarding sexual expression and preserve children's innocence. The dilemma is that too much comfort may lead to relaxing appropriate limits and jeopardizing innocence, and too many limits may lead to anxiety about sexuality and avoidance of the topic—at least in the parent's presence. We believe that focusing on developmental differences between child and adult sexuality helps resolve this dilemma.

Young children are innocent in that they are curious, playful, open, spontaneous, sensual, and excited. Making children comfortable about childhood sexuality is fully compatible with setting limits regarding sexual behaviors. Innocence is preserved because innocence, as defined above, is the hallmark of child sexuality.

## References

Finkelhor, E.E. 1981. Sex between siblings: Sex play, incest, and aggression. In *Children and sex: New findings, new perspectives*, eds. L. Constantine & F. Martinson. Boston: Little, Brown.

Ford, C.S., & F.A. Beach. 1951. *Patterns of sexual behavior.* New York: Harper.

Fox, R. 1980. *The red lamp of incest.* New York: Dutton.

Friedrich, W., P. Grambsch, D. Broughton, J. Kuiper, & R. Beilke. 1991. Normative sexual behavior in children. *Pediatrics* 88 (3): 456–64.

Gagnon, J., & W. Simon. 1973. *Sexual conduct: The social sources of human sexuality.* Chicago: Aldine.

Gordon, B., C. Schroeder, & J. Abrams. 1990. Age and social class differences in children's knowledge of sexuality. *Journal of Clinical Child Psychology* 19: 33–43.

Gunderson, B., P. Melias, & J. Skar. 1981. Sexual behavior of preschool children: Teacher's observations. In *Children and sex: New findings, new perspectives*, eds. L. Constantine & F. Martinson, 45–61. Boston: Little, Brown.

Kendrick, D., & M. Trost. 1987. A biosocial theory of heterosexual relationships. In *Females, males and sexuality*, ed. K. Kelley, 59–100. Albany: State University of New York Press.

Kinsey, A., W. Pomeroy, & C. Martin. 1948. *Sexual behavior in the human male*, 36–192. Philadelphia & London: Saunders.

Money, J., & M. Lamacz. 1989. *Vandalized lovemaps.* Buffalo, NY: Prometheus.

 **Article Review Form at end of book.**

What are the specific steps teachers and schools could take to provide safe and inviting learning environments for all students? How can curriculum changes improve the educational experiences of homosexual students?

# Gay Students in Middle School

**Norma J. Bailey
and Tracy Phariss**

*From* Middle School Journal

In 1993, the National Middle School Association resolved to encourage middle schools to gather information on school policies and programs on the needs and problems of gay, lesbian, and bisexual youth so these schools can "organize and conduct staff development initiatives designed to elevate staff awareness and sensitivity in order to ensure safe and equitable school environments for youth of every sexual orientation." Why is it necessary for NMSA to include this among the resolutions which focus its efforts during the coming years?

Maturation of all young people, including gays and lesbians, has been occurring earlier in successive generations. Although the problem of sexual-minority youth engaging in high-risk behaviors and the failures of schools to address these problems are more acute later in adolescence, they are becoming more prevalent and relevant at the middle level. Studies have shown that the mean age of coming out of sexual-minority youth is declining, at least in urban areas.

Studies also show that homosexuality, or the struggle with sexual identity, is a middle-level issue. Most gay and lesbian youth report having experienced the feeling of being "different" long before the onset of puberty, some as early as first grade. A comprehensive 1979 national study of over 4,400 gay men and lesbians found the majority of gay and lesbian adults reported knowing about their homosexuality before age 18, about 30 percent knowing before age 13.

Many studies have shown that gay and lesbian youth are self-identified (recognize their same-sex attraction and have same-sex fantasies) before they have had a same-sex experience, just as heterosexual youth could identify themselves before opposite-sex activity. A 1989 study found first homosexual attraction at average age 9.6 for males and 10.1 for females, with first homosexual fantasy at average age 11.2 for males and 11.9 for females.

A large-scale 1992 study of nearly 35,000 junior and senior high students from diverse ethnic, geographic, and socioeconomic strata in Minnesota reported that at age 12, 25.9 percent of students were "unsure" about their sexual orientation; at 13, 17.4 percent; at 14, 12.2 percent; and at 15, 7.0 percent (declining to 5 percent at age 18). Educators clearly avoid this issue to the detriment of their young adolescent students.

There seem to be several barriers to making changes which would allow for development of services to meet the needs of gay and lesbian youth. These include a lack of courage from adults, both gay and non-gay; a lack of information available about the needs of these young people; and the failure of school systems to confront controversial matters, especially in the area of youth sexuality.

Educator James T. Sears approached the task of making changes occur by listing several steps that he believed socially responsible educators must take to have a positive impact upon the quality of life in school for all students, especially for gay and lesbian youth:

- First, educators must examine their own attitudes toward homosexuality. When people become comfortable with their feelings, they more

Reprinted from THE EDUCATION DIGEST, October 1996, Ann Arbor, Michigan.

easily educate themselves about this subject.

- Second is educating others about homosexuality, with particular emphasis on replacing myths with accurate information. This means communicating with the school board, parents, and community groups, as well as with students.

- Third, concerned educators must be responsive to the needs of gay and lesbian youth. This means providing young people with a nonjudgmental atmosphere in which they can process their feelings and come to terms with their sexuality and know that they are "okay," as well as providing a curriculum and educational resources which should include information about sexual orientation and people who are gay and lesbian.

- Fourth, Sears believes that professional educators, regardless of their moral or political convictions, are duty-bound to protect and promote the human and civil rights of all people within the classroom. This implies enforcing responsible standards of professional and student conduct in terms of verbal and physical harassment of gay and lesbian students, as well as combating the ignorance and fear engendered by the AIDS health crisis.

- Fifth, educators should encourage hiring and provide support for gay and lesbian educators who will be healthy role models for such students.

- Finally, Sears contends that educators, as articulate citizens of the community, must speak out in favor of legislation that bars discrimination against homosexuals. He believes, "The struggle for social change must begin with a critical examination of arbitrary, narrow, and socially constructed categories in our lives as well as an assessment of how those categories affect the lives of those around us. Only when human beings accept themselves and respect the dignity of others can a genuine commitment to social justice be possible."

Kevin Jennings is Executive Director of the Gay, Lesbian, and Straight Teachers Network, a national organization that brings together gay and straight teachers to combat homophobia in their schools as well as to support gay teachers (contact GLSTN, 2124 Broadway, Box 160, New York, NY 10023; phone 212-387-2098). Jennings describes several specific steps that he believes teachers and schools can take to provide safe and inviting learning environments in schools. They are:

1. **Guarantee equality.** Schools should add "sexual orientation" to their nondiscrimination statements in all school publications as a way to communicate their commitment to equal treatment for all.

2. **Create a safe environment.** Schools must make it clear that neither physical violence nor harassing language like "faggot" and "dyke" will be tolerated, just as they are not for any other group. Clear harassment policies, which include sexual orientation, must be developed and then publicized to the entire school community, so that the consequences of and procedures for dealing with such behavior are clear to all.

3. **Provide role models.** Studies consistently show that personal acquaintance with gay and lesbian people is the most effective means for developing positive attitudes toward acceptance. Both gay and straight students benefit from having role models such as openly gay and lesbian teachers, coaches, and administrators. Straight students are offered an alternative to the stereotypes with which they have often been raised. Gay and lesbian students get the chance, often for the first time, to see healthy gay and lesbian adults, which gives them hope for their own future.

Schools need to create the conditions necessary for gay and lesbian faculty to feel safe in "coming out." If no role models are available from within the school community, the school can bring in presenters from a local gay and lesbian speakers bureau or from a college gay and lesbian student association.

4. **Provide support for students.** Peer support and acceptance is the key to any student's feeling of "belonging" in the school. "Gay Straight Alliances," groups which welcome membership from any student interested in understanding issues of sexual identity, regardless of sexual orientation, have been the key to creating such an atmosphere in many schools. Counselors must also be specifically trained in the needs of gay and lesbian youth in order to provide the support that students struggling with their sexual identity so desperately need.

5. **Provide training for faculty and staff.** School staff need to be equipped to serve all the

students with whom they work, including gay and lesbian ones. Understanding the needs of gay and lesbian youth, and developing the skills to meet those needs, should be expected of all staff members. Schools must provide the ongoing training necessary for the staff to fulfill this expectation.

6. **Reassess the curriculum.** Teachers need to incorporate gay and lesbian issues throughout the curriculum—not just in classes such as health education, where students would learn about the continuum of sexual orientation, but in the other classes taught in the school.

For example, when discussing hate crimes or civil rights issues in a social studies class, include examples related to gays and lesbians. If you would address the fact that Langston Hughes is a black author because of the impact of his race on his work, then also address the fact that Walt

Whitman was a gay author because of the impact of his sexual identity on his work.

This identification also provides positive role models from history for our gay and lesbian youth. Teachers can also work to undo the "hidden heterosexism" of the curriculum, such as the exclusive use of opposite-sex couples in math word problems and foreign-language exercises.

7. **Provide appropriate health care and education.** While being gay is not a "health issue" (any more than being heterosexual is), health education on sexuality and sexually transmitted diseases should sensitively address the particular issues of gay and lesbian people.

8. **Diversify library and media holdings.** Often, the school or classroom library is the first place students turn to for accurate sexuality information. Yet, too often, few or no works on gay and lesbian issues are

found there. It is important that library holdings are up to date, present accurate information about homosexuality and a positive view of gay and lesbian life, and are catalogued so students can easily access the materials.

The National Middle School Association is not promoting homosexuality. It is simply stating that if the middle school's mission is to meet the needs of all young adolescents, then the needs of sexual-minority youth must also be met. There is a great deal we all have to learn in order to meet these needs. NMSA is simply acknowledging these needs and encouraging us to get started. May we, teacher by teacher and middle school by middle school, have the courage to continue this process "in order to ensure safe and equitable school environments for youth of every sexual orientation."

 **Article Review Form at end of book.**

Compare the ideal version of the adoption process with what actually happens. What child characteristics, aside from age, often complicate adoptions of older children?

# Will These Kids Ever Be Wanted?

## The new adoption crisis

**Amy Engeler**

From the doorway it looked like a typical summer party—balloons, sodas cooling on ice, stacks of pizza boxes on the kitchen counter, kids playing games. But an odd electricity in the air hinted that something unusual was about to begin in the Overbrook Presbyterian Church just outside Philadelphia that steamy June morning. Demetria, a girl of about eight, meandered among the folding chairs waiting for the right moment to flash her winning grin. A shy kindergartner named Omar nervously picked at his thumb, never looking up. Only Eva, a poised 4-year-old with cornrow pigtails rocking away on a toy horse, seemed oblivious to the tension.

They were among 37 children, all in foster care, brought to this rented church hall to attend the adoption world's version of a singles' party. Instead of boy meets girl, at this "match party" the children hoped to find parents who might eventually take them home.

As they wandered around the airy hall, the children's ex-pressions were neutral, carefully hiding their hopes and anxieties. To their social workers, these youngsters were tough cases. While foster parents often adopt their charges, these particular children were not wanted permanently in their foster homes. Some had emotional problems, others had as many as three siblings they needed to remain with, a few stood on the brink of adolescence, others suffered from childhood problems like hyperactivity or Attention Deficit Disorder.

If the little ones didn't quite grasp the significance of the party, the older children were fully aware that their future hung in the balance and that, scrubbed, braided, and neatly dressed, they'd be scrutinized by some 60 prospective parents who now perched on chairs arranged beneath the basketball hoop, searching their faces for a spark of connection.

## Everybody Wants an Infant

According to estimates, there are some 100,000 children living in foster homes across the country who are hoping to be adopted—40 percent are African American; 40 percent are Caucasian; 12 percent, Latino; the rest, a mix. No one knows how many of these kids will end up stuck in the foster-care system until they reach independence at 18, but unfortunately, the odds of them finding permanent homes diminish with each passing birthday. Most adoptive couples want infants and are willing to spend an enormous amount of time and money finding one. The waiting list for a white infant in the U.S. can be years, with some private adoption agencies charging fees as high as $40,000 to find a newborn. Many couples give up on waiting for a white American baby, and look instead in countries like Russia; still the costs and time spent can be staggering.

Some couples, however, don't have the time, money, or emotional stamina to search for an infant and instead decide to look for a slightly older child they can adopt from the foster-care system. Usually, these prospective parents come through the so-called front door of the system, using a public adoption agency within their local Department of Social Services

"Will These Kids Ever Be Wanted? The New Adoption Crisis" by Amy Engeler, *Redbook*, July 1997, pp. 76–104. Reprinted with permission of the author.

(DSS) and paying under $1,000. Or they select a private agency, often a nonprofit with religious affiliations (Catholic Charities, for instance) for maybe a few thousand dollars more. Once they've chosen an agency, a social worker guides them through the state requirements for an adoption license and then helps them search for a child. He or she also acts as their representative with the children's caseworkers, who are often employees of the local DSS, or of a private agency under contract to it.

The success of the parents' search depends in large part on how well these public and private agencies network—through mailings about available children and through events such as this match party, hosted by the National Adoption Center, a 25-year-old private nonprofit organization in Philadelphia that promotes the adoption of older children and those with special needs. Parties like this one, held annually by NAC, give parents a rare, up-close look at the children and remain popular despite controversy: Many social workers worry about the youngsters' comfort as they are scrutinized like pet-store puppies, but concede that this is one instance in which the end may justify the means.

That argument seems to be finding support from the White House. Last year, after Hillary Clinton admitted to a news-magazine that she and her husband have considered adopting, President Clinton took up the cause of youngsters who languish in the foster-care system. Pointing to America's poor rate of adoption—only 27 percent of foster children awaiting adoption are placed in permanent homes each year—he challenged the government to help at least double the rate under a program now called Adoption 2002, and budgeted $10 million in state grants for new model programs—like this match party—that speed adoptions.

## Please, No More Rejection

Although all but two of the children at the party were black, most of the prospective parents milling around the church hall were white, and nervous. Many were childless couples in their late thirties or forties with infertility problems. Some, with children in tow, sought adoption as a solution to secondary infertility. Others were seeking a child of a specific sex.

Unbeknownst to the children, some parents were searching for a "Janine" or a "Tyrone" they'd been specifically invited to meet. Several were on the lookout for a pair of boys, an impish 10-year-old named Jack* and his brother Rob,* 13, who'd come to the attention of the county child welfare office four years earlier when they arrived at school without jackets on a winter day. A subsequent home visit found their father long gone and their mother high on drugs. The boys were packed off to a foster home a few towns away.

For two years their mother visited frequently and promised to take them home. Then her appearances dwindled as she failed to stay in a drug treatment program. In February 1996, her parental rights were terminated by an orphans' court judge, freeing the boys for adoption, a prospect that filled them with happiness and panic. As much as they wanted their term in foster care to be over, they still loved their mother and felt bad about leaving her.

Jack and Rob's caseworker from the county Office of Children and Youth originally registered the boys with the Pennsylvania Adoption Exchange, a state-run registry of available children. Several couples inquired about them immediately. One seemed ideal to the boys' caseworker, but they backed out rather abruptly after meeting Jack and Rob, saying they'd decided not to adopt after all.

That last rejection, a few weeks before the match party, didn't help the brothers' spirits as they shuffled into the church hall. Following a volunteer to a table, they each picked up a name tag with a red border (meaning they were free for adoption) and green dot (indicating they were siblings and must be adopted together). Then they stepped into the room and froze as if a spotlight had been trained on them, as one adult after another turned toward them, the only white children at the party. Jack looked terrified, on the verge of tears. Rob, blank-faced, calmly nudged him forward into the crowd.

From the sidelines, a graying, middle-class couple watched the boys edge across the floor to the football toss. Ellen and Howard Adams* hadn't wanted to adopt children as old as Jack and Rob, yet their distress seemed poignant. The party's shopping-for-a-child nature made them uneasy too. In her starchy pink shorts and camp shirt, Ellen, 43, a dietitian, held her back straight as a yoga teacher's. Howard, a 45-year-old salesman, was sweating in khakis and loafers.

In Ellen's case, it was chemotherapy for breast cancer that left her unable to conceive. The Adamses considered adopting a Chinese baby but were startled by the cost, and they were uncomfortable raising a child of

*Names changed to protect privacy.

another race. Taking an older child out of foster care was the only way for them to adopt a white child, so they signed up with an agency and began the process for obtaining a license to be adoptive parents: two months of parenting classes, followed by a police check and a visit from their social worker, who then composed a four-page "home study" that would serve as the couple's "resume" when they applied for a child.

At first, the Adamses conducted their search by flipping through binders of photographs. They picked out ten children they would have liked to adopt, but within weeks they were rejected for all of them, with no reason given other than the boilerplate phrase "The child has been placed with another family." Though their agency told them it's rare to get the first child a couple applies for (and explanations for why a couple isn't chosen are almost never offered) the Adamses worried anyway. Was it Ellen's health? Their ages? They figured the match party offered an opportunity to meet the children's social workers and hoped that talking to them one-on-one would help.

After the first ice-breaking games, the prospective parents were led to a nearby chapel to be briefed by NAC staff: There was to be no dominating a particular child. No talk about adoption. No asking kids if they wanted to come home. "If you see a child you are interested in, talk to the child's social worker," said Chris Jacobs, supervisor of exchange services for NAC. "Then when they receive your home study they can put a face to the name."

She held up a green form which parents could turn in after the party with the names of children who appealed to them. If the

match worked, the parents were assured the paperwork would move rapidly ("We hope to get some of the children placed before school starts," Jacobs said), but most of the prospective parents fanning themselves in the pews knew better.

## What's Money Got to Do with It?

In principle, the adoption process is simple: Prospective parents are interviewed and briefed about the child's history and then, hopefully, approved by a child's caseworker. If a brief visit with the child goes well, a weekend visit follows, and then another. If the child remains eager to make the match, the parents negotiate a monthly subsidy from the state with the child's caseworker (about $342 for a 2-year-old to $363 for a 9-year-old to $1,000 for a teen with Down's syndrome, until the child is 18). These subsidies, meant to encourage adoptions of special needs kids, cost the government substantially less than foster care. Some parents feel uncomfortable taking them, afraid someone might accuse them of adopting for the money, but they are encouraged to at least put it away for college. The child then moves in with the family 6 to 18 months later, the adoption is finalized by the court.

In practice, however, the process couldn't be more confusing. As President Clinton said last December, children typically wait three years to be placed for adoption, sometimes longer. Delays are due in part to poor record-keeping (the Administration of Children's Services in New York, for example, didn't even become computerized until 1996) and to overworked social workers with unrealistic hopes for a perfect

match. A caseworker who cares deeply for a child may turn down 15 interested parents in the hopes that a wealthier, more loving family will come along (or one of the same race, even though the law forbids such discrimination). Yet with each passing birthday, the number of parents willing to take a child declines. While a 4-year-old may attract 20 inquiries; a 10-year-old may receive only one.

Addie and John Brynildsen of rural western Pennsylvania—she's a student teacher; he's a computer programmer—tried to adopt at least a dozen children over the past year. In several instances, their caseworker's calls were never returned by the children's caseworkers; twice their home studies were requested for children who weren't available; one computer registry they tried was outdated by at least four months. "We're learning that the right hand doesn't know what the left hand is doing," says John. "Our experience shows me that we almost gear our system to keeping children in foster care instead of trying to get them a home."

One of the system's major flaws is that agencies are financially rewarded for keeping children in foster care. Each day a child remains in foster care the agency overseeing his or her case collects a stipend—typically between $7 and $21, sometimes much more—which ends when a child goes to live with adoptive parents. What the Clinton Administration will propose under Adoption 2002 is a new system of incentives in which agencies would receive bonuses when they place a foster-care child for adoption. For now, though, it's no surprise that the stipend system sometimes stalls adoptions and creates bad blood between prospective families and the social workers.

## The Party Starts to Swing

As the smell of grilling hot dogs filled the air, Demetria stood at the face-paint table, applying yellow to her lips, while Omar clung to his foster father's shirt, barely peeking out. From the sidelines, Stephanie Hunt watched the kids and every so often jotted down a name, though her attention stayed on a pair of jolly 4-year-old twins and their brothers, ages 5 and 6. Giggling, they chased each other with balloons as not one but two social workers trailed them.

Because of a history of drug and alcohol abuse, Stephanie Hunt might not appear to be the ideal adoptive mother. But her recovery, since 1989, was considered complete by Pennsylvania social services when they gave her approval for adoption. Besides, her own two children were doing great. Her son was away at college and her daughter was a mature ninth grader. Although her life might have seemed full enough to others—Hunt worked and attended college—she yearned to make up for the poor start she gave her children by helping others. In eight months, though, she'd been rejected without explanation for a half-dozen kids. At the party she introduced herself to one social worker after another, trying to dispel doubts they may have held about her.

Meanwhile, the Adamses decided they liked what they saw in Jack and Rob. Though Rob was a bit old for them, the boys seemed free of the behavioral problems so common with children who've lived in foster care. As they dunked basketballs, the Adamses chuckled at their courtside antics:

"Ms. Moss,* Ms. Moss, WATCH ME!" Jack shouted, trying to get a social worker's attention.

"Oh, come on, just shoot, Jack," said Rob.

Jack took a final look at the caseworker, shrugged and shot the ball. He missed, then broke into a broad grin.

Shortly before 2 P.M., the last partygoers filed out, mostly in smiles, and Chris Jacobs collected the green forms. No question, Jack and Rob were the stars of the show. Nine sets of prospective parents asked to be considered for them. "I found that absolutely remarkable," Jacobs said. "Many of those people told us they wanted younger children, but when they saw those boys they changed their minds." Only little Eva generated as much interest. A few children, including a deaf and blind 14-year-old boy, received no inquiries at all.

## A Hitch in the Plan

Now is was time for the social workers and parents to pursue their matches in earnest. The Adamses' home study went out for Jack and Rob, and Stephanie Hunt called her caseworker with the list of children she was interested in. As the summer progressed, nearly 50 home studies were exchanged as a result of the party, yet the first match made—for little Omar—was one that had nothing to do with it: Addie and John Brynildsen were supposed to have met the boy there (their home study had already passed muster), but their car broke down on the way, and the introduction had to come a few weeks later.

Later in June, though the Adamses were still awaiting word on Jack and Rob, they spotted a 9-year-old girl in the Pennsylvania Adoption Exchange book and contacted the girl's case-

worker. Her background, though, was disturbing: As a preschooler, the girl had been sexually abused by both her parents and then, at age 8, had testified against them in court, helping to convict them. As worrisome as this was, after intense soul-searching, the Adamses decided to pursue the adoption.

The papers were about to be filed when the caseworker's boss stepped in to require the Adamses become foster parents to the girl before the adoption. That meant they'd have to earn certification and then take the girl for at least six months as a foster child. The Adamses speculate that the intervention was a veiled attempt by the adoption coordinator to collect more foster-care subsidies on the child. They were furious. Here a little girl was being held in foster care while a family was ready to adopt her.

"That kind of thing happens all the time," says Chester Jackson, a New York social worker. "Basically you do what they say if you want the child—or you hire a lawyer to fight it.'"

The Adamses considered hiring a lawyer, but chose instead to speak directly to the director of the Department of Public Welfare and Children and Youth in Harrisburg. A field representative was dispatched to investigate their claims; a few days later the adoption proceeded. In November, shortly before Thanksgiving, the girl's belongings were stuffed into the Adamses' trunk, and she arrived at their house to a "Welcome Home" banner the neighbors had hung inside the front door.

In the end, out of the 37 children at the party, only one—little Eva—was adopted by a couple she met there; four others were eventually placed with other families. As for the rest, according to

## Why the System Fails: 6 Reasons

1. **Nightmare Bureaucracy.** Getting parental rights terminated, the first step toward adoption, can take years even in a case of abandonment at birth. If there's any chance at all of keeping a family intact, everyone wants to pursue it—family preservation or reunification is a fundamental principle of foster care. In New York, for instance, no legal papers can even be filed until the birth parents are located and given at least six months to reclaim the child. Then a judge must hold a minimum of three court hearings before terminating parental rights. By then, the baby could be two.

   The social workers who oversee these children, usually county or state employees, are responsible for 20 to 80 children each, with the possibility of 100 court appearances a year. This incredible responsibility leads to high burnout rates and turnover; it's not unusual for a child to have three different social workers in one year.

2. **Racial Discrimination.** Although the 1994 Multiethnic Placement Act prohibits racial discrimination in adoptions, experts say many agencies remain unwilling to arrange transracial adoptions. "Race is still a big factor," says Richard Barth, Ph.D., professor of social welfare at the School of Social Welfare at UC Berkeley. "In California, for instance, transracial adoptions are still considered placements of last resort."

   Conversely, many minorities complain that they are not given the same consideration as prospective adoptive parents as are white couples. A 1991 study by the North American Council on Adoptive Children found several barriers preventing minority families from adopting minority children, including unaffordable fees and a prejudice for young, two-parent families with middle class backgrounds.

3. **Social Workers' Expectations.** Some workers view older children with emotional or medical problems as "unadoptable." After a cursory search for parents, they may give up and place the child in long-term foster care. Other workers, taking a special interest in a child, may reject numerous prospective parents as they wait for a "perfect" middle-class family.

4. **Lack of Analytical Studies.** In 1998, Congress mandated the tracking of adoption rates, but the U.S. Department of Health and Human Services just started collecting data last year. "We don't know how many adoptions there are or how they turn out," says Dr. Barth. "We don't know how many prospective parents are out there and what their preferences are. That's one reason adoptions are ruled by tradition and by what people think make good parents. We don't have evidence to support other views."

5. **No National Registry of Available Children.** Social workers and prospective parents in North Carolina don't know, for example, about available children in Maine. Some states have registries, but parents complain that the listings aren't always accurate or up-to-date.

6. **Unrealistic Expectations of Parents.** Infants or toddlers without medical or emotional problems don't exist in the public system. Some parents aren't well counseled about the problems of "special needs" children, nor are they always honest about their parenting capabilities. In the most heartbreaking cases, they may cancel an adoption after having taken a child.

---

Chris Jacobs, their caseworkers ran through the party inquiries and found most of them, including Stephanie Hunt's, wanting in some way—for example, the child had problems the parents weren't prepared for, or absolutely needed a two-parent family. When Hunt's caseworker called about the four little brothers, she was told their social workers insisted on placing them in a house with a father. Not that there were any suitable fathers asking for the boys. As Christmas loomed, the brothers remained in foster care, and Stephanie Hunt continued to search for a child to adopt.

## The Boys' Real Story Comes Out

Eight couples from the match party applied for Jack and Rob, but none impressed the boys' caseworker as much as a couple who hadn't attended the event but had seen the boys' listing in the Pennsylvania Adoption Exchange around the same time. The fact that Richard and Anne*, a contractor and a secretary in their thirties, had survived difficulties—she lost her mother as a child, he had a disability—impressed the boys' caseworker as a qualification to parent kids who'd been through such losses. "I have a good feeling about them," she explained. "They didn't have high expectations of the children. And there was enough of their backgrounds to make me think they could understand where the boys were coming from." And, she added, the couple was open to letting the boys maintain contact with their birth mother since their love for her was still strong.

In mid-July, not four weeks after the party, Jack and Rob left for a weekend visit with Richard and Anne at their home in rural Pennsylvania. The visit went better than anyone expected; on Saturday the boys even asked if they could call Anne "Mom." She said yes, but their eagerness gave her some pause. "I found it quite odd," she said later. "They acted like they knew us all their life."

Jack cried when it came time to leave. And nothing anyone said made him feel better. He rode back to his foster home in misery and spent the next two weeks driving his brother crazy with his nervousness that Anne and Richard might change their minds.

They didn't, and the boys passed a storybook summer, fishing with their new parents, settling into the rambling house, and exploring the surrounding fields and woods. After an eight-year wait for children, Richard and Anne were thrilled with the boys—and realistic. They knew their fine behavior would soon end as the boys entered a (normal) mourning phase for their foster parents and birth mother. They weren't surprised in late September to see Rob return home from school with a bloody nose from a fight. In textbook style, Rob had begun to show his nerves.

From that morning on, a pattern emerged. Every two weeks, Rob was either in the principal's office for fighting or dragging himself home from a scuffle. Richard and Anne doled out punishments—and praise for good behavior. What bothered them was that while the phone rang frequently for Jack, Rob couldn't keep any friends. He spent hours by himself in his room.

In January, just one month before the adoption was to be finalized, Rob announced he did not want to go through with it. "He said he was going to screw it up, that he would rather go from foster home to foster home," Anne recalls. "And he said he was taking Jack with him." She was startled by the timing, but not the message. Unlike Jack, Rob wasn't trying very hard to adjust.

He stopped calling the couple Mom and Dad, using their first names instead or, under his breath, "bitch." He fought constantly with Jack, who took to wearing high-collared shirts to hide bruises on his neck. Richard and Anne did their best to separate the boys, ground Rob, and sit down as a family to talk things out.

But the cause of this growing nightmare was obvious: The calls from the boys' birth mother, which the caseworker had insisted upon before the placement, had increased from one a week to three or four. Rob simply could not accept Richard and Anne as long as his mother was still in the picture. "I found out she was telling Rob that she was off drugs and that she'd be up to pick them up before long and all this crap," says Anne. "He has this fantasy that he is the only one who can take care of his mother. If those calls had stopped earlier then maybe this wouldn't have happened."

Desperate, Anne phoned the boys' caseworker, but the job had turned over twice since the end of August and was now held by a man whom Anne and Richard had never met. They pleaded with him and with their own adoption agency to have Rob placed in a residential treatment center, where he could receive therapy to break the ties with his mother. Anne says she was turned down. The family stumbled through the rest of January and into February, as Rob came home from stores with more merchandise than he had money to purchase, poured dish soap into Richard's coffee, and asked, through other actions, for help in the only way a lonely and troubled teenager can.

As Anne and Richard searched for a solution, they turned to the boys' previous foster parents for advice and learned that Rob's problems were far worse than they'd ever been told. "The social worker had told us he got in fights and stuff at school," Anne says. "She didn't say he was beating on the foster parents." She grew more worried about Jack's safety when she heard that Rob had ground his face into the dirt; one afternoon Rob brought home instructions on how to make a bomb that he'd pulled off the Internet. Then Jack complained that "someone wearing underpants" stood silently in his doorway in the middle of the night. It was creepy and frightened him. Anne went upstairs the following night and found Rob awake, in the hallway outside Jack's room.

"Finally I said to [Rob's caseworker], 'You come and get him or I will deliver him to you,'" says Anne. Instead of putting him in residential treatment where he could get help, Rob was sent to another foster home.

What will happen to Jack? Unlike Rob, Jack hardly remembers living with his birth mother, and since last August, has refused to take her calls. Jack says he loves his new Mom and Dad, as he calls them, and wants the adoption finalized. Though this is the first time the boys have ever been separated, Jack says he does not miss his brother; slowly he's beginning to tell his adoptive parents how Rob brutalized him over the years. Anne and Richard want nothing more than to adopt Jack immediately, but everything is suddenly out of their control.

It's up to Jack's new caseworker to suggest to the court whether he stays with Anne and Richard or is sent to join Rob in the foster home with the hope they might still be adopted together. Despite what Jack, Anne, and Richard have said, and the differences in the brothers' needs, keeping them together continues to be a concern.

"This system sucks—they don't look at the best interests of

the kids," says Anne in disgust. "Are they going to let Rob drag his brother down? Everyone has lied to these kids all their life, even the caseworkers. I'm just going to the hearing and telling them, 'Just decide. I can't take it anymore.' If Jack doesn't stay with us, I give up. No more adoptions."

By now, a year later, the match party is a distant memory for Jack, a minor bump on his way to a permanent home and an event entirely unknown to his current social worker. If Jack stays with Anne and Richard, it may be merely because his caseworker fears no one else will take him—an 11-year-old who's been in the public welfare system since first grade. "You know it's hard to find parents for older children," he says.

But if finding parents for these children were truly the only problem, would match parties such as the one Jack and Rob starred at just a year ago be so well attended? No. The fact is, the public adoption system is so hobbled by bureaucracy and inattention that nothing short of a complete overhaul, with truly innovative programs and financial incentives, will ever see these kids home.

 **Article Review Form at end of book.**

# WiseGuide Wrap-Up

- Boys and girls do not receive equivalent rearing. Despite changes in social attitudes regarding the equality of men and women, many parenting practices continue to encourage daughters to be passive and sons to be aggressive.

- Children are sexual beings, but in a manner quite different from that of adults. Children's sexuality is playful, open, and based on sensuality. Therefore, it is quite normal for children to explore their bodies, use sexual language, and look at others' bodies.

- It is important to deal sensitively with children's displays of sexual behavior in a manner that does not cause shame. However, it is equally important for caregivers to recognize signs of abnormal sexual behavior, such as preoccupations with sexual matters, penetration of bodily orifices, or assaults on others.

- Children who begin to recognize that they are different from their peers in terms of sexuality need supportive environments. These children are in need of information, acceptance, role models, and safety.

- Unfortunately, the U.S. foster care and adoption services are a bureaucratic nightmare. Though designed to assist in the finding of appropriate adoptive families, an assortment of factors often keeps children within the system for a minimum of three years. Older adoptees face many adoption difficulties, including the agencies' desire to keep siblings together, learning and emotional problems, a history of failed placements, and the general lack of adoptive families interested in older children.

## R.E.A.L. Sites

This list provides a print preview of typical **coursewise** R.E.A.L. sites. There are over 100 such sites at the **courselinks**™ site. The danger in printing URLs is that web sites can change overnight. As we went to press, these sites were functional using the URLs provided. If you come across one that isn't, please let us know via email to: webmaster@coursewise.com. Use your Passport to access the most current list of R.E.A.L. sites at the **courselinks**™ site.

**Site name:** Girls Re-cast TV Action Kit

**URL:** http://www.girlsinc.org/programs/recast.html

**Why is it R.E.A.L.?** This web site is an activity page that includes a television action kit. This page is designed to help girls think about how they relate to television and the characters portrayed in the media. Visit the site and complete the activities assigned. Record your findings and discuss them with your teacher.

**Site name:** Socioemotional Development

**URL:** http://www.valdosta.peachnet.edu/~whuitt/psy702/affys/erikson.html

**Why is it R.E.A.L.?** This web site outlines Erik Erikson's concepts, followed by examples for use by school teachers in encouraging healthy socioemotional development in early, middle, and late childhood, as well as in adolescence. Review the suggestions for each stage and visit with a classroom teacher of that grade about the information. How practical are the suggestions? Do you think they would make a major impact if the parents were not involved? Why or why not? Think about the process of identity development of children in other cultures such as the Asian or African American culture. How do you suppose this process differs? Why? What implications would your findings have for teaching these children in American schools?

# Index

**Note:** Page numbers in *italic* indicate illustrations; page numbers followed by *t* indicate tables. Authors of articles are shown in **bold face**.

## A

AAP (American Academy of Pediatrics), 33, 174, 187, 189
Abbott-Shim, M., 162, 164, 165, 169
Abelman, R., 43, 45
ABO (Coombs') test, 27
Abortion
    birth defects and, 2
    fetal rights and, 11, 12
Abrams, J., 208, 209
Absenteeism, child care and, 161
Abstract thought, make-believe play as preparation, 109
Abused Children Have More Conflicts with Friends (R.E.A.L. site), 130
Achievement, role of private speech in, 69, 70
Acting out stories, 41–42
Addams, Jane, 155–156
ADHD (attention-deficit hyperactivity disorder), 70–71, 82–83
**Adler, Jerry, 3–5, 4t**
Adolescence, peer influence in, 119–122
Adoption, 198–199, 213–219
    barriers to, 216–217, 217t
    behavioral problems and, 217–219
    demographics of, 213–214
    foster care and, 213
    rejection and, 214–215
    research on, 217
    role of money in, 215–216
Adoption 2002, 214, 215
Adult-child relationships, 44
Adult children, sibling bonds, 146–147
AFDC (Aid to Families With Dependent Children), 160
Age of fertility (R.E.A.L. site), 15
Aggression
    decreasing, 39–40
    providing alternatives to, 43–44
    tolerance in boys, 202
Agricultural societies, child care in, 154–155
AIDS
    children of homosexuals and, 178
    gay students and, 211
Aid to Families With Dependent Children (AFDC), 160
**Allen, Eugenie, 94–97**
Almy, M., 42, 46
*Altering Fate* (Lewis), 49
Alternative-solution thinking, 42
Altruism, emphasizing, 40, 43
*The Amazing Newborn* (Klaus), 29
American Academy of Pediatrics (AAP), 33, 174, 187, 189

American Psychological Association, 176
American Savings and Loan Association child care program, 171
American SIDS Institute, 33
American Sign Language, 101
Americans With Disabilities Act, 157
America's Homeless Children: Will Their Future Be Different? (R.E.A.L. site), 184
Anderegg, David, 124, 125
Anderson, R. H., 60, 66
Andersson, B. E., 164, 167
Andes, Norma, 139
Andrews, K., 123
Antidepressants, use of, 50–51
Antithesis, principle of, 102
APA Monitor Teaching Today's Pupils to Think More Critically (R.E.A.L. site), 89
Apgar newborn scoring system, 25, 27
Apnea, SIDS and, 32–33
Apple Classrooms of Tomorrow, 77
Apple Computer, Inc., 77–78
*Archives of Pediatric and Adolescent Medicine*, 201
Aschbacher, P., 172, 173
Asher, S. R., 126, 127, 128
Asmus, Kate, 177
Assertiveness
    encouraging in girls, 201
    prosocial, 42
Asthma, 188–189
Atkins, Lori, 5
Atole (nutritional supplement), 194–195
Attention-deficit hyperactivity disorder (ADHD)
    deficits in private speech and, 70–71
    individuality vs. uniformity and, 82–83
Attributions, of positive intentions, 40–41
Atwell, N., 63, 66
Auditory Analysis Test, 86
Authoritarian parenting, learning problems and, 70
Authoritative parenting, competence and, 70
Authoritative strategies, in positive discipline, 43
"Author's circle," 63
Autism, 22
Axons, 20

## B

*Baby and Child Care* (Spock), 96
"Baby fat," 190–192
*Babywatching* (Morris), 30
Bailey, Michael, 178
Bailey, Norma J., 210–212

Baker, K. R., 42, 46
Baker, Laura, 145
Bandaids and Blackboards (R.E.A.L. site), 197
Bandura, A., 40, 45
Bank, Stephen, 142, 144, 147
Bard, Kim, 102
**Barinaga, Marcia, 92–93**
Barnard, Lucy, 57
Barnes, Richard H., 194
Barnett, M., 41, 42, 45
Baron, Naomi S., 58
Barrett, D. E., 42, 45
Barrett, Karen, 30
Barth, Richard, 217
Bassuk, E. L., 179, 183
Bates, E., 109, 114
Baumann, U., 123
Baumrind, D., 43, 45
Bayfield, A., 170, 173
Beach, F. A., 207, 209
Beating Peer Pressure (R.E.A.L. site), 130
Bedford, Victoria, 146
**Begley, Sharon, 32–33, 80–81**
Behavioral genetics, sibling relationships and, 144
Behavioral rules, in make-believe play, 108, 109
Behavioral training, 43
Behavior problems
    deficits in private speech and, 70–71
    homelessness and, 181
    sexual behaviors, 207–208
    subjective nature of behavior ratings, 82
Behrman, R. E., 167
Beilke, R., 205, 209
Bellugi, Ursula, 98
Belsky, J., 30, 31, 161, 163, 167
**Bennetts, Leslie, 200–203**
**Berk, Laura E., 67–72, 107–114**
Berlfein, J. R., 42, 46
**Berndt, Thomas J., 119–123**
Bernstein, Nina, 10
Bibliotherapy, for loneliness, 127
Bickerton, Derek, 101
Binder, Brandi, 21
Binocular vision, 30
Birth defects, 3–5, 4t
    genetic engineering and, 6–8
    prenatal testing for, 6
Birth order, sibling differences and, 144–145
Bivens, Jennifer A., 69
Bjorklund, B., 172t, 173
Blachman, Benita A., 86
Black, B., 129
Blau, D. M., 158, 167
Blood count (hematocrit), of newborns, 27

Blood glucose test, for newborns, 27
Blood incompatibility tests, for
    newborns, 27
Body temperature, regulating for
    preemies, 26
Boldt, Sarah, 138–139
Bolger, K. E., 163, 164, 167
Borke, H., 41, 45
Bornstein, M. H., 112, 115
**Born to Rebel** (Sulloway), 48
Borys, S., 126, 128
*Boston Parents' Paper,* **174–175**
Both, L., 126, 128
Bowman, B., 163, 167
*Boys Will Be Boys: Breaking the Link Between
    Masculinity and Violence* (Miedzian), 201
*The Boy Who Burned Too Brightly* (Welsh),
    82–83
Bradley, Lynette, 86
Brain
    connection between pointing and
        speech, 103
    damage from malnutrition, 193–194
    neurobiology of reading and, 87–88
Brain, development of, 18–24
    child abuse and, 22–23
    complexity of, 47
    end of growth spurt, 23–24
    in first year, 56, 57
    genetic factors, 19–20
    language acquisition and, 98–101
    nerve growth, 20–21
    prenatal, 55
    role of experience, 21–22
    toddlers, 58
Brainerd, C. J., 110, 114
*Brave New World* (Huxley), 51
Brayfield, A., 162, 168
Bream, L., 126, 128
Breast feeding, initial efforts, 26
Breaux, John, 10
Bredekamp, S., 60, 62, 65, 66, 162, 167, 173
Bretherton, I., 109, 112, 114, 115
Bringing Learning Home Alliance, 77–78
Brinster, Ralph, 7
*British Medical Journal,* 84
Broberg, A., 155, 162, 164, 167, 168
Bronchiolitis, 188
Bronfenbrenner, U., 122
Broughton, D., 205, 209
Brown, David, 11, 12
**Brown, J. Larry, 193–196**
Brown, Lyn Mikel, 201, 202
Bryan, J. H., 40, 45
Bryant, D., 162, 164, 169
Bryant, Peter E., 86
Buddy Project (State of Indiana), 78
Buhrmester, Duane, 144
**Bullock, Janis R., 126–129**
Burchfield, B. C., 60, 65
**Burchfield, David W., 60–65**
Bureaucracy of adoption, 217
Burke, C., 63, 66
Burns, S. M., 110, 114
Burton, Barbara K., 4
Burud, S., 172, 173
**Butterworth, George, 102–103**

# C

Caldwell, B., 43–44, 45
Calkins, L. M., 62, 63, 65
Camioni, Luigi, 103
Caplan, Art, 7, 8
Caregivers. *See also* Child care
    influence of, 37
        roles in make-believe play, 111–114
        teaching prosocial behaviors, 39–40
Carolina Abecedarian Project, 162
Cartledge, G., 43, 45
*The Case Against Spanking* (Hyman), 139
Casper, Virginia, 59
Cassidy, J., 126, 127, 128
Categorization, language development and,
    57, 58–59, 92
Centers for Disease Control and Prevention
    (CDC), 187
Cerbone, M. J., 112, 115
Cerebral palsy, 4
Cesarean section, 14
CF (cystic fibrosis), 6, 8
Chace, S. V., 164, 167
*Chain Store Age Executive,* 172, 172t, 173
Chalmers, J., 41, 45
Chard, S., 62, 66
Chasnoff, Ira, 81
Chavkin, W., 183
Cherlin, A., 158, 159, 167
Cherubin, Dan, 178
Chickenpox vaccine, 187
Child abuse
    brain development and, 22–23
    shaken-baby syndrome, 34–35
Child Behavior Checklist, 181
Childbirth, 13–14
    care of newborns following, 25–28
    delivery room, 14
    evaluation and nursing care, 13
    labor room, 13–14
    pain relief, 14
    recovery, 14
Child care
    child development perspective, 161–165
    corporate-sponsored, 152, 170–173
    by female relatives, 154, 157–158
    governmental regulation, 158, 166
    history of, 154–158
    labor force perspective, 159–161
    long-term effects of, 163–165
    public policy and quality/cost tradeoff,
        165–167
    terminology, 154
Child-care centers, 156
Child-focused curricula, 60–65
    multiple intelligences and, 61–62
    Project Approach, 62
    reading strategies/cueing systems,
        63–65, *64, 65*
    writer's workshop, 62–63
CHILDHELP, 34
Children and Television Violence (R.E.A.L.
    site), 151
Children of Lesbians and Gays Everywhere
    (COLAGE), 176, 178

Children's Defense Fund, 170, 173
Chin-Quee, D., 165, 167
Choices, empowering children to make, 44
Chomsky, Noam, 85, 100
Christopher, F. S., 41, 45
Chugani, Harry, 19
Cicirelli, Victor, 146
Circumcision, 27
Clark, M. S., 122–123
Clarke-Stewart, K. A., 161, 163, 167
Classrooms of Tomorrow (Apple), 77
Clay, Marie, 64, 65
Clinton, Hillary Rodham, 214
Clinton, William Jefferson, 214, 215
Cliques, 124–125
Cloninger, C. Robert, 49
Closed-end problem solving, 113
Cognitive development
    developmentally appropriate
        curricula, 60–65
    effects of child care on, 162–163, 165
    effects of crack cocaine on, 80–81
    evaluating intelligence, 55–59
    make-believe play and, 110, 111
    overview, 53–54
    R.E.A.L. sites, 73
    role of private speech, 67–72
    sibling differences in, 144
    undernutrition and, 193, 195
Cohe, Phipps, 33
Cohen, J. M., 123
Cohen, Les, 93
**Cohen, Mark, 6–8**
Cohen, S., 123
COLAGE (Children of Lesbians and Gays
    Everywhere), 176, 178
Colic, crying and, 95, 96
Collins, N., 159, 161, 167
Coltrane, Scott, 134, 136, 137
Committee for Economic Development,
    170, 173
Common cold, 188
Compensated dyslexics, 87, 88
Computer Learning Foundation, 78
Computers
    computer-assisted instruction, 77
    future job market and, 79
    for low-income children, 76–79
Conflict situations
    problem solving in, 42
    sibling feuds and squabbles, 147
Conformity, 105
    cliques and, 124–125
    role in socialization, 116–118
Connecticut Longitudinal Study, 86
**Conners, Mary, 138–141**
Connolly, J. A., 110, 114
Consistency in discipline, 139
Constable, R. Todd, 87
"Cool," 116–118
Coombs' (ABO) test, 27
Cooperative learning, 107
Cooperative play, 113
Corporate-sponsored child care, 152,
    170–173
    assessing, 173t

benefits of, 171–172
employer responses, 170–171, 171t
Corporation for Educational Technology, 78
Corrigan, R., 109, 114
Cost, Quality, and Child Outcomes Study
Team, 162, 166, 167–168, 170, 173
Cost of child care, 161, 170
Cotton, Quincy, 58
Counseling, about discipline, 141
**Cowley, Geoffrey, 98–101**
Cox, Martha, 29, 30
Crack cocaine, "snow babies" and, 80–81
Crain, Stephen, 101
Crary, E., 42, 45
CREB gene, 21
Crib death. *See* Sudden infant death
syndrome (SIDS)
Cross-cultural studies of language
acquisition, 92–93
Crying, 94–97
developmental changes in, 95
infant responses and, 30
problem crying, 95–96
role in language development, 90–91
soothing and, 96
spoiling and, 96–97
variations in, 94–95
Cueing systems, 63–65, *64, 65*
Culture
attitude toward spanking and, 139
make-believe play and, 113–114
sibling bonds and, 146
Curiosity, 59
Curricula
child-focused, 60–65
gay and lesbian issues, 212
prosocial curriculum, 39–40
Cystic fibrosis (CF), 6, 8

### D

Dale, N., 111, 114
Dansky, J. L., 110, 114
Darwin, Charles, 102
Daughters, encouraging assertive
behavior, 201
Davis, R., 60, 65
Dawson, Geraldine, 22, 23
Day care, importance of, 24
Deater-Deckard, K., 158, 162, 164, 166,
168, 169
*The Death of Innocents* (Firstman & Talan),
32, 33
DeCasper, Anthony, 55–56
DeCoster, Vicky, 139
"Defense of Marriage Act," 176
Dehydration, 188
Deich, S., 162, 168, 170, 173
Dendrites, 20
Densmore, M., 172t, 173
Depression, use of drugs to treat, 50–51
Developmental delays, homelessness
and, 179
Devoe, M., 45
DeVries, R., 61, 62, 65
deYoung, Suzanne, 57

Diaper rash, 188
Diarrhea, 188
Diary of a Baby (Stern), 58
Dias, M. G., 110, 114
Diaz, Rafael M., 68, 69
Disabilities: Attention Deficit Disorder
(ADD) [R.E.A.L. site], 89
Discipline, 131
consistency in, 139
divorce and, 175
mother as disciplinarian, 140
parental feelings about, 139
*Parents* magazine poll, 138, 138t
positive discipline, 43–44
positive techniques, 140–141
spanking, 138–139
victim-centered, 42
Distractibility, crack cocaine and, 81
Divorce and remarriage
family stress and, 152
helping children adjust to, 174–175
sibling relationships and, 143
Divorce (R.E.A.L. site), 184
Dixon, Breauna, 178
Dixon, D., 110, 115
Down syndrome, 4–5
Down syndrome (R.E.A.L. site), 15
Doyle, A. B., 110, 114
Dramatic play, as therapy for loneliness,
127
Drugs
"snow babies," 80–81
stimulants for ADHD, 71
use in treating depression, 50–51
Duberstein, L., 157, 158, 159, 160, 161, 168
Dufay, Jo, 12
Dunn, J., 111, 112, 114, 143, 144
Dyslexia, 84–88
myths of, 88
neurobiology and, 87–88
phonological model of, 85–87

### E

Ear infections, 188
Early education, brain development and, 19
Economic issues
in child care arrangements, 160
in learning problems, 74
in parental roles, 137
Education
homelessness and, 181
nutrition and, 195
Educators, responsibility for gay students,
210–212
Egocentric speech, 67
Eisenberg, M., 158, 162, 164, 165–166,
168, 169
Eisenberg, N., 41, 43, 45
Elardo, R., 40, 45
Eli Lilly Corporation, 50, 51
El'konin, D., 111, 114
Emde, Robert, 56
Emotional deprivation, brain development
and, 22–23

Employers, benefits of corporate child
care, 171
"Employers join for emergency child care,"
170, 173
**Engeler, Amy, 213–219**
Engle, Patrice L., 194
Environmental toxins, birth defects and, 3
Enzyme deficiencies, testing newborns
for, 27
Epilepsy, surgery as treatment, 21
Ervin-Tripp, S., 110, 114
Ethical issues
in genetic engineering, 7–8
in postmenopausal motherhood, 10
Evangelou, D., 60, 66
Evans, Richard, 189

### F

Fabes, R. A., 41, 45
Factor, D., 43, 45
Faenza, Michael, 51
Falbo, Toni, 146
Falls, 188
Family day care, 156, 162
Family issues
discipline, 138–141
overview of, 131–132
parenting styles, 133–137
R.E.A.L. sites, 151
sibling relationships, 142–147
television violence, 148–150
Family stressors
child care, 154–167
corporate child care, 170–173
divorce, 174–175
gay parenthood, 152, 176–178
homelessness, 179–182
overview, 152–153
R.E.A.L. sites, 184
Farber, J., 42, 46
Farver, J. M., 113, 114
Fathers
contribution to child development,
134–135
involvement in family care, 133–137
role in child development, 131
Feeding problems, in premature
newborns, 26
Feelings, understanding and expressing,
41–42, 44, 110
Fein, G., 111, 114
Fernald, Anne, 22, 92, 93
Fernandez, H. C., 172, 173
Feshbach, N., 41, 45
Fetal alcohol syndrome, 3
Fetal intelligence, 55–56
Fetal rights, 2, 11–12
Fever, 188
Field, T., 164, 168
Fiene, R., 162, 168
Fiese, B., 112, 114
File, N., 113, 114
Finger pointing, in language development,
102–103

Finkelhor, E. E., 205, 209
Finn-Stevenson, M., 166, 169
First, Neal, 7
*First Feelings* (Greenspan), 30
Firstman, Richard, 32
Fitzgerald, L. M., 163, 167
Fleming-Johnson, R., 129
Fletcher, Jack M., 86
Fletcher, John, 7
fMRI (functional magnetic resonance
    imaging), 87
Foorman, Barbara, 86
**Foote, Donna, 98–101**
Ford, C. S., 207, 209
Forman, E. A., 107, 114
Formants, 92
For-profit child-care centers, 156–157
Foster care, 213, 215
Foster care subsidies, 215, 216
Fostering Speech and Language Skills
    (R.E.A.L. site), 104
Fox, R., 205, 209
Franco, Fabia, 103
Franke, S., 126, 128
Frauenglass, Marnie H., 69
Freigang, R., 126, 128
Fresco (fruit drink), 194–195
Freud, Sigmund, 143
Freund, J. J., 40, 45
Fried, M., 170, 172, 173
Friedman, D. E., 172, 173
Friedrich, W., 205, 209
Friendships. See Peer relationships
Fugitt, E., 43, 45
Fulbright, Robert K., 87
Fults, J., 41, 45
Functional magnetic resonance imaging
    (fMRI), 87
Furman, W., 44, 45, 128

# G

Gagnon, J., 205, 207, 209
Galda, L., 110, 115
Galef Institute, 62, 65
Galen, M., 172, 173
Galinsky, E., 161, 168, 173
Galton, Francis, 144
Game play, 109
Garbarino, James, 202
Gardner, Howard, 61, 62, 65
Garvey, C., 111, 114, 115
Garvin, Ruth A., 68
Gates, Bill, 78
Gay, Lesbian, and Straight Teachers
    Network (GLSTN), 211
Gay marriages, 176
Gay parenthood, 152, 176–178
Gender differences
    in brain organization, 87
    child-raising and, 200–203
    in parental behaviors, 131, 133–137
    in peer relationships, 120
    power differences, 202
Gender equality, child care and, 159

Gender identity development, 200–203
    genetic tendencies, 200–201
    "masculine mystique," 202–203
    minimizing differences, 201–202
    nature vs. nurture in, 201
Genes
    CREB gene, 21
    effects on phonological processing, 85
    role in brain development, 19–20
    stress-activated, 48
Genetic engineering
    birth defects and, 6
    ethical issues in, 7–8
    potentials of, 6–7
    research in, 7
Genetic tendencies
    homosexuality, 178
    shyness, 47, 48
    in social-emotional development, 47–49
George, C., 42, 45
Germ-line therapy. See Genetic engineering
Gestures
    early use of, 90
    finger pointing related to, 103
Gilligan, Carol, 44, 45, 201
Ginsburg, Ruth Bader, 158
Girls and Media (R.E.A.L. site), 220
Giugli, P. E., 183
Glickman, C. D., 129
GLSTN (Gay, Lesbian, and Straight
    Teachers Network), 211
Goelman, H., 162, 167
Goffin, S. G., 41, 45
Golant, Mitch, 136
Goldstein, A., 43, 46
Göncü , A., 113, 114
**Goode, Erica E., 142–147**
Goodkids (R.E.A.L. site), 151
Goodlad, J. I., 60, 66
Goodman, Corey, 19, 20, 21
Goodman, K., 64, 66
Goosens, F. A., 164, 168
Gordon, B., 208, 209
Gordon, T., 44, 45
Gore, John C., 87
Gorman, Kathleen S., 194
Government
    family-friendly policies, 159–160
    regulation of child care, 158, 166
Graham, Josh, 177
Graham, Sarah, 177
Graham-Bermann, S. A., 183
Grajeck, S., 162, 168
Gralinski, J. H., 108, 114
Grambsch, P., 205, 209
Grammar, in language development,
    100–101
Grammar and usage rules, *64*, 65
Grantham-McGregor, Sally, 195
Graphophonemics, *64, 64*
**Grauer, Avery, 204–209**
Graupner, Lida, 103
Graves, D. H., 62, 63, 66
Greenberg, M. H., 155, 169
Green Book (1996), 155
Greenough, William, 23
Greenspan, Stanley, 19, 22, 30, 47, 48, 49

**Gregory, Stephen, 176–178**
Greiner, Jim, 78
Griswold, Robert, 134
Group decision making, in adolescence, 121
*Growing Up With Language* (Baron), 58
Growth cones, 20
*The Growth of the Mind* (Greenspan), 22, 47
Gruber, C. P., 163, 167
Grusec, J., 40, 45
Guddemi, M., 154
Gunderson, B., 206, 209
Gutmann, Miriam, 117

# H

*Haemophilus influenzae* b immunization, 187
**Hager, Mary, 80–81**
Haight, W. L., 109, 111, 112, 114–115
Haith, Marshall, 31
Hall, G. Stanley, 146
Hancock, T., 165–166, 168
Hapworth, Mada, 142
Hapworth, William, 142
Harassment of gay students, 211
Harding, Carol, 31
Harper, E., 172*t*, 173
Harper, Rita, 26
Harris, Margaret, 103
Harris, P. L., 110, 114
Harste, J. C., 63, 66
Hartman, J. A., 60, 66
Hartmann, A. H., 183
Hartmann, E., 164, 168
Hartup, W. W., 44, 45, 123, 128
Harwayne, S., 63, 66
Haskins, R., 39, 45, 166, 168
Hatano, G., 61, 66
Hauenstein, E., 163, 164, 165, 169
Hayashi, T., 183
Hazen, N., 129
Head Start, 156, 158
Health
    advances in pediatric medicine, 187–189
    of gay students, 212
    homelessness and, 181
    malnutrition and undernutrition,
        193–196
    nutrition and, 185
    overview, 185–186
    overweight and, 190–192
    R.E.A.L. sites, 197
    sudden infant death syndrome (SIDS),
        32–33, 185, 189
Health insurance
    genetic testing and, 7
    length of hospital stay and, 14
    minimum hospital stay for childbirth, 27
Healthy Start program (Hawaii), 35
Healy, Jane, 57
Healy, Mary Kay, 140
Hearing
    of newborns, 29
    prenatal development of, 56
    tests for newborns, 27
Heilman, Joan, 142
Helburn, S., 161, 165, 168

Helfgott, David, 48
Hematocrit (blood count), of newborns, 27
Henderson, V. K., 164, 169
Hennessy, E., 164, 168
Heredity, contribution to temperament,
    145–146
Hetherington, E. Mavis, 143, 145
High-frequency sight words, 64–65, 65
Hill, Alan, 78
Hilliard, A. G., 170, 173
HIV (human immunodeficiency virus), 27
Hofferth, S., 155, 157, 157, 158, 159, 161, 162,
    167, 168, 169, 170, 173
Holcomb, P., 162, 168, 170, 173
Holloway, S. D., 163, 168
Homelessness
    children and, 180–181
    demography of, 180
    family stress and, 152–153, 179–182
    health and education, 181
    implications of, 182
    mental health and, 181–182
Homeless shelters, stresses of life in,
    180–181
Homophobia, 177, 202
Homosexuality
    children with gay parents, 152, 176–178
    identity development, 210–212
Honig, Alice Sterling, 39–45, 46
Hopkins, William, 102
Horwitz, Allen, 5
Hotton, Michelle, 141
The House of Make-Believe: Children's Play and
    the Developing Imagination (Singer), 59
Howes, C., 42, 46, 162, 163, 164, 166, 168,
    169, 173
Hoyt, Waneta, 32, 33
Huffington, Arianna, 50–51
Hughes, Langston, 212
Human immunodeficiency virus (HIV),
    testing newborns for, 27
Huttenlocher, Peter, 21
Huxley, Aldous, 51
Hwang, C. P., 155, 162, 164, 167, 168
Hyman, Irwin A., 139
Hymel, S., 126, 127, 128
Hypoplastic left-heart syndrome, 4
Hypothyroidism, testing newborns for, 27

**I**

Identity development
    adoption and, 198–199, 213–219
    gender identity, 200–203
    homosexuality, 210–212
    R.E.A.L. sites, 220
    sexual identity, 198, 204–209
Imagination, symbolic play and, 59
Immunization, 187
Impetigo, 188
Inagaki, K., 61, 66
Individuality, ADHD and, 82–83
Induction, in positive discipline, 43
Industrialized societies, child care in, 155
Infant Behavior and Development (Rovee-
    Collier), 56

Infanticide, 32–33
Infants. See Newborns and infants
Ingersoll, Barbara, 51
Insecurity, about discipline, 139, 140t
Institute of Medicine, 179, 183
Institute of Nutrition of Central America
    and Panama, 194
Intelligence. See also Brain, development of
    development of, 55–59
    dyslexia and, 88
Intentional crying, 95
Intersubjectivity, 113
Intimacy, in peer relationships, 119–120
Iron-deficiency anemia, 196

**J**

Jackson, Chester, 216
Jacobs, Chris, 215, 216, 217
Jaffe, Maya, 178
Jalongo, M. R., 127, 128
Jenish, D'arcy, 11–12
Jennings, Kevin, 211
Jessell, Thomas, 20
Job market
    computer skills and, 79
    homelessness and, 181–182
Johansen, A. S., 173
Johnson, C. M., 183
Johnson, J., 110, 115
Johnson and Johnson Child Development
    Center, 172
Johnston, Richard B., 4
Jones, Teri, 116
Jusczyk, Peter, 93, 99
"Justice Ginsburg takes on affirmative
    action," 158, 168

**K**

Kagan, J., 47, 48, 56, 57, 59, 155, 168
Kahn, Michael, 143, 147
Kahn, Sarah, 55
Kalb, Claudia, 188
Kandel, D. B., 123
Kandel, Eric, 21
Kanter, Rosabeth Moss, 79
Katz, L., 60, 62, 66, 86
Katz, Robert B., 86
Kavanaugh, R. D., 112, 115
Keefe, K., 123
Keefe, N., 162, 164, 165
Keens, John, 33
Keith, B., 159, 169
Kemple, K. M., 129
Kendall, Kim, 116, 118
Kendrick, D., 206, 209
Kidshealth (R.E.A.L. site), 197
Kidsource—Newborns (R.E.A.L. site), 36
Kimmel, Michael, 134
Kindergartens
    origin of, 156
    social development in, 39
Kinsey, A., 206, 209
Kisker, E. E., 157, 169

Klaus, Marshall, 29, 31
Klein, R., 162, 169
Klein, T. P., 183
Kleinman, Ron, 188
"Knowledge workers," 79
Kohlberg, Lawrence, 61, 62, 65, 68, 69
Kontos, S., 162, 168
Koops, W., 164, 168
Koplewicz, Harold, 50
Kopp, C. B., 108, 114
Koren, Gideon, 81
Kosofsky, Barry, 80, 81
Kozol, Jonathan, 179
Krall, Carolyn, 56, 58
Kristal, A., 183
Krogh, S., 42, 46
Kuczynski, J., 40, 45
Kuhl, Patricia, 22, 92, 93
Kuiper, J., 205, 209

**L**

Labeling, positive behaviors, 40
Laboratory tests of newborns, 26–27
Lamacz, M., 207, 209
Lamb, M., 154, 155, 159, 162, 163, 168
Lamme, L., 42, 46
Landau, Steven, 71
Lande, J., 165, 169
Language development, 22
    brain development and, 98–101
    categorization and, 57, 58–59
    crying as part of, 94–97
    effects of child care on, 162–163
    expressing feelings, 44
    foreign language acquisition, 23–24
    grammar, 100–101
    homelessness and, 181
    in infants, 92–93
    meaning, role of, 99–100
    overview, 90–91
    pointing and, 102–103
    prenatal sounds, role of, 98–99
    private speech, 67–72
    process in young children, 98–101
    R.E.A.L. sites, 104
    role of make-believe play in, 110
    signs of problems, 100
    in toddlers, 58
The Language Instinct (Pinker), 98
Laskin, David, 116–118
Lauerman, John F., 32–33
Laychak, A. E., 123
Leach, Penelope, 95, 96, 97
Learning cycle, 61–62
Learning problems
    ADHD (See Attention deficit
        hyperactivity disorder (ADHD))
    attention deficit disorder (ADD), 74
    computers and, 76–79
    deficits in private speech and, 70–71
    dyslexia, 74, 84–88
    economic issues, 74
    neurological bases of, 75
    overview, 74–75

R.E.A.L. sites, 89
"snow babies," 80–81
Leavens, David, 102
Lecht, Charles P., 78
LeClair, Teri, 116
Leira, A., 158
Lennon, R., 43, 45
Lester, Barry, 80, 81, 96
**Levine, Karen, 124–125**
Levitsky, David A., 194
Levitt, Pat, 81
Lewis, Michael, 49
Liberman, Alvin M., 85
Liberman, Isabelle Y., 86
Licensure of child care, 156
Linn, Susan, 34–35
*Listen to the Children* (Zavitovsky et al), 42
Loneliness, 126–128
*Loving Your Child Is Not Enough*
(Samalin), 139
Lowe, C., 183
Lubell, Harry R., 187
Lucariello, J., 112, 115
Lucey, Jerold, 32, 33
Lynch, Stefan, 178

# M

**McCarthy, Laura Flynn, 25–28**
McCartney, K., 158, 159, 161, 162, 163, 164,
165, 168, 169
McGinnis, E., 43, 46, 166, 168
McGroder, S., 161, 169
McKenzie, Beryl, 103
McKeon, Patricia, 125
McNamee, M., 172, 173
Maginnis, Robert, 176
Main, M., 42, 45
Main-effect model of brain growth, 194
Make-believe play
among siblings, 143–144
development and significance of,
108–109
impact on development, 109–111
scaffolding by adults, 107, 111–114
sociocultural theory of, 107–108
Malnutrition and undernutrition
brain damage and, 193–194
correcting and preventing impairment,
196
lack of energy and, 194–195
prevalence of, 193
studies of, 195–196
Maple syrup urine disease (MSUD), testing
newborns for, 27
Markman, Ellen, 99
Marshall, N., 161, 168
Martin, C., 206, 209
Martorell, Reynaldo, 194
Masataka, Nobuo, 103
Masculine mystique, 202–203
Mason, K., 157, 158, 159, 160, 161, 168
**Masten, Ann S., 179–182,** 183
Masturbation, 206

Maternal employment
assessing effects of, 165
corporate child care and, 170–173
family stress and, 152
history of, 155
nonstandard working hours, 158
Mathen, Carissima, 12
Maurer, Daphne, 55, 57
Maximizing perceived similarity, 41
Maynard, R., 166, 168
May-Plumlee, T., 41, 45
Meaning, in language development, 99–100
Meaning and context clues, 64, *64*
Means-end thinking, 42
Measuring Your Child's Speech and
Language (R.E.A.L. site), 104
*Medical Sciences Bulletin,* 50
*Meeting at the Crossroads* (Gilligan &
Brown), 201
Mekos, D., 162, 169
Melhuish, E. C., 164, 168
Melias, P., 206, 209
Melmed, Matthew, 23
Memory
of newborns and infants, 31
recall memory, 57
role of genes in development, 21
rote memorization, 84
Men, shaken-baby abuse by, 34–35
Mendel, Gregor, 47
Mental health, homelessness and, 179, 180,
181–182
Mental schemas, in early learning, 57, 58
Methylphenidate (Ritalin), 81, 82, 83
Microsoft Parent-Teacher Connection, 78
Middleton, D., 107, 115
Miedzian, Myriam, 201, 202
Milburn, J. F., 43, 45
Miliotis, D., 183
Miller, Donna, 11, 12
Miller, Nancy, 78
Miller, P. J., 109, 111, 112, 114–115
Miller, S., 165, 169
Minick, N., 107, 114
Miranda, L., 183
Mirowsky, J., 159, 169
Mirror writing, 88
Misnaming objects, in dyslexia, 86–87
Modeling
of behavior by same-sex parent, 198
of prosocial behaviors, 40
Moll, L. C., 107, 115
Molnar, J., 183
Molteni, Richard, 26, 28
*Mom Loved You Best* (Hapworth and
Heilman), 142
Money, J., 207, 209
Morgan, W. Pringle, 84, 88
Morissette, Paul, 103
Morris, Desmond, 30
Morris, J., 161, 165, 168
Mother-baby bond, 31
Mothers
as primary disciplinarian, 140
in work force, 133–134

Motor control
iron-deficiency anemia and, 196
learning in first year, 56, 57
walking, 58
Motwani, J., 172t, 173
MSUD (maple syrup urine disease), 27
Multi-age curricular models, 60
Multiethnic Placement Act (1994), 217
Multiple intelligences, 61–62
Münchausen by proxy syndrome, 32, 33
Muscle cells, development of, 21
Music, use in relaxation, 44–45
Mussen, P., 40, 46
"My Friends and Me" (prosocial
curriculum), 39–40

# N

Nakayama, Mineharu, 101
NASBE (National Association of State
Boards of Education), 60, 66
**Nash, J. Madeleine, 18–24**
**Nathanson, Laura, 190–192**
National Academy of Sciences, 193
National Adoption Center, 214
**National Association for the Education of
Young Children (NAEYC), 148–150,** 173
National Association of State Boards of
Education (NASBE), 60, 66
National Child Abuse Hotline, 34
National Child Care Survey, 170
*National Enquirer,* 9
National Geographic Society, 78
National Health Care for the Homeless
Program, 181
National Information, Support and Referral
Service on Shaken Baby Syndrome
(R.E.A.L. site), 36
National Institute of Child Health and
Human Development (NICHD) Early
Child Care Research Network, 162, 163,
168
National Institute on Drug Abuse, 81
National Middle School Association, 210,
212
National Television Violence Study
key findings of, 148–149
recommendations of, 148–149
*Nature* (journal), 92
Nature vs. nurture debate, 47–49
about parenting roles, 136
gender differences and, 201
heredity of temperament, 145–146
NCREL (North Central Research
Educational Laboratory), 60, 66
Neel, James, 7, 8
Neemann, J., 183
Nelsen, Jane, 139
Nervous system, development of. *See* Brain,
development of
Neural activity, 18, 19
Neural tube, development of, 19–20
Neural-tube birth defects, 3
Neuroimaging, in studying dyslexia, 87–88

Newborns and infants
    brain, development of, 18–24
    care of preemies, 26
    early responses, 29–31
    first 48 hours, 25–28
    intelligence, development of (*See Intelligence*)
    language acquisition process, 92–93, 98–101
    learning in first year, 56–58
    nonmaternal care of, 163
    overview, 16–17
    R.E.A.L. sites, 36
    shaken-baby syndrome, 34–35
    SIDS re-examined, 32–33
Newkirk, T., 63, 66
Newman, Frank, 19
Newman, L. S., 110, 115
Newport, Elissa, 101
*Newsweek* magazine, 33
*The New View of Self* (Sievers), 47
New York Academy of Sciences, 80
*The New York Times*, 10
NICHD. *See* National Institute of Child Health and Human Development
NICHD Early Child Care Research Study, 163
Nicolopoulou, A., 110, 115
Niefern, Marianne, 135
Non-graded curricular models, 60
Nonprofit child-care centers, 156–157
Nonpunitive discipline, 43
North American Council on Adoptive Children, 217
North Central Research Educational Laboratory (NCREL), 60, 66
Norwood, William I., 4
Nursery schools
    origin of, 156
    social development in, 39
Nutritional supplements, research on, 194–195

# O

Oakley, Godfrey, 3
Object substitutions, in make-believe play, 109, 111–112
**Ochshorn, Susan, 55–59**
O'Connell, B., 109, 112, 114, 115
O'Connor, Sean, 57
**Oekerman, Rebecca, 170–173**
Olenick, M., 163, 168
Only children, 146
O'Reilly, A. W., 112, 115
Osherson, Samuel, 116
Otitis media, 188
Ottenhoff, G., 164, 168
Overweight
    diagnosing, 190–191
    eating habits and, 191–192
    slowing weight gain, 191

# P

Parentese, 22, 90, 92, 99, 100
Parenting, variations in, 38
*Parenting* magazine, 96
**Parenting Q & A, 174–175**
Parents
    attitude toward private speech, 71–72
    benefits of corporate child care, 171
    communicating about sex, 208
    education about discipline, 141
    impact of child care on, 161
    implications of brain research, 19
    infant preferences for, 31
    influence of, 117–118
    issues of discipline (See Discipline)
    recommendations on TV violence, 150
    reinforcing infant responses, 49
    responses to preteen conformity, 124–125
    role in brain development, 22
    role in cognitive development, 53
    scaffolding in make-believe play, 111–114
    understanding infant responses, 29–31
    unequal treatment of siblings, 145
    unreal expectations of adoption, 217
*Parents* magazine, 138, 139
Park, K., 44, 46, 123
Parker, R., 183
Parkhurst, J. T., 126, 127, 128
Parten, M., 113, 115
*The Passions of Fatherhood* (Osherson), 116
Patterson, Charlotte, 177
Patterson, David, 5
Paxil (antidepressant), 50
Pediatric medicine
    asthma, 188–189
    immunizations, 187
    preventive measures, 189
    sudden infant death syndrome (SIDS), 32–33, 185, 189
*Pediatrics* (journal), 32, 33
Peer relationships, 105, 106
    characteristics of friends, 120–122
    cliques, 124–125
    features of friendship, 119–120
    loneliness and, 126–128
    positive and negative aspects, 119, 120
Peers, role in make-believe play, 112
Pellegrini, A. D., 110, 115, 129
Pence, A. R., 162, 167
Pennsylvania Adoption Exchange, 214
Pepler, D. J., 110, 115
Permissive parenting, learning problems and, 70
Perruchini, Paula, 103
Perry, Bruce, 22
Perspective taking, 42
Pertussis (whooping cough) immunization, 187
Pew Memorial Trust, 181
**Peyser, Marc, 47–49**
**Phariss, Tracy, 210–212**

Phenylketonuria (PKU), testing newborns for, 27
Phillips, D., 158, 159, 161, 162, 163, 164, 165, 166, 168, 169, 173
Phillips, David, 11
Phonemes, 84, 85, 99
Phonemological model of dyslexia, 85–87, 88
Phonemological processing, 84–85
Phonological deficit hypothesis, 85–86
Physical examinations, for newborns, 25–28
Piaget, Jean, 57, 58, 67, 68, 108, 113, 114, 115
Piaget (R.E.A.L. site), 73
Pidgin, 101
Pincer grip, 102
Pines, M., 42, 46
Pinker, Steven, 85, 98, 99, 101
Pinkerton, R., 164, 168
Pitch of voice, 100
PKU (phenylketonuria), 27
Play
    game play, 109
    make-believe play, 107–114
    role of fathers in, 135–136
    sexual curiosity, 204–206, 207
    socialization through, 105–106
    sociodramatic play, 110
    symbolic play, 57, 59
Pleck, J. H., 159, 169
Plomin, Robert, 48, 144, 145
Pointing, role in language development, 102–103
Polit, Denise, 146
**Pollitt, Ernesto, 193–196**
**Pollitt, Katha, 9–10**
Pomeroy, W., 206, 209
Popejoy, W. J., 172, 173
*Positive Discipline* (Nelsen), 139
Postmenopausal motherhood, 9–10
Potts, Michael K., 70
**Poussaint, Alvin F., 34–35**
Poverty
    access to computer technology and, 76–79
    effects on development, 17
    undernutrition and, 193–196
Pregnancy, fetal rights and, 11–12
Premature newborns, care of, 26
Prenatal development
    birth defects, 3–5, 4t
    childbirth, 13–14
    fetal rights, 2, 11–12
    genetic engineering and, 6–8
    of intelligence, 55–56
    neural tube, 19–20
    overview, 1–2
    postmenopausal motherhood, 9–10
    R.E.A.L. Sites, 15
    sound, role of, 98–99
    sounds, 90
    uterine environment, 55–56
Preschool children, effects of divorce on, 174

Preschool programs
  brain development and, 19
  for homeless children, 182
Presser, H., 158, 169
Preteens, cliques and, 124–125
Preventive health care, 189
Primary grades, child-centered curricula
  for, 60–65
Principle of antithesis, 102
Privacy, sexual behaviors and, 205–206
Private speech, 53, 67–72
Problem solving
  closed-end, 113
  private speech as tool, 71
  as prosocial behavior, 42–43
Prodromidis, M., 163, 168
Productivity, child care and, 161
Project Approach, 62, 65
Pro-life organizations, 11, 12
Pronouns, use of, 100
Prosocial behaviors, 37, 39–45
  adult-child relationships, 44
  adult focus on, 40–41
  effect of make-believe play on, 110
  positive discipline and, 43–44
  problem solving, 42–43
  relaxation activities, 44–45
  social interactions, 44
  understanding others' feelings, 41–42,
    110
  videotaping, 45
Prosser, W., 161, 169
Protein, importance of, 196
Prozac, use of, 50–51
Public Broadcasting Service, 78
Public policy, implications of brain
  research, 19
Pugh, Kenneth R., 87

## Q

Quality/cost tradeoff in child care, 165–167
Quality of child care, 162–163

## R

Rabinovich, B., 162, 169
Race
  access to computer technology and,
    76, 77
  homelessness and, 180, 182
  sibling bonds and, 146
Rachel and Her Children (Kozol), 179
Racial discrimination, in adoption, 217
Rafferty, Y., 183
Rahe, D. F., 44, 45, 128
Raising a Happy, Unspoiled Child (White), 96
Rakic, Pasko, 20, 23
Ramey, C., 162, 164, 169
Ramey, S., 162, 164, 169
Ramirez, M., 183
Ransom, C., 172, 173
Rashes, 188
Rath, W. R., 183
Ratner, Nan Bernstein, 92

Rawlins, W. K., 122
Reading, dyslexia and. See Dyslexia
Reading Recovery Program, 64
Reading strategies, 63–65, 64, 65
R.E.A.L. sites
  cognitive development, 73
  family issues, 151
  family stressors, 184
  health, 197
  identity issues, 220
  language development, 104
  learning disabilities, 89
  newborns and infants, 36
  prenatal development and childbirth, 15
  social-emotional development, 52
  socialization, 130
Reasoning ability, role of make-believe play
  in, 110
Recall memory, 57
Redirection, as alternative to aggression, 44
Redler, E., 40, 45
Reform movements, roots of child care in,
  155–156
Reichhart-Erickson, M., 163, 168
Reinforcement, overuse of, 41
Reis, H. T., 122–123
Reiss, David, 145
Rejection
  cliques and, 124, 125
  effects of, 106
  loneliness and, 127–128
Relaxation exercises, 44–45
Repetition, in language development, 100
Rescorla, L., 183
Research
  in brain development, 19
  in child care, 161–165, 172
  in development of intelligence, 55
  effects of crack cocaine, 80–81
  longitudinal studies of friendships, 120
  National Television Violence Study,
    148–150
  in private speech, 67–72
  in prosocial behaviors, 40
  in shyness, 48
  twin studies, 48
Respiratory distress syndrome, 26
Reye's syndrome, 188
Reznick, E., 110, 114
Riccitello, Robina, 3–5, 4t
Ricciuti, A., 163, 164, 165, 169
Rising Scores on Intelligence Tests (R.E.A.L.
  site), 73
Ritalin (methylphenidate), 81, 82, 83
Rivera, Juan A., 194
Robbins, P. K., 158, 167
Robertson, M. J., 183
Robert Wood Johnson Foundation, 181
Rocheleau, A., 162, 164, 165
Rogers, D. L., 129
Rogoff, B., 113, 115
Role-taking skills, 41–42
Rosegrant, T., 60, 62, 65, 66
Rosen, Anne, 125
Rosenberg, B. G., 146
Rosenberg, L., 183

Rosenthal, S., 162, 164, 165
Ross, C. E., 159, 169
Ross, D. D., 129
Ross, H. S., 110, 115
Roth, K., 43, 45
Rothbaum, Fred, 204–209
Routman, R., 63, 66
Rovee-Collier, Carolyn, 56
Rovine, M. J., 163, 167
Ruben, David, 133–137
Rubin, David J., 204–209
Rubin, K. H., 127, 128
Rushton, J. P., 41, 46
Rushton, P., 40, 45
Rutherford, E., 40, 46

## S

Saas-Kortsaak, P., 40, 45
Saltz, E., 110, 115
Samalin, Nancy, 139
Savin-Williams, R. C., 122, 123
SBS (shaken-baby syndrome), 34–35
Scaffolding, 107, 111–114
Scarr, Sandra, 154–169
Schilmoeller, G. L., 43, 45
Scholastic, Inc., 77–78
School-age children, effects of divorce on,
  174
Schools
  child care in, 166
  programs for homeless children, 182
Schott, Christopher, 94
Schott, Joann, 94
Schroeder, C., 208, 209
Schulman, Candy, 13–14
Schultz, L. H., 122
Science (journal), 92
Seabron, C., 183
Sears, James T., 210, 211
Second Generation, 178
Segal, T., 172t, 173
Self-direction, as function of private speech,
  68, 69t, 71
Self-esteem
  effect of friendships on, 120
  puberty and, 201
  role of fathers in, 135–136
Selig, Nathaniel, 177
Selman, R. L., 122
Sensorimotor period of intelligence, 57, 58
Sensory activities, as therapy for loneliness,
  127
Sensory development
  hearing (See Hearing)
  prenatal, 55–56
  vision (See Vision)
Separate Lives: Why Siblings Are So Different
  (Plomin), 144
Separation anxiety, crying and, 95
Sex assignment surgery, 201
Sexual identity development, 198, 204–209
  children's behaviors, 204–206
  guidelines for addressing, 207–208
  model of childhood sexuality, 206–207

Shaken Baby Syndrome Prevention Plus, 35
Shaken-baby syndrome (SBS), 34–35
Shankweiler, Donald P., 86
**Shapiro, Joseph P., 176–178**
Shatz, Carola, 18, 20, 21
Shaywitz, Bennett A., 87
**Shaywitz, Sally E., 84–88**
Shen, A., 183
Sher, M. L., 170, 172, 173
Sherer, J. L., 172, 173
Sherman, A., 183
Sherman, T., 45
Shields, Donald, 21
Shinn, M., 162, 168, 183
Shore, C., 109, 114
Short, K. G., 63, 66
Showers, Jacy, 34
Shure, M., 42, 46
Shyness, genetic component of, 47, 48
Shyness (R.E.A.L. site), 52
   *The Sibling Bond* (Bank), 142
Sibling relationships, 131
   among adult children, 146–147
   changing social landscape and, 142–143
   differences between children and,
      144–145
   feuds and squabbles, 147
   importance of, 142
   nature vs. nurture and, 145–146
   parental signals and, 143–144
   unequal treatment and, 145
Sickle-cell anemia, testing newborns for, 27
SIDS (sudden infant death syndrome),
   32–33, 185, 189
Siegel, Linda S., 86
Siever, Larry, 47, 48
Silverberg, S. B., 122
Simon, W., 205, 207, 209
Simultis, Z., 40, 45
Singer, Jerome, 59
Singletary, Jennifer, 139
Skar, J., 206, 209
"Skillstreaming" strategies, 43
Skin infections, 188
Slade, A., 112, 115
Sleep patterns of newborns, 26
SLI (Specific Language Impairment), 101
Smells, infant responses to, 29–30
Smollar, J., 122
Smolucha, F., 112, 115
Snarey, John, 135
"Snow babies," 80–81
Social communication, private speech and,
   68
Social-emotional development
   adjustment to divorce, 174–175
   antidepressants, 50–51
   encouraging prosocial behaviors, 39–45
   long-term impact of child care on,
      164–165
   nature or nurture debate, 47–49
   overview, 37–38
   R.E.A.L. sites, 52
Social identity, "cool" and, 116–118

Social interaction
   opportunities for, 44
   undernutrition and, 194
Social isolation, loneliness and, 126–128
Socialization
   cliques, 124–125
   influence of friends, 119–122
   loneliness, 126–128
   make-believe play, 107–114
   overview, 105–106
   R.E.A.L. sites, 130
   social identity and, 116–118
Social skills training, 43, 128
Social smile, 56–57
Social workers, adoption and, 217
Societal changes, sibling relationships and,
   142–143
Sociocultural theory (Vygotsky), 107–108
Sociodramatic play, 110
Socioemotional development (R.E.A.L. site),
   220
Socratic questions, use of, 43
Something Fishy—Eating Disorders
   (R.E.A.L. site), 197
"Sonic hedgehog" gene, 20
Sound, role in language development,
   98–99
Sound-sorting process, 92
Southall, David, 32, 33
Spanking, 138–139
Sparling, J., 162, 164, 169
Specific Language Impairment (SLI), 101
Speech
   phonological processing, 85
   private speech, 53, 67–72
**Spencer, Paula, 29–31**
Spivak, G., 42, 46
Spock, Benjamin, 96
Spontaneity, sexual behaviors and, 205–206,
   207
Spuhl, Sarah T., 70
Stager, Christine, 92, 93
Staines, G. L., 159, 169
Stanovich, Keith E., 86
Steinberg, L., 122
Steinschneider, Alfred, 32, 33
Stern, Daniel, 58
Sternberg, K. J., 155, 162, 163, 168
Stewart, P., 162, 168
Stewart B. McKinney Homeless Assistance
   Act (1987), 179, 181
Stolley, P., 183
**Stone, Brad, 187–189**
Stone, C. A., 107, 114
Stoney, L., 155, 169
"Story starter," ineffectiveness of, 63
Stranger anxiety, 37
Strange Situation assessment, 163
Stress
   friendship and, 119
   homelessness and, 180–181
   inheritance of stress-related
      abnormalities, 47–48
Strickland, D. S., 64, 66

Stryker, Michael, 21
Sudden infant death syndrome (SIDS),
   32–33, 185, 189
Sugarman, Susan, 59
Sulloway, Frank, 48, 145
Suomi, Stephen, 48
Suwalsky, J., 162, 169
Symbolism. *See also* Make-believe play
   in play activities, 57, 59
Synapses, 20

# T

Talan, Jamie, 32
Tamis-LeMonda, C. S., 112, 115
Tantrums, 95
Task-related behavior, private speech and,
   70
Teachers
   dealing with loneliness, 127–128
   developmentally appropriate curricula
      and, 60–65
   responsibility for gay students, 210–212
   role in cognitive development, 53
   role in make-believe play, 112–114
   role in writer's workshop, 63
   teaching prosocial behaviors, 39–40
Teachman, G., 41, 46
Television violence, 131–132, 148–150
Temperament (R.E.A.L. site), 52
Thalidomide poisoning, 3–4
Theoretical mode of reasoning, 110
Thoman, Evelyn, 94
Thompson, S., 41, 42, 45
Thompson, W., 165, 169
*Thought and Language* (Vygotsky), 68
*Time* magazine, 159, 169
Time-outs, 139
Tinker, Alex, 176, 177, 178
Tinker, Bonnie, 177
Tinker, Connie, 177, 178
Toddlers
   cognitive development of, 58–59
   effects of divorce on, 174
Tolstoy, Leo, 142
Tonniges, Thomas, 189
Torgeson, Joseph E., 86
Townsend, M., 41, 45
Transformational Curriculum, 62
Trost, M., 206, 209
Trovato, C., 42, 46
Truman, Thomas, 32, 33
Tudge, J. R. H., 107, 113, 115

# U

**Underwood, Anne, 32–33, 47–49**
U.S. Census Bureau, 170, 173
U.S. Conference of Mayors, 181
U.S. Department of Health and Human
   Services, 217

# V

Vaccines, 187
Valdes-Dapena, Marie, 33
Valdez, R. B., 183
Vandell, D. L., 164, 169
VanderVere, Joyce, 139, 140
Van Winkle, J., 173
Veiel, H. O. F., 123
Victim-centered discipline, 42
Videotaping, of prosocial behaviors, 45
Violence
    National Television Violence Study,
        148–150
    reducing aggression in boys, 202
Viorst, Judith, 147
Vision
    development in first year, 56
    development of, 21, 22
    effects of brain development on, 23
    of newborns and infants, 30
Vomiting, 188
Vorrath, H., 40, 46
Voucher systems for child care, 166
Vygotsky, Lev S., 53, 67–72, 102–103,
    105–110, 113, 114, 115

# W

Walker, Robert J., 76–79
Walking, mastery of, 58
Walsh, D., 61, 66
Walters, LeRoy, 7
Ward, Cassie, 178

Warner, Rachel, 58
Wasik, B., 162, 164, 169
Waters, E., 44, 46
Watson, Russell, 187–189
Waxler, C. Z., 40, 43, 46
Waxman, P., 172, 173
Weill, J. D., 183
Weinberg, R. A., 155–156, 169
Weinstein, Sharon R., 117
Weiss, R. S., 126
Welfare reform, 160, 166–167
Welsh, David J., 82–83
Werker, Janet, 92, 93
Wertsch, J. W., 107, 115
Westheimer, Ruth, 206
Westin, Karen, 141
Wheezing, 188
Whining, 95
White, Burton, 95, 96
White, L., 159, 169
Whitebook, M., 162, 163, 166, 168, 169, 173
Whitman, Walt, 212
Whittington, S., 112, 115
Whooping cough (pertussis)
    immunization, 187
Willer, B., 157, 169
Williams, G. A., 126, 127, 128
Williams syndrome, 98
Wills, T. A., 123
Wilson, K. S., 164, 169
Wittmer, Donna Sasse, 39–45, 46
Wohlfeiler, Arthur, 187
Wohlfeiler, Vicki, 187
"Women's Figures," 158, 169
Wood, D. J., 107, 115

Wood, D. L., 183
Wooding, C., 112, 114
Woolf, Alan, 188
"Workfare," 160–161
"Workfare means day care," 159, 169
*Working Mother* magazine, 157, 159
*The World of the Newborn* (Maurer), 55
Wright, J. D., 183
Writer's workshop, 62–63, 65

# Y

Yale Center for the Study of Learning and
    Attention, 84
*Yale Children's Health Letter*, 201
Yarrow, M. R., 40, 42, 43, 45, 46
Youniss, J., 122
*Your Baby and Child* (Leach), 95
*Your Child's Growing Mind: A Practical Guide
    to Brain Development and Learning From
    Birth to Adolescence* (Healy), 57

# Z

Zanga, Joseph, 188
Zaslow, M., 162, 169
Zavitkovsky, D., 42, 46
Zellman, G. L., 173
Zigler, E. F., 166, 169
Zoloft (antidepressant), 50
Zone of proximal development, 68, 69, 107
Zukow, P. G., 112, 115

# Putting it in *Perspectives*
## -Review Form-

Your name:_____          Date: _____

Reading title: _____

**Summarize:** Provide a one-sentence summary of this reading. _____

_____

_____

_____

**Follow the Thinking:** How does the author back the main premise of the reading? Are the facts/opinions appropriately supported by research or available data? Is the author's thinking logical?

_____

_____

_____

_____

_____

_____

**Develop a Context** (answer one or both questions): How does this reading contrast or compliment your professor's lecture treatment of the subject matter? How does this reading compare to your textbook's coverage?

_____

_____

_____

_____

_____

_____

**Question Authority:** Explain why you agree/disagree with the author's main premise.

_____

_____

_____

_____

_____

_____

**COPY ME!** Copy this form as needed. This form is also available at http://www.coursewise.com
Click on: *Perspectives.*